Stuart Gordon: Interviews

Conversations with Filmmakers Series
Gerald Peary, General Editor

Photograph by Ben Rock

STUART GORDON
INTERVIEWS

Edited by Michael Doyle

University Press of Mississippi / Jackson

The University Press of Mississippi is the scholarly publishing agency of the Mississippi Institutions of Higher Learning: Alcorn State University, Delta State University, Jackson State University, Mississippi State University, Mississippi University for Women, Mississippi Valley State University, University of Mississippi, and University of Southern Mississippi.

www.upress.state.ms.us

The University Press of Mississippi is a member of the Association of University Presses.

Copyright © 2022 by University Press of Mississippi
All rights reserved

First printing 2022

∞

Library of Congress Cataloging-in-Publication Data

Names: Doyle, Michael, editor.
Title: Stuart Gordon: interviews / Michael Doyle.
Other titles: Conversations with filmmakers series.
Description: Jackson: University Press of Mississippi, 2022. | Series: Conversations with filmmakers series | Includes index.
Identifiers: LCCN 2021034633 (print) | LCCN 2021034634 (ebook) |
    ISBN 978-1-4968-3773-8 (hardback) | ISBN 978-1-4968-3774-5 (trade paperback) |
    ISBN 978-1-4968-3775-2 (epub) | ISBN 978-1-4968-3776-9 (epub) |
    ISBN 978-1-4968-3783-7 (pdf) | ISBN 978-1-4968-3782-0 (pdf)
Subjects: LCSH: Gordon, Stuart, 1947–2020—Interviews. | Motion picture producers and directors—Interviews. | Motion pictures—Production and direction.
Classification: LCC PN1998.3.G67 A5 2022 (print) | LCC PN1998.3.G67 (ebook) |
    DDC 791.4302/33092—dc23/eng/20211201
LC record available at https://lccn.loc.gov/2021034633
LC ebook record available at https://lccn.loc.gov/2021034634

British Library Cataloging-in-Publication Data available

Table of Contents

Introduction   ix

Chronology   xxi

Filmography   xxix

Nude Co-eds in *Peter Pan* Stir Flap on Madison Campus   3
    Frank Ryan / 1968

Sick, Sick, Sick!   5
    Kim Newman / 1985

Dead People Just Wanna Have Fun   7
    Anne Billson / 1985

Lovecraft Re-Animated   9
    Stefan Jaworzyn and Stephen Jones / 1985

Stuart Gordon   14
    John A. Gallagher / 1986

Stuart Gordon's Shock Treatment   24
    David Edelstein / 1986

We Killed 'Em in Chicago   32
    Meredith Brody / 1986

Stuart Gordon: The Ideas, the Philosophy, the *Pit and the Pendulum*   44
    Rick Pieto / 1988

Robot Jox Rides Again   53
    Kyle Counts / 1989

Stuart Gordon   59
    Stanley Wiater / 1990

The Pit and the Pendulum   69
    Steve Biodrowski / 1991

Re-Animator—Stuart Gordon   73
    Maitland McDonagh / 1993

Stuart Gordon: The Force Behind *Fortress*   86
    Joe Kane / 1993

The Future of Stuart Gordon   91
    Dennis Fischer / 1995

Castle Freak   96
    Dennis Fischer / 1995

The Making of *Space Truckers*   100
    Dennis Fischer / 1997

The Wonderful Ice Cream Suit   109
    Judd Hollander and Sue Feinberg / 1998

Dagon and Beyond   112
    Mark Wheaton / 2002

King of the Ants: It's No Picnic   122
    Mark Wheaton / 2003

Screamography: Stuart Gordon   128
    Tony Timpone / 2006

Inside Stuart Gordon's Urban Gothic: An Interview on *Edmond*   137
    Matthew Sorrento / 2006

Stuart Gordon   142
    Paul Kane / 2007

Stuart Gordon, *Stuck*   149
    Nick Dawson / 2008

Object in Mirror May Be Closer Than It Appears: Stuart Gordon Talks About Horror, the Absurd, and *Stuck*   155
    Matthew Sorrento / 2008

Things No One Likes to Talk About: An Interview with Stuart Gordon   159
    James Morgart and Robert Cashill / 2009

Mortal Wisdom: Stuart Gordon   170
    Danny Draven / 2009

Stuart Gordon Talks *Nevermore: An Evening with Edgar Allan Poe*   175
    Robert V. Galluzzo / 2009

An Interview with Stuart Gordon   178
    Christopher O'Neill / 2010

DG Interviews Stuart "*Re-Animator*" Gordon   183
    Joe Bannerman / 2011

Stuart Gordon: H. P. Lovecraft, Ray Bradbury and the Museum of Jurassic Technology   191
    Jeremy Rosenberg / 2012

Stuart Gordon: Gentleman of Splatter   194
    Barbara Crampton / 2012

What Lies Beneath, What Dwells Beyond: The Pleasures and Perils of Adapting Lovecraft   204
    Michael Doyle / 2012

Stuart Gordon on Polanski and Kubrick   219
    Michael Doyle / 2014

The Grimmest of the Grim: Stuart Gordon on *Taste*   229
    Michael Doyle / 2014

Stuart Gordon Discusses *Re-Animator: The Musical*   235
    Tyler Doupé / 2014

Talkhouse Film Contributors Remember Stuart Gordon   238
    Nick Dawson / 2020

Additional Resources   247

Index   251

Introduction

H. P. Lovecraft, that most equitably reviled and cherished of American authors of weird fiction, opens his 1920 short story, "The Picture in the House," by declaring: "Searchers after horror haunt strange, far places." Anyone that possesses even a cursory acquaintance with the film and theater work of Stuart Gordon (1947–2020) knows he committed his entire career to mapping the curious and crepuscular reaches of human experience—and beyond.

Best known for his enduring contributions to the horror genre, particularly his epochal debut offering *Re-Animator* (1985) and its equally lubricous follow-up, *From Beyond* (1986), Gordon also pivoted between the brawny science fictions of *Robot Jox* (1989), *Fortress* (1992), and *Space Truckers* (1996), before winding his talents around the sweet-tempered fantasy of *The Wonderful Ice Cream Suit* (1998) to accommodate such resolutely nihilistic drama-thrillers as *King of the Ants* (2003), *Edmond* (2005), and *Stuck* (2007). One might be hard-pressed to call his diverse output subtle given that Gordon's potent use of symbolism was at times undeniably heavy-handed. Yet each of his films is animated by a singularly subversive spirit, often scrubbing the line drawn between exploitation and arthouse cinema.

In his compelling 1986 profile of the director for *Rolling Stone* (included in this volume), David Edelstein noted that "Gordon inhabits a place where trash, art and politics intersect and where the giddy smashing of taboos is a large part of the fun. He reserves the right to probe the boundaries of taste, because 'good taste' is how societies repress what they don't want to confront—even if those impulses wind up tearing them apart from the inside." Even at their most pungent and prurient, Gordon's films are characterized by their fiendish intelligence. There's always an authentic emotional and political dimension, and a discernible vigor in the way the filmmaker crunches together unflinching violence, queasy sex, and malignant comedy.

Throughout his cinema, Gordon constructed scenes of bold and delicious strangeness. Consider, if you will, the rasping severed head of *Re-Animator* administering oral sex to a naked, screaming co-ed strapped to an autopsy table—a gag labeled "the first visual pun"; the rapacious eel-like lower orders of *From Beyond* soundlessly swimming the air above the tuning forks of the

Pretorius Resonator—and the writhing pineal gland that sprouts obtrusively from a scientist's forehead; the condemned witch of *The Pit and the Pendulum* (1991), who, after ingesting gunpowder, explodes as she burns at the stake, decimating both her executioner and a baying crowd with fragments of her splintering skeleton; the emasculated wretch of *Castle Freak* (1994) awkwardly simulating lovemaking with a horrified child in a gauche gesture at humanity; the oddly moving climax of *Dagon* (2001) in which the near-immolated hero grows fish gills as he drowns; the housepainter-turned-hitman of *King of the Ants* visited by a humanoid insect eating handfuls of its own freshly laid feces; and the hapless pedestrian of *Stuck* facing a protracted death while lodged in the windshield of a car. These are ideas and imagery found nowhere else.[1]

Gordon's career straddled a period in which the cultural status of horror cinema—always a dependably profitable motion picture staple—underwent an appreciable shift. Elitist critics had routinely denigrated the genre, finding no redeeming philosophical or artistic value amidst the crudity of ideas and propensity for violence, viscera, and nudity. Slowly, they began to thaw, and noticed approvingly that filmmakers such as George A. Romero, Tobe Hooper, Wes Craven, and Larry Cohen were creating works that reflected the sociopolitical turbulence of the 1960s and '70s. For Gordon, too, horror and science fiction proved a natural fit for someone whose attitudes were forged from the tumult of his times. Having understood that these forms could masquerade as penetrating commentaries on the questions of the day, his works in theater and film were deliberately designed to be undeviating and visceral, enticing both highbrow and lowbrow audiences. "I have never separated art from having a good time," he told Edelstein, citing Shakespeare's corresponding use of violence and poetry to attract a viable market.

It may seem to some that Gordon arrived from nowhere in making such a big red splash with *Re-Animator*. However, he was in fact already a fully realized and uncompromising artist with an impressive pedigree. Born in Chicago, his early creative life centered on drawing and he worked for six months at a commercial art studio. Arriving in Madison to attend the University of Wisconsin, where he studied theater—Gordon was rejected from the only film course being offered—he eagerly embraced the values of the counterculture. By 1968, he had formed a company, Screw Theatre, which staged a notorious production of *Peter Pan* that featured a ten-minute LSD trip in which a psychedelic lightshow was projected onto the bodies of seven naked women dancers. Despite Gordon and his soon-to-be wife, Carolyn Purdy-Gordon (one of the disrobed females), being apprehended on obscenity charges, he remained unrepentant. In 1969, the pair cofounded the Organic Theatre Company, with Gordon serving as artistic director. Over the next fifteen years, with close to forty plays produced, the group established a formidable reputation amidst the burgeoning Chicago Theater scene.

In 1984, Gordon took a leave of absence from the Organic, having located a literary property he hoped would facilitate his transition to film. "Herbert West—Re-Animator" was a Lovecraft short story written and serialized in six parts in 1922 that detailed the experiments of a medical student who creates a serum that raises the dead with predictably disastrous consequences. Due to its episodic structure, Gordon considered adapting the serial as a pilot for a TV miniseries. He took the first installment and fashioned it into a thirty-minute teleplay. This became the basis of a feature script, which he shot after moving permanently to Los Angeles. Distributed by Charles Band's Empire Entertainment, known for cranking out ambitiously scruffy direct-to-video schlock on indigent budgets, *Re-Animator* opened in America in October 1985, achieving near-instant classic status—having already secured a Special Prize at the Cannes Film Festival. Released unrated in just 129 theaters (or 250, depending on the report), the film made its greatest impact afterward due to the proliferation of VCRs and video stores in the mid-1980s, ultimately earning $30 million against its $900,000 budget.

Now coroneted a progenitor of "splatstick"—films that marry gleeful gore with lacerating humor—Gordon acquired such sobriquets as the "Pop Buñuel" and "Hitchcock on helium." In the wake of this breakout big-screen triumph, Charles Band moved swiftly to bankroll Gordon's next three features. The first of these to appear was *From Beyond*, again an adaptation of an obscure Lovecraft story, this one revolving around the Resonator, a machine which allows anybody standing within its range to see strange life forms that exist beyond our perceptible reality. Unfavorably received by critics, the film also sparked ire amongst some Lovecraft purists for supplanting the author's philosophy of "cosmicism" (fear of the unspeakable horrors of a godless universe) in favor of intrusive S&M kinkiness and a parade of slime-secreting inter-dimensional rubber monsters. Contractually obliged to deliver an R rating, the phallocentric *From Beyond* retains *Re-Animator*'s thrifty number of locations and principals, but somehow feels more pleasingly ambitious, qualities that gained the respect of critic Roger Ebert:

> In its own way, [*From Beyond*] is quite a job. We live in a time when kids are so sophisticated about special effects that they don't get scared by movie monsters, they sit back and evaluate the fake blood and the latex masks. Gordon's mission seems to be to return real fear, real depravity, to the horror film, and he's a genuine stylist. . . . At a time when almost any exploitation movie can make money if its ads are clever enough, this is a movie that tries to mix some satire and artistry in with the slime.[2]

Beneath their gristle of unbridled mayhem, *Re-Animator* and *From Beyond* are commentaries on the perils of intellectual pride since, like *Frankenstein* (1818), they involve scientists who pay a steep price in trying to acquire knowledge, fame, and power. This chafes against Gordon's belief that "[man] should try to know as much as he can,"[3] and is pitched closer to the idea that repressed sexual energy inevitably explodes in destruction. The metamorphosis Barbara Crampton's character undergoes from buttoned-down psychiatrist to leather-clad temptress is mirrored by the salacious Dr. Pretorius's conversion into a shape-shifting entity whose sordid appetites have only deepened. Transformation, a key theme in Gordon's work, is evident in his next film, *Dolls* (1987). The articulate intellectuals are here substituted by youthful protagonists who find themselves in an isolated mansion owned by an elderly couple who punish immoral people by turning them into toys. Harkening back to the cramped histrionics favored by James Whale, Gordon also drew on Bruno Bettelheim in crafting a Grimm's fairy tale intended to appeal to adults, one whose message is "being a parent is a privilege, not a right."[4]

Clearly, Gordon was feeling his way towards reaching a broader mainstream audience. Expressing a desire to make a movie his children could see, he developed the family fantasy *Teenie Weenies* for Disney, which would later be rechristened by the studio as *Honey, I Shrunk the Kids* (1989). Gordon saw this project as a sugarcoated variation on his favorite theme of "a scientist and an experiment that goes horribly wrong."[5] Regrettably, he was forced to withdraw from directing what would prove a popular picture due to pressing health concerns. During this period, Gordon helmed the pulp science fiction actioner *Robot Jox* (1989) for Empire. At a cost of more than $7 million, *Robot Jox* was the most expensive picture by far in the company's modest history. Detailing a future that parallels the Cold War, where robot colossi piloted by humans are pitted against each other, the film proved Empire's swan song. Neither critics nor audiences warmed to its intoxicating blend of comic book adventure and heartfelt antiwar sentiments.

Meanwhile, Gordon directed *Daughter of Darkness* (1990), an atmospheric television movie for CBS. Lensed in Hungary, the story concerns a young American woman who travels alone to Romania in search of the father she never knew (played with palpable relish by Anthony Perkins in one of his final roles) only to discover that he is in fact a vampire. Gordon then shot *The Pit and the Pendulum* in Italy for Full Moon Entertainment (Band's new company after Empire's dissolution), a handsomely mounted adaptation that loosely plundered the work of his great literary hero, Edgar Allan Poe. Set during the Spanish Inquisition, it's a film of considerable intelligence and ambition, as well as a scrofulous allegory for the divisive policies of the Ronald Reagan/George H. W. Bush administrations and institutions such as the MPAA—the latter, an organization Gordon would often come into depressing conflict with. Boasting an admirable attention to historical detail and punctuated with a mordant wit and enough violence to sate the director's more sanguinary fans, the film serves as a biting cautionary tale for our age.

For his next project, the dystopian science fiction prison picture *Fortress*, Gordon imagined an intensely voyeuristic future in which an ex-army officer and his pregnant wife are imprisoned in a maximum security facility by a right-wing totalitarian regime. Crowded with clever ideas, *Fortress* also exhibited Gordon's evolving skills at handling sequences of robust action. *Castle Freak*, a loose reworking of Lovecraft's short story "The Outsider" (1921), was a stately paced study of grief, guilt, and the familial covenants that pain and bind us. The narrative deals with a recovering alcoholic who arrives in Italy with his wife and daughter to finalize the sale of the medieval castle he has inherited, only to discover that they share their decaying abode with a hideously disfigured savage who has escaped from its dungeon shackles. Jonathan Fuller's portrayal of the titular monster, whose tongue and genitalia have been detached by its crazed mother, is remarkable, conveying both animalistic ferocity and a childlike vulnerability that—like many of Gordon's works—veers from the perverse to the poignant.

Gordon exchanged the somber airlessness of *Castle Freak* for the levity and unruly B-picture invention of the freewheeling *Space Truckers*. Hailed as "the world's first science fiction road movie," this outing starred Dennis Hopper as an intergalactic truck driver hired to transport what he believes to be a contingent of sex dolls bound for Earth. The suspicious cargo is in fact a race of destructive biomechanical super soldiers created by yet another of the director's mad scientists. Neither Hopper's presence, nor the sharp wit of Ted Mann's screenplay, were enough to avert the film's excoriation by critics or its ruinous box office. Unbowed, Gordon rebounded with *The Wonderful Ice Cream Suit* for Walt Disney Pictures. This heartening fantasy was adapted by Ray Bradbury from his own short story, which tells of five Mexican-American men who combine their scant finances to purchase a magical white suit that grants the wishes of whoever wears it. Bradbury was delighted with Gordon's film, which faithfully replicates the wistful tone and refined moralizing of its exquisite source.

Throughout the 2000s, the auteurs who had reshaped the landscape of horror cinema throughout the 1970s and '80s enjoyed contrasting fortunes: George Romero was deemed content to regurgitate "pale imitation[s]"[6] of such achievements as *Night of the Living Dead* (1968) and *Dawn of the Dead* (1979); Tobe Hooper was labeled a "fright film pariah"[7] for churning out anonymous efforts that included a remake (in 2004's *The Toolbox Murders*) of a film that had parroted his masterpiece *The Texas Chain Saw Massacre* (1974); Larry Cohen had reverted back to hawking spec scripts like *Phone Booth* (2002) and *Cellular* (2005) around Hollywood offices; Wes Craven delivered compromised and colorless studio product like *Cursed* (2004), *My Soul to Take* (2007), and *Scream 4* (2011); David Cronenberg had all but abandoned the genre to range the artier edges of the mainstream with *Spider* (2002), *A Dangerous Method* (2010), and *Cosmopolis* (2012); while John Carpenter—save for *Ghosts of Mars* (2001) and *The Ward* (2010)—focused predominantly on creating music after a sequence of critical and commercial duds led inexorably to disenchantment and burnout.

During this same period, Gordon generated some of his darkest and most fiercely experimental works, bludgeoning audiences into submission with films that danced sinuously between subtlety and shock. His first contribution of the new millennium was *Dagon* (2001), an amalgamation of Lovecraft's first published short story, "Dagon" (1917), and his classic novella, "The Shadow over Innsmouth" (1936). The film follows a young dotcom millionaire whose boat is scuttled on rocks off the coast of Spain. Forced to seek refuge in a soggy, labyrinthine fishing village, he discovers the residents have disavowed God in favor of an ancient aquatic deity and are mutating into a fish-like species that practices human sacrifice. Having seized upon this twisty and propulsive setup, Gordon created one of his most self-consciously stylish and nightmarish films—shooting it entirely with a handheld camera and displaying no subtitles in a bid to locate the viewer within the confused isolation of its hero. *Dagon* flies in the face of those who claim the irreconcilability of Lovecraft's literature and the qualifications of cinema.

It was followed by a trio of features—*King of the Ants*, *Edmond*, and *Stuck*—that saw Gordon steering away from the supernatural menaces that had stalked his earlier productions in lieu of more recognizably human monsters. Based on the novel by Charles Higson (originally set in London, transposed in the author's screenplay to suburban Los Angeles), *King of the Ants* accents Gordon's implicit concern with the desensitizing effects of cartoon cinema violence in this bruising story of a naïve young drifter who accepts the offer of money from a shady businessman to murder a local accountant. Considerably coarser than most of the director's oeuvre, but far more complex than its unvarnished plot would suggest, this tightly wound thriller is built around Chris L. McKenna's carefully muted performance as the "King of the Ants." A victim of repeated acts of teeth-grinding torture, the retaliatory explosion of bloodshed the novice hitman visits upon his tormentors merely confirms his recent aptitude for violence; the implication being that the potential for perpetrating acts of depravity lurks within each of us.

Edmond, adapted by the Pulitzer Prize-winning playwright and screenwriter David Mamet from his own 1982 one-act play, is another immersive and traumatic viewing experience. An embittered Manhattan businessman abruptly leaves his wife and drifts into a sleazy neon underworld of back alleys, bars, and bordellos. Charting a descent into bigotry, murder, and, ultimately, a kind of fulfillment, *Edmond*—as with *Dagon* and *King of the Ants*—spotlights a character that is seemingly meeting an inevitable destiny. Held together by William H. Macy's committed turn in the eponymous role, the film prospers from the luxury of surrounding its lead with members of Gordon's "repertory company" (Joe Mantegna, Jeffrey Combs, George Wendt, and Debi Mazar). "It manages, in the course of a single tersely delineated story, to say more about the dark pathology of American racism than any five character arcs in *Crash* [2004]," wrote *LA Weekly* critic Ron Stringer in his review, before urging all viewers to approach this timely vision of urban despair with caution.

Gordon's final feature, *Stuck*, is a nauseating horror fable ripped from the pages of the tabloids, and is based on the true story of Chante Mallard, a Texas woman who, while intoxicated, smashed her car into Gregory Glen Biggs, a thirty-seven-year-old homeless man. Biggs became embedded in the vehicle's windshield, with Mallard leaving him there after driving into her garage. Gordon's dramatization of this grisly event exhibits his customary black humor (dismayed that her white-collar victim—who is impaled on a windshield wiper and bleeding over her dashboard—refuses to expire, the self-absorbed driver asks, "Why are you doing this to *me*?") and the abrasive splicing of irony with social commentary (illegal immigrants are the only people who stumble upon this morbid development, but are unwilling to intervene for fear of alerting the authorities). *Stuck* is a bleak and unswerving examination of humanity at its worst, as Gordon reminds us of the appalling cost of losing one's compassion and empathy.

Between *Edmond* and *Stuck*, Gordon supplied two superior installments of *Masters of Horror* (2005–2007), an anthology series for Showtime that gathered some of the most celebrated directors in the genre. The first was an update of Lovecraft's "Dreams in the Witch-House," in which a student who has rented an attic room in a Massachusetts boardinghouse encounters a witch from another dimension. This was followed in the second season by a polished period adaptation of "The Black Cat," which evokes but does not slavishly adhere to Poe's classic tale, incorporating elements from the author's life and placing him at the black, beating heart of the action. The latter boasts an impeccable performance by Jeffrey Combs as a beleaguered Poe battling alcoholism, writer's block, invasive hallucinations, and his young wife's terminal illness. So affecting was Combs in the role, it prompted Gordon to resurrect the character for the 2009 play *Nevermore: An Evening with Edgar Allan Poe*, penned by his frequent screenwriter Dennis Paoli.

Gordon's final work for television was "Eater" (2008), a segment of NBC's *Fear Itself*, starring Elisabeth Moss as a rookie cop assigned to guard a cannibalistic killer overnight in an isolated police station. In his remaining twelve years, Gordon saw his life come full circle with a well-publicized "return to the theater" (in truth he had directed plays apace with making movies). The multi-award-winning *Re-Animator: The Musical* (2011) was hailed by critics as a "superbly performed and perfectly calibrated" revisiting of "a horror classic."[8] It honored the untrammeled insanity of the original film, even designating a special "Splash Zone" for patrons where the first three rows would be duly soaked with blood. A critically acclaimed Los Angeles stage production of *Taste* followed in 2014. This is Benjamin Brand's piquant fact-based play about consensual cannibalism, inspired by the notorious crimes of Armin Meiwes, a former computer repair technician from Germany who killed and ate a voluntary victim he met online. At turns both moving and disquieting, *Taste* verified that Gordon, in almost half a century of relentless ingenuity, had lost none of his transgressive edge.

The thirty-six articles compiled in this volume are spread across more than fifty years. In keeping with other entries in the Conversations with Filmmakers series, the pieces have been drawn from an assortment of magazines, books, websites, and programs. Each was selected for the purpose of not only chronicling the trajectory of a fascinating career—one which succeeded in bringing an unfamiliar archness, complexity, and critical respect to genre cinema, and with them, a host of new viewers—but calling attention to its subject's evolving awareness as an artist. Time and again, Gordon proves an erudite and engaged thinker, articulating the themes, methods, and minutiae of his creativity with honesty and insight. Whether dissecting the reasons why his searing visions often illuminated society's nagging anxieties and misgivings or addressing the charge that slathering vast dollops of slime over his actors was more injurious to scissor-happy censors than buckets of blood, he devotes equal attention and perspicuity to every discussion.

Always an accessible subject, Gordon left behind no shortage of available interviews. Owing to the high number I have curated for this collection, it is inevitable that some of his responses are offered more than once, particularly in regard to the abiding popularity of *Re-Animator*, the achievements of the Organic Theatre, and his affirmation that *Psycho* (1960) is the scariest film ever made. Three interviews (by Dennis Fischer, Paul Kane, and Danny Draven) have been edited slightly on the sufferance of their authors to partially remedy this issue. Others, such as those by John A. Gallagher, Mark Wheaton, James Morgart, and myself, are being published for the first time or in a hitherto unexpurgated form. Happily, the repetitions often yield new surprises, with elaborations that provide an even more comprehensive understanding of his work. When confronted with the same question with little or no variation, Gordon invariably stayed calm and inviting, answering with careful thought as if hearing the query for the first time.

That was especially true when pondering *Re-Animator*, regarded by many to be the apotheosis of the director's career (critic Stanley Wiater suggests in his 1990 piece it is Gordon's *Citizen Kane*).

From Frank Ryan's short opening salvo for the *Petoskey News-Review*—one of Gordon's first published interviews—to his wide-ranging conversations with other notable journalists and authors, the filmmaker was nothing if not consistent in his outlook. He regularly stated his core beliefs as an artist: an abhorrence of censorship and an unwavering faith in the discerning intelligence of the audience. In other interviews, such as Gallagher's lengthy exchange for his book *Film Directors on Directing* (1989) and Draven's 2009 chat for *The Filmmaker's Book of the Dead: A Mortal's Guide to Making Horror Movies* (2015), Gordon articulates his working process, his dependence on storyboards, his steadfast relationships with Dennis Paoli and exhibitor Charles Band, his desire to learn new approaches in "ultra-low" DIY filmmaking, and the appeal he finds toiling in flexible generic forms. "I think that comedy works really well with horror," he told Gallagher. "It's like salt and pepper. You need both spices. But I would never want the comedy to get in the way of the scares or vice versa."

Despite assertions that he lacked the technical flair and all-purpose craftsmanship of a film school-educated contemporary like John Carpenter, Gordon's facility as a visual stylist is underrated. These interviews reveal his passage from theater to film was at times marked by feelings of uncertainty, even inadequacy (Gordon was thirty-eight when he first warmed a director's chair on the set of *Re-Animator*). Like many others, he snatched a handful of flourishes for his maiden effort from two acknowledged masters, Alfred Hitchcock and Roman Polanski: appropriating the swinging light bulb, which in part illuminates the struggle two medical students engage in with a maniacal dead cat, from *Psycho*, and the disconcerting "subjective over-the-shoulder" shots from *Rosemary's Baby* (1968). If, to begin with, Gordon was indeed short on technique, he more than compensated for this deficiency. Note his preternatural knack for extracting strong performances from his actors as well as an ability to create an atmospheric, hermetically sealed world in which to spin his adroitly done stories. Always, he made horror a serious art form.

As editor of *Stuart Gordon: Interviews*, I would like to gratefully acknowledge those who assisted me in the realization of my book. First and foremost, I thank the writers, publishers, editors, and institutions who have granted me permission to transcribe and reprint their articles. Many of them took time to impart their affection and respect for Stuart and his work and checked in with me at regular intervals to inquire about my progress with the project. I also wish to express my indebtedness to the University Press of Mississippi, particularly to Emily Bandy for her guidance and encouragement. I extend a special note of thanks to my wife, Siân, and my children, Poppy and Milo, whose love and tireless support are as essential to me as air, light, and water. The following people also aided me: Jon Abrams, Doug Barron, William Butler, Thom Carnell, Mick Garris, Ron Garver, Trevor Hillman, Alex Humphrey, S. T. Joshi, Jeremy McBain, Pete Mesling, Christopher Micklos, Phil Nobile Jr., Hank Nuwer, Marilynn Preston, Ronald Rand, Debbie Rochon, Ben Rock, Jessica Safavimehr, Mark Shostrom, Shannon Blake Skelton, Adam Torkel, and Peter Tonguette.

Finally, I wish to dedicate this book to the late Stuart Gordon, whose films I have adored ever since my premature exposure to *Re-Animator* as a saucer-eyed eleven-year-old. Many years later, having the pleasure of interviewing Stuart for the first time (one of three dialogues I have contributed to this volume), I told him about that fateful day, how I'd gaped disbelievingly at such sights as a talking head oozing over a denuded female student, and sticky ropes of intestine spewing out of a ruptured torso to lasso Herbert West. It is, perhaps not unexpectedly, an experience that helped inspire and nourish a lifelong passion for horror cinema. My story educed a hearty chuckle from Stuart, followed by a good-natured admonishment of my parents for allowing me "to be subjected to such a movie." I had been looking forward to reminding him of this episode during a final interview, the exchange that was to have concluded this collection, scheduled for March 23, 2020.

On March 21, I was contacted by Carolyn Purdy-Gordon, who thoughtfully informed me that her husband of fifty-two years had been admitted to the hospital that same afternoon after feeling unwell. Carolyn conveyed Stuart's regret at having "to be the fly in the ointment" in postponing our conversation, but added that if he were to be discharged from the hospital in the interim, he would submit himself to me at the agreed time. Lamentably, this was never to be. Stuart Gordon died on March 24, at the age of seventy-two, from multiple organ failure. The loss of this rare talent was deeply felt by genre aesthetes, but their grief pales when measured against that borne by Stuart's family and friends. His many fans must find solace in the not inconsiderable gift of those uncommon films he made, as well as the inexpugnable memories a fortunate few preserve of his audacious plays. One is hopeful that the eloquent accounts and reflections their creator expressed about these works, presented here for your inspection, shall enjoy such an afterlife.

MD

Notes

1. An exception is the 2010 Bollywood remake of *Stuck*, *Accident on Hill Road* (2009), directed by Mahesh Nair, which draws on the same case that inspired Gordon's film.
2. Roger Ebert, *Chicago Sun-Times*, October 24, 1986.
3. David Edelstein, "Stuart Gordon's Shock Treatment," *Rolling Stone*, November 20, 1986.
4. Phil Nobile Jr., "The Badass Interview: Stuart Gordon," *Birth. Movies. Death*, November 21, 2014.
5. Mick Garris, *Post Mortem with Mick Garris*, June 7, 2017.
6. This comes from a review of *Survival of the Dead* (2010) by Cole Smithey, the self-styled "smartest critic in the world," May 25, 2010.
7. Ben Gibbon, "Depth of Field: The Quick Rise and Spectacular Fall of Tobe Hooper," *PopMatters.com*, October 22, 2006.
8. Myron Meisel, "*Re-Animator the Musical*: Theater Review," *Hollywood Reporter*, November 24, 2011.

Chronology

1947 Stuart Alan Gordon is born on August 11 in Chicago, Illinois, the first child of Bernard Leo Gordon (1909-1961), a production manager for Helene Curtis Industries, a manufacturer of personal care products, and Rosalie Lotta Gordon (1910-93), a social worker and later an English teacher. A brother, David George Gordon, is born in 1950, and grows up to be a writer of nature books and a noted bug chef.

1961-65 Attends the Lane Technical Preparatory High School in Chicago, where he majors in art. Following graduation, he works briefly at a commercial art studio.

1965-69 Attends the University of Wisconsin in Madison as a theater major.

1968 Forms a theater company, Screw Theatre, and directs a controversial production of *Peter Pan*. Obscenity charges are leveled against him for the play—as well as vociferous complaints from the estate of J. M. Barrie—and he experiences police harassment for several years afterwards. Marries Carolyn Purdy on December 20.

1969-78 Cofounds the Organic Theatre with his wife using money from their wedding. Over the next fifteen years, with Gordon installed as artistic director, the Chicago-based company mounts thirty-seven plays and tours the world. Notable productions include *Warp* (1971), an epic science fiction trilogy co-authored by Larry Kleinfeld that later has a disastrous run on Broadway; *Poe* (1972), about the life and writings of Edgar Allan Poe; the world premiere of David Mamet's *Sexual Perversity in Chicago* (1974); and the violent "quasi-feminist" swashbuckler *Bloody Bess* (1974), the latter earning Gordon the first of multiple nominations for the Joseph Jefferson Award for Best Director of a Play. In 1975, he wins the award for his acclaimed production of *Huckleberry Finn Part 1*.

1979 Directs a taped presentation of his popular 1977 production *Bleacher Bums*, a play about Chicago baseball fans, for PBS. It wins the Midwest Emmy for Outstanding Achievement for Entertainment—Single Program.

1982-84 Receives his seventh and final nomination for the Joseph Jefferson Award for *E/R* (1982). The play inspires a sitcom by Norman Lear that

	runs for one season on CBS. Develops the comedy movie *Assembly Line* with actor Joe Mantegna, about workers who purchase their factory after it faces a takeover by a larger company. Gordon takes a leave of absence from the Organic Theatre to pursue a career as a film director after the board is appalled at the prospect of his making a horror movie. Begins shooting *Re-Animator* at the S&A Studios, Hollywood, in November 1984.
1985	In January, while *Re-Animator* is being edited, Gordon returns to Chicago to direct a revival of *Huckleberry Finn* at the Goodman Theatre. In May, *Re-Animator* premieres out of competition at the Cannes Film Festival, winning the Prix Special, ahead of its release in America on October 18. That same year, the film also wins First Prize at the Sitges Film Festival and earns a Special Mention Award at the Avoriaz Fantastic Film Festival. Between Thanksgiving and Christmas, he starts shooting his second feature, *Dolls*, at the Dinocittà soundstages located on the outskirts of Rome.
1986	After completing production on *Dolls*, Gordon immediately starts shooting *From Beyond* at Dinocittà from February to April. The film is released on October 24. Over the next year he develops a slate of unmade projects: *Berserker*, a body horror film written for Arnold Schwarzenegger about an athlete who mutates into a monster after ingesting a bad steroid; *Gris-Gris*, a shocker based on the life of nineteenth-century voodoo practitioner Marie Laveau; *Lurking Fear*, a period adaptation of H. P. Lovecraft's tale of a degenerate family of cannibalistic creatures hiding in the Catskill Mountains; *Bloody Bess*, a film version of Gordon's play for the Organic about a noblewoman turned pirate; and *Cops*, a project for TriStar Pictures starring Jim Belushi and based on another Organic play by Terry Curtis Fox.
1987	Begins shooting *RoboJox*, a film inspired by the Transformers toy line, between January and April. Although shot before *From Beyond*, *Dolls* is released after it on March 6 due to the extensive stop-motion animation required to realize the titular terrors. Develops the family fantasy film *Teenie Weenies* for Disney.
1988	Writes, produces, and directs *Kid Safe: The Video*, a thirty-minute horror-themed direct-to-video film made in conjunction with the American Association of Pediatrics and the Kid Safe Project. Unexpectedly becomes ill just two weeks before shooting is to commence on *Teenie Weenies* (now re-titled *Honey, I Shrunk the Kids*). Disney replaces Gordon as director with Joe Johnston.

1989	Develops an unmade half-hour horror anthology series for HBO called *Asylum*. In September, he travels to Hungary, spending three weeks there shooting the TV movie *Daughter of Darkness*, which stars Anthony Perkins and Mia Sara.
1990	*Daughter of Darkness* is broadcast on the CBS network on January 26. Shoots *The Pit and the Pendulum* at Charles Band's fifteenth-century Castello di Giove in Italy between September and October. *Bride of Re-Animator*, a sequel to *Re-Animator* directed by Brian Yuzna, premieres at the Toronto Film Festival on September 8 and is released in the US in February of the following year. *RoboJox*—now re-titled *Robot Jox*—is finally released on November 21 after a frustrating two-year delay.
1991	In March, Gordon pitches an adaptation of Brett Easton Ellis's novel *American Psycho* to producer Ed Pressman. He meets with Johnny Depp, who agrees to star, but the rights are suddenly pulled after the critical and commercial success of *The Silence of the Lambs* alerts Ellis's agent to the new potential of the project. *The Pit and the Pendulum* is released on June 2. That same month, Gordon directs Wendy Hammond's play *The Ghostman* at the Harman Avenue Theatre, Los Angeles. It stars Ian Patrick Williams as a family man driven to the edge of madness by memories of his late father molesting him as a boy. Begins developing a film adaptation of *Iron Man* with Stan Lee and Marvel, as well as a "kaiju" monster movie for producers Paul Maslansky and Benni Korzen called *Tor* about a giant snapping turtle. Both projects drift into oblivion. Begins shooting *Fortress* in Queensland, Australia, in September.
1992	Co-writes *Body Snatchers* with Dennis Paoli, a second remake of *Invasion of the Body Snatchers* (1956), with the intention of directing it. Due to his lengthy commitment to *Fortress*, the job instead goes to Abel Ferrara. Gordon executive produces *Honey, I Blew Up the Kid* and is contracted to develop family films for Walt Disney Pictures. In October, he joins the jury at the Sitges Film Festival.
1993	*Fortress* is released in America on September 3, eventually grossing $40 million worldwide against its $12 million budget, and is nominated for the Grand Prize at the Avoriaz Film Festival. *Body Snatchers*—now featuring additional writing credits for Larry Cohen, Raymond Cistheri, and Nicholas St. John—premieres at the Cannes Film Festival on May 15. Develops the superhero horror film *Faust: Love of the Damned* for Burnett-Chalmers Productions, based on the ultraviolent thirteen-part graphic novel of the same name by David Quinn and Tim Virgil. Works on an unmade adaptation of Dean R. Koontz's 1989 novel

Midnight about townsfolk transformed into emotionless computer-enhanced drones.

1994 Returns to the Castello di Giove to shoot *Castle Freak*. Originally slated for a theatrical run in late October through Pulse Pounders, a subsidiary of Charles Band's Full Moon Entertainment, the film's release is postponed.

1995 Directs the live-action portions of the interactive motion-simulation ride *Aliens: Ride at the Speed of Fright* for Praxis Films and Iwerks Entertainment. Based on James Cameron's *Aliens* (1986), it stars Jeffrey Combs as a marine who is the sole survivor of a Xenomorph attack. *Castle Freak* is released on video on November 14.

1996 Brian Yuzna's *The Dentist*, a horror film Gordon co-wrote with Dennis Paoli, initially to direct himself, is released on October 18. Working with his highest-ever budget ($25 million), Gordon begins shooting *Space Truckers* at Ardmore Studios in the Republic of Ireland.

1997 *Space Truckers* is released in April, grossing a disappointing $2 million. Later that year, Gordon begins shooting *The Wonderful Ice Cream Suit* for Disney from a screenplay written by his friend Ray Bradbury.

1998 *The Wonderful Ice Cream Suit* premieres at the Sundance Film Festival on January 23 and is released on video after playing the festival circuit. In June, Gordon wins the Best Director Award for the film at the Eighteenth Fantafestival in Rome. Directs a Halloween-themed episode of *Honey, I Shrunk the Kids: The TV Show* entitled "Honey, Let's Trick-or-Treat," which is broadcast on October 24. Makes a cameo appearance as "Second Doctor" in John Landis's film *Susan's Plan*.

1999 Co-writes and produces *Progeny* for director Brian Yuzna, which is released on March 30. In December, he directs the play *Kabbalah*, subtitled "Scary Jewish Stories" and based on translations by folklorist Howard Schwartz, at the Lex Theatre, Los Angeles. The stories include a fallen mystic's scheme to transport Helen of Troy across the centuries, a bridegroom whose bride turns out to be one of the walking dead, and a wicked sorcerer's last chance for redemption.

2000 Executive produces *Snail Boy*, a short film by Travis Hottinger, and also appears in the supporting role of Clint's Biker Relative. *Faust: Love of the Damned*, now directed by Brian Yuzna without Gordon's involvement, premieres on October 12 to mixed reviews. In November, Gordon finally begins shooting his long-cherished project *Dagon* in Spain after a fifteen-year effort.

2001 *Dagon* debuts at the Sitges Film Festival on October 12. A second made-for-TV version of Gordon's play *Bleacher Bums* is produced by Paramount Television and Showtime. Directed by Saul Rubinek, it premieres at the Chicago Film Festival on October 18 before airing the following April.

2002 *Dagon* is released on video on July 23. That same month, Gordon starts shooting *King of the Ants*, a neo-noir thriller based on the novel by Charles Higson. Produces *Deathbed*, a horror film directed by Danny Draven about a possessed bed. Agrees to helm the monster movie *Where the Chill Waits*, from a script by the novelist T. Chris Martindale based on his own 1991 book. The project, which concerns four men who encounter the mythological Wendigo, never happens. Attends the first of the annual "Masters of Horror" dinners held in a reasonably priced Los Angeles restaurant. The inaugural attendees are John Carpenter, Guillermo del Toro, Tobe Hooper, Larry Cohen, Joe Dante, Mick Garris, John Landis, Don Coscarelli, William Malone, and Bob Burns.

2003 *Beyond Re-Animator*, a second sequel to *Re-Animator*—once again directed by Brian Yuzna, without Gordon's participation—is released on April 4 to mixed reviews. *King of the Ants* opens on June 13. Acquires the rights to Jack Ketchum's hardcore horror novel *Ladies Night*, in which a tanker truck ferrying a toxic chemical spills its haul onto a New York City street, transforming women into bestial men-killers. Despite his best efforts over the ensuing decade, Gordon is unable to secure financing for the project.

2004 Shoots *Edmond* in Los Angeles from a script by David Mamet. Gordon reveals he is finally working on his own sequel to *Re-Animator* titled *House of Re-Animator*, a riposte to the ineptitudes of the George W. Bush/Dick Cheney administration. William H. Macy is lined-up to play "Dubya" alongside George Wendt as Cheney and Barbara Crampton as the first lady, with Jeffrey Combs and Bruce Abbott returning to play Herbert West and Dan Cain, respectively. Sadly, the film is never realized.

2005 In August, Gordon begins shooting "Dreams in the Witch-House" in Canada, an installment of Showtime's *Masters of Horror* TV series based on the short story by H. P. Lovecraft. *Edmond* premieres at the Venice Film Festival on August 31. "Dreams in the Witch-House" airs on Showtime on November 4.

2006 Gordon returns for the second season of *Masters of Horror*. This time he and Dennis Paoli adapt Edgar Allan Poe's "The Black Cat," starring Jeffrey Combs as Poe, which begins shooting in September. In October, he wins the New Visions Award at the Sitges Film Festival for *Edmond*.

	Arrives back in Canada in November to shoot *Stuck*, a tabloid horror-thriller inspired by a true story.
2007	"The Black Cat" airs on Showtime on January 19. *Stuck* premieres at the Fantasy Film Fest in Germany on August 1. Develops a script called '*68*, a semi-autobiographical love story. It is set amid the riots that occurred during the 1968 Democratic National Convention, in which Gordon, his wife, and other anti-Vietnam War protestors were assaulted by members of the Chicago police and National Guardsmen under the orders of Mayor Richard Daley.
2008	Directs "Eater," an episode of the TV series *Fear Itself* airing on July 3, a remake of a segment of the British horror anthology show *Urban Gothic* (2000–2001). After playing on the festival circuits in both North America and Europe, *Stuck* is given a limited release in the US on May 30. It wins the Silver Raven at the Brussels International Festival of Fantasy Film and the Staff Prize at the San Francisco Film Festival for Best Narrative Feature.
2009	Teaming again with Jeffrey Combs and Dennis Paoli, Gordon directs the one-man play *Nevermore: An Evening with Edgar Allan Poe*. It is mounted at the Steve Allen Theatre, Los Angeles, to coincide with the bicentennial of Poe's birth and continues to tour until 2014. In August, Gordon joins the jury of the Venice Film Festival.
2010	Commits to helming the science fiction script *The Men* while attending the memorial service of its author, Dan O'Bannon, who had succumbed to complications of Crohn's disease in December of the previous year. The story concerns a woman who discovers that Earth is captive to an alien race that took over the planet half a million years ago. In September, Gordon is honored with a retrospective of his work at the MOTELX Film Festival in Lisbon.
2011	Co-writes, co-produces, and directs *Re-Animator: The Musical*, which premieres at the Steve Allen Theatre in March to considerable acclaim, and features music and lyrics by Mark Nutter.
2012	*Re-Animator: The Musical* enjoys a second run at the Hayworth Theatre, Los Angeles, prior to engagements at the New York Musical Theater Festival in July and the Edinburgh Fringe Festival in August. The production wins the Best Book Award from the Ovation Awards and the Los Angeles Drama Critics Circle Award for Best Musical Score. It also secures six awards from *LA Weekly* including Best Musical.
2013	Works on a script with John Strysik, his co-screenwriter of *Stuck*, about the notorious nineteenth-century American serial killer H. H. Holmes. Launches a Kickstarter campaign on October 1 to raise funds for a

	feature film adaptation of *Nevermore*, with a plan to shooting it in the summer of 2014 in expectation of an early 2015 release. The campaign ends on November 1, garnering just $92,804 against Gordon's pledge of $375,000. The project is abandoned. In November, he receives the Michael J. Hein Award for Personal Achievement in Direction at the New York City Horror Film Festival.
2014	Directs *Taste*, a play written by Benjamin Brand, which premieres at the Sacred Fools Theatre Company, Los Angeles, in April. It is based on the true story of "The Rotenburg Cannibal" Armin Meiwes.
2015	In April, Gordon wins a Stage Raw Theater Award for his direction of *Taste*. Cameos as Sherlock Holmes in "Grim Grinning Ghost," Axelle Carolyn's contribution to the ten-segment anthology horror film *Tales of Halloween*, which also features an appearance by Barbara Crampton as a witch. Directs an adaptation of Lovecraft's 1924 short story "The Hound" for *Tales from Beyond the Pale*, a horror anthology podcast that presents "Radio Plays for the Digital Age." Scripted by Dennis Paoli, and featuring a score by Richard Band, the episode stars Barbara Crampton, Ezra Godden, and Chris L. McKenna.
2017	Updates the script of his stage play adaptation of Kurt Vonnegut's comic science fiction novel *The Sirens of Titan*, first performed by the Organic in October 1977. The new production is directed by Ben Rock as the closing show of the Sacred Fools Theatre Company's twentieth season.
2020	Dies on March 24, in Los Angeles, at the age of seventy-two. A remake of *Castle Freak*, directed by Tate Steinsiek, debuts on Shudder on December 3 ahead of a release on VOD and digital HD the following day.
2021	Gordon's memoirs, *Naked Theater and Uncensored Films*, are scheduled for posthumous publication by FAB Press.

Filmography

BLEACHER BUMS (1979)
Production Companies: WTTW and the Organic Theatre Company
Producer: Patterson Denny
Associate Producer: Paul Rocklin
Directors: **Stuart Gordon** and Patterson Denny
Associate Director: Wendy Roth
Teleplay: Roberta Custer, Richard Fire, Dennis Franz, Joe Mantegna, Josephine Paoletti, Carolyn Purdy-Gordon, Dennis Paoli, Michael Saad, Keith Szarabajka, and Ian Williams
Conceived by Joe Mantegna
Photography: Ken Clybor, Raymond O. Meinke, Carlos J. Tronshaw, and R. K. Wells Jr.
Editing: Susan Smeyak
Art Department: Robert Frederick Jr., Vicky Herman, and Michael Loewenstein
Makeup: Eva Agren
Cast: Roberta Custer (Melody King), Richard Fire (Marvin), Dennis Franz (Zig), Joe Mantegna (Decker), Carolyn Purdy-Gordon (Rose), Michael Saad (Greg), Keith Szarabajka (the Cheerleader), Ian Williams (Richie), Dennis Kennedy, William Daniels, and **Stuart Gordon** (uncredited)

RE-ANIMATOR (1985)
Production Companies: Empire Pictures, Re-Animator Productions
Producer: Brian Yuzna
Associate Producers: Bob Greenberg and Charles Donald Storey
Director: **Stuart Gordon**
Screenplay: Dennis Paoli, **Stuart Gordon,** and William J. Norris
Based on "Herbert West—Re-Animator" by H. P. Lovecraft
Photography: Mac Ahlberg (additional photography by Robert Ebinger, uncredited)
Editing: Lee Percy
Production Designer: Robert A. Burns
Music: Richard Band

Special Makeup Effects: Anthony Doublin, John Naulin and John Carl Buechler
Cast: Jeffrey Combs (Herbert West), Bruce Abbott (Daniel Cain), Barbara Crampton (Megan Halsey), David Gale (Dr. Carl Hill), Robert Sampson (Dean Halsey), Gerry Black (Mace), Carolyn Purdy-Gordon (Dr. Harrod), Peter Kent (Melvin the Re-Animated), Ian Patrick Williams (Swiss Doctor), Bunny Summers (Swiss Woman Doctor), Al Berry (Dr. Gruber), Barbara Pieters (Nurse), Annyce Holzman (ER Patient Corpse), Velvet Debois (Slit Wrist Girl Corpse), Lawrence Lowe (Failed Operation Corpse), Robert Holcomb (Motorcycle Accident Corpse), Mike Filloon (Bullet Wound to Face Corpse), Craig Reed (One Arm Man Corpse), Jack Draheim (Tall Skinny Guy Corpse), and Robert Pitzele (Bald OR Corpse)

FROM BEYOND (1986)
Production Companies: Empire Pictures, Taryn Prov
Producer: Brian Yuzna
Associate Producer: Bruce Curtis
Director: **Stuart Gordon**
Screenplay: Dennis Paoli
Adaptation by **Stuart Gordon**, Brian Yuzna, and Dennis Paoli
Based on the short story by H. P. Lovecraft
Photography: Mac Ahlberg
Editing: Lee Percy
Production Designer: Giovanni Natalucci
Music: Richard Band
Special Makeup Effects: Mark Shostrom, Anthony Doublin, John Naulin, and John Carl Buechler
Cast: Jeffrey Combs (Crawford Tillighast), Barbara Crampton (Dr. Katherine McMichaels), Ted Sorel (Dr. Edward Pretorius), Ken Foree (Bubba Brownlee), Carolyn Purdy-Gordon (Dr. Bloch), Bunny Summers (Neighbor Lady), Bruce McGuire (Jordan Fields), Del Russel (Ambulance Driver), Dale Wyatt (Paramedic), Karen Christenfeld (Nurse), Andy Miller (Patient in Strait Jacket), John Leamer (Shock Therapy Technician), Regina Bleesz (Bondage Girl), and Albert Band (Drunk, uncredited)

DOLLS (1987)
Production Companies: Empire Pictures, Taryn Productions, Inc.
Producer: Brian Yuzna
Associate Producers: Bruce Cohn Curtis, Debra Dion, and Michael Wolf
Director: **Stuart Gordon**
Screenplay: Ed Naha
Photography: Mac Ahlberg

Editing: Lee Percy
Production Designer: Giovanni Natalucci
Music: Fuzzbee Morse
Special Makeup Effects: John Carl Buechler
Doll Effects: David Allen
Cast: Guy Rolfe (Gabriel Hartwicke), Hilary Mason (Hilary Hartwicke), Stephen Lee (Ralph Morris), Carrie Lorraine (Judy Bower), Ian Patrick Williams (David Bower), Carolyn Purdy-Gordon (Rosemary Bower), Bunty Bailey (Isabel Prange), and Cassie Stuart (Enid)

KID SAFE: THE VIDEO (1988)
Production Companies: American Academy of Pediatrics, Master Digital, Inc., Novartis Consumer Health, Inc.
Producer: **Stuart Gordon**
Co-Producers: Michael Hirsh, Lisa Lieberman, and Roger Pryor
Director: **Stuart Gordon**
Screenplay: **Stuart Gordon**
Photography: Stephen Ashley Blake
Editing: Jonathan Lapidese
Production Designer: Stuart Blatt
Music: Jonathan Pearthree
Special Makeup Effects: Greg Cannom
Cast: Andrea Martin (Kathy Tudor), Shuko Akune (Tina), Stephen Lee (Ernie), Meshach Taylor (Marty), Joe Flaherty (Count Floyd), Daniel Welk (Jason), Grenelda Thornberry (Witch), John Vulich (Werewolf), Keith Edmier (Mummy), and Greg Cannom (Alien)

ROBOT JOX (1989)
Production Companies: Empire Pictures, Altar Productions
Producer: Albert Band
Associate Producer: Frank Hildebrand
Director: **Stuart Gordon**
Screenplay: Joe Haldeman
Story: **Stuart Gordon**
Photography: Mac Ahlberg
Editing: Lori Scott Ball and Ted Nicolaou
Production Designer: Giovanni Natalucci
Music: Frederic Talgorn
Stop-Motion Animation: David Allen
Cast: Gary Graham (Achilles), Anne-Marie Johnson (Athena), Paul Koslo

(Alexander), Robert Sampson (Commissioner Jameson), Danny Kamekona (Dr. Matsumoto), Hilary Mason (Professor Laplace), Michael Alldredge (Tex Conway), Jeffrey Combs (1st Prole), Michael Saad (2nd Prole), Ian Patrick Williams (Phillip), Jason Marsden (Tommy), Carolyn Purdy-Gordon (Kate), Thyme Lewis (Sargon), Gary Houston (Sportscaster), Russel Case (Hercules), and **Stuart Gordon** (Bartender, uncredited)

DAUGHTER OF DARKNESS (1990)
Production Companies: Accent Entertainment Corporation, King Phoenix Entertainment
Producer: Andras Hamori
Co-Producers: Andrew Laskos and Pál Sándor
Director: **Stuart Gordon**
Screenplay: Andrew Laskos
Photography: Iván Márk
Editing: Andy Horvitch
Production Designer: Tamás Hornyánszky
Music: Colin Towns
Special Makeup Effects: Craig Reardon
Cast: Anthony Perkins (Anton/Prince Constantine), Mia Sara (Katherine Thatcher), Robert Reynolds (Grigore), Dezsö Garas (Max), Jack Coleman (Devlin), Erika Bodnár (Nicole), and Mari Kiss (Elena)

THE PIT AND THE PENDULUM (1991)
Production Company: Full Moon Entertainment
Producer: Albert Band
Executive Producers: Charles Band and Michael Catalano
Director: **Stuart Gordon**
Screenplay: Dennis Paoli
Based on the story by Edgar Allan Poe
Photography: Adolfo Bartoli
Editing: Andy Horvitch
Production Designer: Giovanni Natalucci
Music: Richard Band
Special Makeup Effects: Greg Cannom
Cast: Lance Henriksen (Torquemada), Rona De Ricci (Maria), Jonathan Fuller (Antonio), Oliver Reed (The Cardinal), Jeffrey Combs (Francisco), Frances Bay (Esmeralda), Mark Margolis (Mendoza), Stephen Lee (Gomez), Tom Towles (Don Carlos), William J. Norris (Dr. Huesos), Carolyn Purdy-Gordon (Contessa D'Alba Molina), Larry Dolgin (Sergeant of the Guards), Geoffrey Copleston (Butcher),

Fabio Carfora (Beggar), Barbara Bocci (Contessa's Son), Benito Stefanelli (Executioner), and Fabrizio Fontana (Jew)

FORTRESS (1992)
Production Companies: Davis Entertainment Company, Village Roadshow Pictures, Fortress Films
Producers: John Davis and John Flock
Co-Producers: Michael Lake and Neal Nordlinger
Director: **Stuart Gordon**
Screenplay: Troy Neighbors, Steven Feinberg, David Venable, and Terry Curtis Fox
Story: Troy Neighbors and Steven Feinberg
Photography: David Eggby
Editing: Timothy Wellburn
Production Designer: David Copping
Music: Frederic Talgorn
Special Makeup Effects: Bob Clark
Cast: Christopher Lambert (John Henry Brennick), Kurtwood Smith (Prison Director Poe), Loryn Locklin (Karen B. Brennick), Clifton Gonzalez Gonzalez (Nino Gomez), Lincoln Kilpatrick (Abraham), Jeffrey Combs (D-Day), Tom Towles (Stiggs), Vernon Wells (Maddox), Carolyn Purdy-Gordon (Zed-10), Alan Zitner (Claustrophobic Prisoner), Deni Gordon (Karen's Cellmate), Eric Briant Wells (Border Guard), Dragicia Debert (Bio Scanner Guard), Heidi Stein (Pregnant Woman), Harry Nurmi (Guard #1), Peter Lamb (Guard #2), and Troy Hunter (Guard #3)

CASTLE FREAK (1994)
Production Company: Full Moon Entertainment
Producer: Maurizio Maggi
Co-Producer: Michael J. Mahoney
Director: **Stuart Gordon**
Screenplay: Dennis Paoli
Story: **Stuart Gordon** and Dennis Paoli
Based on the story "The Outsider" by H. P. Lovecraft
Photography: Mario Vulpiani
Editing: Bert Glatstein
Production Designer: Frank Vanorio
Music: Richard Band
Special Makeup Effects: Everett Burrell, John Vulich and Mike Measimer
Cast: Jeffrey Combs (John Reilly), Barbara Crampton (Susan Reilly), Jonathan

Fuller (Giorgio), Jessica Dollarhide (Rebecca Reilly), Massimo Sarchielli (Giannetti), Elisabeth Kaza (Agnese), Luca Zingaretti (Forte), Helen Stirling (Duchess D'Orsino), Alessandro Sebastian Satta (JJ), Raffaella Offidani (Sylvana), Marco Stefanelli (Benedetti), Tunny Piras (Grimaldi), Rolando Cortegiani (Tonio), Carolyn Purdy-Gordon, Suzanne Gordon, Jillian Gordon, and Margaret Gordon (the Gelato People)

ALIENS: RIDE AT THE SPEED OF FRIGHT (1995)
Production Companies: 20th Century Fox, Praxis Films, Iwerks Entertainment
Director: **Stuart Gordon**
Based on the 1986 film *Aliens* directed by James Cameron
Photography: David Breashears and Paul Gentry
Camera Operator: Les Paul Robley
First Assistant Camera: Rick Taylor
Video Assist Operator: John N. Campbell
Music by Richard Band
Original *Aliens* Themes by James Horner
Visual Effects by Dennis and Robert Skotak (*Aliens* footage)
Cast: Jeffrey Combs (Colonial Marine Hyer)

SPACE TRUCKERS (1996)
Production Companies: Goldcrest Films International, Peter Newman Productions, InterAL, Mary Breen-Farrelly Productions, Irish Film Industry, Pachyderm Productions
Producers: Mary Breen-Farrelly, **Stuart Gordon**, Greg Johnson, Ted Mann, and Peter Newman
Associate Producers: Heidi Levitt, Mary Louise Queally, and Morgan O'Sullivan
Director: **Stuart Gordon**
Screenplay: Ted Mann
Story: **Stuart Gordon** and Ted Mann
Photography: Mac Ahlberg
Editing: John Victor Smith
Production Designer: Simon Murton
Music: Colin Towns
Cast: Dennis Hopper (John Canyon), Stephen Dorff (Mike Pucci), Debi Mazar (Cindy), Charles Dance (Nabel/Macanudo), George Wendt (Keller), Sandra Dickinson (Bitchin' Betty), Vernon Wells (Mister Cutt), Barbara Crampton (Carol), Shane Rimmer (E. J. Saggs), Sean Lawlor (Mel), Carolyn Purdy-Gordon (Delia), Graeme Wilkinson (Jackie), Lonny Smith (Jerry), Michael G. Hagerty (Tommy), Dave Duffy (Alex), Birdy Sweeney (Mr. Zesty), Sylvan Baker (Black Pirate), Billy

Clarke (Sam), Vincent Walsh (Rigid), Thomas McLaughlin (Lou), Pat Laffan (Scummy), Conor Mullen (Cop #1), David Ganly (Cop #2), and Owen Conroy (Cop #3)

THE WONDERFUL ICE CREAM SUIT (1998)
Production Company: Touchstone Pictures, Walt Disney Pictures
Producers: Roy E. Disney and **Stuart Gordon**
Co-Producer: Laura J. Medina
Director: **Stuart Gordon**
Screenplay: Ray Bradbury
Based on the short story by Ray Bradbury
Photography: Mac Ahlberg
Editing: Andy Horvitch
Production Designer: Stuart Blatt
Music: Mader
Cast: Joe Mantegna (Gomez), Edward James Olmos (Vamanos), Esai Morales (Dominguez), Clifton Gonzalez Gonzalez (Martinez), Gregory Sierra (Villanazul), Sid Caesar (Sid Zellman), Howard Morris (Leo), Liz Torres (Ruby Escadrillo), Mike Moroff (Toro), Lisa Vidal (Ramona), Mercedes Ortega (Celia Obregon), Jose Hernandez (Mariachi), Pedro Gonzalez Gonzalez (Landlord), Mirnada Garrison (Wife), Michael Saad (Husband), Tony Plana (Victor Medina), Renee Victor (Grandmother), Carol Borjas (Granddaughter), and Thomas Bradford (Paramedic)

HONEY, I SHRUNK THE KIDS (1998)
[Episode: "Honey, Let's Trick-or-Treat"]
Production Companies: Plymouth Productions, St. Clare Entertainment, Walt Disney Television
Producers: Leslie Belzberg, John Landis, Cathy M. Frank, Jonathan Hackett, and Bert Swartz
Associate Producer: Grace Gilroy
Director: **Stuart Gordon**
Teleplay: Matt Kiene and Joe Reinkemeyer
Based on characters created by **Stuart Gordon** and Brian Yuzna
Story Editor: Kat Likkel
Photography: Rick Maguire
Editing: Joan La Duca
Production Designer: John Blackie
Music: Peter Bernstein
Makeup: Samantha Rumball

Cast: Peter Scolari (Wayne Szalinski), Barbara Alyn Woods (Diane Szalinski), Hilary Tuck (Amy Szalinski), Thomas Dekker (Nick Szalinski), Quark (Himself), George Buza (Chief Jake McKenna), Michael Berryman (Hook Hand Man), Sean Smith (David Foaf), Eric Johnson (Ray), A. J. Edmond (Barton Lewis), Farron Dearden (Ernie), Shane Vajda (Rodney, Munson), Vanessa King (Danielle), Catherine Myles (Mrs. Foaf), Daniel Libman (Mr. Foaf), Hilda Doherty (Sweet Old Lady), Gail Hanrahan (Neighbor), Steve Gin (Wolfman), Chelsea Lunan (Angel), David Barrett (Zombie), and Devon Weaver (Cinderella, uncredited)

DAGON (2001)
Production Companies: Castelao Producciones, Estudios Picasso, Fantastic Factory (Filmax), Generalitat de Catalunya – Institut Catalá de les Indústries Culturals (ICIC), ICF Institut Catalá de Finances, Televisió de Catalunya (TV3), Televisión de Galicia, Vía Digital, Xunta de Galicia
Producer: Brian Yuzna
Line Producer: Miguel Torrente
Director: **Stuart Gordon**
Screenplay: Dennis Paoli
Based on the short stories "Dagon" and "The Shadow Over Innsmouth" by H. P. Lovecraft
Photography: Carlos Suárez
Editing: Jaume Vilalta
Production Designer: Llorenç Miquel
Music: Carles Cases
Special Makeup Effects: David Martí
Cast: Ezra Godden (Paul Marsh), Francisco Rabal (Ezequiel), Raquel Meroño (Bárbara), Macarena Gómez (Uxía Cambarro), Brendan Price (Howard), Birgit Bofarull (Vicki), Uxía Blanco (Madre Ezequiel), Ferran Lahoz (Sacerdote), Joan Minguell (Xavier Cambarro), Alfredo Villa (Capitán Orfeo Cambarro), José Lifante (Recepcionista Hotel), Javier Sandoval (Padre Ezequiel), Victor Barreira (Ezequiel Joven), Fernando Gil (Sacerdote Católico), Jorge Luis Pérez (Chico), Ignacio Carreño (Tanner 1), Diego Herberg (Chofer), Óscar García (Imbocan 1), José Manuel Torres (Imbocan 2), Lydia González (Imbocan 3), Lydia Bosse (Imbocan 4), Joan Manel Vadell (Imbocan 5 and Tanner 2), and Richard Stanley (Fish Monster, uncredited)

KING OF THE ANTS (2003)
Production Companies: Anthill Productions, the Hecht Company, Red Hen Productions, the Asylum
Producers: Duffy Hecht and David Michael Latt

Co-Producers: **Stuart Gordon**, Charles Higson, Shawn Simons, and George Wendt
Director: **Stuart Gordon**
Screenplay: Charles Higson
Based on the novel by Charles Higson
Photography: Mac Ahlberg
Editing: David Michael Latt
Production Designer: Georges Moes
Music: Bobby Johnston
Special Makeup Effects: Rocky Faulkner, Dan Gates, Brad Hardin, Glenn Hetrick, Kari Murillo, Lancel Reyes, Reyna Rhone, John Vulich, and Gary Yee
Cast: Chris L. McKenna (Sean Crawley), Kari Wuhrer (Susan Gatley), George Wendt (Duke Wayne), Vernon Wells (Beckett), Lionel Mark Smith (Carl), Timm Sharp (George), Daniel Baldwin (Ray Matthews), Ron Livingston (Eric Gatley, uncredited), Carissa Koutantzis (Maureen), Briana Beghi (Maureen's Daughter), Carlie Westerman (Catlin Gatley), Ian Patrick Williams (Tony), Antoine Jospeh (Drooling Idiot), Shuko Akune (Meade Park), Steven Heller (Gary), Ken "Bam Bam" Johnson Jr. (Apartment Kid), Tino Marquez Jr. (Apartment Kid), Adam Noble (Bartender), and Joe Davis (Big 69, uncredited)

EDMOND (2005)
Production Companies: 120dB Films, Catfish Productions, Code Entertainment, Dog Pond Productions, Fully Loaded Pictures, Muse Productions, Neverland Films, Pretty Dangerous Films, Red Hen Productions, Tartan Films, the Hecht Company, Werner Film
Producers: **Stuart Gordon**, Chris Hanley, Molly Hassell, Duffy Hecht, Roger Kass, Mary McCann, and Kevin Ragsdale
Co-Producers: Lionel Mark Smith, Art Spigel, and Chad Troutwine
Associate Producers: Amy Gunzenhauser, Jade Healy, Jasper Jan, Lorna Soonhee, and Allison Wolf
Director: **Stuart Gordon**
Screenplay: David Mamet
Based on the play by David Mamet
Photography: Denis Maloney
Editing: Andy Horvitch
Production Designer: Alan E. Muraoka
Music: Bobby Johnston
Makeup: Rocky Faulkner
Cast: William H. Macy (Edmond), Julia Stiles (Glenna), Joe Mantegna (Man in Bar), Mena Suvari (Whore), Denise Richards (B-Girl), George Wendt (Pawn

Shop Owner), Rebecca Pidgeon (Wife), Debi Mazar (Matron), Jeffrey Combs (Desk Clerk), Lionel Mark Smith (Pimp), Bai Ling (Peep Show Girl), Dylan Walsh (Interrogator), Bokeem Woodbine (Prisoner), Patricia Belcher (Woman on Subway), Wendy Thompson (Cocktail Waitress), Vincent Guastaferro (Club Manager), Dulé Hill (Sharper), Russell Hornsby (Shill), Aldis Hodge (Leafletter), Barry Cullison (Pawn Shop Customer), Marcus Thomas (Window Man), Wren T. Brown (Preacher), Bruce A. Young (Policeman), Jack Wallace (Chaplain), and Michael Saad (Library Guard)

MASTERS OF HORROR: "DREAMS IN THE WITCH-HOUSE" (2005)
Production Companies: IDT Entertainment, Industry Entertainment, Nice Guy Productions, Reunion Pictures
Producers: Lisa Richardson and Tom Rowe
Co-Producers: Ben Browning, Adam Goldworm, and Pascal Verschooris
Director: **Stuart Gordon**
Series Creator: Mick Garris
Screenplay: Dennis Paoli and **Stuart Gordon**
Based on the short story by H. P. Lovecraft
Photography: Jon Joffin
Editing: Marshall Harvey
Production Designer: David Fischer
Music: Richard Band
Special Makeup Effects: Gregory Nicotero and Howard Berger
Cast: Ezra Godden (Walter Gillman), Chelah Horsdal (Frances Elwood), Campbell Lane (Masurewicz), Jay Brazeau (Mr. Dombrowski), Yevgen Voronin (Brown Jenkin), Susanna Uchatius (Keziah Mason), Donna White (Librarian), Susan Bain (Psychologist), Terry Howson (Attendant), Anthony Harrison (Detective), David Nykl (CSI), David Racz, Nicholas Racz (Baby Danny), Lance Gutterman (2005, uncredited), and Andrea Marino (Voluptuous Woman, uncredited)

MASTERS OF HORROR: "THE BLACK CAT" (2006)
Production Companies: Starz!, Industry Entertainment, Nice Guy Productions
Producers: Lisa Richardson and Tom Rowe
Co-Producers: Ben Browning and Adam Goldworm
Director: **Stuart Gordon**
Series Creator: Mick Garris
Screenplay: Dennis Paoli and **Stuart Gordon**
Based on the short story by Edgar Allan Poe
Photography: Jon Joffin
Editing: Marshall Harvey

Production Designer: Don Macaulay
Music: Richard Ragsdale
Special Makeup Effects: Gregory Nicotero and Howard Berger
Cast: Jeffrey Combs (Edgar Allan Poe), Elyse Levesque (Virginia Poe), Aron Tager (George Graham), Patrick Gallagher (Barman), Christopher Heyerdahl (Rufus Griswold), Ian Alexander Martin (Mr. Fordham), Ken Kramer (Doctor), Eric Keenleyside (Sgt. Booker), and Ryan Crocker (Policeman)

STUCK (2007)
Production Companies: Prodigy Pictures, Amicus Entertainment, Tumidor
Producers: **Stuart Gordon**, Jay Firestone, Ken Gord, and Robert Katz
Associate Producers: Julie G. Moldo and Zenon Yunko
Director: **Stuart Gordon**
Screenplay: John Strysik
Story: **Stuart Gordon**
Photography: Denis Maloney
Editing: Andy Horvitch
Production Designer: Craig Lathrop
Music: Bobby Johnston
Special Makeup Effects: Mike Measimer
Cast: Mena Suvari (Brandi Boski), Stephen Rea (Thomas Bardo), Rusell Hornsby (Rashid), Rukiya Bernard (Tanya), Carolyn Purdy-Gordon (Peterson), Lionel Mark Smith (Sam), Wayne Robson (Mr. Binckley), R. D. Reid (Manager), Patrick McKenna (Joe Lieber), Sharlene Royer (Tiffany), Bunthivy Nou (Gloria), Suzanne Short (Receptionist), Wally MacKinnon (Beat Cop), John Dartt (Cop), Liam McNamara (Thin Young Man), Shuko Akune (Hospital Voice Menu), John Dunsworth (Cabbie), Marguerite McNeil (Mrs. Pashkewitz), Jeffrey Combs (911 Operator), Martin Moreno (Pedro), Lorena Rincon (Estela), Mauricio Hoyos (Luis), and Brian Johnson (Bouncer, uncredited)

FEAR ITSELF: "EATER" (2008)
Production Companies: Fear Itself Productions, Industry Entertainment, Lionsgate Television
Producers: Ben Browning, Adam Goldworm, and Jonathan Hackett
Co-Producer: Steve Best
Associate Producer: Randy S. Nelson
Director: **Stuart Gordon**
Series Creator: Mick Garris
Screenplay: Richard Chizmar and Jonathon Schaech
Based on the short story by Peter Crowther

Photography: Alwyn J. Kumst
Editing: Marshall Harvey
Production Designer: Stephen Geaghan
Music: Bobby Johnston
Special Makeup Effects: Gregory Nicotero and Howard Berger
Cast: Elisabeth Moss (Danny Bannerman), Russell Hornsby (Sgt. Williams), Stephen Lee (Marty Steinwitz), Stephen R. Hart (Duane "Eater" Mellor), Pablo Schreiber (Mattingley), Joe Desmond, Andrew Krivanek, Troy O'Donnell (Cops), Franco Imbrogno (Cop, uncredited), Kieran Martin Murphy (Cop, uncredited), and Marie Zydek (Tortured Woman, uncredited)

As Writer and/or Producer Only

Honey, I Shrunk the Kids (1989)
Co-Story Writer
Honey, I Blew Up the Kid (1992)
Executive Producer
Body Snatchers (1993)
Co-Writer
The Dentist (1996)
Co-Writer
Robo-Warriors (1996)
Based on Characters Created by
Honey, We Shrunk Ourselves! (1997)
Based on Characters Created by
The Dentist 2 (1996)
Based on Characters Created by
Progeny (1999)
Co-Writer and Executive Producer
Snail Boy (2000)
Executive Producer
Bleacher Bums (2002)
Co-Executive Producer and Co-Writer
Deathbed (2002)
Producer and Executive Producer

As Actor (in Other Director's Films)

The Arrival (1991, dir. David Schmoeller)
Biker

Susan's Plan (1998, dir. John Landis)
Doctor #2
Snail Boy (2000, dir. Travis Hottinger)
Clint's Biker Relative
Bread and Roses (2001, dir. Ken Loach)
Party Guest (uncredited)
The Crystal Lake Massacres Revisited (2009, dir. Daniel Farrands)
Walter Finkelstein
Chastity Bites (2013, dir. John V. Knowles)
Mr. Rowland
Trophy Heads (2014, dir. Charles Band)
Stuart
Tales of Halloween: "Grim Grinning Ghost" (2015, dir. Axelle Carolyn)
Sherlock Holmes

Stuart Gordon: Interviews

Nude Co-eds in *Peter Pan* Stir Flap on Madison Campus

Frank Ryan / 1968

From the *Petoskey News-Review*, October 2, 1968, p. 10. Reprinted by permission.

The critical review of the children's classic *Peter Pan*—featuring a supporting cast of nude co-eds—was still out today.

The University of Wisconsin student version of James M. Barrie's tale reopened for a special one-day stand Monday, and "critics" among the selected audience of fifty-two included Madison Police Chief Wilbur Emery and Dane County District Attorney James C. Boll.

Boll, after a command performance, ruled the production obscene and four of the co-eds dropped out in fear of prosecution. But Tuesday night, despite possible prosecution, *Peter Pan* went on for two more packed audiences of 500.

"No one has the right to censor a work of art except the audience," said producer Stuart Gordon of Chicago, a drama senior. There were no arrests.

Their judgment on whether drama senior Stuart A. Gordon's version of the play is esthetic or obscene will determine the future of the show, which has an eight-minute sequence with nude co-eds.

The nudity, Gordon says, is to depict innocence.

Boll said he would meet today with Wisconsin Chancellor H. Edwin Young to discuss the show's future—or lack of one.

It first played a week ago, but closed after one performance amid controversy and concern among cast members they might be charged in obscenity warrants. Monday's show was held after the cast said they wanted to know whether they could perform on a regular basis without being prosecuted.

The university administration, including Young and President Fred Harrington, boycotted Monday's show. A spokesman said Harrington and Young "don't want to go to a private showing of their co-eds in the nude."

Gordon was asked why he didn't portray "innocence" with something like long, flowing white gowns instead of nudity.

"We tried long, flowing white gowns," he said. "They looked silly—like some crummy painting from 1880."

Sick, Sick, Sick!

Kim Newman / 1985

From *City Limits*, January 10–16, 1986, p. 17. Reprinted by permission.

"To ask an actress to be naked on a table and have somebody bleed on her is not an easy thing to do," chuckles Stuart Gordon, a graduate of the theater in Chicago who has made his debut film with *Re-Animator*.

In this grossly funny film based on a series of short stories by H. P. Lovecraft, medical student Herbert West invents a glowing green serum which, if injected into the brain, brings the newly dead back to animated and angry life.

"I'm a big horror movie fan. We sat down and said, 'We have to have as few characters as possible and as few sets as possible. It's got to be cheap!' So, we had to cut the World War I story and the scene with the cannibal boxer and the baby's arm.

"We've started talking about a sequel. The plan is that West is going to work for the CIA. There's an underground laboratory in which all the famous people have been frozen. The main event is going to be him bringing back Albert Einstein and Marilyn Monroe. The one he is not able to get near is John F. Kennedy."

If the prospect of a zombie Marilyn seems daunting, Gordon has very firm ideas about horror and humor.

"My feeling is that the comedy is built into the story. The line West keeps saying—'I guess he wasn't fresh enough'—must be the only laugh Lovecraft got in his whole life. I also felt that if the movie was unrelentingly grim its effect would diminish. It was always supposed to be funny. I always felt that West was a funny character.

"I think it's an old-fashioned horror film. It's got a lot in common with old Frankenstein movies. It's a monster movie. The idea was to take modern effects and apply them to an old-fashioned horror film. The stories were pretty gory. If you were to make a film without the gore elements, I don't think today's audience would stand for that. They want to see it all, and so we showed it all."

"All" includes a severed talking head with indecent designs on the heroine, zombie cats splattered on walls; assorted murders and autopsies; and a victim constricted to death by a zombie's snakelike entrails.

Asked if there was any idea too sick for the film, Gordon replies, "No, heh-heh-heh!" The game was to try and go beyond what had been done before. "My favorite movies are those where you get the sense that the people who made them are capable of anything. That gets you real scared."

Researching the film, Gordon visited several morgues and is glad he did "because I found that the way morgues have been portrayed is completely inaccurate. In movies, they have drawers that pull out of the wall and there's a body in it. I never saw that.

"I found that doctors' attitudes and morticians' attitudes are exactly opposite. A mortician will do everything that he can to pretend that a person is alive; a doctor will do everything he can to keep you alive, but as soon as you're dead you are basically a piece of garbage.

"There's absolutely no respect for a corpse. One of the basic ideas in horror movies is that dead bodies, when they're brought back to life, are always angry. I think that's because of the bad treatment they get from doctors.

"The stuff that they're doing in this movie—trying to reactivate the brain—is being researched right now. To a doctor, what West is doing is completely understandable. Twenty years ago, when somebody's heart stopped, they were considered dead. Now they've got all sorts of things that can start a heart going.

"Death is no longer cardiac arrest. Death is brain death. So the new frontier is being able to conquer brain death, which is what *Re-Animator* is all about. The idea of some sort of drug that can do that is probably the way it will work out.

"I don't think it'll glow and be green, but it'll be something."

Dead People Just Wanna Have Fun

Anne Billson / 1985

From *Time Out*, January 15–21, 1986. Reprinted by permission.

It was in one of the most dilapidated and furthest-flung reaches of that monstrous edifice known as the National Theatre that I met Stuart Gordon, creator of an unnamable motion picture called *Re-Animator*. His greeting to me was not unfriendly, but one could only guess at the unspeakable depravity festering behind that bearded and amiable countenance . . .

The film was awarded a Special Critics' Prize at Cannes. So, the French liked it? "They loved it!" exclaimed Gordon. "They said I'm the next Jerry Lewis!" He chuckled. It was a sound that lodged in the very marrow of my bones . . .

H. P. Lovecraft wrote "Herbert West—Re-Animator" in 1921/22. It was first published in serial form in a little-known magazine called *Home Brew*. Lovecraftians will already be aware that West doesn't re-animate Donald Duck; he re-animates corpses. "The story covers a twenty-year period," explained Gordon. "In the film it's compressed into two weeks. There were a couple of episodes so gory we couldn't include them. There's one episode in which West revives a Black boxer, and the guy goes running out of the house, and comes back on all fours carrying a baby's arm in his mouth . . ."

Re-Animator is Gordon's feature debut, though he has a healthy track record as a theater and TV director. Brian Yuzna, his producer, arranged for Empire International Pictures to provide post-production facilities in exchange for distribution rights. Empire is the haunt of the Band brothers; Richard Band composed the *Psycho*-esque score, while Charles is busy mutating into a Roger Corman for the 1980s, building up a stock company of filmmakers and actors who specialize in science fiction and fantasy.

Gordon and Yuzna have both been signed up for further forays into Lovecraftland. Edgar Allan Poe has been much plundered for the screen, notably by Corman in the 1960s, but adaptations of the old H. P. have been rarer. Gordon puts this down to the author's tendency to write things like, "'And then, the *unspeakable* horror . . . the *unmentionable* . . . the *dot dot dot* . . .' And if you're making a movie, you've got to show *something* on that screen." As well as all his *ultimate abominations*, Lovecraft also displays an inordinate fondness for *italics* and names with lots of consonants strung together, such as *Cthulhu*.

Lovecraft was raised by maiden aunts in Rhode Island and grew up into a hypochondriac with a morbid fear of fish. "Whenever someone tried to serve him a plate of fish, he would run out of the house," said Gordon. "There's a story of his that we're going to be doing called "The Shadow Over Innsmouth," about a town in which all the people are turning into fish . . ."

Re-Animator is short on fish, but long on mad doctors (two) and zombies (lots). It also features a severed head with a crush on the heroine and a headless torso with a lot of guts. Gordon, although he confesses to a weak stomach, did his research in pathology rooms and mortuaries.

"I found that the way death was portrayed in the movies is very inaccurate. The way that they portray dead people is to paint them white with dark circles under their eyes. That's not right. . . . The first time I looked in a morgue, they were opening these large lockers, and all of them were *jammed* with bodies—no white sheets—and the *smell* is not to be believed. And the colors of the bodies were like rainbows. Just as each person is an individual in life, the same is true of death, depending on how you die. And the attitude of a doctor to a dead body is that it's toxic, it's disease-ridden; it's garbage or shit . . ."

Gordon reckons *Psycho* is still the scariest movie ever made. "When I really start to get scared is when I realize that the director is capable of anything. I also don't like the idea of those films in which, as soon as they have sex, people are murdered. My feeling is they should have sex *after* they're murdered . . ."

My ears were again assailed by that unearthly chuckle, and I sloped off into the howling night. Life is a hideous thing, as Lovecraft himself once wrote, and even now my tormented brain echoes dementedly with Stuart Gordon's parting words: "*Dead people just wanna have fun.*" Dot dot dot.

Lovecraft Re-Animated

Stefan Jaworzyn and Stephen Jones / 1985

From *Shock Xpress*, no. 3 (January-February 1986), pp. 1–3. Reprinted by permission.

During the early 1920s, reclusive Providence author H. P. Lovecraft was approached by G. J. Houtain to write a series of six connected horror stories to run in Houtain's new professional magazine, *Home Brew*. The fee would be five dollars per episode. Lovecraft complained about "the burthen of hack labor" and "the arid waste of ochreous commercialism," but finally agreed to work for the rock-bottom price. Houtain called the series *Grewsome Tales* and the first installment, "From the Dark," appeared in issue one of *Home Brew* in January 1922. Twenty years later, the series was reprinted in the classic pulp magazine *Weird Tales* under the title "Herbert West—Re-Animator," and subsequently appeared in the collection *Dagon and Other Macabre Tales* [1965, Arkham House].

Stuart Gordon, a young alumnus of Chicago's Organic Theatre, originally considered developing the stories into a play, then as a pilot for a TV miniseries. With the help of producer Brian Yuzna, the project finally ended up with Charles Band's Empire Pictures, who gave Gordon a paltry million-dollar budget and the opportunity to make his directorial debut on *Re-Animator*.

The finished film was described by the *Los Angeles Times* as "equal parts Mary Shelley, Alfred Hitchcock and Andy Warhol . . . a real throat-grabber, and quite simply the best horror picture to come along in ages." *Re-Animator* went on to win the Prix Special at the 1985 Cannes Film Festival and First Prize at the Festival of Cine Fantástico de Sitges in Spain. In November, it received a screening at the London Film Festival, and Stuart Gordon was whisked into town to promote his suddenly hot exploitation movie. We spoke to him about *Re-Animator* and his forthcoming projects . . .

Shock Xpress: How do you feel about *Re-Animator* being cut for British release?

Stuart Gordon: I don't approve of censorship. I think people should be allowed to decide what they see and what they don't. As long as the advertising makes it clear what the nature of the film is, then it's every man for himself.

Shock Xpress: Why was it released without a rating in the USA?

Gordon: We submitted it to the MPAA who told us we'd have to cut the last three reels for an R. We'd have had a very short movie if we'd gone along with that. Also, the feeling was that what makes it special is the outrageousness of it, and trimming the movie back would lose the whole point of it. So, to Empire's credit, they released it intact, though it makes it a lot harder to distribute.

Shock Xpress: How has that affected the US box office?

Gordon: There are certain theaters that won't run it, certain TV and radio stations that won't broadcast the ads, and some papers that won't print them, so it does have an effect. But it's done very well despite being unrated.

Shock Xpress: It must add a certain amount of interest . . .

Gordon: I think so. I prefer going to movies where I don't know what the limits are. That's when I get really scared—when I know the people who made the film are capable of anything.

Shock Xpress: The unrated version succeeds very well in capturing the escalating madness of Lovecraft's story.

Gordon: I believe *Re-Animator* is very true to Lovecraft. When we did the first drafts of the script we only used the first couple of parts, but when Brian Yuzna, the producer, became involved, he said that we should use the whole story. I said, "Don't you think that's a bit excessive?" and he said, "Yes, let's do it." So we did, and there's a point in the movie where you think, "This is as far as it can go," but it just keeps on going.

Shock Xpress: Which is the essence of Lovecraft's original. Why did you change the ending?

Gordon: It's still very similar—West being destroyed by an army of re-animated corpses. We took a lot of liberties in terms of compressing events, which take place over twenty years in the story, and I thought it best to keep the action in the morgue as far as possible. There are some things I'd have liked to do if we'd had a bigger budget . . .

Shock Xpress: There's a great black sense of humor in the film which is missing from the story.

Gordon: I think Lovecraft's story is pretty funny. My favorite line is, "I guess they weren't fresh enough," which is a recurrent theme, and I believe Lovecraft intended it to be funny.

Shock Xpress: You've said that you had a great deal of trouble tracking down a copy of "Herbert West—Re-Animator." Did you have any problems getting the rights?

Gordon: The story is public domain. Copyrights are being contested for all of Lovecraft's work, but a lot of it's now becoming public domain. It's a very weird situation. But this story had no copyright, neither by Lovecraft nor the magazine. (Note: In *Dagon and Other Macabre Tales* it is copyrighted 1939, 1943, and 1965). I wrote to the estate asking permission, and they said, "It's all yours." In the USA, it's been out of print for some time—I had to order it from a library. When it arrived after a year, they wouldn't let me take it away, and the copy literally crumbled in my hands as I turned the pages. It was like the *Necronomicon*.

Shock Xpress: What made you pick "Herbert West—Re-Animator"? Simply the fact that it was out of copyright?

Gordon: Someone recommended it to me. I wasn't familiar with it, and they told me it was a modern-day *Frankenstein* [1818], so I started tracking it down. Compared with his other work, it's very action-packed. The problem with Lovecraft is that he often gets into this "unspeakable and indescribable horror" stuff, which is hard to portray on screen.

Shock Xpress: Have you seen any of the other Lovecraft adaptations?

Gordon: I saw [Roger Corman's 1965 film] *The Haunted Palace*. I think that's got the same problem—how can you equal what's left to the imagination?

Shock Xpress: Do you feel you've done justice to Lovecraft with *Re-Animator*?

Gordon: The story is very close to the original, and I think the intentions are similar. We've updated it, but all the main routines are Lovecraft's. I always enjoy it when the audience laughs at the line, "I guess it wasn't fresh enough." I hope the film may result in the story being reprinted in the USA.

Shock Xpress: Will you attempt any more Lovecraft adaptations?

Gordon: I'm working on one now, based on "From Beyond," which we'll be shooting in January. It's another of his "indescribable horror" stories, and we've had a difficult time deciding what we'll be showing visually. We're using the story, which is only nine pages long, as the opening scene of the movie, and we're taking it from there. I feel what we're doing is true to the spirit of Lovecraft, that we're taking his ideas and sticking closely to them.

Shock Xpress: Where will you be filming *From Beyond*?

Gordon: In Rome.

Shock Xpress: Isn't that where you're making *The Doll*?

Gordon: Yes. We're shooting that in Rome and it's coming along real well. It's based on an original story by Ed Naha, though the title is now *Dolls*.

Shock Xpress: What's it about?

Gordon: It concerns witches who turn people into dolls and send them off to murder other people. There's an entire army of little living dolls . . .

Shock Xpress: Sounds like *The Devil Doll* [1936]. Have you ever seen it?

Gordon: With [Lionel] Barrymore? Yes, I've seen it. I've also seen *Twilight Zone* episodes about dolls that come to life, and I think my film's a throwback to those older movies—except we're using the effects available to us today.

Shock Xpress: Are you using American or Italian technicians for the effects?

Gordon: I'm using John Buechler, who's doing a great job.

Shock Xpress: What kind of effects? Stop-motion?

Gordon: No, it's all being done on the stage, very similar to *Re-Animator*, which was all done right there while we were shooting. My background is in live theater, and I feel most comfortable working with something that can be done on set. It makes it more believable if you can have the actors appear with the creatures, rather than say, "Imagine you're seeing this or that."

Shock Xpress: Which actors are you using for *Dolls*?

Gordon: A combination of English and Americans. Guy Rolfe is starring, and Hilary Mason. Rolfe was *Mr. Sardonicus* [1961], one of my heroes, and Mason played the blind medium in *Don't Look Now* [1973]. The other actresses are Bunty Bailey—she's in the A-Ha video ["Take On Me"], where she turns into an animated cartoon—and Cassie Stewart.

Shock Xpress: What about the Americans?

Gordon: Two of them were in *Re-Animator*: my wife, Carolyn Purdy-Gordon, and Ian Patrick Williams, who had a tiny part at the beginning. I'm working with the others for the first time—there's a girl of seven called Carrie Lorraine, who I think is terrific, and Stephen Lee, who was in *Crimes of Passion* [1984], and who's very funny in this film, sort of a John Belushi-type.

Shock Xpress: Why are you filming in Rome?

Gordon: The idea is to get as much of the money onto the screen as possible, and Rome has excellent facilities—great art direction, spectacular crews. We're using Mac Ahlberg as cinematographer again, but the rest of the crew is Italian. Mac Ahlberg is great. I'm really excited by the look we're getting for *Dolls*.

Shock Xpress: Do you see yourself becoming a genre director, and do you want to be known as one? You've done three horror films in a row now . . .

Gordon: I like horror films. I'm a horror movie fan, so it doesn't bother me. But I'm going to be following up with a science fiction film.

Shock Xpress: Which is what?

Gordon: It's a top secret project, I can't really discuss it.

Shock Xpress: What are your favorite genre films?

Gordon: I still think the scariest movie made is *Psycho*, which I don't think has been surpassed. I think that all the *Friday the 13th*-type films are just replays of *Psycho* without the originality that Hitchcock had. I like *Alien* [1979] a lot, and *From Beyond* is going to have some similarities to *Alien* in that you're never going to know exactly what the monster looks like; it's going to keep changing.

Shock Xpress: Did you enjoy John Carpenter's *The Thing* [1982]?

Gordon: I thought the effects were fascinating, but I don't think it was very scary.

Shock Xpress: It's quite Lovecraftian ...

Gordon: My problem with it was that there was no one in it you cared about, and when that happens it means you don't get scared.

Shock Xpress: If *Re-Animator* is the big success that everyone thinks it's going to be, would you consider re-animating Herbert West for a sequel?

Gordon: Well, you can't keep a good monster down. I'd be up for another *Re-Animator* movie if it works out.

Stuart Gordon

John A. Gallagher / 1986

From *Film Directors on Directing* (Praeger, 1989), pp. 89–99. Reprinted by permission.

Re-Animator (1985), *From Beyond* (1986), *Dolls* (1987)—the films of Stuart Gordon are marked by his imaginative direction and macabre sense of humor, along with stunning special effects and consistently fine acting. The Chicago-born filmmaker has brought an impressive background to his horror and fantasy product, having founded Chicago's acclaimed Organic Theatre Company in September 1969. Under Gordon's direction, the Organic Theatre developed and debuted such plays as *Bleacher Bums*, which became the longest running show in Los Angeles theater history; *E/R Emergency Room*, later the basis for a CBS-TV series; and David Mamet's *Sexual Perversity in Chicago*, which was adapted into the feature film *About Last Night* (1986).

Gordon's first feature film, *Re-Animator*, based on a short story by H. P. Lovecraft, has already become a horror classic. A jury of leading French film critics named *Re-Animator* the best science fiction, horror, or fantasy film of the 1985 Cannes Film Festival and Market, and it was invited to the London Film Festival, which has rarely screened such grisly fare. Gordon followed with another Lovecraft adaptation, *From Beyond*; a horrific fairy tale, *Dolls*; and a large-scale sci-fi epic, *Robot Jox* (1989).

My interview with Stuart Gordon took place in New York in August 1986. He had already completed *From Beyond* and *Dolls*, and was in the early planning stages of *Robot Jox*.

John A. Gallagher: How did your background with the Organic Theatre help your film work?

Stuart Gordon: We borrowed very heavily from movies in the kinds of plays we did. A lot of times the Organic reviews would say, "This is a movie being done live on stage." We used movie effects on stage and people weren't used to seeing that happen. So, I guess I've been making movies for years. I just haven't been putting them on film. I do feel that the technical side of moviemaking is the easiest thing to pick up, and I'm lucky in the background I had at Organic because I think the hardest thing is the script and working with actors. In theater, you realize pretty quickly that the whole show is the acting. The actor has a tremendous amount of power. By flickering a light, a good actor can convince you that a planet is blowing up on stage. If the acting is good, you'll go along with the simplest effect. I still think good acting is the best special effect.

JAG: Your films have a very effective blend of comedy and horror.

SG: I think that comedy works really well with horror. It's like salt and pepper. You need both spices. But I would never want the comedy to get in the way of the scares or vice versa. What I really like to do is build up some tension and then let the audience release it with a laugh—and then start up again.

JAG: The audience seems to care about the characters in your movies.

SG: I think it's crucial to a horror movie, or *any* movie, that you like the people. You care about them, and when something bad happens to them, it upsets you. So many horror films don't give a shit about anybody, and then you're just watching the technical side and the effects. I think the effects are just there to aid the acting and if the audience is with the characters you don't have to spend hundreds of thousands to do an effect. The acting and the script are the key ingredients. If you've got those together, everything else will be forgiven.

JAG: What movies influenced you?

SG: Definitely *Psycho* (1960). I still think that's the scariest movie ever made. One of my all-time favorite monster movies is *The Bride of Frankenstein* (1935). If we do a sequel to *Re-Animator*, we'll call it *Bride of Re-Animator*. I like the original *Alien* (1979) a lot. I wasn't crazy about *Aliens* (1986). I didn't think it was scary. For me, what was so great about the initial film was you didn't know what it was you were up against and every time you saw it, it was something else. With the sequel, you know exactly what it was and all the mystery was gone. It just became *Rambo* (1985). It could have been Viet Cong or anything, just a shoot-'em-up. If I were going to do a sequel to *Alien*, I would have to have a new alien in it. I think *Aliens* fell into a trap that happens with a lot of sequels. The marketing philosophy is just "give 'em more of the same." So, instead of one alien, it's a hundred aliens. Just make it bigger and do everything the same. The one thing I liked about the movie was [Sigourney Weaver's character, Ripley, fighting the monster while inside] the forklift, because it was new. My feeling is, when you start to do sequels and remakes of good movies, you're already falling into a no-win situation. What I would want from a sequel would be a similar feeling. Since I thought *Alien* was such a scary movie, I would hope that the sequel would be scarier. I felt that way about *Return of the Jedi* (1983), that it was basically *Star Wars* (1977) done over with more money.

JAG: How did *Re-Animator* come to be made with Empire?

SG: It was an arrangement between Empire and the producer of the film, Brian Yuzna. In exchange for post-production facilities, Empire would have the right to distribute the film. Initially, Empire was taking a back seat, and then as we started shooting it and they saw dailies, they got more involved. They made suggestions and gave us more than was in the original bargain. They ended up letting John Buechler work on the effects, although Tony Doublin and John Naulin did a great job. It was one of those projects where it was the more the merrier. They also suggested we get Mac Ahlberg as director of photography, and that turned out to be a very good decision.

JAG: What was the budget and schedule on *Re-Animator*?

SG: *Re-Animator* cost about one million dollars and we shot it in Los Angeles in four weeks, a real fast shoot. With both *Re-Animator* and *From Beyond*, we were able to rehearse before we started shooting. My background being theater, it was really essential to me to have time for the actors where that's all you're thinking about. Especially when you're dealing with effects, your concentration has to go to all the technical things and the actors are left alone. So, the fact that the actors knew what they were doing before we started shooting made it all work.

JAG: Did you shoot *Re-Animator* on location or on a set?

SG: Most of it was done on a stage. I did a lot of research and visited several morgues, taking pictures. The set is based on the brand new Cook County Morgue in Chicago. I had visited the old morgue, which had this creepy, decrepit look, and when I went back to get some pictures it had been torn down and they'd built a new one.

JAG: The Al Capone Memorial Morgue?

SG: Yeah, right! The guy that ran it wanted to do a whole exhibit of famous Chicago murders, but he got overruled by the city council. He's quite a character. He originally told me that if I wanted to shoot *Re-Animator* in the real morgue, I could, and he would even allow me to use *real* corpses.

JAG: Can you imagine, under the hot lights?

SG: The old morgue smelled like a cat had died, and after you left there you had that smell with you for two weeks. The new morgue is very futuristic with a ventilation system that changes the air every thirty minutes. We ended up basing our set on the new morgue with its hi-tech look, since we've seen the creepy old morgue in so many movies. In *Re-Animator* and *From Beyond*, we had medical advisors who made sure our doctors and nurses were doing everything correctly and gave it a real sense of believability. My concern when you're doing a fantasy film is that there has to be some basis in reality. If you're gonna expect an audience to go off and believe something, you have to give them the real world first. If things get too crazy, they'll throw their hands up and say, "This is nuts!"

JAG: In *Re-Animator*, how did you get the reagent to glow?

SG: The stuff really does glow. It's called Luminol and it's used in flares. It comes in tubes in a glass capsule. You break the glass and it glows. We could only find it in these plastic tubes, so we had to break open hundreds to get enough for the movie. We did a test and found it really photographed well. It looks like an optical effect in the movie, but it was really done live. In *Re-Animator*, that's the only leap of faith that you're asking the audience to make, which is to believe this stuff can bring the dead back to life. Everything else is as believable and real as we could make it.

JAG: How did you get the sound of the crazed cat?

SG: They took an actual cat's screech and put it through these machines, lowered the pitch, and raised the sound to give it an unearthly quality.

JAG: The way you make the dead walk in *Re-Animator* is jerky and awkward, as though if a dead person actually got up that's the way they'd walk.

SG: Again, it was talking to doctors. One of the things I really appreciate about Lovecraft is that he really did his homework when he wrote these stories. He wasn't just some horror writer coming up with these weird ideas and writing them the next morning. In the story "Herbert West—Re-Animator," he explains what kinds of chemicals would be used in the serum. In doing research I found there is work really being done that is identical to what West is trying to do in *Re-Animator*. The doctors' point of view is that this is not horrible but life-extending. They used to believe that when your heart stopped you were dead, and now they've got adrenaline and electroshock and all sorts of ways to bring the heart back after it's stopped. Why not be able to do the same thing with the brain? In the movie, they talk about the six-minute limit and brain death. That is something that people are trying to break now. There's a lot of work being done with people who fall into icy water and are literally clinically dead for half an hour, then get revived, and there is no brain damage. The same thing with *From Beyond*: all this stuff about the pineal gland that Lovecraft had in his original story is all turning out to be true. I talked to some people doing pineal research, which is now a very hot topic. Lovecraft came upon this in the twenties, and it's taken over fifty years for the scientists to catch up to him. A lot of the ideas we threw into the script turned out to be correct. The idea that the pineal gland might be the key to curing mental disorders like schizophrenia is something we put in the movie and found that, yes, this research is being done. Lovecraft really was a science fiction writer more than a horror writer. Everything has a scientific basis in his work. One of the big questions about Lovecraft was that he did not believe in the supernatural. There's a great Arthur C. Clarke quote—"Magic is unexplained technology"—and that's where I think Lovecraft is working.

JAG: How did you determine the visual look of *From Beyond*?

SG: The biggest problem was how we should create this other world, the beyond. Lovecraft gives you a few hints in the story with violet and purples, but what Mac Ahlberg ended up doing on the photography was almost like *The Wizard of Oz* (1939). The scenes that take place in the real world are almost black and white, but when we go into the beyond, there are suddenly all these intense colors.

JAG: What was the budget on *From Beyond*?

SG: About two and one half million, because we shot it in Italy. The value there was such that if we shot the picture in the United States it would have cost fifteen million. The technical expertise there is tremendous. Our art director, Giovanni Natalucci, had just finished doing *Once Upon a Time in America* (1984) and *Ladyhawke* (1985). The crew had worked with Sergio Leone and Federico Fellini. It's a great value there for a fraction of what it would have cost here.

JAG: Did you name Ted Sorel's Dr. Pretorius character in *From Beyond* after Ernest Thesiger in *The Bride of Frankenstein*?

SG: Yeah.

JAG: *Re-Animator* was released unrated, but I know you really had to battle with the Motion Picture Association of America to get an R rating on *From Beyond*.

SG: There are no rules. It's unlike the old Hays Office, where you used to know exactly what was allowed and what wasn't. If you had a woman's garter belt showing, you knew you were in trouble. With the MPAA, they're the first to tell you that they are not censors. They are basically there to let an audience know what to expect when they buy a ticket. They have these ratings, but it's all based on how these six people feel about the film they're watching and what they call the "cumulative effect." There are certain areas of concern: sex, violence, drugs, foul language. When they first saw *From Beyond*, they said, "You have ten times too much of everything, and there's no way we're ever gonna give you an R." At first I was depressed because it was as if they were saying the whole concept of this movie was unrateable, that it was too disquieting to be rated. I argued that this is the way horror movies are supposed to be, that the audiences will feel cheated if they're not scared to death. I ended up making very small trims, not removing any sequences. This actually ended up making the movie stronger. In a way, it left more to the imagination and gave you just enough of the idea of what was going on, and to see enough to get your mind spinning. So, the audience didn't have enough time to study an effect and figure out how it was done, or look for seams on the prosthetics. After resubmitting time and again to the MPAA, I think they got used to the shocks. Our last message was to cut one frame from a scene, so we really got down to fighting over frames. There's an R-rated version of *Re-Animator* that was done without my involvement that is like an episode of *Masterpiece Theatre*. All it needs is Alistair Cooke to introduce it. They've cut out anything they thought would be objectionable to anyone and put back in all the expositional scenes I'd cut because they really weren't necessary to tell the story. It's very talky, very little action.

JAG: Do you storyboard?

SG: Definitely. My background before I started working in theater was commercial art. I had been an apprentice in a commercial art studio for six months and hated it. I stopped drawing. Working in movies gave me a good opportunity to draw and I used that drawing ability to do the storyboards for effects sequences. I only do boards for the effects scenes though. I'll storyboard the way I'd like to see it done in the best of all possible worlds. Then I'll show it to the effects guys and they'll suggest any changes to make it easier or even possible, but usually I'll shoot pretty much what I draw.

JAG: How is your working relationship with Dennis Paoli, the co-writer of *Re-Animator* and *From Beyond*?

SG: We go all the way back to high school. We had a comedy group together, and we used to write sketches and perform them. It was a summer job. Dennis and I are real simpatico. I think he has a real feel for character and comedy, as well as understanding how horror movies work.

JAG: How did you like shooting *From Beyond*, *Dolls*, and *RoboJox* at Empire Studios in Rome?

SG: Great. Dino De Laurentiis originally built this enormous soundstage on the outskirts of Rome called Dinocittà. John Huston did *The Bible* (1966) there, and movies like *Barbarella* (1968), *Cleopatra* (1963), *Romeo and Juliet* (1968), and *The Taming of the Shrew* (1967) were shot there. It's fun to take a little tour because they still have the remnants, like a piece of Barbarella's spaceship. The soundstages are bigger than anything at Cinecittà. In fact, I haven't seen anything in Los Angeles bigger than these stages. When Dino left Italy they were taken over by the government for nonpayment of taxes, and were seldom used until Empire bought them. *From Beyond* and *Dolls* were the first pictures made there under the Empire aegis. The house in *From Beyond* was built next to this ancient temple Dino built for *Red Sonja* (1985). Empire left the *From Beyond* set standing, so they have the Old Dark House set, and they'll do the same thing with *RoboJox* so they'll have a standing futuristic set. Charlie Band announced he wants to do a Universal Studios-style tour. The Italian press calls it "Horrorland," but we dubbed it "Bandland."

JAG: How involved is Charles Band in your Empire films?

SG: Very involved. He chose the short story "From Beyond" and always wanted to be kept abreast of all the various changes in the script. He visited the set a lot. He keeps his hand on things but never interferes. He's a very positive force. He's quite a good director. My only regret is that he hasn't directed more pictures.

His picture *Trancers* (1985) was terrific. His father, Albert, was on the set of *From Beyond* as a producer and his experience was really invaluable. He's worked with John Huston on films like *The Red Badge of Courage* (1951) and *Face of Fire* (1959). He's done a lot of work in Italy, so he knew the best way to utilize the crew's talents. Empire is very much a family. It's not like these big studios where you have to go through committees before you reach the top. You can just go and sit down with Charlie Band and he'll either like something or he won't, and if he likes it, the next thing you know you're making the movie. One thing he always says is, "There's no such thing as a development deal at Empire. There's no time for it." You either make the movie or you don't, and usually it has to be ready in two weeks! Now we're getting bigger budgets and longer schedules. *RoboJox* is seven million, the biggest budget Empire has ever had.

JAG: What are the plans for *Bride of Re-Animator*?

SG: We've come up with three or four different ideas for plots. Trying to outdo the first movie is the name of the game. I think eventually there *will* be one. We just have to decide what the story is we're going to tell, although with the title *Bride of Re-Animator* we have to focus on Meg Halsey, Barbara Crampton's character.

JAG: How would you describe *Dolls*?

SG: It's a horror movie fairy tale. I viewed it as a version of "Hansel and Gretel," which is a very frightening story about abandoning children, although the storyline is more akin to *The Old Dark House* (1932). It's about some evil toymakers who turn people into dolls, and then send these dolls out to murder. So, you have an army of homicidal dolls running around this house. The effects for *Dolls* are primarily stop-motion animation by Dave Allen, who did *Young Sherlock Holmes* (1985).

JAG: What kind of research did you do for *Dolls*?

SG: I had been reading a lot of Bruno Bettelheim, particularly his book *The Uses of Enchantment*, which discusses the importance of fairy tales. He really debates these people who say fairy tales are too violent. His attitude is that it's a scary world out there, and fairy tales are a way children are prepared for that world. We're taught in fairy tales that, yes, there are monsters and horrible things that can happen to you, but if you are brave, strong, and good, and don't give up, you can succeed. He feels those lessons are important and to minimize it takes the whole punch and point out of fairy tales. The idea of doing a movie that, rather than toning down those elements, really plays them to the limit, was something I found very interesting. When I came upon Ed Naha's treatment at Empire, I got turned on by the whole thing.

JAG: *RoboJox* is your largest undertaking to date.

SG: It's about this futuristic society where nations settle their differences with gigantic robots battling it out, piloted by these robot jockeys representing their entire country. They sit in the heads of the robot and are a combination of warrior and astronaut, the best of the best. Their nation's fate rests on their shoulders. These battles take the place of football games as well as warfare. It's like the Super Bowl every time these guys come out. I think it's an interesting metaphor. It's set in a post-nuclear era, although it's not *Mad Max* (1979), one hundred years after nuclear war. The world has rebuilt itself to some degree, but things are still pretty shaky. People have decided they're never going to allow another war, so now international disputes are settled in these battles.

JAG: What was the inspiration for *RoboJox*?

SG: The idea occurred to me from looking at the illustrations on the boxes of those Japanese robot toys, with the maintenance crews scrambling over these giant robots. It's a ready-made fantasy that no one has really tapped into yet. It's just waiting for a chance to be up there on the screen, not in the form of an animated cartoon, but live-action where the sense of size could really be created. Kids are already enjoying the robot toys and playing on their own, but now we'll be able to use the magic of moviemaking to create the illusion of these metal giants. It's a great fantasy for a kid to have that kind of power and size. Initially, Empire was skeptical about the kind of budget we'd need, but eventually they got intrigued by the idea. The effects are similar to *Dolls*, only in reverse. With *Dolls*, Dave Allen creates the illusion of things being small, and in *RoboJox* he's doing things huge, but it's basically the same set of stop-motion tricks that are being used. There are some great battle scenes, as well as what I feel is missing from a lot of science fiction films—the human story. I don't want the people in the film to be like the robots. There has to be some real flesh and blood emotions that the audience can relate to. The idea is to let the audience drive the robots and let them play with these giant toys. It has to measure up to pictures like *The Empire Strikes Back* (1980), a movie that will appeal to children but that parents can enjoy as well; a real family experience.

JAG: You're also doing your first non-Empire picture this year, *Gris-Gris*, scripted by Dennis Paoli.

SG: Yeah. *Gris-Gris* is set in New Orleans and it's about the granddaughter of Marie Laveau, the voodoo queen of New Orleans. I've been doing a great deal of reading about voodoo, and I'm realizing that in many ways it's like theater or film in that it only works if you believe. Voodoo magic can be as light as a love potion, or as heavy as a curse that can kill you. All of the material that Dennis Paoli has used comes from the research, and after reading some of the accounts, it's hard *not* to believe. People today are very curious about other forms of religion and the power of the supernatural. Voodoo is a field that is about to have a wide interest. A person who practices voodoo would say it's like nature. Is nature good or bad? Nature can kill you. You can be struck by lightning and die, or you can bask in a beautiful, sunny day. Voodoo is the same way. It's channeling natural forces to do what you want done, but there are elements that are extremely disquieting. The voodoo god is a large snake that is called Zombie. Supposedly, the legendary Marie Laveau fed this snake babies which were brought to her by people who were repaying debts for favors rendered. So there's a dark side to it, but it can also be very positive, used to help people or cure them. There's a voodoo ceremony in *White Zombie* (1932) that is pretty accurate. The big thing in voodoo is the Goat Without Horns, which is the human sacrifice, something that supposedly was fairly common. The imagery is extremely strong. What they call "fixing" somebody, putting a curse on someone, for example, has people writhing around with things moving under their skin, dying, and having snakes come out of their mouths and spiders come out of their ears. Horrible stuff! As well as being very frightening, *Gris-Gris* is a very sensual piece.

JAG: And Barbara Crampton is going to play the pirate queen *Bloody Bess*.

SG: She's very happy about that. She's a perfect choice for the role. Empire is signing her to a three-picture contract. We sat down the other day and tried to figure out exactly what a Barbara Crampton movie is, and decided it should be a movie where she goes through a transformation—like she does in *Re-Animator* and *From Beyond*—where she starts out as one thing and becomes another by the film's end. *Bloody Bess* is about this very proper English girl who is kidnapped by pirates and ends up becoming their leader, sort of a swashbuckling version of the Patty Hearst story.

JAG: You're also planning another Lovecraft picture, *Lurking Fear*.

SG: Yeah. *Lurking Fear* is a Lovecraft story set in the 1920s in upstate New York's Catskill Mountains. It's about a family that has degenerated into ape-like cannibal creatures through inbreeding. They've burrowed these tunnels underneath the mountains so they have secret passageways. Whenever there's a thunderstorm, which is fairly common in this region, it drives them absolutely berserk, and they go running around tearing people apart and dragging them into the tunnels.

JAG: Borscht Belt comics?

SG: Yeah! (Laughs) Actually, the thing I find most interesting about it is that the hero of the story is H. P. Lovecraft himself, who'll probably be played by Jeffrey Combs. We're talking about Barbara Crampton as a fast-talking twenties reporter, like Glenda Farrell or Joan Blondell. Jeffrey and Barbara would work together to solve the case.

JAG: Crampton and Combs also starred in *Re-Animator* and *From Beyond*.

SG: My background being in theater, I'm used to working with a company of actors, and I really like that approach for film—especially doing movies as crazy as the Lovecraft stories. You don't want to spend all your time trying to explain to somebody why something is important, or why they should do something that seems ludicrous. Barbara and Jeffrey know that if they work with me, I'll ask them to do all sorts of odd things. I really like the idea of doing a series of Lovecraft movies that have an ensemble company in them, sort of like the old Roger Corman Poe movies with Vincent Price. Jeffrey Combs is my Vincent Price!

JAG: What is *Berserker*?

SG: We just found out that we're going to have to change the title. There's another movie called *Berserker* coming out. This guy called up and said, "Excuse me, we're calling our movie *Berserker*." I said, "Okay, we'll call ours *The Real Berserker!*" We originally wrote it for Arnold Schwarzenegger. He came and saw *Re-Animator* and really liked it. Afterwards, we were talking and he said, "Write me a horror film. I'd love to make one with you." Dennis Paoli and I came up with this idea about an athlete who's been taking steroids and finds out what the side effects are. He has a choice—he can stop taking them and die, or he can be a berserker. So, he becomes a monstrosity that is completely out of control. We sent it to Arnold, and his manager sent us a message saying that Arnold doesn't want to play a monster; he only wants to play heroes. What I tried to get across was this guy *is* the hero, someone the audience really sympathizes with being put in this terrible situation. The idea was to let Arnold really show some new sides of his acting ability. To have Arnold Schwarzenegger be in jeopardy for a change, to have him betrayed by his own body, would really be interesting. I think the problem with a lot of his movies is that you're never worried about him. You're just waiting for him to tear the other person to pieces.

JAG: What appeals to you about working in genre pictures?

SG: The thing that was great about the Organic Theatre was that we did all kinds of plays. I'd like the same thing to be true about my movies. One of the great things about genre movies is that as long as you follow the rules of the genre you can do anything you want and say anything you want. There's a tremendous amount of freedom. I got into a conversation with a friend that the horror films are really the subconscious of the movies. Even in the fifties when things were very repressive in mainstream movies, the horror films were dealing with fears and concerns that people were afraid to talk about, films like *Invasion of the Body Snatchers* (1956) and *The Thing* (1951). I find it very liberating to work on horror films, especially at Empire where I've never ever been censored by anyone. In fact, I'm encouraged. They say, "This isn't weird enough!"

Stuart Gordon's Shock Treatment

David Edelstein / 1986

From *Rolling Stone*, November 20, 1986, pp. 109–112, 154. Reprinted by permission.

After Jeffrey Combs sucked the eye out of Carolyn Purdy-Gordon's socket, it took the effects guys at least six tries before they got the little jelly ball to land so that it stared up at the camera. The magic of movies! Too bad it was the first shot director Stuart Gordon had to snip out of *From Beyond* when the Motion Picture Association of America slapped his new film with an X rating. X means a lot of theaters in the country won't show your movie. It means fourteen-year-olds can't get in, no matter how much they whine. Gordon still speaks fondly of the eyeball suck-and-plop, however, and of the conversation he had with an MPAA woman. "What on earth," she asked him, "were you thinking of when you zoomed in on his mouth as he was sucking out her eye?"

We're in the editing room of Empire Entertainment in Los Angeles, and as the gory footage runs on a viewing screen behind him, Gordon confesses, "I didn't even tell her that the woman onscreen was my wife and that it wasn't very pleasant for her, either." He takes a deep breath and adds, heartily, "But if your wife won't put up with it, who will?"

Plenty of people. For instance, Combs—who also played Herbert West, the wacko med student in Gordon's rollicking horror farce *Re-Animator*—not only sucks out eyeballs and munches brains in *From Beyond*, but walks around with a four-inch pineal gland sticking out of his forehead (that is, until someone bites it off).

"Stuart," says Combs, "is the Ozzy Osbourne of directors."

"There is a side of me that likes to break through clichés and wake people up," says Gordon. "I find that fun. I think that's part of what art is supposed to do—to make you see or experience things in ways that you haven't before."

Most of Gordon's shenanigans have nothing to do with biting off heads (or pineals). At Chicago's Organic Theatre, where he was artistic director for sixteen years, he was famed for his rambunctious originals—sci-fi epics, comedies, musicals, adaptations of big books.

Today, if you go by number of projects, Stuart Gordon is one of the hottest directors in Hollywood: *From Beyond* opens this fall; *Dolls*, a fairy tale about killer toys, will be released in January; shooting begins this month on *RoboJox*, a sci-fi epic; and after that comes a voodoo shocker, *Gris-Gris*. Empire Entertainment, his principal backer, has just announced three more Gordon films (among them *Bloody Bess*, about a noblewoman turned pirate), and on the other side of the tracks, the director has development deals with both Tri-Star and Disney. (The latter will produce *Teenie Weenies*, the first film of Gordon's that he'll let his two little girls see.)

He likes to spread himself around, this guy. In person, the bushy, burly Gordon seems gleeful and receptive—a big, friendly child. ("Mikhail Gorbachev comes off that way, too," points out William J. Norris, a former Organic actor who co-wrote *Re-Animator*.) It's only when someone says, "You can't do that," that Gordon gets ornery.

At the moment, his task is to win an R for *From Beyond* without—literally—ripping the guts out of it. The first time he submitted the picture, the MPAA pretty much laughed and said, "Are you kidding?" The second time, after Gordon cut the eyeball scene and still got an X, an Empire executive pressed the bearer of bad tidings for details. "I wouldn't know where to begin," was the reply. It didn't help that this was the week the cover of *Time* featured the report of Attorney General Edwin Meese's commission on pornography and violence.

But Gordon never flinches. "We'll just keep sending it back," he says. "They're freaked out by the movie now. They just have to get used to it."

The approach has worked before. His wife, Carolyn, didn't give in until the fourth time he proposed. He had to fight just to meet her—they made contact their first week at college when Gordon, drunk, dialed her number at random and wanted to chat. (Now she gets hideously murdered in his movies. Think about that the next time you get a crank call.)

Further back, Gordon's mother wouldn't let him go to horror movies, so he made a point of seeing as many as possible. "They became the forbidden fruit," he told a New York science fiction and fantasy convention, which was swarming with pimply kids whose parents probably thought they were out dribbling basketballs. Forbidden fruit, for many people, is the sweetest.

Stuart Gordon grew up in a poor section of Chicago, where his mother indulged him, but life on the streets was pretty rough. He never quite got over his strict, all-male high school, and by the time he got to college—the University of Wisconsin in Madison—he had thrown himself into the late-sixties counterculture. Gordon showed up everywhere in jeans, a motorcycle jacket and boots, and, more tellingly, formed Screw Theatre, a company that railed against middle-class complacency and the Vietnam War.

He made the national news (and Johnny Carson's monologue) in 1968, when he staged *Peter Pan* with naked Never Neverland fairies (his future wife, Carolyn, among them). "I thought nudity would suggest innocence," says Gordon, blandly. The inspiration for the production was the 1968 Democratic National Convention, in Chicago, where Mayor Daley gave his police license to bust the heads of antiwar demonstrators. In *Peter Pan*, the pirates became cops; Peter and the Lost Boys hippies; Wendy, Michael, and John straight, suburban kids; and flying became tripping. "'Think lovely thoughts and up you go,'" says Gordon, quoting. "The lines were there. Without changing one word of dialogue, we made a political cartoon out of J. M. Barrie's play."

After the second performance, the police nabbed Gordon and Purdy for public obscenity. The case was dropped, but the university theater department told Gordon that if he wanted to continue directing, he'd have to submit his scripts to a faculty panel and have a professor at every rehearsal. "At which point I said, 'I guess I just graduated,' and left school." He never got his degree—although the college now, in light of his success, claims him as its own.

"Stuart's favorite word of praise," says critic and playwright Terry Curtis Fox, "has always been 'outrageous.' They did *The Adventures of Huckleberry Finn* at the Organic, and what's interesting is that Huck is in a lot of ways Stuart. Like Huck, there was a point at which Stuart said, 'Alright, then I'll go to hell!' This is a man who put his wife on stage nude at every conceivable opportunity."

In Screw Theatre's darkest hour, help arrived from Paul Sills, director of Chicago's acclaimed Story Theatre troupe, who read of Gordon's troubles and invited the company to take up residence in a Chicago church. "They had an enlightened congregation," recalls Sills, "and they let Stuart tear all the pews out."

From Sills, Gordon learned to choose strong stories and develop original projects with a resident acting company. According to playwrights who worked with the theater, now renamed the Organic, actors, not writers, had the most power in shaping material; among Gordon's quirks is a mistrust of words. Despite his counterculture impulses, he wanted a genuinely popular theater—a theater that would appeal to both highbrows and lowbrows.

"I have never separated art from having a good time," says Gordon. "My feeling is that something is a classic because it has pleased audiences for many years. There's a wonderful book on Shakespeare by Anthony Burgess, where he makes the point that Shakespeare was concerned with selling tickets the same as any other producer. He knew he couldn't just have people reciting poetry, so he had scenes of people plucking out eyes or tearing out tongues; he has a woman making love to a jackass. You have to grab people. Roosevelt said the first job of a president is to get elected. The first job of a producer is to get an audience."

At first, audiences were lean, and at the end of every week, the company would divide up the meager booty. The commercial breakthrough was *Warp*, a muscular three-part sci-fi adventure in which characters traveled through space, time, and alternative dimensions (making wisecracks all the while). In his sixteen years at the Organic, Gordon oversaw thirty-seven original plays and adaptations, among them David Mamet's *Sexual Perversity in Chicago*; *Bloody Bess*; Terry Curtis Fox's *Cops* (which Gordon will direct for Tri-Star with Jim Belushi); *Bleacher Bums*, an improvised ensemble comedy set at Wrigley Field that has been playing in Los Angeles for seven years; and *E/R Emergency Room*, which became a TV series. The theater helped launch the careers of John Heard, Joe Mantegna, Andre De Shields, and Dennis Franz of *Hill Street Blues*.

A friend of Gordon's once dubbed the place "the take-off-your-clothes, scream, and bleed theater." William J. Norris says, "Stuart's big line was 'If it can be done on film, it can be done on stage, only better.' And all the bruised bodies and broken bones were a testament to the fact that sometimes you can do it and sometimes you can't."

By the time Gordon left to pursue filmmaking in 1984, the Organic had a budget of over $1 million a year and attendance that cut across class lines. All that was missing were nibbles from Hollywood. While Gordon was casting around for a film project, a friend mentioned six stories by H. P. Lovecraft written under the general heading "Herbert West—Re-Animator." Gordon, who has lots of doctors in his family, began to haunt the Cook County Morgue.

Re-Animator became a Gothic horror comedy about a dedicated young med student who gives life (or a crazed, blood-frothing version of it) to corpses. Poor Herbert: every time he injects his Day-Glo-green re-animating fluid into the brain of something dead, it gets up and tries to bash his head in. Some gratitude. This means the whirling corpses must be killed all over again (with bone saws, axes, et cetera). *Re-Animator* has a headlong pace and a giddy sense of its own absurdity (though it never condescends to the genre), along with wicked, straight-faced turns by Combs, Bruce Abbott as his sweet, frazzled straight man, and David Gale as a plagiarizing neurosurgeon whose head gets hacked off—his body spends the rest of the film dragging his noggin around, brains dripping.

The showstopper of *Re-Animator* is the infamous scene in which actress Barbara Crampton gets trussed to an operating table and given head by . . . the head. (Writer Dennis Paoli called up Gordon in the middle of the night and announced, "I've just written my first visual pun!") As Crampton remembers, "Stuart approached it like any other scene. He just said, 'He's gonna pick up the head, and it's gonna lick your ear and lick your breasts and then make its way down between your legs, and then Jeffrey [Combs] is gonna come in.' And I said, 'Oh, c'mon, Stuart, are you kidding?' And he said, 'No, seriously, it's gonna be great, really.' He was totally serious." She adds, "There's something a little *off* about Stuart. But that off-ness is part of his genius."

The final punchline is not the scene itself but critic Pauline Kael's delirious account of it, which is said to have appalled the strait-laced *New Yorker* editor William Shawn: "Barbara Crampton, who's creamy pink all over, is at her loveliest when she's being defiled; lying there in the morgue with the head moving around on her, she's like a nude by Fragonard or Boucher floating on a ceiling."

Now *that's* criticism.

The highbrows and lowbrows went nuts for *Re-Animator*; it was the folks in between who missed out on not just one of the best horror films of the decade but one of the best *farces*. The movie didn't do as well as expected at the box office (although it's been boffo on videocassette) largely because, executives at Empire think, it was released without a rating—the alternative to an X but for all practical purposes the same thing, since it means that no one under eighteen gets in. (Studios prefer no rating to an X, which signifies pornography in people's minds.)

"They never even said, 'You'd have to take this out or take that out,'" recalls Albert Band, executive vice president of Empire. "They said, '*Blehhhhhhh*.'"

Although the MPAA insists that it's not in the business of censorship (it's administered by the film industry, not the government), an X rating (or no rating) means a measurable loss of revenue. It's not just that some major theater chains won't show X and unrated pictures; scores of newspapers and TV stations won't even run ads for them. The final impact is on ticket sales. "It's well known," says G. Michael Ridges, president of Empire, "that exhibitors will often turn the other way and sell tickets for R-rated movies to your average fourteen-year-old, but with X or unrated films, enforcement is very strict." That enforcement cuts deeply into Empire's target audience.

Empire, an exploitation house with higher pretensions, has provided Stuart Gordon with a home to experiment in film the way the Organic allowed him to experiment on stage. The stakes are higher, however, and, unlike the Organic, Empire isn't a not-for-profit company. With *From Beyond*, the studio did not intend to make the same mistake twice. It couldn't afford to.

Empire Entertainment is the child of thirty-four-year-old Charles Band, who combines the gee-whiz enthusiasm of a Marvel Comics buff (he's even made a deal with *Fantastic Four* artist Jack Kirby to create two new characters) with an uncanny instinct for hawking his low-budget schlock. He jumped on the video bandwagon early, joining forces with video-industry giant Vestron. Largely as a result of that partnership (and the spectacular returns on low-budget sleaze in video), Band had the funds to take a swing at the moon.

"Charlie," according to an associate, "wants to be a mogul, a Sam Goldwyn. There's no way he wants to be [schlock-movie titan] Roger Corman. He wants to be much more respectable than that." Last January, Band surprised Hollywood by paying $20 million for Dinocittà, Dino De Laurentiis's massive studio complex outside Rome (where Band's father, Albert, a producer, director, and former assistant to John Huston, moved the family in the late fifties). The company now has a whopping production schedule; its motto is: "A thousand films by the year 2000." ("I wish it were 'A hundred *good* films by the year 2000,'" says one Empire insider.)

How can Empire, with no real blockbusters behind it, throw around such money? It hinges on "presales." Most Empire productions evolve in a curiously backward fashion—first a concept, then the artwork, then the sale of foreign and video rights, *then* a script. Preselling is Empire's art, and its posters, designed to Band's specifications, its glory. The posters send the message to overseas distributors that Empire understands its target audience and knows how to bait the trap. Screaming titles like *Decapitron*, *Erotikill*, *Berserker*, and *Breeders*, they boast leggy women, fearsome creatures, kinky action, and playful hints of sadism; each is calculated to plug directly into a pulp lover's subconscious.

The problem is that the movies themselves have largely sucked. (Remember *Troll*? *Eliminators*? *TerrorVision*?) Band realizes that, and he's been trying to upgrade his screenplays and spend more money on talent. But cash flow is tight these days, even with Vestron pumping in millions for video rights. Empire has sold a lot of movies it hasn't yet made, and the money has been spent. Now, more than ever, it needs a big hit. And the man who seems most likely to come up with one is Stuart Gordon.

Unless, of course, his movies get released without ratings.

The ratings board, unfortunately, is more likely to sanction clean, bloodless violence—death without sting—than Gordon's lavish gore. Sylvester Stallone can mow down scores of Vietnamese, have audiences cheering the killing and get an R. But a film by Stuart Gordon will never make murder look clean, easy, and fun.

"Violence," says Gordon, "should *horrify*. If it doesn't, there's something wrong with it. It should not be seductive. If you're going to show violence, you should show a lot of the stuff that goes along with violence—the suffering, the blood, the mess. When I staged my first fight scene, I did some investigating and found that most serious fights last one punch, and the person who throws it usually breaks his hand. The other guy's jaw breaks."

From Beyond doesn't waffle in its commitment to making you retch. Based on a Lovecraft story, it's about scientists who want to go beyond the five senses and who discover a dormant sensory organ in the brain—the pineal gland. When they stimulate it with a machine called a Resonator, they come in contact with a feverish, wildly sexual dimension, and, like drug addicts, are drawn again and again to the forbidden fruit. The first to pass entirely into the beyond is Dr. Pretorius (Ted Sorel), a brilliant sadist who spends the rest of the movie turning into squiggly, slimy creatures and trying to maul a lady psychiatrist (Barbara Crampton). Pretorius wants to go further, to feel things more deeply, than any human who's ever lived (or died).

From Beyond has little of *Re-Animator*'s gung-ho momentum or puckish wit. Gordon is shackled by the pace of his grisly special effects, which unfurl while the actors stand frozen in their tracks. Trying for a tone of crawly sexual menace, he forsakes the comic invention he's famous for. (At the Organic, and in his first film, he nurtured his actors' improvisational instincts and compulsively added slapstick business).

This is a much straighter horror film, freakishly unnerving, and loaded with grotesque sexual imagery—the flesh conforming to the most depraved human urges. On the surface, Gordon seems to be condemning sexual liberation, but the movie is really a Lovecraftian warning: in a repressed culture, normal desires have a way of swelling up and overwhelming you.

"I don't think it's an accident that all of H. P. Lovecraft's stories are set in Massachusetts, the center of Puritanism," says Gordon, who, along with Dennis Paoli, has vowed to film as much of Lovecraft as he can (next comes *The Lurking Fear*). "Lovecraft was examining the Puritan mentality, which on the surface is very proper and strait-laced and moral, and underneath is possessed by demons."

Indeed, it's the witch-hunting impulse that fascinates both author and director—the sadistic (and deeply sexual) urge to punish anyone who steps out of line. A favorite story of Lovecraft's concerns the Order of Dagon, an early free-love settlement wiped out by Puritans. And Gordon thinks the witch-hunting impulse is among us again, most visibly in the shape of Ed Meese. He likes to shake up the Meeses.

Gordon inhabits a place where trash, art, and politics intersect and where the giddy smashing of taboos is a large part of the fun. He reserves the right to probe the boundaries of taste, because "good taste" is how societies repress what they don't want to confront—even if those impulses wind up tearing them apart from the inside.

"There is something about Pretorius that I like," says Gordon. "In Frankenstein movies, they always say, 'He delved into things that man was not meant to know,' and that was his big sin. I don't believe that. I believe that man can know as much as he can know, and that he should try to know as much as he can. Where Pretorius becomes a monster is that he does it at the expense of other people."

There isn't enough of Pretorius in *From Beyond*, and he's the juiciest, most frightening character. In Gordon's work, the obsession with transcendence is a legacy of the drug culture that helped to shape his talent. "What people wanted in the sixties was to be transformed, to become something better than they were, and it meant you were going to lose something in order to do it. In a sense, *From Beyond* is about that, too. The problem—and this may be one of the lessons of the sixties—is that that usually ends in the person destroying himself. Although, when you look back at it, a lot of the people who are gone now achieved some truly spectacular and wonderful things."

What's refreshing about Stuart Gordon's work is that you can squeal, gag, and laugh your way through it and then sit down and talk—if you're so inclined—about Puritanism, the philosopher Descartes (some of Pretorius's lines are almost direct quotations), the lessons of the sixties, or the number of gallons of slime the effects people used (160, if you're interested).

This time, he did it his way. With *From Beyond*, Gordon gracefully wore the MPAA down, giving up about thirty seconds of graphic footage but cleaving stubbornly to the film's major shocks. Oh, sure, he cut away from a masturbation scene; obscured some lower-frontal nudity during the whipping of a woman; pared down a shot of his wife poking at Jeffrey Comb's pineal gland with a pair of forceps (the gland plays peek-a-boo); trimmed the brain-eating scene (you still get the idea); took a few frames out of a head being twisted off.... And, after the fourth submission, Empire had its precious R. *From Beyond* is now playing in major markets and will wind up in your neighborhood sooner or later.

In their modest home in North Hollywood, the Gordons have a big, friendly dog, a cat, and a barbecue in the backyard. Outside, police surveillance helicopters sometimes circle overhead, their lights traversing the lawns of the Gordons' neighbors in pursuit of fleeing suspects. Inside the house, however, you find a normal, all-American family—except that your normal, all-American husband doesn't cast his wife as a bitch or torture her in his movies.

"I hope we keep acting that part of our personalities out on the screen and not in real life," says Carolyn Gordon.

After all, a lot of couples don't have that luxury.

We Killed 'Em in Chicago

Meredith Brody / 1986

From *Film Comment* 23, no. 1 (January–February 1987), pp. 68–75. Reprinted by permission.

In the fall of 1985, an audacious, completely unheralded, unrated horror movie, *Re-Animator*, popped out of nowhere and left its appalled and delighted viewers reeling with questions: Who is this Stuart Gordon? Where had he gotten so smart? And was there more where that came from? Nobody expected such self-aware wit from Empire Pictures, a prolific schlock house that had lived by founder Charles Band's credo: "2000 pictures by the year 2000!" Band has turned out pictures sausage-style, presold to foreign and videocassette markets, and made at a price. But *Re-Animator* was a cut above: gory, scary, and dependent on shock effects, to be sure, but also cunningly contrived, slyly funny, and astonishingly assured for what was a million dollar-minus directorial debut.

There had been virtually no advance word of the movie—it escaped rather than was released—and at the peak of its popularity had played only in about 250 theaters, and even those were of the second rank, the chains that will take unrated pictures. Gordon was unable to flack the film or bask in his sudden glory, because he was in Rome shooting his second picture for Empire, *Dolls*, between Thanksgiving and Christmas. Then "in true Corman fashion," as Gordon says, he shot *From Beyond* (based, like *Re-Animator*, on an H. P. Lovecraft story) on the same old dark house set (redressed from American colonial to Victorian English style), in forty days, from February through April of 1986. Within a year, Stuart Gordon had three movies in the can.

So who was this Stuart Gordon, who was not a graduate of USC/UCLA/NYU, the hallowed halls of TV, or a member of the Writer's Guild? Who had written A and B before he demanded to direct C? In Pauline Kael's first and last review of an Empire picture, in the November 18, 1985, *New Yorker*, Kael cited Gordon as one of the founders of Chicago's Organic Theatre in 1969. Gordon directed nearly forty plays there in sixteen years, including his *Bleacher Bums*, which not only ran forever in Chicago, but also received a respectable run in New York and ran seven years in Los Angeles. Another Gordon original, *E/R* (for "Emergency Room"), ran for three years and inspired a Norman Lear sitcom.

In the late sixties, Chicago was noted more for its Second City satire than as a hotbed for new theater that it is perceived to be now—after David Mamet's sojourn at the Goodman Theatre, and John Malkovich's turn at the Steppenwolf Theatre, and William Peterson's at the Remains. Gordon says that he was encouraged to start there by Paul Sills, then working at the Body Politic, who called him up and said, "There's two theaters down here now; if you start one, we can call it a scene!"

Gordon was born in Chicago, in 1947. His father, an executive with Helene Curtis, died when he was thirteen, and his mother, who had been a social worker before she got married, became a high school English teacher to support Stuart and his younger brother. His father had originally wanted to become an architect and so interested Gordon in art, which he majored in at the legendary Lane Technical High School (he still has his letter sweater, which he says, "fits as long as I don't button it"). After graduation, Gordon worked for six months at a commercial art studio, long enough to realize he didn't want "to develop one particular style and spend the rest of my life doing that." So off he went to the University of Wisconsin at Madison, three hours northwest, but, as Gordon says, "a whole different world."

Gordon spent his first couple of years "just taking general courses—things I never thought I would have any use for, like anthropology. It turns out you always have use for them. Anthropologists will go into a village, study it, and take photographs, and take records.... When I'm preparing or working on a play or a movie, I do the same thing. When we went into the bleachers at Wrigley Field, it was like an anthropologist visiting this weird tribe of characters who have these weird rituals that they perform—it was a community, just the way the Ururumbu tribe was. We did a lot of field trips working on *Re-Animator*—hospital wards, morgues. None of it is wasted; it's the little details, those things that are totally insignificant, that make something believable."

Ironically, he took a theater course because he was turned away from the only film course. "It was full, I couldn't get in, and so I was looking for something else to do, and there was an acting class that was open, and I took it, and it turned out to be one of the best classes I ever had. It was a Stanislavski method acting class. One of the requirements was that you had to appear in a play—the play they were doing was *Marat/Sade*—and I got cast as a loony. I think I had two lines in the whole thing, but that play really changed my life. I had always thought of theater as a bad movie."

After *Marat/Sade*, Gordon recalls, "I wrote a play called *The Game Show*, which took *Marat/Sade* to the next logical step. The audience was locked in the theater and seeing a play that was kind of like *Let's Make a Deal*. The audience members were brought on stage as contestants, and were beaten, raped, and even murdered. I had plants in the audience, chosen seemingly by chance; we had locks and chains on the doors of the theater so that people would think they couldn't escape, but they were breakaway chains. The first night, the audience got so freaked out that they rioted and attacked the actors. The show actually got produced a few times after that, but I didn't direct it. One critic said, 'This is the most exciting piece of theater I've ever seen in my life, and it should be closed immediately!'"

His junior year summer, "Like a junkie, we did four plays in two months. We did one called *Vis*, which was an adaptation of *Titus Andronicus*. 'Vis' is Latin for violence or viscera—and in the play they rape a girl and cut off her tongue and her hands. We did this as an outdoor production in a burned-out building, and we had the whole audience sitting around a sort of pit. We did it non-verbally. We set it in a sort of post-nuclear holocaust time, kind of like cavemen, with grunts and groans, with all sorts of blood effects . . ."

And, "We did a production of *Who's Afraid of Virginia Woolf?* in a real apartment. We started it at 2 a.m., when it was supposed to be actually happening, and the audience followed us around from room to room, ending at 6 a.m. We did one play that was an adaptation of *Hamlet* that was done as a Western. Instead of moving the sets, I moved the audience around, on these bleachers that were on rollers, from scene to scene, and in for close-ups, and back for long shots. This was a real exciting time—just-try-anything time—and so I was shocked when we got into trouble with *Peter Pan*."

Inspired by the 1968 Democratic Convention, during which Gordon had been tear-gassed by Mayor Daley's police, the student company politicized their *Peter Pan*. Peter and the Lost Boys were hippies, whose "flying" became metaphorical drug trips, during which liquid light shows were projected on nude dancers (among them Carolyn Purdy, later to marry Gordon). "*Peter Pan* seemed very conventional compared to some of the other stuff we had been doing—we had a lot of nudity in the other productions and had never had any problems with it. That it was *Peter Pan* really freaked people out; we even got nasty letters from J. M. Barrie's estate in London." Gordon was arrested for public obscenity, and although the case was eventually dropped, the university told him that he could only continue producing plays there if he submitted scripts to a faculty review committee and allowed a faculty advisor to be present at all rehearsals. Gordon refused, and left six credits shy of graduation—although he notes that they've now put him on the alumni list.

Gordon, Purdy, and a number of others followed him off campus and formed the Organic Theatre. Its first official production was *Richard III*, but they continued to be harassed by the police who, looking vainly for flesh, would close down productions for building code violations, and forced the Organic to move to five theaters in three weeks. When Paul Sills and Chicago beckoned, the Organic didn't look back.

Sills (whose mother, Viola Spolin, was an influential teacher of improvisational theater) helped them find space in a Methodist church. When he later moved to New York to start his Story Theatre, the Organic moved into the space he'd vacated and became the Organic Theatre at the Body Politic; they stayed for three years.

"The first play we did in Chicago was an adaptation of *Animal Farm*," recalls Gordon, "which started out with sort of an open space. During the course of the play, we started putting up walls between the actors and the audience made out of camouflage netting. By the end of the play, you could hardly see the actors—they were imprisoned. We followed that with the *Odyssey*, which was a non-verbal production—I think there were three words spoken in the whole show. Then we moved to the Body Politic and did an adaptation of *Candide*—commedia dell'arte, with a lot of clowning around—that we took to New York.

"The first two times we went to New York, we got killed. We did it at Joe Papp's Public Theatre, which he was just moving into, in an un-renovated theater that was just a mess. We said, 'Let's just leave it as it is' and hung a banner over the entrance that said, 'This is the Best of All Possible Worlds.' Chicago was considered to be very unhip, and we were a bunch of hicks from Chicago, and we came back after having our asses kicked in New York and did a production called *Poe*, which was about the life and writings of Edgar Allan Poe. Actually, it was based on his mysterious disappearance for forty-eight hours just before they found him in a pauper's hospital, delirious, in someone else's clothes, with no identification; the mystery is what happened to him. It was a delirious nightmare version of his life and writings mixed together, one turning into the other. It was our first attempt at horror."

After *Poe*, Gordon moved into science fiction with *Warp*, Organic's first hit. Inspired less by sci-fi movies than by Marvel Comics, *Warp* featured a bank teller who is told he is really Lord Cumulus, Avenger of the Universe, and that only he can save the world. "Actually, the entire universe," Gordon corrects. "He ends up going into the fifth dimension, where it turns out he has superhuman powers, and gets involved in cosmic battles right there on stage. It was epic."

Originally conceived of as a seven-play cycle, *Warp* was done as a trilogy, "increasingly grandiose, which is the way comic books work—the villains get bigger and more powerful," Gordon says. The three original productions "were put together literally with Scotch tape and string," and ran for over a year in Chicago.

Then artist Neal Adams (later to do conceptual drawings for *From Beyond* and *Dolls*) came in and redesigned the costumes and sets. "We took it to Broadway and got killed. This was 1973, four years before *Star Wars*, and sci-fi was regarded as junk. One guy started his review with, 'I hate science fiction, I hate anyone who likes science fiction, and I hate this play.'

"It was an open-ended run, but we closed in about a week. We came back to Chicago and had to find ourselves a new theater—since we were all going to be rich and famous in New York, we let somebody else take over our theater. We found the Uptown Center at Hull House, a wonderful theater but in one of the worst neighborhoods in Chicago, Uptown, and people were afraid to go there. But we moved there, and we lived there, and the kids were born while we lived there—Suzanne in '77, Jill in '82."

In 1973, Gordon and the Uptown did an adaptation of Ray Bradbury's *The Wonderful Ice Cream Suit*. Bradbury came to see it, got up on stage at the end, disrobed, and put on the suit, saying it was the best production he'd ever seen. With that imprimatur, Gordon took it on a successful US tour.

Bloody Bess, a quasi-feminist pirate swashbuckler written by Gordon, Dennis Paoli, and John Ostrander, followed in 1974. One member of the company was an expert fencer and designer of stage combat, and the Uptown wanted to exploit his skills. "We were reading all these revenge tragedies," Gordon says, "and we couldn't relate to them. Most of them were about a woman losing her virginity and having to kill someone. Actually, the boyfriend has to kill someone; the girl usually goes mad. We discovered that there were two women pirates, Anne Bonny and Mary Reed, and based a story on their lives. The week before it opened, Patty Hearst was kidnapped, and her story absolutely mirrored everything that was happening in our play; people started criticizing us for trying to make money out of Patty Hearst's misfortunes, but we'd written the story—about the daughter of a governor of a Caribbean island, kidnapped by pirates, who ultimately becomes the leader of the pirates—before any of that happened."

A great success, *Bloody Bess* was invited to play the Mickery Theatre in Amsterdam as a guest of the Dutch government. The show launched the troupe on its first European tour. "It was like the Rolling Stones, with lines around the block. Pirates are to Europeans what cowboys are to us, folk heroes, and *Bloody Bess* was perceived like Sergio Leone—someone else doing one of our stories.

"Then we came back and did *The Adventures of Huckleberry Finn* in two parts, two full plays," says Gordon. "Twain wrote the book in two sections, put it aside for two years, and then came back to it. The first half of the book and the second are very different in tone, and though the characters are the same, the style of the two plays are very different. Like *Warp*, you had to come back a second time to see it. (We were in Uptown, and we were always trying to get the audience used to coming up there!) We brought it to Europe the next year,

'75, and then toured it through the US for the Bicentennial. We wanted to take it down to the Mississippi on the *Delta Queen*, a paddle-wheeler, but never got it together." Gordon did get to direct a new production of it in January 1985, as a guest of the Goodman Theatre in Chicago, right after he shot *Re-Animator*.

Then came *Sexual Perversity in Chicago*, the first professional Equity production of a work by David Mamet. "We actually helped put that play together—originally it was in two scripts, which we combined into one. One was called *Sexual Perversity*, which was a series of blackout sketches that were various people in different locations all talking about sex, and it had some wonderful dialogue, but there were no characters, really. And the other one was called *Danny Shapiro and His Search for the Mystery Princess*, about a guy and a girl meeting and eventually breaking up. We ended up putting the two plays together and using the dialogue from *Sexual Perversity*; we created the two friends and gave them the dialogue from this other play, with Mamet."

Gordon liked *About Last Night*, though he says he would have liked to have directed the movie. "It was true to the basic idea of the play . . . the conflict of fantasies: true love and living happily ever after fantasy versus 'Playboy, you're missing out on all this great sex' fantasy. I would like to have seen more of Mamet in the movie; also it would have been stronger if they hadn't stuck a happy ending on it."

Another success for the Organic—"It was kind of a landmark for us"—was the 1976 *Cops*, written by Terry Curtis Fox, then a theater critic for the *Chicago Reader* who now credits Gordon with getting him to "put up or shut up—if you know what's wrong with what we do, why don't you write a play for us." So, *Cops* was done "in realistic style," per Gordon. "As the audience walked into the theater, there was this greasy spoon restaurant in full swing on the stage, cooking real eggs—with people walking in and ordering food—and you smelled the coffee and the bacon. Then the gunfight breaks out in the middle of the play—we had all sorts of bullet squibs, and other movie effects—breakaway stuff that we had flying over the counter. The audience literally dove under the seats." Currently writing for *Hill Street Blues*, Fox is developing *Cops* with Stuart as a Tri-Star movie to star Jim Belushi. Says Gordon, "Jeff Sagansky had seen the play and understood exactly what it was supposed to do. He said, 'Just make it as outrageous as the play.' The other studios wanted to turn it into *Dirty Harry* or *The French Connection* [both 1971], but why do just another cop thing if you can do it differently?"

"One of the great things about working at the Organic," Gordon says, "was getting to meet terrific people. We did a production of *The Sirens of Titan* [1959], and Kurt Vonnegut came and worked on it with us. We did *The Great Switcheroo*, a production of three of Roald Dahl's short stories from *Switch Bitch* [1974]. It's about these guys who live next door to each other who are in lust with each other's wives. The wives are not into swapping, so the men decide they are going to switch without the wives knowing. Two guys realize that they are the same size; they start wearing the same aftershave lotion, and so forth. They have to explain in great detail their lovemaking techniques to each other, so that they can duplicate them. We also did *Uncle Oswald*—it would make a wonderful movie, too—and *Mrs. Bixby and the Colonel's Coat*. Dahl came with Patricia Neal, and they loved it."

In 1977, Gordon and the Organic did *Bleacher Bums*, the story of the long-suffering Chicago Cubs fans who camp out in the cheap seats at Wrigley Field. The play scored long runs at home and in both New York and Los Angeles, and had a TV production. "*Bleacher Bums* was the first time the theater ever created a work without a playwright in residence, using improvisation as the thing," Gordon says. "We went back to New York with *Bleacher Bums*, and this time, the third time, was the charm—we got wonderful reviews. We did it at the Performing Garage; then moved it to the American Place Theatre, and it ran for six months in 1978. I felt that we had finally conquered New York. We got back up after being kicked and tried again. Now things have completely gone full circle, and anything that comes from Chicago is considered wonderful!"

Chicago's Public Television station, WTTW, offered Gordon the TV adaptation of *Bleacher Bums*. "That's the first time I really had a chance to work with cameras, and that was a real good experience, just to sit down and work it out shot by shot. I worked with Pat Denny—a wonderful director who has gone on to become one of the main guys at WTTW. We ended up sharing an Emmy for direction on *Bleacher Bums*. PBS picked it up. We were always trying to get *Theater in America* to do some of our stuff, and they wouldn't. They were focusing on New York theater, so it was kind of funny to come in the back door with *Bleacher Bums*, which was one of the most popular plays done on PBS."

The Organic was nothing if not eclectic and often was accused of attempting projects "that should have been movies. We did an adaptation of *The Beckoning Fair One*, a great ghost story [by Oliver Onions] that is also kind of a sexual thing, a love triangle. A writer moves into a haunted house that has a female ghost, a succubus, who is jealous of his girlfriend. Every time his girlfriend comes into the house, terrible things happen to her. Like a movie, we built a haunted house set that could do all kinds of tricks, and set a lot of effects. In one scene, the girl walked up a staircase, her foot went through the step, and she laughed about it. ('How clumsy!') When she pulled her foot out, after what seems like a few seconds, it was torn up and bloody with big slivers stuck in it. We had two makeup guys concealed underneath the stairs. It ended up with her being completely destroyed, torn up, and eaten!"

Uptown went on to plunder film genres, doing a pornographic musical called *Fornicopia* in 1980, and an adaptation of Raymond Chandler's *The Little Sister*. In 1978, Uptown discovered the Buckingham movie theater on Clark Street, deserted since the forties. The troupe secured a group of angels to buy it and a matching grant from the NEA to renovate it (most of which was done in secret to avoid the endless political red tape generated by the Chicago Buildings Department). They opened on a cold May day in 1981 (spring is called "June" in Chicago), "with no heat, with an adaptation of Mary Renault's *The King Must Die* [1958] that featured a lot of nudity—of course!"

Next was *Doctor Rat*, an adaptation of William Kotzwinkle's [1976] book. "With *Doctor Rat*, we kind of retuned to the *Game Show* idea. All of the characters in *Doctor Rat* are laboratory animals, so I put the audience in cages. Then the animals have a revolution, open up all the cages, and encourage the audience to join them on stage. Some nights we got over 100 people on stage—they really did play along. There's a scene at the end where all of the animals are gassed to stop the revolution, and the audience members all died on stage—it looked like Jonestown. These people had come to the theater in nice clothes and everything, and there they were, lying on this grungy stage.

"After *Doctor Rat*, we were just about to fold, the theater had its back to the wall, no income, and the last two shows had bombed. We did *E/R*, which got absolutely slammed by the press. Jill was born on opening night—it was the only time I ever missed an opening night—and Jill brought us some good luck, because *E/R* ended up running three years. It took almost a year to write, after talking about the idea for years with Ron Berman. We were visiting doctors and talking to nurses working in emergency rooms, and then coming back and improvising based on these stories that we compacted all into one night.

"We did a tape of *E/R*, which I sent to some people at Norman Lear, who liked it enough to cut a deal. They hired us to be advisors and consultants and so forth, and they actually listened. I liked the show—it was interesting to watch the evolution. When the show started it was very close to the play—a comedy in which patients are dying and doctors are making mistakes. By the time the TV show was happening, *Re-Animator* was being shot as a film; I was visiting the *E/R* set at Universal and going to locations to shoot *Re-Animator*."

Gordon next adapted *The Forever War*, a [1974] novel by Joe Haldeman, a Vietnam vet who wrote up his experiences in a science fiction context—Vietnam in outer space. Gordon had been disturbed by the philosophical implications of *Star Wars*, which he thought made war look like fun, like a video game, and blew up entire planets without showing any blood. "It must be the highest body count movie ever made, but it's clean, incredibly clean; it's like a nuclear war, like dropping a bomb on a city and you don't see the results. And it ends with them all getting medals at the end. Having gone through the sixties and Vietnam, I was horrified.

"Then I came across Haldeman's book, which is a futuristic war, but is written from the point of view of somebody who's actually been in a real war and doesn't like it. It's a wonderful book. It would be a great movie, and now with all the Vietnam movies somebody should make it. I'd love to do it.

"The last sequence of *The Forever War* takes place on a planet in the middle of nowhere that is to be held at all costs—sort of like the Alamo. They're attacked by aliens, and they don't know who these aliens are. We had screens and video effects. It was a real big project, technically very involved, and not cheap. A lot of people asked, 'Is this a movie?' But we always did things on stage that people thought should be done as films. Or shouldn't be done at all."

Gordon's awareness that he did theatrical projects that were filmic in nature, and his positive experience with TV, prompted him to try filmmaking. He worked on two scripts with Lenny Kleinfeld that were never produced. "We wrote one called *Sweetheart* based on the Karen Silkwood story. After a doctor's girlfriend is murdered, he does an autopsy on her and discovers that she's been killed by radiation poisoning. Then we did *Lucky* with Dennis Paoli, a story about a childless couple that has a little dog they treat like it's their kid. When they have a baby, the dog gets jealous and tries to kill it. Only the dog and the baby know what's up. *Lucky* was based on our own experience—we had two dogs, little West Highland terriers, and one bit Suzanne in the face when she was a baby. No damage, but it scared the shit out of me, and I never felt the same way about the dog again. Anyway, it became a battle between the dog and the baby, and the baby wins, because the baby is smarter. I thought I'd use a lot of subjective camera."

With *Re-Animator*, Gordon returned to literary inspiration rather than nursery inspiration. "We were having a discussion one night about vampire movies—*Dracula* with Frank Langella, *Love at First Bite* [both 1979]—everybody was doing Dracula to death. I said, 'I wish somebody would do *Frankenstein*.' Carolyn's brother's girlfriend said, 'Have you ever read "Herbert West—Re-Animator?"' and I'd never heard of it. It is an H. P. Lovecraft story, and I thought I'd read all of Lovecraft, but the book was out of print. It was in a six-part serial in a collection that had never been reprinted—because Lovecraft didn't like it. He said that he just wrote it for the money. I put in a request for it at the Chicago Public Library, and then forgot all about it. About a year later, I got a postcard saying I could come and read it, but only at the library.

"The pages were literally crumbling in my hands as I read it, so I had it xeroxed. I was still thinking theatrically, but then Dennis Paoli and Bill Norris and I decided to do it as a half-hour TV pilot. The story is set around the turn of the century, and we realized that automatically made it about six times more expensive, so we decided to put it in the present day. I wanted to set it in Chicago, using the Organic Theatre Company, and thought our chances were better on TV. We got close to selling it a couple of times—once to Tribune Entertainment, which ended up going with *Tales from the Darkside* [1983–88]. We were told the half-hour format was not saleable, and so we made it an hour. I've got thirteen episodes—one of them about starting an ambulance service to get bodies easier.

"Bob Greenberg, who had been after me for years to come out to Hollywood, convinced me that the only market for horror was in features, and introduced me to Brian Yuzna, a producer. I showed him the hour-long pilot and the thirteen stories; he looked over the material—the pilot went up to the point where Dean Halsey is killed, re-animated, and sent to the madhouse—and said, 'You've got to put in this headless guy.' I said, 'Then we've used up everything, we don't have anything for the sequel.' And he said, 'Hey, there isn't going to be a sequel unless you kick out the jams in the first one.' And I said, 'Isn't that excessive?' and he said, 'Yeah.'"

Yuzna convinced Gordon that, with all the special effects, it made sense to shoot *Re-Animator* in Hollywood. He made a distribution deal with Empire in return for post-production services, unusual for Empire, which cranks out the goods after the orders are written. The movie was already in production when Charles Band started to get excited about the rushes and brought in cinematographer Mac Ahlberg, special effects man John Buechler, and composer Richard Band. Then Charles Band started talking to Gordon about future projects with Empire. The picture was shot on "the oldest soundstage in Hollywood," the S&A studios, where Mary Pickford once worked, and where they swore to Gordon that the soundstage was haunted.

Editing on *Re-Animator* began while Gordon went back to Chicago to direct *Huckleberry Finn* at the Goodman, and to choose someone to run the Organic—now a thriving concern with an annual budget of over a million dollars. Gordon took a year's leave of absence to stay in Los Angeles to prepare his current *Dolls*, from an original script by Ed Naha, and *From Beyond*, based on another Lovecraft story. The year's leave is now permanent.

Though *Dolls* was shot before *From Beyond*, most of the latter's effects (four times as many as in *Re-Animator*) were done on the stage. Because *Dolls* required extensive stop-motion animation work, *From Beyond* was released first, in the fall of 1986. Empire did not want to release another unrated or X-rated movie, and despite its sexual content, *From Beyond* got an R after four edited submissions to the MPAA Ratings Board. Gordon claims that the cuts were trimmed time onscreen, rather than whole shots lifted out. By the fourth viewing, he thinks the board grew accustomed to the shock values. Technically, the film is flawless, but philosophically it is both disturbing and intriguing, but after the totally unexpected, loony, rapid-fire jolt of *Re-Animator*, it disappointed.

From Beyond seems classically structured, more evenly paced. Patiently, you wait for the next horrible mutation of the Mad Doctor Pretorius, whose Resonator has caused his adorably phallic pineal gland to burst through his forehead. Touchingly, his assistant sighs, "Five senses just weren't *enough* for him."

Dolls also doesn't deliver quite the frisson that *Re-Animator* did. Gordon calls *Dolls* "comedy-horror in the tradition of *The Old Dark House*." Well-acted, funny, and mildly resonant of Bruno Bettelheim's *The Uses of Enchantment*, *Dolls* lacks *Re-Animator*'s sass. Is it unreasonable to wish that these three films could have been released in reverse order? Gordon is now faced with expectations that seem unfair, given the time-dollars parameters of the films.

Gordon refers to the year that he shot those three movies as having the same junkie feel of the summer in Madison when he directed four totally different productions—"try anything time"—in two months. And he's already shooting his fourth Empire picture in Rome, *RoboJox*, the company's most lavish and ambitious project to date. It is a post-apocalyptic fantasy in a future in which national disputes are settled by battles between gigantic robots piloted by robot jockeys, or "robo-jox." Ron Cobb, who designed *Conan the Barbarian* [1982], designed the hardware; Dave Allen, of Industrial Light and Magic, who was nominated for an Oscar for *Young Sherlock Holmes*, is doing the stop-motion work; Giovanni Natalucci, who did *Ladyhawke* and *Once Upon a Time in America*, is the art director. Gordon's wit might be obscured by the very weight of these special effects, but he says, "It's about the people, not about machines."

Not to worry. Empire and Gordon have a three-picture deal: *Bloody Bess*, based on the female pirate play he did at Organic; *Berserker*, about a wrestler who takes bad steroids that turn him into a killing machine, and originally intended for Arnold Schwarzenegger ("But," Gordon sighs, "I hear Arnold won't play villains anymore!"); and another Lovecraft story, *The Lurking Fear*, in which the main character is Lovecraft himself. Not to forget the possibility of a *Re-Animator* sequel, called *Bride of Re-Animator*, in which Gordon takes on marriage. There's also a voodoo story called *Gris-Gris* set in Haiti, the development deal with Tri-Star on *Cops*, and *Teenie Weenies* at Disney, an Ed Naha script about children shrunken to less than an inch in height who have to make it home across their suddenly dangerous back yard.

Teenie Weenies came about, Gordon says, when he and Brian Yuzna realized they hadn't made any movies that they would allow their children to see. Having once turned out plays that were like movies, and re-animated by an open field, Stuart Gordon might make more movies that either kill audiences or free them from their cages—and at the pace he produced plays.

Stuart Gordon: The Ideas, the Philosophy, the *Pit and the Pendulum*

Rick Pieto / 1988

From *Slaughterhouse Magazine* 1, no. 3 (Spring 1989), pp. 13–20. Reprinted by permission.

In this issue, we focus the *Slaughterhouse* Prime Cuts grinder on Stuart Gordon, one of America's most violently original filmmakers; a man of highly principled vision who succeeds at communicating his message, at one level or another, to everyone that experiences his films. He also has great taste in magazines. *Slaughterhouse* caught up with Gordon during pre-production on his current cinematic project, Edgar Allan Poe's "The Pit and the Pendulum."

Stuart Gordon: I really liked the first issue. I'm glad that *Slaughterhouse* is getting off to a good start.

Slaughterhouse: I bet you say that to all the pretty magazines. "The Pit and the Pendulum" is such a personal and private story. How are you visualizing it?

Gordon: In Poe's story, a man is arrested by the Inquisition for crimes that he knows nothing about—and then goes through hell. In researching the Inquisition for the film, we were fascinated by Torquemada, the Grand Inquisitor. He was a Dominican monk who was responsible for putting two thousand people to death at the stake, and by burning them to death. We were playing around with the idea of him as the Leonardo da Vinci of torture, and that he comes up with more and more elaborate ways to torture and kill people. In our story, he falls in love with the wife of a baker and, being a monk, he cannot justify these feelings within himself. He decides that she must have bewitched him. He then has her and her husband arrested as witches. The husband ends up being tortured in the pit with the pendulum.

Slaughterhouse: Do the tortures become progressively more bizarre? In the story, there's basically the pit, the pendulum, and the rats.

Gordon: Absolutely. We are going to stick pretty close to Poe's story as far as the pit and the pendulum are concerned, and being rescued by the rats. But the things that lead up to that . . . we've been doing a lot of research and we found that the actual tortures that were used by the Inquisition were far more horrifying than anything that we could dream up. It was very formalized. There were three levels of torture. We will be taking our audience through all three levels. They—the torturers—wanted you to confess. If you were a particularly hard case, you would have to go to the next level, and so forth. The first level of torture is being forced to watch other people being tortured, knowing that this will be done to you if you do not confess. The second level is what they called "light torture," which means there is no permanent damage inflicted. You won't end up a cripple. At the third level, they just don't worry about any of that. Their attitude was that the body is a temporary thing. They're trying to save your soul, which is eternal. The body is not important. Whatever they have to do to the body to save the soul is justified.

Slaughterhouse: You've stated that horror is becoming more involved with telling stories of personal horror, stories of the individual. "The Pit and the Pendulum" definitely fits that description.

Gordon: Yeah, the idea will be to get the audience to identify with the innocents that are thrown into hell; for the audience to take it on a very subjective level. The other thing is that there is a horrifying mundanity in the way these guys approach things. One of the things that I found in the research was a schedule of torture—you know, what a day of torture would be like for the torturer. They had their hour for lunch during which they would leave their victim strung up. They'd just sit down and eat in the torture chamber, and then go back to work. It was that kind of nine-to-five job. They had a doctor in attendance to make sure that the torturers did not kill the victim, because that would ruin the chances of the person confessing—if he dies. One of the things that I learned is the difference between an executioner and a torturer. Their jobs are exactly the opposite.

Slaughterhouse: What kind of sources did you go to for your research?

Gordon: There are several very detailed books about the Inquisition, but I also did a lot of reading about witch trials and witchcraft, and so forth. The idea of the Inquisition—it's incredible how long it lasted. It started in Spain in 1492 and it did not end until about 1810! It went all through Europe. All of the various witch trials that eventually happened in America were kind of a direct outgrowth of the Inquisition.

Slaughterhouse: When I read Poe's short story, I instantly thought of Jeffrey Combs as the prisoner. Is there any chance that he'll be cast that way?

Gordon: I don't know. I have a role in mind for Jeffrey, but not as the prisoner. I think Jeffrey is going to play the scribe that is always in attendance at the tortures, to take down the confession, and also to make sure that the rules of torture are followed. The idea of him being the very persnickety bureaucrat in the midst of all this horror—and he's just keeping the records on it all—I think that that would be fun.

Slaughterhouse: Are you going to use any of your other actors, like Barbara Crampton?

Gordon: I'm not sure about Barbara, but I'm hoping to cast Hilary Mason. There's an actual witch in our story, and she was such a wonderful witch in *Dolls*, that it's hard for me to imagine anyone else playing this part. In *The Pit and the Pendulum*, the baker's wife is thrown into this cell with a witch, and then learns some actual witchcraft in order to save herself.

Slaughterhouse: What type of special effects are you going to go for?

Gordon: The effects are going to be very realistic in terms of portraying the actual methods of torture.

Slaughterhouse: You're basing them on the actual devices?

Gordon: Oh, absolutely, and the makeup will be extremely unsettling and believable—very real. There are some hallucinations that some of the characters have. Toward the end of the story, we will see some pretty bizarre things take place.

Slaughterhouse: That fits the story. It's an intense, subjective experience.

Gordon: Yeah, that's the thing Poe was able to do. You know, most of his stories are written in the first person. As the reader, you're always wondering if this is actually happening or if this is happening in the person's mind.

Slaughterhouse: Is your interest in Poe an outgrowth of your interest in H. P. Lovecraft?

Gordon: My interest in Poe preceded my interest in Lovecraft. I was a fan of the Roger Corman movies; that's what really started me reading Poe, and, of course, I'm a fan of Corman's original film version of "The Pit and the Pendulum."

Slaughterhouse: Will there be any allusions to the Corman version in your film?

Gordon: This isn't definite yet, but I'm hoping that we can get Vincent Price to play a cameo. There's a wonderful part as the pope, and I can't imagine a better person to *bless* our production than Vincent Price. I did theater before I did film, and we did a play called *Poe*, which was based on the life and writings of Edgar Allan Poe. We actually did two productions of it. We did one in 1972, and then we revived it in 1982. I'm pretty familiar with his career. But getting back to the film at hand, our *Pit and the Pendulum* is in production right now. We're designing it and we're starting to cast it, which is why, at this point, no one is really set in any of the roles yet. The plan is to begin shooting in the middle of March [1989].

Slaughterhouse: Who's doing the effects?

Gordon: I'm talking to a lot of different effects people, and getting an idea of how they would approach it, before we decide which company will handle it. There are quite a lot of effects, particularly fire effects; a lot of burning at the stake, torturing people with fire.

Slaughterhouse: What happened to *RoboJox*?

Gordon: I just finished the film, just before Christmas. I think that they are going to be testing it for a bit. The plan is to release it in late spring or early summer.

Slaughterhouse: Really? I just read . . .

Gordon: Yeah, *that* article in *Cinefantastique* was about six months old when it hit the stands, and the situation has improved considerably. The film actually wasn't even finished when that came out. They were correct in what they were saying, but that was ancient history. What happened was Trans World, which essentially took over the film from Empire, put the money into it to complete it properly. The movie is now done—thank God! (Laughs) It came out great. The special effects are seamless, all done inside the camera. [The robot puppets are] very, very believable. I mean, no matter how good a blue screen shot is, you're always aware that there is an optical process going on. But this way, the way Dave Allen shot them, using real mountains, skies, and sunlight—I mean, it just *killed* everybody! We were out there almost a year, shooting that. The results are just stunning.

Slaughterhouse: It intrigued me to hear you say that you made *RoboJox* for children, how you were fascinated with the Transformer toys. But, on the other hand, your films are always politically progressive, with different subtexts going on. How did you juggle the two, making a children's film and keeping the subtexts?

Gordon: I think the worst thing that you can do with kids is talk down to them. I think kids pick up on a tremendous amount of material that we aren't even realizing. So, my attitude was to keep it clear and simple, but not simplistic. The characters, I think, are real people, and the world they're in is a real world. There's a lot there. If they want to see that, they can, and if they don't, well, they don't. The story is clear enough that a ten-year-old can enjoy it, but I also think his parents will enjoy it, too. I remember going to see those movies they hardly make anymore, where the whole family can go together and enjoy a film, rather than taking the kids to a *Care Bears* movie or something where the parents get bored. I think there is a real need for movies like that. The idea, as you said, was inspired by toys, but being an adult who loves the toys myself, I wanted to keep the grown-ups happy, too.

Slaughterhouse: Continuing with the "kids" theme: how is the *Teenie Weenies* project for Disney coming along?

Gordon: They changed the name from *Teenie Weenies* to *Honey, I Shrunk the Kids*, because it sounded too much like *Care Bears* or something. I think that they're finishing the effects on it now, but I had to drop out of that one. The timing was not good. I had just come back from doing *RoboJox*—too much, too soon. I had to take a break. But they did complete the film, and followed the original plans and so forth, and have even been testing the movie, and it's been doing very well. I'm going to receive a story credit on it. All of the planning on it was done under my supervision. You know, people used to say Disney made children's films, and he would say, "No, they're family films." I think that that is playing to the widest possible spectrum that you can. I think that is why Disney's films are still so wonderful today.

Slaughterhouse: You once said that horror films could address issues that other forms could not. Is that what originally attracted you to horror films?

Gordon: Well, I think the greatest thing about horror films is that they help people deal with their fears. The most central fear—that I think we all have—is the fear of death, which is exactly what horror films address. In our society, we spend most of our time trying to avoid that issue, and pretend that it doesn't exist. Horror films confront it directly. They give an audience a chance to take these things which are lurking in all of our subconscious, and put it right out there in the open. I think that's a much healthier thing to do. You can exorcise your own demons.

Slaughterhouse: Given that horror has the ability to confront and address issues that other forms cannot, what would you like to see horror dealing with during the [George H. W.] Bush regime?

Gordon: There are several things that I think will be needed to be stated. I think that the idea of caring for people will be needed. I like horror films where you can identify with the characters, feel for them, and care for them. I think that is something that is going to have to be stated again and again. It is kind of interesting that this last John Carpenter film, *They Live* [1988], is a terrific political statement dealing with that very issue: the idea that our society is breaking down into the haves and the have-nots, and there's nothing in between. With *The Pit and the Pendulum*, you've got the whole moral majority kind of thing, which is what the Inquisition is all about, that there is only one way to think and that anyone who thinks any other way is dangerous and possessed by Satan and has to be destroyed. I think that that is very much a part of what is going on today.

Slaughterhouse: Another thing I get from your films, especially from *Re-Animator* and *From Beyond*, is this need that individuals have for some sort of transcendence. In *From Beyond*, Dr. McMichaels and Dr. Tillinghast would turn on the Resonator and a whole new world would appear to them. They're taken out of their ordinary reality and placed into a new world.

Gordon: I think it is Nietzsche that they always quote: you know, "That which does not kill you makes you stronger." I think that ties into horror films, too—you know, [it's] going through the experience that strengthens you. In *The Pit and* *the Pendulum*, our heroine, as I said, is accused of witchcraft and in order to save herself, she has to transform into a witch. She has to become the very thing that *they* want her to be. In order to do that, she has to go through a tremendous and painful transformation. The real witch is able to teach her some things, and recognizes that there is a kindred spirit there. Our heroine is then left to pick up the mantle and take it further.

Slaughterhouse: It's interesting that you use the phrase "pick up the mantle," because you use that in referring to another film I really hope that you make called *Gris-Gris*, based on Marie "voodoo" Laveau's life.

Gordon: What happened was, unfortunately, at the time we started talking about *Gris-Gris*, there had been a whole series of voodoo films coming out. What started upsetting me was that, although none of these films were really successful in presenting voodoo on screen, they all had elements that were similar to our script. Eventually, I decided that I had to just put it aside, because by the time it would have come out it would be seen as just a rip-off of all these other films.

Slaughterhouse: But did you put elements from the mother/daughter relationship in *Gris-Gris* into the witch and the wife relationship in *The Pit and the Pendulum*?

Gordon: I had never thought of it that way, but I think you're right. There is a similarity there, the idea of an innocent girl having to protect herself through the use of the supernatural.

Slaughterhouse: What horror films work for you?

Gordon: Well, I tell you, I think the best film of last year was David Cronenberg's *Dead Ringers* [1988]. I don't know if I would call it a "horror" film, although it was definitely horrifying. Cronenberg really is the master of horror. I also really liked *The Fly* [1986]. The criticism that people had of Cronenberg up until that point was that he was so cool and his characters were never very compelling, whereas with *The Fly*, Jeff Goldblum's performance was outstanding and had such a wonderful humanity about it. That made the movie all the more frightening; this nice guy going through all of these terrible things. But *Dead Ringers*... Jeremy Irons's performance was just fantastic, and I hope that he gets nominated for an Academy Award. *Dead Ringers* was one of those films that make you want to wash your hands when it's over, and that might be too much for them. The Academy doesn't want their violence to be upsetting, which I think is amoral. To me, that is what pornography is. You have violence without pain and without mess, and making it look like fun. I think that's the worst thing that you can do. Violence should be horrifying as hell. People should be saying, "Boy, I don't ever want to do that, or have that happen to me." I still think *Psycho* is the scariest movie ever. I don't think anyone has ever topped that. What's so scary about it is that [Hitchcock] broke all the rules, which is what I love to see in a movie. I'm so tired of movies where you know everything that's going to happen in the first ten minutes. In *Psycho*, he took all of the audiences' expectations and twisted them 180 degrees. Killing off the star thirty minutes into the movie leaves the audience absolutely panicked. I love that feeling, when you have no idea what is going to happen next. Just like real life.

Slaughterhouse: *The Fly* has often been interpreted as being an AIDS allegory. Much the same can be said about *From Beyond*.

Gordon: Yeah, I think that's true. That was definitely in my mind when we were working on it. It was interesting because the original story is only about five pages long and I was trying to figure out what was the inspiration for the story, what was Lovecraft writing about here? The story is about being aware of these invisible creatures which can kill you. In reading about Lovecraft, I discovered that this man was an extreme hypochondriac, [who was] very afraid of becoming sick. The idea that these invisible creatures in the air are actually viruses ... first it seemed kind of wimpy to me, but then I thought about AIDS. It's exactly the same thing—you know, the fears that are running through society about AIDS is a very strong thing. Again, it's one of those issues that no one wants to deal with, and the only place that you can discuss it is in a horror film. I mean, *Torch Song Trilogy* [1988] had to be set in the past, because they didn't want to have to deal with AIDS. But if you put it into the context of a fantasy, it suddenly becomes manageable. People are always thinking about things like that, and they need a way to express it.

Slaughterhouse: You were talking about a need to care for people during the Bush regime. Does this enter into your thoughts in *The Pit and the Pendulum*?

Gordon: Yeah, I think very much so, in that if the hero of the story has committed any crime at all, it's to turn his back on all of the suffering that's going on all around him. In the beginning of the story, he's going to where they burn people at the stake in order to sell bread. The fact that he is benefiting from people suffering, in a sense, is his crime. We've seen this before, in Nazi Germany, and now we are seeing it again with these right-wing, moral majority types. We're getting back into racism, anti-Semitism, and all of those sorts of things. The Inquisition used the same tactics to create the common enemy, so everyone could hate the same group and thereby bring the country together. That philosophy is used all of the time.

Slaughterhouse: At one point you were working on Lovecraft's "The Lurking Fear" and "The Shadow Over Innsmouth."

Gordon: "The Shadow Over Innsmouth" is the one that we did the most work on, but "Lurking Fear" never got beyond a treatment. We had a script for "Shadow" and we were in pre-production. We even had makeup designs and drawings. I worked very closely with Dick Smith on that one. He actually did some sculptures of some of the characters for us, which are fantastic. Bernie Wrightson did some production designs for us. Unfortunately, what we found was that the project was going to cost twice as much as we had originally estimated. It's an entire town filled with monsters. A kid comes to a New England fishing village and discovers that the townspeople have been mating with amphibious creatures that live on the reef outside the town. The offspring look normal when they are children, but the older they get, the more fish-like they get, until, eventually, they slither off into the sea. When the town learns that this guy has discovered their secret, they all come after him to kill him. It's a film project involving literally hundreds of monstrosities, each more repulsive than the last one. The finale takes place on the reef outside the town, in the ocean. Those elements contributed to the budget going too high for a horror film. I'm hoping that it's eventually going to get made, but it's going to take a while to find a company that's willing. It's interesting, I've run across a lot of people that want to make that story—going all the way back to Fritz Lang. Roger Corman's *Humanoids from the Deep* [1980] is inspired by it, but it hasn't ever been filmed as Lovecraft wrote it.

Slaughterhouse: What about this female swashbuckler project called *Bloody Bess*?

Gordon: Yeah, bad timing on that. We were taking that around right after Roman Polanski's *Pirates* [1986] came out. So, it bit the dust. The last thing people want to do is to make a parrot movie. In fact, one company even said that they would make the film, but as space pirates! (Laughs) I kind of felt that was disappointing. One of the things about *The Pit and the Pendulum* that I like is the chance to do a period piece. For the last few years, Hollywood has avoided anything set further back than the fifties. I see this as an opportunity to show that there is an interest in other times, and that a project like this can be commercial. Again, horror has the ability to take subjects and, by making them fantastic, you can deal with them. I think the same thing is true with putting the setting in the past. It makes the oppression something that we can manage a little easier. If we were to do a movie about torture in El Salvador, it would be much harder to take than a piece about the Spanish Inquisition. It gives you a little distance, which I think will be helpful.

Slaughterhouse: Are you thinking of doing a number of Poe stories in the same way that you've done a number of Lovecraft stories?

Gordon: There's a number of Poe stories that I would love to do. One of my favorite Poe stories is "William Wilson." It's a story about a guy and his conscience. I don't think that it's ever been filmed yet. Poe's the greatest. His writings are one of those things that you can keep going back to and get more out of each time.

Slaughterhouse: One last question and it's kind of off the wall. Have you ever read the German psychoanalyst Wilhelm Reich?

Gordon: I've read articles about him, but I've never read his stuff.

Slaughterhouse: Your work really seems like a horror version of his psychoanalysis and his philosophy. He had this thing called an Orgone Box, which resembled your Resonator in *From Beyond*.

Gordon: Right! That's true! (Laughs) We had him in mind when we were working on that. He was the kind of scientist, the kind of visionary, that we envisioned Dr. Pretorius as. Pretorius was kind of a cross between Reich and the Marquis de Sade, I guess. Maybe with a little Aleister Crowley mixed in.

Slaughterhouse: Hmmm, I ran out of questions.

Gordon: Well, *The Pit and the Pendulum* should be finished in around a year from now. Then I can talk about it with hindsight.

Robot Jox Rides Again

Kyle Counts / 1989

From *HorrorFan* 1, no. 2 (Summer 1989), pp. 54–58. Reprinted by permission.

It's been uncharitably described as the film that broke Empire's back—the costliest, most ambitious, most troubled production of Charles Band's career as head of that once-prolific, low-budget grindhouse. The deal memo for the movie in question, *Robot Jox* (formerly *RoboJox*, a title that sounded a bit too much like *RoboCop* to suit Orion Pictures), is dated October 4, 1985. When the futuristic fantasy film is released in April by Trans World Entertainment, three and one-half years will have passed since director Stuart Gordon first conceived the project.

The reasons for the prolonged delay are numerous, all related to the toppling of Band's Empire beneath the weight of a staggering $46 million in debts. Whether due to inferior product or the company's attempt to distribute its own films, Band was forced to relinquish control of Empire and regroup under the banner The Bandcompany (its video arm called Full Moon Productions), where Gordon has an office on a film-by-film arrangement. (TWE now owns the Empire catalog, including films that were not yet complete at the time of the takeover.)

Gordon conceived *Robot Jox*—he slips now and then and calls it *RoboJox*—while making *Dolls* in Rome. "I'm a big fan of the Japanese Transformers toys," he explained from his office, which overlooks Sunset Boulevard. "While there have been animated cartoons based on these giant robots, no one has ever attempted a live-action feature about them. It struck me that it was a natural fantasy for the big screen—and a terrific opportunity to take advantage of the special effects that are available today."

When Gordon brought the idea to Band, Band's first reaction was that it was too big a picture for Empire to tackle. But he later changed his mind and suggested that Gordon team up with stop-motion effects wizard Dave Allen (who contributed several shots to *Dolls*) and film a brief test to determine if the film could be done well—and believably. Not only did Band want to see if Allen's effects had the right stuff, he also had plans to use the footage to presell the movie.

Gordon approached science fiction writer Joe Haldeman to write a screenplay based on Gordon's original story—itself based on the story of Achilles from Homer's *Iliad*—having worked with him two years prior on an ambitious stage adaptation of Haldeman's most celebrated book, *The Forever War*. Dennis Paoli (co-author of Gordon's *Re-Animator* and *From Beyond*) put the final draft through various rewrites.

"Joe is part of an air force think tank to develop weaponry for the future," explained Gordon, "so he was able to incorporate a lot of actual existing technology into the script and to hypothesize where it might all lead. Then we started storyboarding the film. The reaction to Dave's footage was excellent, and Charlie was able to get the project rolling on a projected $10 million budget—a huge budget for an Empire film. I think Charlie saw it as Empire's chance to move up into larger-budget films."

Six months passed from the time the test footage (which would become *Robot Jox*'s opening title sequence) was put together to the time funding was raised. What that figure doesn't take into account, Gordon said, is that the planning for the film was also going on during that period. "This film needed almost a year of pre-production. We had to set the script and storyboard the effects sequences, then those sequences had to be broken down shot by shot for budgetary purposes. We ended up doing some simplifying and trimming, which is something that happens on every effects picture. You never have enough money to do everything that you want to do. The actual budget ended up being about $6.5 million."

The film takes place fifty years after a nuclear war has almost destroyed the Earth. War has been outlawed, and all territorial disputes are now settled by single combats fought by towering robots manned by pilots, or "robot jox," with each warrior representing his country. The technology that would normally have been used to develop warfare is now being used in service of what has come to be known as "The Games." According to Gordon, "It's almost like a sporting event in that it's televised worldwide on a regular basis and people bet on the outcome. They even have bleachers on the battlefield for the fans."

In this future world there are two alliances: the Market—the United States, Europe, and Japan—and the Confederation, which includes the Soviet Union and all of the Third World Countries. Like the board game Risk, each side expands its territory by winning a robot battle.

The robot jock, who is trained like a fighter pilot, has taken on a superstar quality. He's contracted for ten fights—even though only one robot jock, a John Wayne-type character named Tex Conway, has made it through all ten. The hero of the film is a robot jock who fights under the name Achilles (played by Gary Graham, Tom Cruise's older brother in *All the Right Moves*). As the film opens, Achilles is about to go into his tenth battle—if he wins he can retire. His opponent is Alexander (Paul Koslo—"the man you love to hate," joked Gordon), characterized as a ruthless, cold-blooded warrior who always kills his adversary. A fighter for the Confederation, he's also been the victor in nine bouts.

The Games are staged like a gunfight, with the robots starting out at opposite ends of the playing field, about a mile apart. Armed with canons and lasers and rockets, as they walk toward one another each begins his high-powered assault on his opponent. When the robots get close enough to touch, the referees—who fly above the arena in a craft called a "Ref Floater"—shut down all the robots' long-range weaponry. At that point, only hand-to-hand combat is permitted. As the robots are transformer machines—the most sophisticated kind in existence— they have the ability to turn into different kinds of fighting machines, including a tank and a space rocket (a submarine mode was considered but dropped due to its prohibitive expense).

During the battle, Alexander finds Achilles's weak spot: his heart. In an effort to protect the fans from a secret weapon Alexander has fired, Achilles deliberately throws his robot in front of the projectile. The impact knocks him off balance and he falls into the bleachers, crushing several hundred spectators. Even though it is clearly an accident, Achilles is so shattered by the experience that he quits The Games, vowing never to fight again.

The referees replace him with a female robot jock named Athena (Anne-Marie Johnson, Howard Rollins's wife on the TV series *In the Heat of the Night*). She's a "tubie"—a new breed of female pilot genetically engineered using designer genes. Achilles falls for Athena, but she doesn't really understand his feelings. "It's simply not part of her genetic makeup to care about anyone," explained Gordon. "He realizes she has no chance against a seasoned fighter like Alexander, so he decides to come back rather than see her killed. That infuriates her, because she's gone through hell to be chosen for this battle. That's all I'll tell you about the story, other than the last half hour of the movie is solid action."

Kevin Altiere designed the menacing Confederation robot for the opening sequence (Tom Sherman contributed the skeletal remains of various fallen robots, one of which utilized pieces of Tupperware), the plan being to keep him on board for the duration of filming. But he left to take a job with DIC Animation Studios before production resumed. "The further we got into production, the clearer it became to be that the person we needed to do the design work was Ron Cobb," said Gordon. "One of the things I liked about Ron's design work is that his futuristic machinery looks like it would actually function. Ron is, like Joe Haldeman, a Vietnam veteran, and he also has a tremendous interest and expertise in weaponry and machinery."

Steve Burg was brought in to assist Cobb with the robot detailing, since Cobb had a limited amount of time to devote to the project. Despite a report in *Cinefantastique* that "everything went to pot" when Cobb departed, Gordon insisted that the transition was virtually seamless. "We were constantly referring to Ron's drawings, and Steve continued to report back to Ron to show him what he was doing and to get Ron's approval. As a matter of fact, Ron and Steve hit it off so well that they've worked together ever since."

Robot Jox began principal photography at Empire's Rome facilities (since sold off) in January 1987, and wrapped in April. Gordon then turned over the post-production effects to Allen, who had selected El Mirage, a dry lake bed near the Mojave Desert, as the site for filming of the live-action robot skirmishes. (Some stop-motion work would be done at Allen's Burbank studios; the live-action filming made use of the five-foot, fifty-pound cable-controlled models of Achilles and Alexander.)

"There wasn't too much choice as far as shooting outdoors because Empire didn't own a local stage we could work on," Allen explained. "And even then it would have to have been huge; we would have had to hang and paint a cyclorama and then put tables out and light everything artificially. We would have been into a tremendous set rental situation over an extended period of time, which would have been a huge cash drain."

El Mirage was chosen for its brilliant blue skies and unobstructed panorama, but the year of on-again, off-again shooting that transpired—Allen and his crew would make a total of three trips out to the desert location—proved to be anything but smooth sailing. The weather was so temperamental, Allen considered it a good day if he got two or three good shots in the can. "The heat wasn't so bad, but as we were in a geometrically unstable area, we were at the mercy of the elements," Allen said. "We had to contend daily with clouds, rain, dust storms, and hellishly high winds—our outhouse got blown over constantly. Sometimes the dust was so bad you couldn't see in front of you. When that happened, we'd go back to the motel or drive back to LA. When it rained the lake bed would fill up and our cars were in danger of getting stuck."

Numerous delays caused by the weather—and requests made by Gordon for additional effects—made location shooting more costly than Empire budgeted for. Still, Allen bristles at the suggestion that his unit work might have set the film back. "The location shooting was probably more expensive than [Empire] expected, yeah. However, the problem wasn't that we were breaking the bank, but that we weren't getting money sent to us regularly enough. If by week four we didn't have a check, we had to go back to LA. Rain or shine, I still had to put up ten or twelve guys in a motel."

Even though Empire was clearly in the midst of severe financial woes by this time, Allen insists that he was never pressured by Band to finish. "He understood what we were battling, which was the weather. Empire's loan money was costing them interest, but we weren't that expensive—our effects came in at less than 25 percent of the total budget."

How was Gordon able to maintain control over the production if he wasn't present at the El Mirage site?

"I did go out to the desert site a couple of times, just to kind of say hello and check in. But my feeling was both Dave and I were involved with the storyboarding. We both knew shot for shot what was supposed to be happening and I felt confident that I could turn it over to Dave and he would do it as planned—which he did. Dave is an artist in his own right and has to be given his own measure of control—to run things as he sees fit. It was very much a sharing of the power.

"Otherwise I was in constant communication with Dave during the post, even while I was in pre-production on *Teenie Weenies* for Disney [a project Gordon had to turn over to Joe Johnston when a bout of high blood pressure dictated a three-month rest]. He would be sending me footage as he was shooting it, and I would make suggestions. I also supervised the footage as it was edited into the picture. I know he and his crew went through hell out there, but the results were so spectacular that it was worth it."

Gordon scoffs at the industry talk that *Robot Jox* was responsible for the fall of the Band Empire. "I don't believe that this picture sunk Empire, though it certainly didn't help," he admitted. "It is true, however, that it was the most expensive picture Empire ever produced—three or four times their normal budget. It also had the longest post-production schedule. But even if everything had gone like clockwork, it would still have required a year of post. Charlie had envisioned that *Robot Jox* would put Empire on the map, financially speaking. Unfortunately, we were not able to get the movie done in time to save the company."

Gordon is currently developing a half-hour anthology series for HBO titled *Asylum* ("Each week we go down a corridor of this insane asylum and open a different cell door—we learn what it was that drove that particular person mad"), but the gleam in his eye at the moment is his new version of "The Pit and the Pendulum," scripted by Dennis Paoli, which will be shot at the [Incer De] Paolis Studios outside Rome. For his version, Gordon plans to "go back to Poe," as the 1961 AIP film used very little of Poe's twenty-page story.

"I happen to like the Roger Corman/Vincent Price version, but today's audiences demand a different approach to the material. We can get much more visceral about things now. Corman had to avoid some of the elements of Poe's story that were considered a little much at the time the movie was made. I'm doing research about the Spanish Inquisition, specifically torture—the various methods used back then and its rules. All of that will be in this movie. I also did a lot of reading about Torquemada, the Grand Inquisitor of the Inquisition. In his day, he was known as the Leonardo da Vinci of torture—he was constantly looking for new ways to take people apart."

Realizing the almost fiendish glee with which he has been discussing the rather unsavory business of torture, Gordon stopped and smiled. "No wonder people expect to see my hands dripping with blood when I answer the door."

Stuart Gordon

Stanley Wiater / 1990

From *Dark Visions: Conversations with the Masters of the Horror Film* (Avon Books, 1992), pp. 77–87. Reprinted by permission.

From time to time, a new talent appears on the horror scene and is responsible for a motion picture that quickly earns a reputation as a landmark in the genre. In 1985, the film destined to become a classic was *Re-Animator*.

Its first-time director was Stuart Gordon.

Like his colleague Clive Barker, Gordon entered the world of moviemaking from the theater stage. As founder and artistic director of Chicago's Organic Theatre, Gordon already had twenty years' experience of what it took to get an audience's attention. Working with producer Brian Yuzna and screenwriter Dennis Paoli, he blasted his way into the field with a movie based on some obscure stories by an otherwise famous horror writer, H. P. Lovecraft. To say the least, it was an impressive debut for all concerned.

In his cinematic version of these Lovecraft tales, Gordon takes the idea of a young scientist bringing the dead back to life to the ultimate in shock. *Re-Animator* contains such bizarre images, and gory scenes so outrageously grotesque, that audiences either had to laugh out loud or left the theater in utter disgust. Ultimately, the movie would gain a cult reputation, partially because of the infamous scene where the head of an undead doctor attempts to perform an unnatural sex act with the strapped-down, nude heroine. Regardless of how mainstream audiences may have reacted to *Re-Animator*, the fact remains that *cineteratologists* now regard it as one of the most important films of the 1980s, just as George A. Romero's *Night of the Living Dead* was a taboo-breaker for the 1960s.

Stuart Gordon's career has continued to climb, though perhaps not as quickly as fans of his premiere film would have liked. His second film, *From Beyond* (1986), was also inspired by the writings of H. P. Lovecraft, and in many ways is just as shocking as *Re-Animator*. However, Gordon's third film, *Dolls* (1987), was basically a Grimm's fairy tale for adults, while such long-delayed projects as *Robot*

Jox (1989) have so far been unreleased in this country. Another Lovecraft film, *The Shadow Over Innsmouth*, literally never made it off the drawing board, even though such veterans as artist Bernie Wrightson and Dick Smith were involved in the pre-production stages.

I had my conversation with Stuart Gordon as he was preparing to get production underway with a new version of Edgar Allan Poe's classic tale, "The Pit and the Pendulum."

Stanley Wiater: Oliver Stone once said that to be a successful director of horror films, you have to be a "visual sadist." Do you have any response to that interpretation?

Stuart Gordon: I think you have to be a masochist as well, because you have to know what scares you and be able to return the favor.

Wiater: Oliver Stone directed two horror films early in his career, and he felt that he didn't have the right stuff it took to be a horror director. I was wondering if there is any particular talent that separates horror directors from mainstream directors?

Gordon: In my own case, I was affected very much by horror films when I was a kid. I was scared to death; I had nightmares that would last for weeks after seeing a film. My parents, because of that, told me that I wasn't allowed to go see them, which of course only made me want to see them more. In reading other interviews, it seems to be true of a lot of people who make horror films. So, I think that is a good preparation; you know what scares you and it's a sort of therapy turning it around and scaring someone else.

Wiater: Was it the idea that you didn't enjoy being scared or that you *did* enjoy being scared? Sam Raimi told me that he didn't enjoy being scared, and this was his way of getting back at his own fears, to confront them.

Gordon: I think that's true. I think that you *have* to have an overactive imagination. One thing that I've found about horror movies is that whatever you can imagine is far worse than what you can portray. The thing that really scares you in a movie is when suggestions are made to your mind, and then your mind does most of the work. It's an unpleasant feeling; you feel like you're going to throw up or pass out. But when it's over you feel a kind of relief, and it's a positive feeling. It's like a rollercoaster ride: after it's over, you always say, "Well, let's do that again!" I think the ideas are similar, the idea of facing your own death and surviving.

Wiater: When you were a youngster, was it a particular group of films? I can date myself by saying that I was watching *Thriller* and *The Twilight Zone* as a very young lad, as well as the Roger Corman films with Vincent Price in the early sixties that made an indelible impression on me.

Gordon: One of the films that really scared me was *The Tingler* [1959], directed by William Castle. I was out of there. I didn't stick around for the end of that movie, I was gone! I think the earliest one I can remember is *Abbott and Costello Meet Dr. Jekyll and Mr. Hyde* [1953]. I saw the movie again recently and realized that the movie ends with Abbott and Costello turning into monsters, so it didn't have a very comforting ending. This movie didn't end, it just kept on going. I think that's what scared me.

Wiater: Continuing with childhood influences, in literature you were obviously well associated with H. P. Lovecraft.

Gordon: No, actually it was in college, which would put it in the late sixties. But I was a fan of horror and ghost stories since I was a kid. I remember reading *Dracula* in Chicago in the summer when it was really hot and muggy. I would sleep with all the windows shut and locked. That book was so scary that I would just sweat it out. I kind of agree with Oliver Stone: I think it takes a certain type of person. I would even go further to say that all people who direct horror films look the same, too.

Wiater: Describe that please?

Gordon: Sort of large, heavy-set sometimes, usually with beards. I keep running into various versions of myself all the time. (Laughs) There was one article I read about Stephen King that he was sort of using his writing to get back. He wasn't one of the kids that fit in. He wasn't the most popular. He gets revenge by taking people apart in his stories. I think that could be part of it, too, that your imagination triumphs over your problems.

Wiater: Why horror? I know you were a founder of the Organic Theatre in Chicago and obviously it wasn't Grand Guignol or a horror theater.

Gordon: Well, we did some plays that were definitely horror plays. We did a play based on the life of Edgar Allan Poe. We did a ghost story, *The Beckoning Fair One*, and we did use some blood effects in our shows. I like to do other things besides horror movies as well. I think it's almost Freudian in a way: my father died when I was young, and I think horror movies deal with death in some form or another, and sometimes it's the ability to triumph over or conquer death. I think there is a definite connection between my father's death and my having done the movie *Re-Animator*.

Wiater: Sometimes writers and filmmakers go to extremes, of course. I'm talking about people in the horror genre trying to belabor the point that they had "normal" childhoods and normal parents.

Gordon: You could say the same things about axe murderers. They seem so "normal." Your next-door neighbor seems so normal, always keeps himself to himself, and then chops up his whole family. I think that "normal" exterior is a good camouflage. Then, instead of going out and chopping up your family, you do it on film.

Wiater: So many people like to think that horror movies and horror fiction are a bad influence. Why are some people so obsessed with protecting our "precious youth" from horror?

Gordon: It's funny, because I think the way they go about protecting them does a lot of damage—particularly the MPAA. If you are going to murder someone in a movie, they want it done with no fuss and no mess, no blood. The lesson they are teaching is that violence is painless and fun. My feeling is that if you are going to show violence in a film, you should see how it *really* is. It should be ugly and upsetting, and there is a lot of blood. Anyone who's seen a newsreel knows how much blood there is when someone is shot or stabbed. When you portray violence without the reality, I think you are encouraging it. The argument is 180 degrees opposite of what they intended. I think that children should be protected in that they, and their parents, should know the content before they go see it. But I think as long as you give them fair warning, it is up to the individual to make the choice.

Wiater: Do you think that in today's moral climate, things are getting worse instead of better?

Gordon: Yes, I definitely do. I think the standards of the MPAA are getting much more strict, and they're not allowing certain things to be shown anymore under an R rating. I've gotten into arguments with them over this scene or that scene. I would compare it to another film, and they would say that if that film was being rated today it would be rated differently. One of the ones that they are most upset about is *Friday the 13th* [1980], that they gave the initial film an R rating back whenever that was, and now it has sequels that they have to deal with.

Wiater: How is that affecting your current film projects? Do you have to pre-censor your imagination because you are dealing with a lot of money and the producers will say, "Why even try because it's going to get cut out by the MPAA?"

Gordon: You do run into that. Oftentimes, though, I think you can find alternate ways of shooting something so that the audience will still get the idea without showing everything, and sometimes it's more effective.

Wiater: When you did *Re-Animator*, which was shot in 1984 and released in 1985, did you say at that point, "The hell with it, we're just going to do it?" It's really hard for me to fathom how in today's climate *Re-Animator* could be made, and I'm wondering how it could have been made even six years ago.

Gordon: I think we were incredibly naïve. We were concerned, but when we were making the film, we thought we could get an R rating, believe it or not. One of the worries that we had was the male nudity because we were told that if you have any full frontals of men, then it is automatically an X rating. So, we went to great trouble to make sure that you didn't see anyone's genitals. They even created these things for the actors to wear called a merkin, which is sort of a codpiece. We never used these things, but when we got to the last day of shooting we were doing a sequence and someone said the actor was exposed. So, we said, "Let's put a merkin on him." It turned out that the prop guy had thrown them out because we never used them. What we ended up doing was painting it black. That was how naïve we were. (Laughs) It turned out, when we showed it to the MPAA, that they said no way would they give it an R rating. I think if we had tried to cut that film, we would have ended up with a twenty-minute film.

Wiater: Correct me if I'm wrong, but when the movie came out on cable, wasn't it the unrated version, or was it the R version? If memory serves, Cinemax or Showtime was actually showing the unrated version, but with their own R rating over it.

Gordon: No, that's right: they did show the unrated version on cable TV. I think that it should have been an R-rated film, anyway.

Wiater: When Orson Welles made *Citizen Kane* [1941], and whenever he made a film after that, people would say, "Okay, Orson, tell us more about *Citizen Kane!*" Are people saying that to you: "Stuart, we know you've made other films, but tell us more about *Re-Animator*"—as if that is your *Citizen Kane* already?

Gordon: It was a very strong introduction of my work and it does stick with people. That doesn't bother me. I also think it has to do with the fact that it's been around the longest and it's taken all these years for an audience to be developed.

Wiater: You're probably aware that the gonzo critic Joe Bob Briggs has called *Re-Animator* "the drive-in film of the decade."

Gordon: That's terrific! I didn't know that.

Wiater: Tell me about your made-for-television movie called *Daughter of Darkness*. I was wondering how that experience was, in the sense that you had to go by the standards and practices of network television right from the outset?

Gordon: I was curious to see what was allowable on TV. The most intriguing thing that I found out was that most made-for-TV movies are trying to appeal to a female audience, because in all their research they found that it is the women who turn on the TV and prefer made-for-TV movies. Horror films are notoriously a guy's thing, so there was an interesting challenge to see if I could interest a female audience. In a sense, *Daughter of Darkness* is sort of a cross between one of those Barbara Cartland romance-type books and Bram Stoker.

Wiater: That was shot overseas, I believe.

Gordon: Yes, it was shot in Budapest, although it's set in Bucharest, Romania. One of the other things that happened was that about less than a month before *Daughter of Darkness* aired the revolution took place. So the film, which we had done a great deal of research on to try to get it as accurate as possible, suddenly became a period piece. It became a sort of historical epitaph.

Wiater: It starred Anthony Perkins, and I know you're a big fan of *Psycho*. Did you swap anecdotes, or did he tell you any anecdotes about *Psycho* and working with Hitchcock?

Gordon: Yes, he did, he was full of wonderful stories. He worked with some of the greatest directors, and he is a fascinating fellow. He is also a great fan of the horror genre and has great knowledge of it. He told me a funny story about Hitchcock when they were doing *Psycho*. He and Martin Balsam had been rehearsing the scene in which the detective is questioning Norman Bates about the woman who had been staying at his guest hotel. Balsam kept interrupting Perkins, not letting him finish his lines, asking the next question before he could answer the one before. They liked that, and later in the day Perkins was looking through the storyboard that Hitchcock had done on that scene and discovered that the entire scene was shot in close-up, which meant that there could be no overlapping of the dialogue. He said to Hitchcock that he would like to show him the scene that they had been rehearsing. Hitchcock said that he didn't really have time right now, and Perkins said, "No, I really think you need to see this." Finally, Hitchcock realized that something was going on and he said, "What's the problem?" Perkins told him that he thought it would be better if he shot it with a two-shot instead of a close-up. He realized in that moment that here he is telling Hitchcock how to shoot a piece. In a long, ominous moment, Hitchcock takes the storyboard and tears it up. He said that the stories of Hitchcock being so immovable and such are just not true. Hitchcock was much more flexible and he did listen to actors.

Wiater: Let me continue with that thought on directors—Hitchcock being an obvious one to name about influences.

Gordon: Well, Hitchcock, definitely. I think *Psycho* was a curious movie because it broke all the rules. I'm a big fan of Roman Polanski. *Rosemary's Baby* was a great film, and I watched it a lot before I directed *Re-Animator*. His work in that movie is so subjective that it makes the audience become Rosemary. I also love Stanley Kubrick's work. His work in *The Shining* [1980] I think is great, the way he moves the audience through the story. The cameras are constantly in motion.

Wiater: Are there some other directors outside the horror genre, or was it always the horror directors?

Gordon: There are other areas I enjoy. I am a big fan of the Marx Brothers and Fellini. I think both their movies are full of surprises. The worst thing for me in a movie is when you know everything that is going to happen in the first five minutes of the film. It's like it was written by a computer. So I like it when they mix it up, pull the rug out from under you. When the directors surprise and startle you.

Wiater: This gets to the humor in your films. I think George A. Romero's films are very humorous, as are Polanski's and Kubrick's, with a lot of black humor that I think only the sophisticated viewer appreciates.

Gordon: When Hitchcock referred to *Psycho*, he always referred to it as a comedy. It took me seeing it three or four times before I started picking up on the comedy. He said there was a very thin line between getting someone to laugh and getting someone to scream. One thing that I've learned is that laughter is the antidote. When you think you don't have to laugh, then you are basically blowing away the intensity. You have to be careful when you do that, you don't want to be laughing at the expense of the fright. It's best if you can alternate the two, build up the tension, and then release it with a laugh. It is a double degree of challenge. You're walking a tightrope, and if something becomes inadvertently funny, the whole thing is over. The thing I have found is that you'll never find an audience that wants to laugh more than a horror audience. I did a lot of comedies in Chicago, and a lot of these audiences are just going to sit there with their arms folded like, "Make me laugh." Whereas in a horror movie, you welcome any chance to laugh—something that takes you away from the oppressive scariness of the piece. So, it's always a good idea to give the audience that moment.

Wiater: One unfortunate situation for you is that *Robot Jox* has been held up for so long. Is there still a possibility of that film being released?

Gordon: That's true. It has been finished for over a year now. If it had been released when it was supposed to have been, it probably would have done well. The premise of the movie is one that comes out of the Cold War—two superpowers—and the world is a whole new ball game. It's been released on video in Great Britain and done extremely well. In fact, it did better than *Lethal Weapon II* [1989]. But I'm still keeping my fingers crossed; I haven't written it off yet. It's too bad. I think movies have life spans.

Wiater: I would like to know a little bit about your relationship with Dennis Paoli. I understand that you have known him for many years, and it's unusual for a director and a screenwriter to work on more than one or two films. What is that special chemistry you have—beyond your obvious friendship—that you work together?

Gordon: Dennis and I go all the way back to high school together. We wrote comedies together as part of a comedy group called the Human Race. We were able to work our way through school doing this. I think the fact that we are such good friends allows us to be honest with each other. We kind of complement each other. Dennis's strong suit is dialogue and mine is stories, so we are a good team. The bottom line is that we enjoy working together.

Wiater: What is the fascination that keeps you interested in the horror, fantasy, and science fiction fields?

Gordon: I like stories that take you somewhere that you've never been. They take you somewhere and show you something new and exciting. Science fiction, fantasy, and horror are the bread and butter; that's what they thrive on and they explore. I like stories where anything's possible. I think movies are like dreams, and they don't need to be ruled by reality.

Wiater: What about the sense of telling the philosophical truth? Both Romero and David Cronenberg have stated in interviews that it is only in horror films that you can speak about the unspeakable in terms of death and decay. Cronenberg's *The Fly* was a good example.

Gordon: I think that is one of the great strengths of horror and fantasy films. But when they do talk about these things, they have to talk about them in parables, in a way. They couldn't talk about AIDS in *The Fly*, but everyone could feel what it was really about. The parable is like the Bible, where the exact details of the story are exaggerated or invented. But I think with any form of great art you have to tell the truth. I agree with the idea that there are certain topics that people would not be able to talk about unless done as a parable.

Wiater: It's the same thing with humor, which brings me back to your work. As you mentioned Hitchcock with *Psycho*, the idea that these are comedies, I have always found that comedians understand death and horror better than anybody else.

Gordon: That's true. When I was doing the research for *Re-Animator*, I talked to a lot of pathologists and discovered that they have very funny, very black outlooks. It's the same thing that if you're going to do a job like that day in and day out, you *have* to be able to laugh. I think that's one of the reasons why *Re-Animator* ended up the way it did, trying to incorporate that approach, that view of humanity that comes from hanging out in the morgue.

Wiater: In terms of *Re-Animator*, are there things that you yourself determined were too off the wall or over the edge?

Gordon: We pretty much threw everything in there that we could think of. There was very little self-censorship, although we did cut a particular scene. Earlier on in the movie, there is an autopsy and they are removing the brain from a corpse. During that sequence, I talked to a pathologist who explained—move for move—how things were done, which we shot in great detail: cracking open the skull and using a corkscrew-type device. This scene went on much longer than it probably should have. The reaction from the audience was kind of weak, and they had a hard time recovering from this. So, that scene was cut way back.

Wiater: Let me switch over to *Dolls*, which I enjoyed a lot, but with the running time, and maybe I'm just falling into a black hole by saying this, was that film cut? Is there a longer version of *Dolls* or was it meant to be a relatively short running time?

Gordon: It *is* a short film. Part of that was that this was the first film I did in Italy, and they work at a quite different pace. It's not that they're not—they're wonderful craftsmen and artists, but they have their own way of working. We found that we had to cut things or never shoot them in order to make our schedule. So, that film is short due to the reality of the situation. But the things that were cut I wouldn't say were necessary for telling the story. I don't think this film could have been much longer and worked as well. It's interesting that you mentioned that because I've talked to a lot of people who have seen the film, and I've never met anyone who complained about it being too short. The original script was longer, but I think that the film is as long as it needs to be. It's a satisfying film.

Wiater: Would you like to go back to H. P. Lovecraft if that opportunity presented itself?

Gordon: There are so many wonderful stories! I think a lot of people are finally picking up on that. It's too bad that he's not around to appreciate the fact that he *is* appreciated.

Wiater: Films have been based on H. P. Lovecraft stories before. What do you think he would have thought of your interpretations if he were alive today?

Gordon: I think he would be a little shocked by some of the films because he approached things with a sort of Victorian view. He was much less explicit when writing a story. But I think he would have been pleased overall.

Wiater: Is it true that today's audience has forced you to always be explicit? You can no longer go for just the hand on the back, or the shadow on the wall, to make an audience be scared?

Gordon: I think you ultimately have to show them something if there is something to be seen. You can't just go with the Lovecraft "cop-out." He would talk about this *thing*, but he would never say exactly what it was. Film is images. I think it is still possible to scare an audience with suggestion. Like I said, imagination is the greatest weapon that you've got. I think it's the combination of both those things. You should show the audience just enough to get the idea of what they are seeing, but not too much. I used to think with horror movies that the movie was over as soon as you saw the monster. No matter how horrible something is, once you've seen it you feel better. So, it's the anticipation of the horrible thing that really scares you. When that moment comes you really have to deliver it and knock someone's socks off.

Wiater: But is there a point where there won't be anything left to scare an audience with? Are we going to reach the point where they say, "We've seen everything in the horror film and even Stuart Gordon can't give us a new chill?"

Gordon: No, I don't think we will. The horror movie has been around forever. Before the horror movie was the horror story. The new filmmakers will come up with more scares. When Romero did *Night of the Living Dead* people were running out of the theater, and now it's being shown on network TV uncut. I think the same thing will be true of *Re-Animator*: that it will eventually be looked at as a period piece. So, I have faith in my future generation. And that's part of what you do, you always try to top what has been done before. You see what the level is and top it. That's what filmmakers are doing all the time.

Wiater: Sam Raimi told me when they did *Evil Dead II*, they went to every horror movie they could find, and said, "Now we have to top everything that is best about these movies."

Gordon: Exactly! And the only way you can go is further. The imagination is always working.

The Pit and the Pendulum

Steve Biodrowski / 1991

From *Cinefantastique* 21, no. 6 (June 1991), pp. 12–13. Reprinted by permission.

The past two years have not been kind to Stuart Gordon. After bursting onto the horror scene with outrageously inventive films like *Re-Animator*, *From Beyond*, and *Dolls*, his career hit a few snags: first, his jump to mainstream success was delayed when illness prevented him from directing *Honey, I Shrunk the Kids* (though he did receive co-story credit and will executive produce the sequel); then *Robot Jox*, his low-budget attempt at action-packed science fiction, fell into distribution limbo after the collapse of Charles Band's Empire Productions, finally emerging a year later only to prove itself hardly worth the wait.

But now Gordon rebounds from those setbacks with *The Pit and the Pendulum*, a film that takes the graphic intensity and black humor of his Lovecraft adaptations and sets them in the more tangible world of Edgar Allan Poe. Lance Henriksen stars as Torquemada, of the Spanish Inquisition, a role originally intended for Peter O'Toole. Jonathan Fuller and Rona De Ricci are the young innocents falsely accused of witchcraft when the Grand Inquisitor's dormant lust is aroused by a beautiful woman. Jeffrey Combs, Oliver Reed, and Carolyn Purdy-Gordon (the director's wife) make cameo appearances. Band's new company, Full Moon Entertainment, produced the film for Paramount, which provided financing in exchange for theatrical and video distribution rights. A March video bow was scrapped to explore theatrical release possibilities.

Last year saw a spate of Poe-inspired productions, but the idea of adapting "The Pit and the Pendulum" occurred to Gordon before then. "I'd always been a big fan of Edgar Allan Poe's writings and also of Corman's films," said Gordon. "It seemed like there was a whole new generation out there coming to Poe fresh, so I thought it was time for new adaptations of his work. I guess other people felt the same way!"

Gordon chose to adapt this particular story "because it's so visual and action-oriented—perfect for film. Also, the idea came out of a visit I made to the Tower of London. I realized the things that people actually do to each other are far scarier than anything you can fantasize about—the worst monsters are people. It struck me that 'The Pit and the Pendulum' is set during the Spanish Inquisition, a period that is extremely cruel and frightening, and a film of that could be truly horrific." Knowing that major studios would be hesitant to tackle such grueling subject matter, Gordon pitched the idea to Band. "We had done several pictures together in Italy, but had never taken advantage of the location—we were always pretending to be in America."

To expand Poe's short tale into a screenplay, Gordon collaborated with Dennis Paoli, who had previously co-written Gordon's Lovecraft adaptations. "Poe's story is very short, around fifteen pages, so it would not sustain a feature," said Gordon. "Using Corman's influence, we borrowed things from 'The Cask of Amontillado,' and one of the characters is buried alive. We ultimately get to Poe's tale in the last half hour," Gordon laughed.

"Also, we focused on the character of Torquemada, which was not part of Poe's story, and used a lot of our research. We discovered that Torquemada invented the Inquisition, and he approached it very meticulously. He formalized everything. He wrote, I think, twenty-eight books on the rules of torture, and he had all of the trials transcribed. So, there were these incredible records of everything, and we were able to incorporate a lot of that into the film."

The project went through a long period of development, which included a one-year hiatus when the original financial backing fell through. "It took all kinds of strange turns," recalled Gordon. "Originally, the financing was coming from Vestron, who wanted a major star. We approached Peter O'Toole about playing Torquemada, and he was interested. The only problem was that he was not able to leave Great Britain during the time we wanted to shoot. There's some kind of custody arrangement with his son, which means that he has to reside in England during certain months of the year. So, we ended up moving the whole production to Elstree Studios, built the sets, and cast English actors—and were ready to make the movie when the bottom fell out because Vestron went down the tubes."

With the production on hold, Gordon lost his star, but O'Toole's approach to the character remains an important influence on the finished film. "O'Toole had some interesting ideas about how Torquemada should be played, which were terrific, and we ended up using them," said Gordon. "Torquemada does not see himself as a villain. He sees himself on a mission from God. So, rather than playing him as this snarling, evil presence, we decided to make him a very driven man who has this sense that God is speaking directly to him, which gives him the right to disregard the pope and everyone else in order to do what he thinks has to be done."

Ultimately, Gordon thinks the delay benefited the film. "Charlie worked out an arrangement with Paramount and did several videos for them, such as *Puppet Master* [1989]. He showed them a copy of the *Pit and the Pendulum* screenplay, and they ended up giving him double what the normal video budget would be, with the hope that it could be released theatrically. But that budget was about half of what we had a year ago. We went back to the original plan to shoot in Italy, at a castle which Charlie owns. Doing that, we were able to cut some corners financially and ended up with a movie that has greater scope than our original one would have. We recast it with American actors, a lot of them members of my 'repertory' company. It worked out better in the long run. When I look back, I'm glad that we didn't shoot it a year ago.

"The great thing about postponing the picture," Gordon continued, "was being able to come back to the script a year later and re-read it. We realized that a lot of material would have been lost on the audience. We had this information about the wars with the Moors going on in Spain and Queen Isabella trying to unite Castile and Aragon into one country. All of that stuff was interesting background, but it really had nothing to do with our story. We realized that for an audience today—many of them don't even know there was a Spanish Inquisition—we needed to portray the Inquisition, and to focus on the characters. It ended up strengthening the script."

Gordon's direction is typically graphic. Makeup effects, including several unsettling torture scenes, were devised by Greg Cannom (*The Exorcist III*). Gordon's fans, however, may be surprised to find that context often prevents the violence from going over the top. "We tried to balance it out with other things," said Gordon. "The violence is upsetting because it really happened. You don't have to worry about some creature from beyond biting your head off, but the idea that somebody could arrest you—and do whatever he wanted to you—is very scary. One of the things we debated was whether the torture would be too much. We decided we had to be very careful."

One of the elements Gordon used to balance the film is the kind of macabre humor he derives from taking horror so far that it goes past the point of absurdity. (In one scene, for instance, a witch, prior to being burned at the stake, swallows gunpowder, so that her body explodes and kills her executioner.) In fact, Gordon's version of *The Pit and the Pendulum* seems almost like an inversion of the old: whereas Corman played straight man to Vincent Price's tongue-in-cheek performance, Gordon often goes for the laugh while Henriksen plays it straight.

"That was intentional," said Gordon. "The subject is so bleak and disturbing that if you did it without humor it would be impossible for an audience to sit through—it would be too depressing. I think you need black comedy or gallows humor in this movie; you need that release. I like to move from horror to comedy, to break the tension and then build it again."

Another way Gordon provides a distance from the unsettling events onscreen is by introducing a small fantasy element: some of the witches being tortured are genuine. "We deal with witchcraft in a very positive way, as the religion of Mother Nature. We wanted to add a little magic, which gives you a way to escape the torture, but we wanted the magic we're portraying to be based on something factual. So, we tried to limit it to ESP and the kind of phenomenon being studied today, like out-of-body experiences, rather than turning someone into a toad."

Although Gordon used such devices to make the subject matter palatable to an audience, he doesn't soft-peddle Torquemada's tyranny and torture, which he saw as an integral part of the film's theme. "In my other pictures, the fantasy was able to give you distance. With this picture, I felt there was an important message there. I've been feeling that our society has been moving in an Inquisition-like direction, with all of the recent stuff that's been going on with censorship and the fundamentalists getting so much power. Some of the ideas for this film were influenced by the stuff that's happened with Jim Bakker and Jimmy Swaggart—the hypocrisy of that Holy Roller type. Now is a good time for people to be told this story as a cautionary tale."

Re-Animator—Stuart Gordon

Maitland McDonagh / 1993

From *Filmmaking on the Fringe: The Good, the Bad and the Deviant Directors* (Citadel Press, 1995), pp. 149–58. Reprinted by permission.

In 1985, when Stuart Gordon was simultaneously promoting *Re-Animator*, which had come out of nowhere to be the surprise horror hit of the year, and casting the lead in *Dolls*, which he was about to shoot for Charles Band's Empire Pictures, he cut an imposing figure.

Gordon's background was a publicist's dream, simultaneously highbrow and naughty. As a student at the University of Wisconsin, he was arrested on obscenity charges springing from a production of *Peter Pan*. Founder of Chicago's Organic Theatre,[1] where he directed David Mamet's *Sexual Perversity in Chicago* and the long-running *E/R* (which was later adapted into a sitcom starring Elliott Gould). In all, a welcome change of pace, a horror movie director who didn't have to be embarrassed he'd made a movie about mad scientists and walking corpses because he didn't have to prove he could do something *serious*.

But that's not to say Gordon is easy to get a handle on. His work at the Organic was summed up by one critic as "take-off-your-clothes, scream, and bleed theater," and the same could be said of his movies. But ask him what picture he's enjoyed recently, and he'll tell you he loved *Into the West* [1992], a contemporary fairy tale about two boys and a white horse. In fact, he once spoke of making his own magical horse movie, *Florian*, and said he'd like to do it for Disney. *Disney*? Who could imagine Gordon there?

Almost ten years later, with Gordon ensconced in a tastefully beige-on-beige office on the Disney lot, it's hard to remember what a shock *Re-Animator* was, how far it stood above the crowd of reductive slasher pictures that dominated genre filmmaking in the eighties. In fact, almost as hard as it is to believe that the man who made his first, gleefully offensive film a hit by spattering blood on every available surface works in this pristine office in the Animation Building at the intersection of Dopey Drive and Mickey Avenue, in the heart of the politically correct fascist state that is Disney. *Re-Animator* was mean, funny, and really gross—a Feydeau-esque farce with the stakes raised absurdly high (if you opened the wrong door, you were less likely to find your wife in bed with her physician than your prospective son-in-law cavorting with a revivified corpse) and its humor sunk absurdly low, all adapted from the work of the prissiest horror writer who ever lived, the comically repressed H. P. Lovecraft.[2]

But *Re-Animator* begged the question of what Gordon could do as an encore; this was, after all, only his first film. He went back to the well of Lovecraft with *From Beyond*, a loose gloss on an insubstantial story, and at various times was said to be doing others, including "The Shadow Over Innsmouth" and "The Lurking Fear." In fact, Gordon once spoke of hoping to do a series of Lovecraft films, like the series of adaptations of Poe stories that helped Roger Corman's name in the sixties. Nothing ever came of them, or of many other Gordon projects announced by Charles Band's company, Empire, which soon went down in a mass of debt and poor planning. In fact, Gordon has directed only six films to date, and one of them is responsible for his Disney birth. That honor goes to the one that got away, *Honey, I Shrunk the Kids*, the children's picture Gordon wrote as *Teenie Weenies* and was set to direct. He was forced to bow out at the last minute, but the picture became a hit and landed Gordon a nonexclusive deal to develop family films for Disney.

He's got a good deal at Disney, a badge of success and respectability many filmmakers would kill for, but not much has actually come of it yet. The bulk of his work has been for Charles Band, whose associates, though certainly competent filmmakers, don't include one with anything resembling the promise Gordon showed in *Re-Animator*. Paul Bartel has said that anyone who makes more than two films for Roger Corman comes to a bad end; the same could pretty much be said of Band, though Gordon's career isn't spiraling downward into sixth-generation sequels. His most recent picture, a futuristic prison movie with Christopher Lambert called *Fortress*, did knockout numbers in Australia, but its US release was a hit-and-run affair. This interview includes material taken from several conversations about Gordon's work.

Maitland McDonagh: What interested you about the H. P. Lovecraft story that became *Re-Animator*? Your background, after all, was in serious theater, not exploitation.

Stuart Gordon: Someone suggested that I read the story, and I had a real hard time finding it. Finally, I went to the library and put in one of those call slips, and about a year later they sent me a postcard saying they had found it in one of their archives. It was in a special collection, so I couldn't take it out, but I was welcome to come in and read it. And I was able to make a xerox; after a while, I started handing around xeroxes of xeroxes. I think the sexual aspect intrigued me. People had sort of played with it in *Dracula*, and I was thinking that one of the most horrifying taboos is still necrophilia. The idea of reversing it, instead of making love to a dead person, having a dead person make love to you, seemed like a pretty interesting approach. When Dennis [Paoli] wrote *that scene*[3] he called me up, real excited, and said, "I've just written the first visual pun!" As a matter of fact, some of the first artwork that was done was based on that scene, and it was like something someone would draw on a bathroom wall.

Originally, we—myself, Dennis Paoli, and William Norris—conceived it as a serial; we started out thinking that maybe it could make a good TV show, something like a miniseries that would run at midnight on Saturday nights, maybe on HBO. So, we took the first of the six parts and tried to sell it as a pilot. We found that the word was out that nobody was interested in half-hours, so we said, "Okay, we'll make it an hour." We added the second segment, took it around, and were then told that nobody wanted to do horror on television. That's when we decided that we should really think in terms of a feature.

Right around that time is when I first met Brian Yuzna, who produced the film. He read Lovecraft's story, looked over what we had done, and recommended that we put all six of the segments together. Once Brian got involved, the attitude was that television would just hold us back because we'd never be able to show the things we wanted on the air. Brian's take, and I have to say that I agree with him, was that the only way you can make your mark in horror is to go beyond whatever's been done before. I looked at just about every horror film that had been made in the last five years, got some good ideas, then we sat down and wrote *Re-Animator*.

MM: Did you see *Re-Animator* as a stepping stone, a way to get your foot in the door of the movie industry so you could do something more serious than a horror movie?

SG: Oh, people were always saying to me, "Don't you want to make a *serious* film; don't you want to make a bigger statement?" But I feel that I did make a statement, that there's a lot going on in *Re-Animator*. Working within the horror genre is like writing a sonnet or something; there are rules you have to follow, but once you follow those rules, you can say whatever you want to say. In an exploitation movie or a horror movie, as long as you have enough action, enough T & A [tits and ass], you can make it about whatever you want. That's also one of the nice things about working on a low budget; you don't have a big studio worrying about the implications of what you're doing. *Re-Animator* was made for about a million dollars.

I love horror movies; my parents never allowed me to see them, so naturally I fell in love with them. But they gave me nightmares as a child, especially William Castle's *The Tingler*. Of course, I saw that again recently and couldn't figure out what I had gotten all upset about. I think it's a psychological thing, rather than what you actually see. If you get the feeling that they're going to do something you've never seen before, that there are no holds barred, then your imagination starts to run wild and you get yourself into a state before any shocks have actually been delivered on screen. I think that's why *Psycho* is such a terrifying movie. It breaks the rules right up front, and then you're left there thinking *uh-oh*, because you don't know what this guy might do next. David Cronenberg movies always scare me, because they give me that feeling. When I walk out of the theater, I'm always saying to myself, "Now, what exactly was I so scared of?" But while I'm in the theater, I'm just sitting there and anticipating: "Oh, no! He's going to do something *really* disgusting now!" With his films, there's something automatic: about ten minutes in, I get creeped out.

MM: Horror directors often profess to be more interested in humor and tell you about how they were the class clowns ...

SG: That's true. You know, having mentioned *Psycho*, Hitchcock always referred to it as a comedy. I couldn't understand what he meant for the longest time, but then one day I looked at the film and saw how many funny things there are in it. Like when Norman cleans up after the murder in the shower ... it's like a Top Job commercial. Or when the car refuses to sink into the quicksand; it gives that little jump, like a burp.

I don't think, though, that you can be funny and scary at the same time. That's one of the things I'm starting to discover. You can do one or the other, but not both; they kind of cancel one another out. In *An American Werewolf in London* [1981], [John] Landis was doing them simultaneously, rather than alternately, and the picture kind of devoured itself. It was a risky project, and I don't think it quite worked. I think *The Howling* [1981] does work on that level; there's a lot of funny stuff in it, but [Joe] Dante doesn't do it simultaneously with the scary stuff.

MM: Were you always aware that you were shooting an unrated film, and did you have any idea what that would mean commercially?

SG: At the time we were shooting, we were trying for an R, believe it or not. There were certain things we were very careful about, and when I look back, I wonder why we went to all the trouble. There was a big concern about genitalia, for example, particularly male genitalia; the rule seems to be that you can show a woman frontally nude, but not a man. We, of course, had all these naked corpses running around, and the special effects guys built merkins for them so there was an overabundance of pubic hair covering everything up. We ended up not using merkins because I thought they were silly, and I felt we could construct the shots in such a way that it could be fixed in the editing.

On the last day of shooting, we did a sequence in which this nude corpse is fighting with Dan and Megan. Brian was watching and he got really upset; he was screaming, "All you see is this guy's thing bouncing up and down! You've got to get one of those merkins on him!" We went to get one and discovered that the effects people had thrown them all away. So, we decided that the way to solve the problem was to paint the guy's privates with Streaks and Tips—you know, the hair-coloring stuff. Once we did that, you still saw the guy's thing, but it was painted black; I guess you could sort of pass it off as a shadow. But by the time the film was finished, it didn't matter anyway.

At a certain point, we realized that there was no way the MPAA was going to give us an R. We actually submitted the film, just to see what they would say, and they told us that we would have to cut everything after the second reel. If we'd done everything they "suggested" there would have been about half an hour of film left. So, the decision was made to see if we could make the film fly without a rating. There were some instances in which we ran into problems, particularly with the TV ads, even though there's nothing *in* them that would actually offend anybody. It's just the fact that the film they're advertising is unrated.

MM: Dolls scare the hell out of me, so naturally, I find *Dolls* really disturbing.

SG: And those dolls are nasty, with their little saws and hammers and such. I find dolls pretty creepy, too. When I was going to the University of Wisconsin, there was a doll museum on the top floor of this historical society, and I always knew that under no circumstances would I want to be trapped there when the lights went out. The dolls were like the ones in the movie—you know, these Victorian porcelain dolls—but some of them had been through fires and had their faces sort of charred. The wax ones had partially melted. They were pretty bad, a scary bunch of dolls. When I was a little kid, a friend of the family came over with a ventriloquist's doll. He took him out of the suitcase, and I was out of the room. Gone! That's all I had to see, just him taking this guy out of the suitcase.

When I was making the movie, my daughter, who's now ten, visited me on the set one day. The idea of dolls being something that could hurt her had never occurred to her, until Dad came along with the idea to make this stupid movie. So, there were like a thousand dolls in this room, and she was looking at them all and looking kind of nervous. Finally, she said, "Dad? Are all of these dolls bad?" And I said, "Oh, yes, they are. They're very bad dolls." And she said, "Even this one here, with the white buttons?" So, suddenly, the light goes on, and I realize what she's getting at. "Is that the one you want? No, she's not a bad doll; she must have gotten in here by mistake." She still has that doll.

MM: With *From Beyond*, you returned to the material that had served you so well in *Re-Animator*...

SG: But it was a very different experience from *Re-Animator*. For one thing, Empire had a great deal to do with choosing the story, and I've always felt that the reason they went with "From Beyond" is that Charlie Band loves machinery.

The story involves this invention that we call the Pretorius Resonator and the scientists work on this machine. When people are within the field of the vibrations produced by the Pretorius Resonator, they're suddenly aware of all these things that are around us all the time but are normally invisible to us. And, of course, in the Lovecraft story these things are all monsters.

But from that point on Empire really let us run with the story, which was great. We decided that since this was a machine that stimulates the pineal gland, it would also stimulate the sex drive of the characters in the story; they find themselves getting very turned on after they've turned on the machine. The character that Barbara Crampton plays starts out as a very puritanical professional woman, and she ends up in black leather doing a kind of *Belle de Jour* [1967] nymphomaniac routine.[4]

MM: You still managed to get an R, where you had failed with *Re-Animator*.

SG: We went through a real wrestling match for that R. The first time the MPAA saw *From Beyond*, their reaction was that it was triple X and far worse than *Re-Animator*. We had thought that if we toned down the amount of blood we used and replaced it with slime, we might be able to slide past them, but as it worked out, they didn't see it that way. They thought the movie was more upsetting than *Re-Animator*. The quote I got back from the MPAA after the initial screening was: "Nonstop violence from beginning to end." When you ask them what you should change and they say, "Everything," it's kind of rough. We submitted the film four times, making small changes each time, hoping they'd get used to it, but these people sit in the dark too much. One woman started scolding me, asking me what I was thinking of. I felt like I'd been called into the principal's office.

MM: Your next film, *Robot Jox*, was extensively delayed. Didn't you have trouble with the title?

SG: Yes. It started out as *RoboJox*; in fact, I always like to say that the *t* in *Robot Jox* is silent. We were threatened by Orion over the title, because of *RoboCop*. They claimed we were interfering with their ability to do business; that they had spent all this money on their title, and we were somehow getting a free ride. The thing that I found upsetting about the whole business is that we had started our movie before they started theirs. But it took us so long to finish *Robot Jox* that they were ready to do the *RoboCop* sequel by the time that we got our movie out. It was delayed a good three years. I swear, *Robot Jox* had the worst bad luck, I think, of any movie ever. It started out with Empire being taken over by Credit Lyonnais, and then becoming Epic. We had finished shooting the live action and were just beginning the miniature work, and they had to decide whether or not to finish the movie or just scrap it. That took six months; everything just ground to a halt. And then they decided, yes, they did want to finish the film.

The other thing was the effects were done in an *interesting* way. Normally you shoot miniatures in a very controlled situation in a studio, but ours were shot on location in the high desert, near Edwards Air Force Base. It was like *Lawrence of Arabia* [1962]. Originally, it was supposed to take three months, and it ended up taking over a year. They had flooding. They had sandstorms. By the time the movie came out, it was three years later and the world had changed; the cold war was over. Transformers were not the new toy anymore. And the theatrical run of the movie was not a success. What saved *Robot Jox* was video. When it finally came out on video, people started seeing it. The ten year-old kids it was really designed for appreciated it, and it was a huge video release. It's been sitting on the New Releases shelf for two years, and it's shown on cable all the time. That's the thing I like about video: it's a great equalizer. In the video store everything is equal; they're all on the shelves together. It doesn't matter whether the movie had the benefit of all this P-and-A money or not. It takes a little longer for the buzz to get around when the money isn't there, usually about two years. *The Pit and the Pendulum* is now finally getting discovered, two years later, but at least people are watching it. In the old days, once you had a theatrical release that was it. So, I'm pretty grateful. Ninety percent of the people who have seen my movies have seen them on video.

MM: *The Pit and the Pendulum* reunited you with Charles Band, after the dissolution of Empire.

SG: Right. It was produced by his new company, Full Moon Entertainment. Originally it was scheduled to be done a year earlier, with money from Vestron. Peter O'Toole was set to play Torquemada, and we were going to shoot in England. We had sets, costumes, the whole works, but, when Vestron went under, the whole project collapsed about two weeks before the beginning of principal photography. The project was put on hold. Charlie was able to get Paramount interested, though the money they put up was far less than we had agreed on with Vestron. What Charlie had up his sleeve was that rather than shooting on soundstages, we could shoot at a real castle, *his* castle on the outskirts of Rome. As it turned out, this gave the movie a tremendous sense of realism; the location contributed enormously to the atmosphere. Obviously, shooting in a real castle isn't like shooting on a set. At three to five feet thick, the walls don't move. But most sets don't have ceilings or authentic floors, and all that was there. The sense of place is very important to Poe's story, so, in the end, we didn't mind the inconveniences.

MM: How did *Bride of Re-Animator* come to be made without your involvement?

SG: Brian Yuzna really wanted to direct. He had the rights to the sequel, and my feeling was that I wished him well. I knew they were trying to get an R-rated sequel, and I didn't really see how the sequel could top the original working under that constraint.

I went pretty directly from *The Pit and the Pendulum* to *Fortress*; one just went right into the other. In fact, I think it was *The Pit and the Pendulum* that persuaded

Village Roadshow, who produced *Fortress*, to consider me as the director. They saw similarities between the two projects: the idea of imprisonment, the torture devices, and so on. They said they wanted the futuristic equivalent of the Inquisition.

They're the largest entertainment company in Australia. In the past, they've been mainly distributing movies, but in the last few years, they've started producing them as well. What they've wanted is to have one of their pictures break into the international market and not be perceived as an Australian film. They also own these wonderful studios in Queensland, where it's like working at Universal. They built it in conjunction with a theme park, so there are little trams driving around pointing things out to people, rides, and so forth. One of the reasons they wanted us to shoot it there was that they wanted to have a production going for people to look at.

This movie needed a complete rewrite. The script needed a complete overhaul to bring it down for budget for one thing, but also to deepen the characters and all those other things. And then we had to jump right into casting. We needed guys who looked like convicts, and we needed lots of them.

Anyway, we had a very short period of time to prep the picture, and we *had* to deliver it on schedule because of the presales. They were expecting that the movie would be finished within a year, and the original goal of starting photography in August was completely unrealistic. Thank God it was pushed to October. Even so, with all the special effects, that was barely enough time. I mean, this prison was the star of the movie—it's the title role—and to come up with the design of this thing, to create the illusion of this enormous prison, was a huge project. Making this movie was like a trapeze act where you just hope that the other trapeze is going to be there by the time you're going to need it.

MM: Although *Fortress* isn't exactly like *Re-Animator* or *Dolls*, it's not hard to see how you came to make it. On the other hand, your fabulous, beige, wall-to-wall-carpeted office on the Disney lot is a little incongruous. How did this happen?

SG: It's funny; I remember really clearly how it all began. I was with Brian Yuzna in his backyard, and he was really upset because his kids had gone to see a movie called *The Journey of Natty Gann* [1985], which was directed by a neighbor [Jeremy Kagan] whose kids went to the same school as they did. The director's kids invited the entire class to come to an advance screening, and Brian's kids came home afterward and said, "Dad, how come we never get to see any of your movies?" which knocked his nose a little out of joint. That said, Brian will actually show his kids anything. He had his son sitting in on dailies for *Re-Animator*, which I couldn't have imagined doing with my daughters. My eldest daughter loves horror films, but my middle daughter, the one who wanted the doll with white buttons, is *terrified* by them, and the slightest little thing will set her off and give her nightmares. Brian's kids seem to be fine; they aren't axe-murderers, at least not as far as I know. But anyway, his movies weren't the kind of thing you'd invite a whole class full of other people's children to, and that was what got to Brian.

So, we started talking about it, saying, "Why don't we come up with an idea for a movie our kids could see?" And we started talking about little kids playing in the backyard, because that's where we were having this discussion. And, all of a sudden, this idea kind of came together, about kids who get shrunk so they're teeny-tiny and the adventures they have trying to get across the yard, and we brought it over to Disney.

Now, this was right at the time the new guys—Jeffrey Katzenberg, Michael Eisner, and David Hoberman—took over. Hoberman was a junior executive at this point, so he was the one we took the idea to, and he liked it. The original title was *Teenie Weenies*, and we got Ed Naha, who had written *Dolls*, to collaborate with us on the script. Poor Ed ended up doing seventeen drafts, but eventually we got the green light. The movie was going to happen, and I was going to direct it. We went into pre-production and planned it all out, and worked with the designers, found a director of photography, got all the effects people on board. And about two weeks before we were going to start shooting, I got sick and had to drop out.

I was replaced by Joe Johnston, who pretty much inherited all this work I had done. He didn't really have any breathing room; they wanted to make the schedule, so he took all the planning we had done and made the movie. And I'm glad he was very faithful to our concepts; there were a few departures, but for the most part it was really our movie. And then the movie did extremely well.

MM: Even with a funny title [like *Honey, I Shrunk the Kids*].

SG: Yeah. When I first heard that title, I *hated* it. In my mind, the movie was about the kids, and that title was about the parents. But the title turned into one of those things that becomes part of the collective consciousness of our society. You see variations on it everywhere—"Honey, I did such-and-such." So, I ended up really liking it.

MM: Who came up with it?

SG: The funny thing is, I don't know. Probably somebody in marketing. Jeffrey Katzenberg *hated* the title *Teenie Weenies*; that was something he made very clear from the start. I suggested *The Itsy-Bitsies*, which wasn't any more appealing. His biggest problem with the title was that he thought it sounded like a little kids' movie, which I think is probably true. He wanted to appeal to more of a teenage audience, and *Teenie Weenies* sounded as though it was aimed at third-graders. You know how kids are at that age; it's very important to them to differentiate themselves from younger kids, so we understood that the title had to be changed.

There's another thing you have to take into account. At the time *Honey, I Shrunk the Kids* was made, calling something a family film was the kiss of death. Anything called a family film was nowhere; even Disney had stopped making them. As a matter of fact, *Honey, I Shrunk the Kids* was the first live-action Disney, as opposed to Touchstone,[5] film that had been made in ten years. I thought that was *great*.

MM: That the guys who made *Re-Animator* . . .

SG: Yeah! That the guys who made *Re-Animator* got Disney back into family films. Working at Disney has certainly always been a dream of mine. When I was a kid, I used to love Disney stuff. I think every American of my generation was kind of brainwashed by the Disney TV show. Disney's always really been a special kind of thing. And you know what? Walt Disney himself always used to say that they didn't make kids movies, they made family films. That was a big distinction in his mind: that Disney made movies that had things in them that everybody could enjoy together, the whole family. So, he didn't want the movies just to be kiddie pablum.

You have to remember, the older Disney movies did things that shock people, even today: Bambi's mother died; they shot Old Yeller. I read an article about *Old Yeller* [1957], and apparently a lot of people at the studio tried to convince Disney to give the movie a happy ending. He said, "This is the book we bought. This is the way it ends. This is the movie we're going to make." So, I think it's a wonderful thing that we were able to help get the studio back into that kind of filmmaking.

And then it was time for the sequel [*Honey, I Blew Up the Kid*]. I hate these sequels where they just do the first movie over again . . .

MM: The "give us the same picture but different" syndrome.

SG: Right. Give us the same picture, but spend more money on it. *Honey, I Shrunk the Kids Again*, really expensive. I find that kind of thing really irritating and boring, so I started thinking about what else we could do with the premise. There was a script I had been sent, actually about the same time as I started working on *Honey, I Shrunk the Kids*, called *Big Baby*. It was, naturally enough, about a giant baby, kind of an homage to *The Amazing Colossal Man* [1957].[6] And it struck me that without a lot of work, this script could be turned into the sequel to *Honey, I Shrunk the Kids*.

My only complaint with the way the sequel turned out is that I didn't feel there was enough danger in it. They were afraid to put the baby in danger; you know, the MPAA has a specific sanction against children in danger. But my feeling was the child didn't really have to *be* in danger; you just had to *think* the child was in danger. There was one sequence cut from the movie, in which the baby is approaching these high power lines, and everyone is terrified that the baby is going to electrocuted. They're trying to get the baby to stop, shouting, "Don't come near these things," and the baby eventually grabs hold of the power lines and is tickled by the electricity and starts laughing. It was a great scene, because you get all the tension—"My God, the baby's going to *fry*"—and then you get this overwhelming relief. And as soon as you think about it, you realize the child was never really in danger; he's too big to be electrocuted by these puny little power lines. Anyway, here I am at Disney, charged with developing family films.

MM: Does the difference between working with a studio like Full Moon and working with a studio like Disney really come down to money, or is there something else?

SG: Actually, I think there are a lot of similarities between the two places; I find them similar in many ways. They're both driven by fantasy, and with Charlie Band you have a guy who's a kid in a very real way. You know, when Katzenberg said that thing about finding the child within you, he could have been talking about Charles Band. The thing that's wonderful about Charlie is that nothing's impossible. No matter how little the budget may be, he'll figure out a way to do what he imagines. Charlie loves miniature things. I kid him sometimes and say we make little monster movies. He says, "Well, when our budgets get bigger, our monsters will get bigger too." But money is a big difference [between Full Moon and Disney]. They've got tons of money here, which can sometimes drive you even crazier; you *know* they've got it, but this is a very tight-fisted studio. At Full Moon, you *know* there's no money, whereas here, there's obviously tons of it . . .

MM: But they won't give it to *you*.

SG: That's right. Infuriating—so close and yet so far. As a matter of fact, I once had to refuse to get on an airplane until they paid me. This was when I was working on *Honey, I Shrunk the Kids*, and everyone was impressed that I was working at Disney. Somehow the fact that I was working at this big studio was supposed to be enough—you know, why did I want to get paid, too? I said, "Well, I got paid at all the other places I worked. It would be nice if I got paid here, too."

There's another thing about working at Disney: have you seen the building with the seven dwarves on it, the Team Disney building? That phrase, "Team Disney," is very important around here; everyone is on the team, and you're doing things by committee. One of the nice things about working with Charlie Band was that once he gave you the go-ahead, you made *your* movie. Still, being here, in this building, is just like a dream. This is where it all happened. This is where Walt's office was. All the great animated cartoons were made here.

MM: There's a widely circulated story told about Disney: it involves a director in a story meeting, so frustrated by the interference that he had either a nosebleed or a stroke, depending on the version. I've heard that story was about you.

SG: It was a nosebleed. I didn't have a stroke, thank God. But blood started spouting from my nose like a projectile. It was really pretty intense.

MM: Was it really from the aggravation?

SG: Well, from the stress you know . . . high blood pressure. That's why I had to stop and drop out of *Honey, I Shrunk the Kids*. A nosebleed is a blood vessel blowing in your nose because the pressure is too great and it won't hold. My doctor said the next one would be a little higher up, and that I had to decide whether I wanted to make this movie or whether I wanted to live. I didn't have a lot of conflict about making that choice. High blood pressure is curable, so I had to get healthy. In a way, the incident was a good thing, because it made me deal with my health. But I'd be lying if I denied that it was also a huge disappointment, especially when *Honey, I Shrunk the Kids* became this blockbuster. Still, ultimately, I can't complain. It's done great things for me.

MM: Do you keep up with what's going on in the marginal areas of moviemaking?

SG: To some degree. I was recently on the jury at the Sitges Festival in Spain, and that was a chance to meet a lot of directors from all over the world who are making some amazing movies. A lot of them are being done on very low budgets, and seeing that was really a turn-on, really revitalizing. It's like those old cowboy movies where'd they say you're the fastest gun in town, but someday some punk is going to show up, and he's going to be just a little bit faster than you. I had that feeling at Sitges. I met Peter Jackson, who made *Braindead* [1992].[8] I had always thought that *Re-Animator* held the all-time record for blood-spilling; we used thirty gallons of fake blood. So, I asked Peter how much blood *he* had used, and the answer was *three thousand* gallons. This young punk was just a little bloodier than me. I guess it's my turn now to use six thousand gallons, or sixty thousand.

MM: Or resign yourself to being the elder statesman.

SG: I'm beginning to think you've got to go in a different direction now. I think gore movies have pretty much run themselves out, lost their ability to scare you. Jackson's movie is a joke, a comedy. Anyway, I've always felt the best special effect is good acting. The night after *Braindead* was screened, we saw *Reservoir Dogs* [1992], which had a lot less blood but is a lot more upsetting. It's *really* upsetting, and I think it's because you believe it. I really wasn't sure I was going to be able to sit through that torture scene[9], and I later discovered that Wes Craven and Rick Baker had both left. Compared to what you see in a typical slasher movie, the scene is *nothing*, but because you totally *believe* it, it's just horrible.

I'll tell you something I've discovered. A lot of the people who make horror films are kind of chicken, like Wes Craven walking out of *Reservoir Dogs*. We can't really take it. As kids, we were scared to death by all these movies and had nightmares; I had nightmares for *years* about some movies. So, maybe what we're doing is an attempt to get even.

Notes

1. Several Organic alumni have turned up in exploitation, including Richard Fire, Gordon's successor, who wrote John McNaughton's *Henry: Portrait of a Serial Killer* [1986]; Dennis Paoli, Gordon's frequent screenwriter; and actor Tom Towles, who's appeared in *Henry*, *The Borrower* [1989], and the 1990 remake of *Night of the Living Dead*.

2. In adapting Lovecraft's little-known serial "Herbert West—Re-Animator," Gordon and screenwriter Dennis Paoli tampered little with the story but plenty with the tone. Where Lovecraft—a reclusive, anti-Semitic racist; a misogynist hypochondriac; and a prude of near-pathological proportions—specialized in dodging anything that suggested sex behind baroque prose, Paoli and Gordon went at the subject, um, head-on. Sexual hysteria is a conscious subtext in Lovecraft's work—conspicuous by its overt absence, to be sure, but conspicuous all the same and *Re-Animator*'s finest invention must be the scene in which the naked girl is abused on a hospital gurney by the head of a walking dead man.

3. The scene in which Dr. Hill's re-animated head molests Megan, the movie's heroine. If not the first visual pun, even in horror films—the "arm chairs" in *The Texas Chain Saw Massacre* come to mind—it's certainly the best.

4. Barbara Crampton, who was also the female lead in *Re-Animator*, was featured in a layout in *Playboy* magazine inspired by her work in *From Beyond*.

5. Touchstone is a division formed by Disney to handle more adult films.

6. Coincidentally, this classic movie, about a man whom radiation turns into a giant, was directed by Bert I. Gordon, no relation. The colossal man, who has outgrown his wardrobe, spends the film dressed in an oversized diaper and attacks Las Vegas, just like the giant toddler of Randall Kleiser's picture.

7. Designed by postmodern architect Michael Graves, the Team Disney building looks perfectly normal from the back. From the front, one can stare in amazement at the seven dwarves, arranged along the façade like bulbous caryatids. When it rains, the water stains make it look as though the dwarves have urinated in their pants.

8. New Zealander Jackson has made four films to date: *Bad Taste* [1988], in which aliens come to Earth to turn us into fast food; *Meet the Feebles* [1990], a puppet movie about the scabrous behind-the-scenes scandals at a popular TV show; and *Braindead*—re-titled *Dead Alive* for its US release—a zombie comedy of unparalleled grossness. His newest film, the true murder story *Heavenly Creatures* [1994], is an entirely different sort of thing, a delicate study of two teenage girls lost in a dream world of their own devising. A critical hit, it's a change of pace that bodes well for Jackson.

9. Gordon is referring to the scene in which a smiling psychopath (Michael Madsen) cuts off the ear of a bound cop then threatens to douse him with gasoline and burn him alive.

Stuart Gordon: The Force Behind *Fortress*

Joe Kane / 1993

From *VideoScope* 2, no. 7 (January–March 1994), pp. 10–11. Reprinted by permission.

Your Phantom of the Movies spoke with Stuart Gordon shortly before *Fortress*'s release in September 1993, the first time we'd had the pleasure of picking the cult auteur's brains since *From Beyond*'s emergence back in 1986.

Joe Kane: Could you tell us about the genesis of *Fortress*?

Stuart Gordon: It was a script that was sent to me a couple of years ago. Originally, it had been written for Arnold Schwarzenegger and it was over at 20th Century Fox. But Arnold decided not to do it. Fox put it into turnaround, and it was picked up by an Australian company called Village Roadshow. They decided to do it with a much smaller budget and contacted me because of my background in low-budget films. I came in and had some ideas about the script. The main character, Brennick, was written like Arnold, so you didn't have to worry about him at all. It seemed important to me that this guy be much more an everyman, so the audience could relate to him and put themselves in his shoes, going into this incredibly horrific prison. A little bit later, I got a call from Christopher Lambert saying he had read the script and liked it very much, and would I be interested in talking about him starring in the movie. That idea really appealed to me a great deal.

JK: Lambert doesn't come off as a superman.

SG: He's a wonderful actor. A lot of these leading men types, especially the action stars, do not want to portray themselves being afraid. They think it's gonna make them look weak. Whereas Lambert realizes that being a hero is doing something even though you *are* afraid.

JK: Loryn Locklin's character also depends on her wiles.

SG: We did not want another damsel in distress. In the original, she was not in prison with her husband. The whole thing about the babies was something that was added after I got on board. Originally, I think his crime was he had broken a robot. To me, it was important, the idea of a husband and wife working to save each other. It gave the film a lot of heart, and a romantic quality.

JK: What kind of shooting schedule did you have?

SG: Forty-five days. Lambert had gone to the Cannes Film Festival and came back with money to make the movie. It was one of those things where we had to have the film finished within a year. From that point on, it was like a race. Because of all the special effects and everything that had to be built and designed, preparation was very, very quick. We got the go-ahead in June and started shooting at the beginning of October. Normally, a movie like this would have six months to a year's preparation.

JK: The fortress itself is pretty complex.

SG: What we did before we started was we visited some of the new prisons that have been built in California. We modeled the fortress after a super-maximum security prison in northern California called Pelican Bay, where they send the worst 2 percent of the prison population. It's brand new, very futuristic, with a lot of electronic surveillance equipment—one of the scariest places I've ever been. We had to sign a release saying that we understood that if we were taken hostage, they would not try to rescue us. We had to wear stab-proof vests. Then they told us, "They always go for the *eyes* anyway!" As it turns out, it was one of the safest places I've ever been. You start feeling sorry for them after about five minutes. They keep them in their cells for about twenty-two and a half hours every day. It really is a place where they kind of break them down. And it's very quiet. Most prisons are very noisy places, but there you can hear a pin drop.

JK: In most futuristic prison films, the interiors are dark. But in *Fortress*, they're fairly bright.

SG: That's the way it is because, again, they need enough light for the video cameras. There's less interaction between the guards and the prisoners, and more reliance on electronics, computers, and so forth. So, we just kind of took that to its logical conclusion, with one person running the whole prison.

JK: It's good to see actors like Jeffrey Combs and Tom Towles, who are really charismatic in what could have been background roles.

SG: They interviewed a lot of prisoners; they did their homework on this. Lambert was actually locked in a cell for a while.

JK: Was the idea of the Intestinator [a device convicts are forced to ingest that administers intense pain for infractions and even death in the event of an escape attempt] in the original script?

SG: No, that was something that was added. Again, all of the technology in the movie is based on reality. They do have things like this—tracking devices on prisoners' wrists, which don't emit pain, but, if they attempt to escape, a loud-pitched noise registers on their equipment. So, the idea of the Intestinator is it prevents people from taking the thing off.

JK: You don't find out immediately what the Kurtwood Smith character's secret is.

SG: Right. He did a wonderful job. From the beginning, he was concerned this guy was gonna end up being just another typical bad guy, and he wanted to give him a little more depth. You end up feeling sorry for him. He's a victim. The whole idea of relationships with people is something that's been denied him. In a way, it's his falling in love that does him in. There's a kind of tragic quality about him. And the whole thing about the amino acids is something they've been working on. NASA's actually experimenting with it for space travel, so people wouldn't have to sleep or eat when they go on long journeys. You find out, when you research, the weirdest stuff you can dream up actually exists.

JK: What about the fortress itself?

SG: In actuality, there are supposed to be eleven cell blocks stacked on top of each other. We built one, which was four stories tall. It was the largest set ever built in Australia.

JK: It also supplies a lot of stunt opportunities.

SG: Both Christopher and Vernon [Wells] did their own stunt work, almost entirely. The only time Lambert and I got into a fight was when he got angry with me when I didn't want him to stand in front of that truck at the end with the flamethrower, when it was coming at him. We shot that scene very early on. I said to Chris, "It's going to be very hard for me to finish the movie if you get run over by a truck." Eventually, we compromised: the stunt guy did the first take, and he did the second take—and the second take was the one we ended up using.

JK: Any sequel possibilities for *Fortress*?

SG: We're already planning it. I think *Fortress 2* is going to have something to do with their child being captured and they have to break *into* the fortress. The new fortress is gonna be orbiting Earth, like a space station. Another project is called *Faust*, which is based, of course, on the legend, but also on an underground comic book about a psychotic superhero who sings James Brown music as he kills people.

JK: Were you disappointed when *The Pit and the Pendulum* didn't get a theatrical release here?

SG: I *was* disappointed. I was very proud of that film, although, eventually, I think most people see things on video anyway. People have discovered the film and a lot of them want to talk to me about it. Paramount had the opportunity to release it theatrically, but instead they chose to do *Pet Sematary Two* [1992]. They felt the name recognition would be enough to fill those seats. When I talked to them, I said I thought that "The Pit and the Pendulum" was a fairly well-known story. They said people think they've already seen it because of the Corman movie. I said that was around 1958. The problem with a lot of these little movies is getting them out there. I think video is the film's second chance. It's kind of a great leveler. After a while, you're just another title up on the shelf there, right alongside all of the big movies. It just takes a little longer. I'm glad that people are finally seeing it.

JK: The opening scene is a classic, where they flog the corpse.

SG: They really used to do that, I found out. Again, we did a lot of research. The stuff they were doing was far more horrific than anything you can dream up. And they kept very accurate records during the Inquisition; they were like the Nazis. They've got transcriptions of all the trials and all that stuff. Jeffrey Combs's character was a scribe and took down what everyone was saying under torture.

JK: Have you done any theater recently?

SG: I did a play about a year ago called *The Ghostman*, written by Wendy Hammond, about a coal miner in Utah, a Mormon. His father dies and all of a sudden he starts having these weird hallucinations in which he becomes convinced that his father had sexually abused him as a child. Of course, everyone is telling him this is impossible, as his father was one of the elders of the church. Wendy decided to make it into a coal miner, because she thought if she made it about a woman everyone would think it was just a hysterical girl.

JK: Any chance of *The Ghostman* becoming a film?

SG: It's one of those things where the subject matter seems to be so upsetting to people that it's very hard to get a company to produce it. What I've noticed is if you put something into a fantasy context, you have a better chance of getting it produced. You have to put it into a science fiction or horror context to be able to deal with some of these things.

JK: What recent films have you enjoyed?

SG: My favorite film of last year was *Man Bites Dog* [1992].

JK: Did you see *Dead Alive* [aka, *Braindead*]?

SG: Yes. I met Peter Jackson, actually. The first thing I had to ask him was how much blood he used in his movies. *Re-Animator* had the all-time record—thirty gallons. He told me he used three *thousand* gallons. So, I said, "Okay, you win!" That's gonna be a tough one to top. [*Dead Alive* is] a hilarious movie, actually.

JK: A movie we enjoyed was Joe Dante's *Matinee* [1993].

SG: Yeah, I liked that movie too.

JK: Surprisingly, it didn't do too well theatrically.

SG: You know what it was? I took my kids to see it, and they asked, "What's a fallout shelter, Dad?" The idea that these kids were worried about World War III—kids today, thank God it's not something that's a part of their life. I used to have nightmares—I'm sure you did too—about seeing a mushroom cloud over Chicago. The scenes in the movie where all the kids have to get under their desks, I can remember doing that. And I always thought like the kid in the movie does: "What's this gonna accomplish? If it's an A-bomb, it's goodbye!" But to an audience of kids today, there was too much that had to be explained to them, I think—that and all the William Castle references. For those of us who were there, it was a terrific movie.

JK: Have you seen any John Woo films?

SG: I like his films. Talk about fantasy—those are kind of the ultimate fantasies. They remind me of playing with guns when I was a kid. In a John Woo movie, if you do a somersault, nobody can shoot you. And your guns are never out of ammo. Another movie I liked a lot last year was *Reservoir Dogs*. Seeing John Woo, I could see where [Quentin Tarantino] was getting a lot of his stuff. What he added, I thought, was pain. The opening scene, where Tim Roth is shot [and collapses into] the back of the car? How many movies do you see where someone gets shot? But this was the first time it was ever really horrifying. There is all this uproar right now about violence and I think it's such jive. The problem with most violence in films is that they *don't* show you the blood; they *don't* show you the pain. They make it seem like it's easy and fun. I saw *Reservoir Dogs* at a film festival. Wes Craven was there—and he had to leave! I came up to him afterwards, and said, "Wes, *it's only a movie!*"

The Future of Stuart Gordon

Dennis Fischer / 1995

From *Samhain*, no. 50 (May–June 1995), pp. 10–12. Reprinted by permission.

Stuart Gordon is currently prepping his biggest science fiction film ever, *Space Truckers*, which is being independently financed for between $16.5 and $17.5 million. The plot concerns a small independent space truck operator who is forced by a big genetics consortium to smuggle a huge, secret load through the solar system down to Earth.

A number of top-notch designers have been prepping the film, including Ron Cobb (*Alien*, *Conan the Barbarian*), Bernie Wrightson, and Bruce McCall (*National Lampoon*). Additionally, Gordon promises that rather than take the film off into *Star Trek*/*Star Wars* territory, he has consulted with NASA scientists to make the film as scientifically accurate as possible. Hence, he explores ideas about how tomorrow's astronaut workers will deal with problems such as zero gravity in ways that no SF film has since *2001: A Space Odyssey* [1968].

I recently had the opportunity to chat with Gordon about his recent projects, which have increasingly, from *Robot Jox* on, turned to science fiction (*Honey, I Blew Up the Kid*; *Fortress*; *Body Snatchers*; and now *Space Truckers*). *Robot Jox* was written by science fiction great Joe Haldeman, who made a big splash in the science fiction field with his first SF novel, *The Forever War*, which won a Hugo Award as Best Science Fiction Novel of the Year.

Dennis Fischer: Are you still planning to do a film version of *The Forever War*?

Stuart Gordon: That's a dream of mine. I'm still hoping to do the film at some point. What I found out is that Richard Edlund has the rights to *The Forever War* at Boss Films, and I have spoken to him about the idea of working on it with him, but that's a huge undertaking. That would be a $50 million movie to do that.

DF: How did you feel about the public perception of *Robot Jox*?

SG: It's funny, it caught on when it got to videotape and when it started to be shown on cable almost more than just about any other film. What I've discovered is that it has become a huge film for ten-year-old boys. I keep running into kids who love it. I run into these kids who give me the Robot Jox salute, and they want to know when the sequel is coming out. Maybe one of these years, that'll happen. The original idea on *Robot Jox* was that it was a family film. It was intended to be a little departure from other films, and in a way it was the beginning of what became *Honey, I Shrunk the Kids*: the idea of using science fiction as a way of making a family film in the science fiction vein.

DF: What was it like working with Haldeman?

SG: Working with Joe Haldeman was great because Joe did give it a reality, which I liked. Looking back on *RoboJox*, the film's original title, I wish we had more money to do some things a little better than we did, but it was a very ambitious movie to have done for a budget of $6 million. I keep looking back and I think that we were able to do it at all is an achievement.

DF: I thought the lead who starred in the *Alien Nation* TV series [1989–90] was quite good.

SG: Gary Graham is great. He's terrific. Gary is an actor who could do a job on *Space Truckers* as well.

DF: One problem I had with the film is that I thought much of the satire and many of the characters were too broad.

SG: It was broad. We wanted to keep it simple enough for kids to follow it, but we didn't want to make it too simple so that parents would get turned off by it. Some of the negative feedback on the movie was that people were expecting to see something like *Re-Animator* and it wasn't. It was a very different kind of film. But I think if you take it on its own terms, I think you'll enjoy it.

DF: How did *Fortress* come about?

SG: *Fortress* was originally a project for Arnold Schwarzenegger. He decided not to do it, and it had originally been budgeted at around $50 million, I think. It went into turnaround and then it was picked up by Village Roadshow, the Australian company, who wanted to do it for about a fifth of the budget. Actually, it was Arnold who recommended me for that job. He was a fan of *Re-Animator*, and he had suggested to John Davis, who was the producer on *Fortress*, to bring me in. I read the script and realized that we would have to rethink sections of it to bring it into that budget, but I liked the idea of doing a movie about prisons. I think that it's a topic that's very timely, even more so today than when we did the movie. [America is currently gripped by an anti-crime fever centering around the slogan, "Three strikes and you're out," meaning that after committing three felonies the felon is then jailed for life.] The thing that is really interesting is that we visited a lot of prisons when we were working on *Fortress*, and more prisons were built during the Reagan/Bush administrations than in the entire history of the United States, and most prisons—the day that they opened—had twice as many prisoners as they were designed to hold. It's a completely impossible situation. Even the wardens that we talked to said it was crazy.

What we realized is that most of the prisoners are non-whites. I think 70 percent of the prisoners are non-whites, so what you essentially are seeing is almost like a race war. Taking people off the streets and locking them up. A large percentage of them are there for drug offenses. The "War on Drugs" was what it was called, but it really was a war on people who were non-white. Most of the people in prisons are not there for selling drugs, but for holding or using drugs. I asked one of the wardens what was the answer to this problem, and he said, "Change the laws," which I thought was an amazing answer coming from a law enforcement person, but I think that's true. What we're getting into now with this "three strikes" thing is going to be absolutely impossible. One of the things I learned is that it costs something like $27,000 a year per prisoner to incarcerate someone. The cost of this is going to bankrupt this country. It turns out that the money you're spending on the prisoners is more than you're paying the guard to guard them. It's scandalous, I think. *Fortress* was a way to show that. If you did a documentary about prisons, no one would want to see it. But if you do it as an action movie, you can have a tremendous audience.

DF: Did you have any trouble with the MPAA?

SG: We submitted the movie only once, and their first reaction was that the movie was NC-17. We appealed—actually, we just said we were going to appeal it—and as soon as we did they realized that somebody hadn't seen it who should have seen it, and they ended up giving us an R rating. So, I never had to make any cuts in the picture. The thing that's funny is that they asked me to do a version of the film for Great Britain that is more violent than the original film, which surprised me because Great Britain is cracking down on so-called "video nasties." But what I think they wanted was to make sure that the movie would be released on video with the equivalent of an NC-17, because they felt it was so borderline in terms that it is a very violent movie. They wanted to make sure that little kids would not be able to see it. But it was funny because it's the first time anybody has come to me and said, "We'd like to see more violence."

DF: Was it difficult to create *Fortress* on the budget that you had?

SG: That whole prison had to be created from scratch. My favorite comment from people when they see the movie is, "Where did you shoot this? Where did you find this place?"—which I like. To me, the best special effects are the ones where you don't even realize they are special effects at all. On *Fortress*, what we did was build one cell block full-size—which was a big set, it was three stories tall. It was the largest set ever built in Australia, but the idea was that these were stacked on top of each other, and that there were eleven of those on top of each other, and that was done through miniatures which Paul Gentry supervised. The miniature was about as big as this whole office, almost thirty feet long. So, it was a very large miniature and we were able to put cameras inside of it and move through it with a motion control system, and we were able to combine that optically with the full-sized set. We placed the full-sized set inside the miniature when we needed to, so it really did create the illusion of this enormous place. It took a lot of planning. What is really great about *Space Truckers*, and about *Fortress*, is that we had time to really get everything right before we started shooting. We're not in a situation where we can waste a penny. Everything has to be exactly right. We have to know everything is going to work before we start it.

DF: What was the biggest difficulty for you on the film?

SG: One of the big problems on *Fortress* when we went into it was the idea of the laser bars. In the script, it called for the idea that each of the cells—rather than having steel bars to keep the prisoners inside—had lasers, a grid of lasers. The question was, how could we possibly do this? It would mean we would have to do an optical for every shot of the cell. In daylight, you can't see them very well. So, in some scenes, you can't see the lasers, but you still see glowing dots on the wall where they emanate from. What we ended up doing is the cinematographer, David Eggby, came up with the idea of using Scotchlite, making rods out of Scotchlite, and doing it in the camera, which allowed us to have characters walking in front of them. It turned out to be a tremendous saving; it saved us probably half a million dollars right there by being able to do things on the set.

DF: How did you become involved in scripting the new *Body Snatchers*?

SG: I was going to direct it originally, but, again, everything always happens at once. You have three projects going along and all of a sudden they collide. That's what happened with *Body Snatchers*, *Fortress*, and *Honey, I Blew Up the Kid*. I ended up doing *Fortress* and left *Body Snatchers*, and Abel Ferrara came in and directed it. I thought he did an exceptional job. I was very pleased with his work on the film.

DF: I had a problem with setting this version on an army base because everything seems so soulless and mechanical already. There's no contrast.

SG: We did that deliberately, because we felt people would be a little more paranoid—who is a pod person and who isn't? It would be a little harder to tell on an army base. What I think all three [*Invasion of the Body Snatchers*] movies are about is conformity. When you're in the army, everybody has to dress the same, cut your hair the same; everybody has to be the same. That, we felt, would make it a little bit more difficult to figure out who was who. What we were going for in the third one was the idea of the disintegration of the family, and it is the first time that that idea has been used in a body snatcher movie. Our goal was to make it seem like it was about the parents when, in actuality, it was about the daughter. You see her parents get taken over by something and she ends up being abandoned in the center of the movie. It's interesting that I've noticed, although it wasn't a conscious thing at the time, that both *Fortress* and *Body Snatchers* deal with attempts to destroy a family. Even this last movie that I just finished, *Castle Freak*, has the same theme running through it: that of a family that is being split apart.

DF: So, what scares Stuart Gordon?

SG: I am beginning to think that maybe that is really my central fear, personally. To me, the idea of a family being destroyed is a very upsetting idea. So, maybe that's why I'm working it out in those movies.

DF: Whatever happened to *Gris-Gris*, your voodoo project?

SG: *Gris-Gris* was a voodoo project that was brought to me by a producer named Peter Newman [who is now the producer of *Space Truckers*]. We worked on the script, Dennis Paoli and I did several drafts of it, but at a certain point we showed Peter "The Shadow Over Innsmouth," and he liked that idea better. And so we began developing "The Shadow Over Innsmouth" together.

DF: Horror fans have long been anticipating your adaptation of Lovecraft's "The Shadow Over Innsmouth." Will we see it?

SG: We were unable to get that film made because the budget was too high. It didn't fit into your horror movie niche, it was a bigger project, and it was so strange. What people kept saying to us was that if it was about vampires or werewolves, you would have no problem here. But since this is about people turning into fish, this is a little bit too weird for us to be able to put this kind of money into the project. Well, to me, that's what makes this interesting. You haven't seen this before.

Gordon's latest project is *Castle Freak*, produced by Charles Band's Full Moon Productions. Gordon was given a guarantee that he would have final cut, allowing him to make the film as intense as he liked without worrying about external censorship. The film deals with an American family in a European castle who encounter the much abused title character, who turns the family's notions of what's right on its head.

Meanwhile, work continues briskly apace on *Space Truckers*, with completion expected sometime in 1996. The film is being independently financed and will arrange a distribution deal upon completion. It could well become the most memorable trek through the solar system ever committed to celluloid. One thing is for certain, it's liable to pave the future path for writer-director Stuart Gordon.

Castle Freak

Dennis Fischer / 1995

From *Cinefantastique* 26, no. 4 (June 1995), pp. 32–34. Reprinted by permission.

Director Stuart Gordon's previous films in collaboration with Charlie Band—*Re-Animator, From Beyond, The Pit and the Pendulum*—are the ones most beloved by horror fans, who should rejoice that his latest feature, *Castle Freak*, is a hell-for-leather assault on audience sensibilities.

Castle Freak is the story of an American family that inherits a castle in Italy and discovers that somebody has been left behind in one of the dungeons. The wretch has been very, very seriously tortured and maimed, arousing the family's pity. However, the family finds itself pulled apart at the seams when the "freak" gets free and becomes obsessed with their teenage daughter.

"It's really a return to an old-fashioned horror movie," commented Gordon. "Our goal was to really make a scary film. One of the things Charlie Band and I talked about a lot was how long it had been since either one of us had seen a movie that scared us. I sometimes think that *Re-Animator* was one of the reasons that people are now doing sort of comic horror films, but I miss movies that really are scary."

Re-Animator excelled at combining humor with gut-wrenching horror, giving the film genuine visceral impact. "That's one of the things that *Re-Animator* imitators forgot, which is you have to do both," continued Gordon. "One of the things I always found was that comedy works well with horror, but you have to really build tension for it to work. With *Castle Freak*, there is some comedy in the movie, but it's more of a real hide-under-your-chair kind of movie."

Part of what drew Gordon to the project was Band's agreement to release the film unrated, long thought to be a risky move in these censorious times. According to Gordon, that "basically gave me the license to go crazy and do whatever I wanted to do. So, we pushed and stretched the envelope even further."

Gordon predicted it will be a very disturbing film to a lot of people. The movie reunites *Re-Animator* stars Jeffrey Combs and Barbara Crampton. Jonathan Fuller, who played the leading man in *The Pit and the Pendulum*, plays the freak himself.

Fuller is singled out for high praise: "He was in makeup six hours a day for this role. Jonathan is an incredible physical actor. I first worked with him on stage in Chicago, where we did a production in which he had to learn gymnastics to play the part, which he did incredibly well.

"So, when I knew I was going to be doing this movie, I went to him because I knew this was going to be an incredibly demanding part, physically. This is a guy who has been twisted, every bone in whose body has been broken and healed badly. It was clear to me that this wouldn't just be a stuntman walking around wearing a hockey mask.

"Also, the character has a great deal of sadness about him at times, like the great monsters [such as] Karloff's Frankenstein. There's a pathos there as well as horror. I realized we really needed a wonderful actor to play the freak, and it turned out that one of Jonathan's great heroes of all time was Lon Chaney. So, the idea of being able to tackle a Lon Chaney role, even with the rigors of that makeup, would have driven anybody else crazy."

The elaborate makeup for the film was executed by Optic Nerve. Added Gordon, "Jonathan, when I cast him in the part, read the script and called me up and said, 'Thank you for thinking about me,' and I said, 'If you can say that at the end, I'll accept it. I'll accept the thanks.' The last day he came over to me and said thanks. He's a real gentleman."

According to Gordon, it was a difficult shoot on a short four-week schedule. The film was lensed in the same fifteenth-century castle where Gordon had shot *The Pit and the Pendulum* for Full Moon. "It's not a soundstage," commented the director. "Physically, the demands of the production shooting in a castle like that were difficult. It was very demanding physically on all of the actors, because they all have to go through a lot.

"We shot the film in a very short amount of time. The whole shooting schedule was four weeks, which was about the shortest shooting schedule I've ever had. I think *Re-Animator* was about the same schedule."

Castle Freak was written by Dennis Paoli, Gordon's high school buddy and longtime writing partner who also wrote *The Pit and the Pendulum*, *From Beyond*, and collaborated on *Re-Animator*. "The project was quick and came together fast, but sometimes when that happens, it becomes very good," said Gordon. "Everything just kind of fell into place. The script turned out as a tight little script, and a very scary one."

Due to the recent problems at Full Moon, the film remains in a kind of limbo, as does the still-unproduced *The Shadow Over Innsmouth*, a Lovecraft adaptation also scripted by Paoli after Paoli and Gordon's plans to make a voodoo project called *Gris-Gris* fell through.

Hope for *The Shadow Over Innsmouth* was revived when Charlie Band wanted to produce it. Said Gordon, "There have been so many false starts on that. There were a lot of people that needed to be dealt with and deals needed to be worked out, and turnaround costs that had to be paid off and all of this stuff, and he [Band] went through all of the legal tangle to make it happen.

"But now, with the situation at Full Moon, it may have to be put off again. So, I'm still keeping my fingers crossed that we're eventually going to get this movie made."

Gordon noted that his relationship with Band has been a good one. Their stars rose together with the success and notoriety of *Re-Animator*, which helped establish Empire as a potential force to be reckoned with. Despite Band's claims that *Re-Animator* was produced by Empire, however, Gordon asserts that *Re-Animator* was an independent production that Empire picked up for distribution. Said Gordon, "Brian [Yuzna] was the producer of *Re-Animator*, but he made a deal with Charlie to distribute it in exchange for Charlie providing post-production facilities. That really was the way things worked out."

Despite *Re-Animator*'s financial success, very little of the money it generated made it back to Yuzna or his investors who were understandably upset. As a consequence, the investors threatened to sue him, and he in turn threatened to sue Empire and Charlie Band. Gordon had signed a three-picture deal with Band, but his former producer declined to work with him again after the matter was settled out of court.

Gordon noted that he and Yuzna remain friends and are discussing doing more projects together. "As a matter of fact, Dennis Paoli and I just wrote a script together for Brian to direct for Trimark called *The Dentist*," said Gordon. "We've been talking about combining forces on other things—including another *Re-Animator* sequel. Another is a project of seven films based on the Seven Deadly Sins with seven different directors doing each of the sins. Brian is one of the organizers of this project, and he would be directing one and I would be directing one. So, Brian and I are still very good friends and I've been very happy with the work he's been doing as a director. I think he's been doing some very exciting work."

Yuzna went on to direct *Bride of Re-Animator* without Gordon's participation. Gordon gave this reaction to Yuzna's sequel: "I thought that he did things differently than I would have done them. I have kidded him about this, because one of the major questions about that was: how did Herbert West ever become a doctor? They keep referring to him as 'Dr. West' in the sequel. I can't imagine a university giving this guy a diploma. But Brian has his own take on things, and it's a unique one.

"He also took the rest of the Lovecraft stories as a basis, which I thought was pretty good. We have been talking about a third one, which I would possibly direct."

Gordon's *The Pit and the Pendulum* was initially a very ambitious project for Vestron with a budget of about $6 million, and Peter O'Toole and Sherilyn Fenn set to star. When Vestron went under, the project would have gone down the tubes except for Band, who resurrected it on a budget of under $2 million. Gordon is very pleased with the film, particularly with Lance Henriksen's performance.

Gordon noted that *Castle Freak* has not been caught up in Full Moon's recent financial difficulties. "My movie is really in kind of a strange place because it really was not part of the deal with Paramount," said Gordon. "It was something that Charlie wanted to do because he wanted to do it. So, there was no completion bond company involved in *Castle Freak*. It was so small that it flew below the radar in a way.

"Paramount, I think, likes the film, and what they're saying is, '[Perhaps] we'll take this.' But all of this must now get sorted out, which is what Charlie is in the process of doing. My sense of this is that he will be back on his feet by the end of the year [1995], and that his new mission will be family films, although he may still do the Full Moon movies. Those other movies still do extremely well overseas and have done pretty well here, too, as direct-to-video product."

The Making of *Space Truckers*

Dennis Fischer / 1997

From *Cinefantastique* 28, no. 10 (April 1997), pp. 14–24. Reprinted by permission.

When Stuart Gordon was a child, he dreamed of being an astronaut, but his poor eyesight put the kibosh on those plans. The closest he came was watching Kubrick's *2001: A Space Odyssey*, which had a huge impact. "I still think it's the best space movie ever made," said Gordon. "I saw that movie about 100 times. I remember my reaction the first couple of times I saw it was just a religious experience. I mean, that movie was just out there; it was pure cinema—it really speaks in images, almost no words. There's about twenty minutes of dialogue in the whole movie. And the fact Kubrick did as much homework as he did! The movie has not dated, and yet here we are almost at 2001, and it still seems a very believable movie. The science in it is great."

Gordon always wanted to direct a space movie that would follow the rules of space. "It sort of bothers me in *Star Trek* that they walk around and there's no sense of them being in a spaceship," he said. He is also a fan of *Alien*, another solemn science fiction film, which conveyed the concept of future astronauts just being working-class guys doing a job that happens to be in outer space. For *Space Truckers*, he has combined the two influences and added a playful, twisted sense of humor.

Unlike a lot of studio pictures, *Space Truckers* had only one screenwriter, Ted Mann. Mann, who worked on *Civil Wars* and *NYPD Blue*, concocted the story of independent space trucker John Canyon (Dennis Hopper), who transports genetically engineered pork to the far reaches of the solar system when he is coerced by a corporation into shipping a secret load past Earth's defenses to the home planet. He is joined in his quest by novice trucker Mike Pucci (Stephen Dorff) and waitress Cindy (Debi Mazar) after accidentally killing corporate flunky Keller (George Wendt).

"Ted and I just knocked out the scenes of the story together, and he would go out and write a draft," Gordon explained. "We would go over it together, and make changes. It was done very much in tandem. We were both frustrated astronauts, so we were on the same wavelength. The trick came in later when we had to start dealing with the budget and realized that certain sequences as written would not be affordable, so Ted and I would go back and think about how we could do this simpler. Instead of having five locations, could we do the sequence in two?"

According to Gordon, the solutions he and Mann found often improved the sequences. "For example," he said, "in the earlier drafts, the InterPork henchmen hijack John Canyon's load, and there was this elaborate scene of him having to couple his rig to the back of their booster and work his way across the cargo, break into the tow truck, where there's a fight, and it ends up with one of these characters getting sucked out through the window. The sequence was very elaborate, and we realized that it was beyond us.

"In the simplified version, we loved the idea of the guy going through the window and so we hung onto that idea, but we reset the scene in the diner, and rather than it being a henchman, we made it into Keller, who is the major bad guy in the first third of the movie, the George Wendt character, and the sequence had a lot more impact as well, because it was somebody who really was a formidable adversary, rather than some minor character that you don't really know. It's one of the best sequences in the film, I think."

This alteration "tightened everything that came after it," said Gordon. "It accelerated the action and the tensions and the urgency." The characters are now responsible for the death of a dispatcher from the corporation, so they are forced to go on the lam and have a lot more at stake. In the process of eluding the police, they run into a group of space pirates, led by their Cyborg captain Macanudo (Charles Dance) and his henchman Cutt (Vernon Wells), and eventually they discover that Canyon's truck is harboring BMWs—Bio-Mechanical Warriors, which are part of the corporate plot to take over the Earth.

Once the story was in place, Gordon elaborately planned out how to visualize it unlike any previous space opera. To achieve this, he brought in a variety of artists, like Ron Cobb, Bernie Wrightson, Hajime Sorayama, and Bruce McCall. Bringing these visions together and designing the overall movie is first-time production designer Simon Murton. "We deliberately did not want to use other films as references," Gordon explained. "Instead of going with a sterile, white NASA feeling, we went the opposite, into bright colors and a commercialized feel. In *2001*, they built the wonderful set that spins 360 degrees. In our film, that became the diner, which looks like a Bob's Big Boy, so there's the juxtaposition of science fiction and the familiar."

Another important element in the design of the film came from costume designer John Bloomfield (*Waterworld*). According to Gordon, they started by looking at the actual spacesuits. "We have a book called *Space Gear*; it went through the whole evolution of the spacesuit from a study point," he said. "We also wanted the suit to look—rather than a real high-tech perfect suit—like a beat-up, used suit that John Canyon got with his used truck. It's like when you change a tire: the gear you've got in your car is not pristine; it's well used and some of the pieces are missing." The result is a cross between a spacesuit and an old diving suit. "It's really a kind of clumsy, bulky-looking thing," Gordon recalled, "and then he did a more modern, spiffed-up version for what the new models are like. They're the slimmed-down, high-tech version."

Bloomfield did a lot with plastic. "We moved away from natural materials and went for a lot of bright colors and corporate logos," said Gordon. "The entire costume is covered in logos, kind of taking this idea about how people wear logos on their clothes. Basically, the logo becomes the clothes. In this futuristic world, we are walking billboards.

"He's a very witty designer," Gordon continued. "A lot of the things he did were strange but familiar at the same time. You see a lot of things like cowboy hats and baseball caps, and things that have been with us a long time and will probably be with us a few years from now, so that you can look at these guys and recognize them immediately as truck drivers. But they don't look exactly like any truck drivers you've ever seen before."

Once the film was written and designed, it needed to be cast. Gordon selected Dennis Hopper to play John Canyon because he was a fan of Hopper's work and needed someone who conveyed the impression of being a veteran of life, a quintessential maverick. Hopper proved interested in playing a sympathetic character for a change. "Dennis Hopper has really been quite wonderful," said Gordon, "because what he did from the very beginning is [he] made it very clear that he wanted John Canyon to be a real person. I felt that his decision was right on the money. He felt that there was so much stuff in the movie that was strange and funny and weird, that there had to be somebody in there who grounded it. He really underplayed him and made him a very real guy and resisted getting too big with him, because if you do that, it's like a parody of a parody and you end up with nothing. He wanted to be someone who the audience could relate to and think, 'This is me in this situation.' It's a very rich portrayal. The fear in something like this is that it could turn into something like *Spaceballs* [1987]. In order for there to be real tension, there had to be characters that you cared about and were worried about, and Dennis was able to do that.

"He contributed a lot of things," Gordon added. "The hat he wears is something that Dennis came up with. The costume designer had come up with a whole bunch of hats, and one of the hats that he made had a brim that would snap off so that you could wear it inside a space helmet. Dennis took a look at it and just unsnapped it and wore it like that, and the result is a hat that looks very much like a rebel soldier's did in the Civil War when he wears it with the short brim, which I think really set up the sense that John Canyon was an independent trucker, a postmodern rebel. Visually, he's telling us who this guy is.

"One of the best lines in the movie is something that Dennis came up with right on the set that was not scripted at all: after they have made a daring escape, Mike says, 'That's some of the best driving I ever saw.' Dennis just turns to him and says, 'Pedal to the metal and played footsie with fate.' The whole crew just sat there with their mouths hanging open, which was great.

"He was very much there for us. He was also supportive of the whole process when there were delays. Other movie stars would have gotten nervous and gone with another project or bailed, but Dennis stuck with us. Dennis brought in Stephen Dorff, and Stephen really idolizes Dennis. Stephen had some questions about whether a film called *Space Truckers* would be a good career move, and Dennis said to him, 'You can have fun with this,' and they really kind of bonded in a kind of father-son relationship."

Dorff (*Backbeat*) plays Mike Pucci, who makes a deal with Cindy the waitress that if he can get her to Earth, she will marry him. "Stephen Dorff is like a young Dennis Hopper," Gordon said. "In the story, his character starts out wanting to work for the big corporation, but by the end of the movie he is an independent trucker. He becomes a young John Canyon. There's even a line in the movie where John Canyon says, 'I don't want you to end up like me.' Stephen Dorff says, 'Heaven forbid.' At that point, you know he will.

"Stephen Dorff is like Dennis in that he approaches things very realistically. If he can't believe it, he can't do it. He took what was a very sketchy character in the script and fleshed him out to make him real. He caught on to what we're going for. 'White trash in space' is how he put it; trailer park guys who are in space."

Cindy is played by Debi Mazar (Spice in *Batman Forever*). Claimed Gordon, "I could actually say that the part was written for her. Ted Mann and she worked together on a TV series called *Civil Wars*, where she played a secretary in a divorce attorney's office. I used to watch the show and became a big fan of hers. When we were working on the first couple of drafts, the part was very bland and uninteresting, and Ted and I were talking about some ways to develop the character, and at one point, one of us mentioned why don't we take it to Debi Mazar? And from that point on, the part just took on a life of its own. She came in and read the part. There were no doubts that she should play that part."

Gordon originally went with Ron Houser for the part of Captain Macanudo, who has been partially disintegrated and rebuilt, his inner workings visible through a transparent plastic shell. But the actor was replaced partway into shooting. Explains Gordon, "He is a wonderful actor, but it was one of those situations where his style of acting was at odds with what everyone else was doing. While everyone else was trying to ground their performances for the audience, Ron went in the opposite direction a bit."

To replace him, Gordon went with Charles Dance, who had also been under consideration for the part. "Charles Dance was a happy accident in a way," Gordon recalls. "We were staying at the same hotel as he was, in London, and ran into him in the lobby one day and described the movie, and he said, 'Let me look at the script.' About a week later, I got a call from him that he wanted to play Captain Macanudo. I found out later that he liked the script, but wasn't sure as this character was very different from anything that he had ever played before, and he showed it to his teenage daughter who said, 'This is great, Dad. You should do this.' That convinced him. No one has ever seen him play comedy before, and he's wonderful. He had to undergo four to six hours of makeup every day to play the part, but again, he found a way to humanize a character who could have been just a cartoon. And there is this almost sexy quality about him as well, even though he's half-man and half-machine. There is still a charisma that comes through all that makeup. By the end of it, you really like him. It's funny; he saw the movie in Spain, and his wife said it was just terrible the character was not going to be around if there's a sequel. I said, 'Well, in this kind of movie, being blown up does not mean you won't be around for the sequel.'"

Also on hand is Barbara Crampton, who starred in Gordon's first few features. "Barbara Crampton is an old friend," he said. "We were trying to find an actress to play a very small but pivotal role, and we needed a sense that she and Debi Mazar were related to each other. Barbara is a wonderful mimic, and after spending a little time with Debi, she was able to get the accent down, so the two of them seemed like they were two peas from the same pod."

With script, pre-production, and cast apparently in place, Gordon went to Ireland to shoot—when disaster seemingly struck. "We went to Ireland because we were promised half the budget from our investors provided we shoot there," Gordon explained. "Then, less than half a month before we started, it turned out the Irish producer who had promised £7 million had only £2 million."

Gordon credits his American producers, Peter Newman and Greg Johnson, for not abandoning the project. "I assumed that was it," said the director, "but they went out and scrambled and found other producers, and the movie never even had to shut down. The Irish government helped the film, which was made under Section 35, by which the Irish government would put up a portion of the film's budget in exchange for filmmakers using Irish facilities and labor. But this was the first time that the government ever granted two Section 35s. For the first Section 35, we did not meet the terms, because the producer had not provided the correct amount of money. So, the Irish government said, 'We will allow you to post a second time for new investors to help you complete the film.' A new producer, Morgan Sullivan, came on board, one of the most renowned Irish producers, and he straightened out the mess and got us back on track, along with Peter Newman and Greg Johnson, and Guy Collins brought Goldcrest in with a lot of investors. Goldcrest would only come in if we did all the post-production work in London, so this is the first movie where I had to do the post-production as well as the production away from home. What was originally to have been a three-month stint became over a year abroad."

Regarding working in the UK, Gordon reported, "I like Ireland very much, and the crew was sensational. This was not an easy movie to make. Every single shot had some level of difficulty—if it wasn't zero gravity, it was creatures or prosthetics or pyro. It was never just simply two people sitting in a shot. The schedule was not that different from an ordinary film. We had an eleven-week period, which is still pretty tight for a normal movie, and our crew was very disciplined and quick and had wonderful attitudes. There never was any grumbling or complaining."

Murton remembers it a little bit differently. "There were a lot of moments when we thought it wasn't going to make it," he said. "I had to send out letters for me and my crew, saying, 'If we don't get paid, we're leaving.' That happened a couple of times, because sometimes we were three weeks in arrears, and they were trying desperately to bring money in. It certainly wasn't a very smooth road, but we fought hard enough and it came through. My hat goes off to the American producers who kept it going, when we thought, 'Well, that's it.' What they went through would send a lot of other people into the loony bin."

Initially, the production rejected Ireland's Ardmore Studios because it did not have a stage large enough to encompass the scope of the production. However, it soon became apparent that Ardmore was the only true studio setup in the country. Production designer Murton wanted a large stage for the Regalia interior. "I'm a great believer in using light to build a set," he said. "If you can't build it physically, we can use some good old theatrical tricks to make it work, and sometimes you need the space to throw light through stuff, and we didn't have that [at Ardmore]. We started looking in other areas. The only thing that was big enough was these old ex-meat storage places; unfortunately, they ended up being a very dangerous site because they have all this insulation that was highly flammable. Someone should have booked up Ardmore just in case, but we didn't because we thought we were going somewhere else, so time was wasted."

Gordon became concerned that if production did not begin on time, he might lose his cast. "Our start date would have to be pushed back about six months," he recalled, "and our reaction was, 'We have commitments to people to start at a specific time,' and so we explored ways of making the film. One was converting a warehouse into a studio, and the space [available] was a huge meat carving facility with these gigantic refrigerators, which were about the size of a large soundstage. Unfortunately, the costs of converting it would have been the whole budget of the film; also, the time to get it ready would take up the six months that we'd be waiting to get into Ardmore, so we decided to use the extra time to work and plan some more."

Another key member of the *Space Truckers* production was Paul Gentry, an experienced effects man with films such as *The Muppet Christmas Carol* [1992], *The Addams Family* [1991], and *Last Action Hero* [1993] to his credit. He had worked with David Allen on *Dolls* and *Robot Jox*, and also worked previously with Gordon on *Fortress* and photographed the Iwerks interactive *Aliens: Ride at the Speed of Fright* ride, which Gordon directed. "Stuart thought the *Aliens* ride film was a training ground, a dry run for *Space Truckers*," explained Gentry. "A lot of things we did for *Space Truckers*, we did on that ride. Stuart hadn't a lot of experience with paramilitary soldiers firing weapons—you didn't see those kinds of things in *Re-Animator*, so it was great. I introduced him to certain things which he didn't know the camera could do, just little tricks of the trade, such as the use of lightning strikes, which is a very basic tool of the industry, but it's interesting to use it in a battle scene. Traditionally, lightning strikes are used to create lightning effects. Of course, you can change the color of it, which makes it more the color of a gun-flash, so you can have several lightning strikes going off in the background, and then you have soldiers firing in the foreground, and it makes it appear much bigger than it is because you have flashing all over the place. It creates a lot of excitement, and it's something Stuart hadn't used before, and on top of that you throw in white frames in editorial."

One of the biggest problems faced by the special effects crew in *Space Truckers* was zero gravity, which, Gordon notes, "is something you don't see in too many space movies any more. It's expensive and very time consuming, but we felt that it was important enough to spend the time to do it. Unlike Ron Howard, we couldn't afford to send people up in the Vomit Comet and get real zero gravity, so we had to find another way to do it. Some of the solutions were very simple. Sometimes we used string; other times we would turn things upside down. The best solution sometimes was to have the actors play weightlessness, and we were able to convincingly portray weightlessness just by the way they moved their bodies."

To assist with the weightless wire work, Gordon hired a stunt coordinator from *A Chinese Ghost Story* [1987] and *Mighty Morphin Power Rangers* [1993–96], Koichi Sakamoto, who had done work in Hong Kong, Japan, and the United States, and who spoke English. Many of the stuntmen on the project were Asian martial artists and acrobats. "We had a perfect stunt team: Apple Stunts, it's called," said

Gordon. "They did some amazing things. We had a sequence where a guy takes a punch and flips end over end for thirty feet into a wall. This was all done right there live on the set. As a matter of fact, in terms of zero gravity, there was very little in the way of optical effects."

Recalled Gentry, "Koichi and I did these augmented scenes of this whole battle going on. We had limited time, only four days, and we all realized we needed two weeks for this elaborate sequence because it's so difficult setting up these stunt shots. One guy [Tatsuro Koike], absolutely the most fearless stunt guy I've ever seen, was slamming into this or that. He looked like he'd just broken his neck. You'd yell, 'Cut! Tatsuro, are you alright?' You'd think he's dead, and he'd just look up and smile. 'That okay?'

"It's going to be hard to watch *Space Truckers* and not see the same faces scene after scene, doing any stunts that are going on. Tatsuro we had in any costume imaginable—it was funny. If you do things safely, and with a certain amount of care, it takes time. These things can't be rushed; it's counterproductive. We barely got through them by the skin of our teeth."

Since there was not a lot of money left over for wire removal, most of the wire work had to be hidden by the cinematographer while on the set. "I think it's a testament to Mac Ahlberg, our cinematographer, who's an expert at this," said Gordon. "Part of the solution was built into the set design. Simon Murton was aware we'd have to hide wires, so he designed the set to have all kinds of strips on it. It fakes your eye out, allows the background to camouflage the wires."

"I wanted the lines in the set going the other way to make the sets look wider," said Murton, "but they had the problem that they weren't going to have enough money to do wire removal. Stuart wanted to do realistic space freefall and, in reality, we should have had the set on a gimbal, but we never had the money nor the time to do it properly. So, we came up with something like the space shuttle where they have these Velcro pads absolutely everywhere so they can stick things like cameras or paraphernalia to the walls to keep them from floating around and bumping into things. We just did all these vertical lines to help camouflage the cables. I'd say 70 percent of the time it works. The other 30 percent it didn't. Sometimes you see it; sometimes you don't."

Gordon employed simple misdirection to prevent viewers from spotting the wires. "When you're looking at somebody floating, the audience always looks above him for the wires," the director explained, "but if you shoot upside down, tilting the camera in some strange way, the wires are below, where you're not expecting to see them. There are a couple of shots in the movie where the wires are clearly visible—they are not hidden at all—but nobody has ever spotted them because they are looking in the wrong place. There are places where we did have to do some wire removal, but I think the total number of wire removal shots in the whole movie was something like three, thanks to Mac and Simon's ingenuity, which saved us a fortune."

Filming in Ireland proved a fairly copacetic experience. The shore of Dublin Bay ended up filling in for White Sands, New Mexico. The Dublin Civic Center, considered an eyesore by the inhabitants because its modern design clashes with the pastoral countryside, proved an ideal location for a hospital scene. The Irish and English crewmembers largely got along, but the resumption of hostilities during post-production created some nervousness on the part of the director.

As Gordon noted, "I was there when the truce was on, and it was really some of the best feeling between England and Ireland, and then right as we started post-production, the bombings started again. It was done outside of Ardmore in Ireland and also in London, and I was going back and forth between the two on a regular basis. There was a bombing about a block away from where the post-production house was in London, which was nerve-wracking. There were a lot of discussions because half the crew was Irish and the other half English, and they had all been able to work together as a team, and all of this broke out again, and there were a lot of discussions about how to solve this problem. As an American, this seemed like something that should be settled fairly easily, and they would look at me like I was an idiot. It is very complicated, and there doesn't seem to be any easy answer."

Having finished post-production, *Space Truckers* now must find its audience. It has been aided in this regard with good word of mouth from festival appearances, which is scheduled to be followed by overseas distribution early this year. "It was very well reviewed at the Sitges Festival," claimed Gordon. "It also played the Tokyo Festival; although I was not present there, the report I got was that it was very well received there—spontaneous applause and a lot of laughs."

Naturally, Gordon is concerned with how his film, which is yet to find a US distributor, will be marketed. "We're showing it to the studios now and hoping we'll have a deal soon," said Gordon. "It's a strange movie, the largest-budgeted independent one in some time. I think we have to make the right deal for the picture; we can't just give it away, because it has a pretty big sized price tag on it. We have to find the right company who understands it, because it's not your typical movie. It requires a very creative campaign to let people know what it is. I hear people say, 'Is this an action movie or is it a comedy?' The answer is yes. There has never been anything like this before, and that makes marketing people a little nervous."

The Wonderful Ice Cream Suit

Judd Hollander and Sue Feinberg / 1998

From *Cinefantastique* 29, no. 12 (April 1998), pp. 10–11.

Whoever came up with the saying "clothes make the man" was righter than they knew, as author Ray Bradbury proved in his comically poignant tale "The Wonderful Ice Cream Suit," which is coming to the screen nearly forty years after it was first written.

It is the story of six impoverished Mexican-Americans who become entranced with the purest white suit they have ever seen, thinking it will make all their dreams come true. Bringing the tale to life are Joe Mantegna (*House of Games*); Edward James Olmos (*Stand and Deliver*); Gregory Sierra (*Barney Miller*); Esai Morales (*La Bamba*); and newcomer Clifton Gonzalez Gonzalez (*The Replacement Killers*). Also featured are veteran actor Sid Caesar as the tailor who, along with Howard Morris, sells the group the suit (Caesar and Morris co-starred on the landmark TV series *Your Show of Shows*). Rounding out the cast are actress-comedienne Liz Torres, Mike Moroff, and Lisa Vidal.

As Bradbury described the plot: "They collect their money, buy one suit, and move into a tenement room and live with [it]. Each of them gets to wear the suit one night a week. On the seventh night they flip a coin to see who gets the suit." However, things don't go as they planned, and before the film is over, each person will find out just how important the suit is in the scheme of things. The film will be released by Disney's Buena Vista Division; it is the first Disney original live-action feature made expressly for the home video market.

Bradbury got the idea for the story from his boyhood experiences in the 1930s: "Until I was eighteen or nineteen, I was wearing my brother's and my father's clothes," he recalled. When he graduated from Los Angeles High School, he wore a suit that his uncle had been wearing when he was killed in a holdup. "My family was on government relief when I graduated. What else [could I do] but wear the suit, bullet holes and all? . . . With the first money I earned, I went and bought some clothes for myself." In 1944, he lived for a time in a tenement in Los Angeles where he would see friends coming and going across the border from Mexico. "I noticed they borrowed clothes from one another and bought them together as we had done."

First published under the title "The Magical White Suit" in 1958 by the *Saturday Evening Post*, the story has previously been adapted for television and the stage (the latter includes a straight dramatic adaptation by Bradbury himself and a musical version for which he provided the book). One of the most acclaimed versions of the play came from Chicago's Organic Theatre Company in 1973. The company's cofounder, director Stuart Gordon, came across Bradbury's story, obtained the rights, and mounted a production, which included such people as Joe Mantegna, Dennis Franz (*NYPD Blue*), and Meshach Taylor. "They were incredibly talented, and I always had a feeling these guys were going to hit it big," Gordon recalled. The show was immensely successful, and the company toured all over the world with the production. "It's a very universal story," Gordon remarked. "Everywhere we went, even if they couldn't understand the language, they understood the play."

In one of the most recent Los Angeles productions of "The Wonderful Ice Cream Suit," the work found a fan in Roy E. Disney, the vice chairman of the board of directors of the Walt Disney Company and head of the studio's animation department. "[He] kept coming to see the play, and they finally [purchased the rights] to it," Bradbury noted. The film's rights were acquired close to two years ago, and Bradbury was hired to write the screenplay. Gordon, who in Bradbury's words "directed a beautiful production," was tapped to direct the film version. Bradbury and Gordon worked closely together on the project, with Gordon encouraging the author to "give as much input as he wanted. I think it's rare that you have an author there with you when you're working on a movie," he noted. Gordon's directing credits include H. P. Lovecraft's *Re-Animator*, [a winner of] the Critics' Prize at the Cannes Film Festival, *Fortress*, *Castle Freak*, and the upcoming *Space Truckers* with Dennis Hopper. He is also the co-creator of *Honey, I Shrunk the Kids* and executive producer of the sequel, *Honey, I Blew Up the Kid*.

Another Organic alumnus who signed on to the project was Joe Mantegna, who recreated his stage role as "Gomez," the ringleader of the group that purchases the suit. "It's an actor's dream come true to be able to put this character and this play to film," Mantegna said. "I've got twenty-four years of acting and life experience in this role." It's Gomez who sets the story in motion by deciding that, to be someone important, you have to look the part. One day, in the window of a tailor shop, he spies a perfectly white suit and decides that's the answer to his prayers. Lacking the money to buy it by himself, he rounds up three men who all have the same build: Martinez (Gonzalez), Villanazul (Sierra), and Dominguez (Morales)—described in the press materials as "the innocent, the intellectual and the romantic," respectively. Gomez convinces them to pool their meager resources ($20 each) to buy the suit.

But, as Gordon explains, there's a problem. "There's a fifth guy in the group, Vamanos, played by Olmos. They let him in because he's the right size, and they need his money. He's a complete slob. He's like this street person who lives in a trash dumpster. And the suit is pure white, and [the rest of the group] are convinced he's going to destroy it. They give him a bath and give him all these rules: 'No smoking, no drinking, no eating juicy tacos,' and he, of course, breaks [them], and they're chasing after him trying to save the suit." At one point the piece becomes a very physical comedy, a factor that Gordon found appealing. "I'm a big fan of the Marx brothers, but it has lots of fantasy elements as well."

Another appealing aspect that attracted Gordon to the project was the chance to do something that wasn't pure science fiction. "Heads don't explode in this one," he joked. "Bradbury's work is very poetic, and so is this. Things that happen [to the men] when they wear the suit are not realistic or possible. But they're so magical." Gordon wasn't the only person to work against "type." As he noted: "Edward James Olmos is playing the dirty guy, Vamanos, which is a real first for him. [He's] usually thought of as a very serious actor, but here he gets a chance to be a clown and is absolutely hilarious in the movie."

Although no release date has been set as of yet, Gordon thinks the film will probably hit screens sometime in the late spring or early summer of 1998. He's actually partial to Cinco de Mayo Day—May 5th. "That would be kind of appropriate," he noted. "I'm real pleased with what we got. I also know that Ray is very pleased with it. He says it's the first time that any of his work has really been produced word for word. He's always been rewritten."

Gordon sees *The Wonderful Ice Cream Suit* as a family film everyone can enjoy (which is different from what he considers a "kids' film" made strictly for young children). Thus far, the film has been very successful in test screenings. "We've been screening it as I've been working on it," Gordon noted, "and the reactions have been terrific. [Because] it's very simple and very visual, I think everyone can relate to it. Here's this white suit, and here's this dirty guy ('Vamanos'). At one of the screenings, a little kid—he must have been three or four years old—yelled out, 'Don't let him touch the suit!' It just builds and gets funnier and funnier as it goes along. I've got very high hopes for it."

Dagon and Beyond

Mark Wheaton / 2002

From *Fangoria*, no. 214 (July 2002), pp. 26–29. This interview appeared in the magazine in a different, shorter form. Reprinted by permission.

Fangoria: How long ago did you actually know you were going to make *Dagon* at Fantastic Factory?

Stuart Gordon: It was about three years ago—it was when the Fantastic Factory was just being started. Brian [Yuzna] called me and said, "How would you like to make *Dagon* as one of our first films?" This was a project that we'd been working on since *Re-Animator*. It was a script that originally was written in 1985. It was the project that was supposed to follow *Re-Animator*, but instead we did *Dolls* and then *From Beyond*.

Fangoria: How much did this movie change from the original script after incorporating parts of "The Shadow Over Innsmouth" into it?

Gordon: Well, the script had to be rewritten for Spain because we reset it. Originally, Lovecraft's story was taking place in New England. So, that was the biggest change, but in terms of the structure of the story, it pretty much stayed as originally written. I think the only thing that we really added was the flashback. It was so funny; I had completely forgotten that the script even existed. I was going through some old papers and I found an outline for it. I called up Dennis Paoli and said, "This outline is terrific. You should write this." He said, "Stuart, I did!" He'd *written* it. Brian Yuzna had hired him to write the script right after *Re-Animator* was a big success. "Innsmouth" had always been my favorite Lovecraft story, so it was a real labor of love.

Fangoria: The movie starts with images from the short story "Dagon" rather than from "The Shadow Over Innsmouth."

Gordon: Well, we combined the two stories. One of the things was that we always felt the title, *The Shadow Over Innsmouth*, was quite a mouthful. *Dagon*, we thought, was a stronger title. The whole opening dream sequence is very much like "Dagon," of finding the carvings on the wall, and so on and so forth.

Lovecraft always came back to certain themes. "Dagon" was the first story he ever wrote [in July 1917]. It was his first published story and he came back to those themes—the idea of the "Deep Ones"—many, many other times including in "The Shadow Over Innsmouth" [published in April 1936], one of his last stories, which was much more detailed and intricate.

Fangoria: Turning Lovecraft on its head?

Gordon: Actually, I think *Re-Animator* is pretty close to Lovecraft's story. "Herbert West—Re-Animator" was one of Lovecraft's least favorite stories. He hated it, because I think he was paid to write it. So, he felt he was whoring or something. His other stuff he would *write*, and then submit them to magazines, but this is one that he was hired by the magazine to write as a serial. So, he always dismissed it as something he had just done for money.

Fangoria: Was this for *Weird Tales*?

Gordon: It was actually a magazine called *Home Brew* that he wrote it for. [In regard to *Dagon*], we tried to stay very faithful to Lovecraft. I went back and reread both stories very carefully when we were working on the script. When we put the flashback in initially, we had it as a much more expanded flashback. We even showed them going to the South Seas Island and meeting the native tribe that was worshipping Dagon, but it turned into a whole other movie. It became an *Indiana Jones* kind of thing. Then, working with Brian Yuzna, we boiled it down and focused on the town and the impact of this on [its inhabitants].

Fangoria: What kind of changes did you have to make to set the film in Spain?

Gordon: Brian called me from Spain. He was exploring a region called Galicia, which is where the head of Filmax [Julio Fernández], who produced the movie, comes from. It's the northwest coast of Spain, on the Atlantic Ocean. It's very different from what you would imagine Spain to be like. It's Celtic. They play the bagpipes there. The music sounds like Irish music. It's really interesting. It rains all the time there. It's very much like our Pacific Northwest—like Seattle, where it's constantly raining and very green. It's foggy. It actually has a feeling somewhat like New England, which was perfect for the Lovecraft thing. There are all these legends about that region, having to do with witches, ghosts, and so forth, so it was really a perfect counterpoint. I went to Spain with Brian and we toured Galicia and discovered all kinds of interesting things, like these structures there they call "hórreos." They're these odd-looking little buildings that are on stilts and they store food in these things—this was before they had refrigeration. So, in the original script, when [Paul and Ezequiel] got captured, we had them thrown into a jail. We then said, "Why don't we just stick them in one of these hórreos?" The other big change was one of the favorite dishes in that region is a dish called Pulpo Gallego, which is octopus. It started hitting me that, unlike Lovecraft's story where the creatures are changing into things that he describes as "frog-fish" creatures, the idea of them turning into octopi seemed much more interesting. We started working in that direction, the idea that these creatures' bones were softening, which was why it was difficult for them to walk as they got further and further along in their mutation.

Fangoria: Can you talk about some of the production design on *Dagon*, but also working with David Marti and his special makeup effects studio DDT?

Gordon: Well, they did a lot of the work on the designs as well, although we had several other conceptual artists that worked on the project with us. There was a guy named Rafael Garres, who is a comic book artist who designed a lot of the creatures. David Marti, who runs DDT, did a lot of the design work, too. What an enormous job he had. At first, I thought we were going to need several companies to do the work. It turned out that DDT was able to handle everything, which was amazing.

Fangoria: How much of the movie is on location with actual exteriors and how much of it was stuff built up on stages?

Gordon: No, there were no exteriors that were built. Everything was real, though our art department went in and made them look more funky and run down. Some of those places, in reality, are actually quite pretty. This town, on a sunny day, is a very charming place to be. When it got overcast, all of sudden it started getting this creepy vibe. They added to it by boarding up the windows and adding ambience. The other thing we had to do was cover up all the crosses in the town and turn them into tridents, which was our symbol for the Dagon-worshipers.

Fangoria: Who designed the pyramid that they use to summon Dagon?

Gordon: Again, I think it was Rafael Garres who designed that. We had a great production designer on this movie, Llorenç Miquel. He was great in terms of finding these locations and transforming them. Like the scene at the end of the movie with the pit, that whole temple is a real place. It's actually a really weird story. It was originally a mansion and there was an underground catacomb that was built—the whole thing that he goes through is also real—and it opens up into that big room with the pillars. It was owned by an eccentric millionaire who, we found out, used to have orgies down there. After he died, he donated it to the church, which was really bizarre, and it's now a nunnery! The nuns let us use it on the condition that we would not disturb them while they were praying. It was a very, very odd place. I've learned that since we made the movie, it's been torn down and they're building a restaurant there.

Fangoria: What about the pit itself?

Gordon: Yeah, that pit was built. It was Llorenç taking this area with these pillars and so forth, and then adding this section of the mouth of the pit there. Then the actual pit itself was built on a stage. It was about a forty-foot-deep pit with a water tank at the bottom of it. So, it was actually two locations that we were able to combine through the magic of editing.

Fangoria: A lot of directors talk about how difficult it is to work in water and in rain, but you do both in this movie. Can you talk a little about the challenges of doing that and how you worked around it?

Gordon: Well, it was one of those things that sounded like a really good idea when we were writing the script. But as soon as we got into the reality of it, I was cursing myself for having agreed to this because it was really, really hard. Working on the water, especially the stuff we did with the sailboat, which was near a real reef, if the water got too rough, there was the possibility that the sailboat really would be wrecked. Since we had rented this sailboat for the movie, we couldn't let that happen. Our captain would say, "No, no! We can't get this close today. You're going to have to shoot something else." We were very dependent on the weather. There were some days when we would go out, and they'd be in the rubber inflatable raft, and the waves were so high it was like we were shooting *The Perfect Storm* [2000] or something. They were twenty feet up above us and then they'd be twenty feet below us. It was insane—and those were our actors! They weren't stunt doubles. The raft had been deflated, so it would look like it was losing air, but I started realizing how dangerous this was. I was about to call them in and they started *whooping* like they were on a rollercoaster ride. So, we kept on shooting.

Fangoria: Was all that material shot off the coast of Spain as well?

Gordon: Yeah, we shot in real water. The area where we shot a lot of the water sequences out on the ocean was in the Costa Brava, which is closer to Barcelona. Then we had to match it with the ocean that we found when we got to Galicia. When we got there, we discovered that it was one of the most rainy and stormy winters that they had ever had in that region. There were some days where we just couldn't shoot because the storms were too intense. Our sets were literally getting blown apart. It was very challenging, but we had to have the constant rain, so we had our own rain machine with us. What would always happen is that it would be pouring rain while we were setting up the shot and as soon as it was time to shoot, the rain would stop! Then we had to crank out our own rain to shoot with. So, everybody was always soaking wet and freezing cold because we shot this in December and January. It was a crazy thing to be doing. But Ezra Godden, who plays Paul, was such a great sport. He was so brave and stoic about it all—never complaining—so how could any of us complain? This was the guy who was in the worst situation. We all had to rise to the occasion as well.

Fangoria: How did you come to cast him and some of the other principals?

Gordon: You know, I looked all over the place for both him and Barbara. I cast here in LA; I cast in London; I cast in Spain. I found Ezra in London, he's actually British, and he'd been in *Band of Brothers* [2001], the HBO series. He just really had the quality [I needed], and I thought he brought a lot of comedy to the role. One of things he told me early on was that he's a huge fan of Harold Lloyd, the silent movie comic who's always hanging on the faces of clocks. I said, "What a great image for this guy. Why don't you play him as Harold Lloyd?" I guess that's when the glasses appeared. So, he came up with a lot of really funny business and physical comedy that was not written into the script. It was amazing. Raquel Meroño, who played Barbara, is a big Spanish television star. She's on a series there that's kind of like *Beverly Hills 90210*. She's very, very well-known. We couldn't walk down the street with her without people trying to get autographs. Originally, the role was written for an American, but I couldn't really find an actress that could play that part without making her seem like a ball-buster. She's a very take-charge kind of girl at the beginning of the movie. Raquel manages that with a great deal of good spirit, so you like her for it. She's strong and gutsy, but also fun. So, we rewrote the role to make her Spanish-speaking at some points.

Fangoria: Some of the costumes are very nautically inspired and looked like they may well have been forged beneath the deep by some Atlantean sort of tribe.

Gordon: Oh, you're talking about Macarena Gómez, the girl who plays Uxía. One of the elements that is in Lovecraft's story is the idea that there's these gold artifacts that are from this civilization from under the sea. We don't really show very much of this undersea world, so we had to suggest a lot with the design of these things, including things like Uxía's crown, the dagger that she uses, the chair that she sits in. Again, it was Rafael Garres who designed these things and he incorporated natural sea shapes. The crown that she wears is actually a form of seashell, the one with all the spikes on it. I guess it's some kind of weird sea anemone or something. So, he incorporated that into the design. What we wanted was a very otherworldly quality.

Fangoria: Was there any feeling of completing a trilogy of Lovecraft films by making *Dagon*?

Gordon: This is the third one that I've done with Brian, so the thing that was great was working with him again. I had worked with him in other capacities over the years, as a writer [on *The Dentist*] or as an executive producer on *Progeny*, but this was the first time since *From Beyond* that we worked together where I was the director, he was the producer, and Dennis Paoli was the writer. So, it was kind of a reunion of the group. It was quite wonderful. But it was a project, as I said, that we started a long time ago and to actually, finally, be able to make this movie after talking about it and dreaming about it for so long . . .

Fangoria: How has the three of y'all's relationship changed over the years?

Gordon: I think our relationship has stayed pretty much the same. We're all friends. Brian is great, because the thing is he's the opposite of your typical studio where they always try to tone everything down. Brian will keep saying, "I think you can make this a little bit weirder. Let's see if you can make this *more* bizarre. Is there some way to make this scarier? Is there some way we can make this *more* outrageous?" He challenges you. I always say we bring out the worst in each other.

Fangoria: So, he never puts any kind of restrictions on you?

Gordon: Oh, no, not at all. The only restrictions we had were time and money. The budget was what it was—which was about $3 million—and we had a certain amount of time to make the movie. There were some things that had to be cut, because we just could not afford to do some stuff that I thought was great. But we had to really decide what was essential to tell the story.

Fangoria: Since *Re-Animator*, you've been associated a great deal with Lovecraft. As people's regard for him has changed, has your opinion of him changed or the way you read his books?

Gordon: It's funny, because I've gotten to know his books pretty well and there are certain themes that keep coming through his writing. Someone recently gave me a book of letters that he wrote, which were very interesting—and kind of shocking in some ways. Lovecraft had many fears. He feared fish, for example, and hated them, which is a lot of the reason I think he wrote these stories. The most disgusting thing in the world to Lovecraft was a fish. But the second most disgusting thing to Lovecraft was a Jew. He was very anti-Semitic, which is what I was finding in these letters. If he was alive today, he'd be considered a white supremacist. He was on the side of Hitler when World War II was about to begin. That I found very shocking, because I'm Jewish myself and Lovecraft would probably have wanted nothing to do with me if he were alive today. But I think that the fear of *different people* is one of the things that run through his stories. The idea that people are different scared him. He was uncomfortable if anyone wasn't White Anglo-Saxon Protestant. A lot of his stories have to do with the intermingling of races, and in this one it's actually of species, and the idea of tainting the purity of the blood. He took these fears and turned them into fantastical stories. Although I'd probably want to have very little to do with this guy personally, his stories are so extraordinary. I think they are the scariest things ever written, because this is a man who took his fears and used them and channeled them into great storytelling.

Fangoria: Has there ever been any attempt to suppress his xenophobia or has it always been out there?

Gordon: I think the people who know Lovecraft *know*. I've heard comments about him being anti-Semitic before, but I never realized to what extent it was until I saw these letters. And then these letters were really [revealing that], you know, this guy was *completely* supporting the Nazi Party.

Fangoria: What is *King of the Ants*?

Gordon: *King of the Ants*, although it sounds like it should be a story about people turning into insects, is actually a *Reservoir Dogs*-esque crime story. It's based on a book by Charles Higson. It's about a housepainter who becomes a hitman, and where the title comes from is one time [some gangsters are out] to scare him. They say, "You're just an ant. We could *crush* you." And he says, "Well, I'll be King of the Ants, then."

Fangoria: Are you producing the film?

Gordon: I'm producing and directing it.

Fangoria: Is that in pre-production right now?

Gordon: It is. We've had a lot of good casting—Ron Livingston and George Wendt, Stacy Keach has just come on board; Nastassja Kinski is interested in playing one of the roles. So, it's turning into quite a project.

Fangoria: What about *Deathbed*?

Gordon: Yeah, *Deathbed*. We just finished shooting that. It's a small movie that I executive produced for Full Moon Entertainment and Charlie Band. It's a great script; a ghost story. I think the title says it all: it's a haunted bed, written by John Strysik, who is a big Lovecraft aficionado. He was one of the writers of a book called *The Lurker in the Lobby* [2000, Wizard's Attic], which is a book about all the Lovecraft movies that have been made. That's how I met John.

Fangoria: What's the storyline of *Deathbed*?

Gordon: It's about a young couple who move into a loft and discover, hidden away, is an old antique bed. What they don't realize is this bed was used by a serial killer at the turn of the century, and the spirits of the victims still haunt it, and it starts having an effect on the two of them. They start having these strange dreams, the ghosts actually start appearing to them as the victims cry out for help. It's a classic ghost story—very scary! We've got a terrific young actress named Tanya Dempsey playing the lead role. I'm real pleased with it. Danny Draven, who's been working with Charlie, directed it, and he did an incredible job.

Fangoria: What made you want to take this project to Charlie Band, as it's been a little while since you've worked together? What was it about *Deathbed* that screamed out that it would work well at Full Moon Entertainment?

Gordon: You know what it was? It was meeting Danny Draven. He came to my office a couple of months ago. He said he always wanted to meet me and he brought me some of his films. I looked at them and they were pretty good. I asked him about them, and he told me that they had been shot in like eight days on digital video and that he had basically created a studio in his apartment building. He has one guy doing the sound work in one apartment, one guy doing the music in another, and so forth. They just [worked] from apartment to apartment, assembling the movie. That seemed so amazing to me, and he was so full of energy and excitement, I just got very intrigued by the whole thing. I had this script, which was very contained. Most of the story takes place in this one location in the loft, and I realized that this could be done in that manner. So, I got the script to Charlie, who said, in typical Charles Band manner, "Wow, I can't believe I've never thought of this title!" Charlie always thinks of the title first. When I did *Castle Freak*, there was a poster in his office. I walked in and it just said *Castle Freak*, and looked like Quasimodo was whipping a girl tied to a wall or something. I said, "What's the story?" He said, "I don't know. There's a castle and there's a freak." So, we sat there, and Charlie said, "I've had *Death* in so many titles, but I've never thought of *Death-bed*." The thing about working with Charlie is there's no such thing as development. Most movies take forever to get made, but Charlie said, "Let's make it!" A week later, we were shooting it. It was unbelievable! We shot the movie in two weeks and cut it in two weeks. Post will be finished in a couple of weeks.

Fangoria: Because of the new technology these days, you really can shoot a movie in eight days...

Gordon: I know. It was amazing to me. We did *Deathbed* in nine days. We actually went one day over. To me, it's the fastest—you know, *Re-Animator* was shot in eighteen days, so that was twice as long—but I think it all really relates to the material, to the script. There are some scripts that, yes, you can do quickly. There's a joke that Charlie Band and I would always have with each other. He would come up to me and say, "Stuart, how long is a movie?" I'd say, "It's about ninety minutes." He'd say, "How long is a day?" I'd say, "Twenty-four hours." He'd say, "Then you should be able to make two or three movies a day."

Fangoria: With such a swift pre-production on *Deathbed*, how did you find a bed that quickly, one that would be perfect as the title character in the movie?

Gordon: This movie was kind of blessed in a strange way. In a lot of ways, I have to give credit to John Strysik, because it turned out that one of his best friends collected antique beds. As soon as we started working on it, he emailed me a photograph of the bed that we ended up using in the movie, which has this very interesting, circular design headboard that was actually made in the 1890s. There's something about it that is very ghostly, so that was great. One of the other things that happened was the guy we had cast to be the serial killer ghost didn't show up when his day of shooting came. We were all sitting there like, "Hey, Stuart, do you want to play this part?" We didn't know what to do and then [John] got on the phone. He had a friend who was this crazy performance artist named Dukey Flyswatter [real name Michael David Sonye]. Dukey, I guess, has been in several horror films, and John went, "I don't know why I never thought of calling him before." Dukey just came down to the set and, suddenly, he was *in* the movie. He ended up being the best ghost in the movie. He's got a great face. We didn't have to do much in the way of makeup on him. He's a pretty intense-looking character. He kind of looks like Mr. Hyde or something. He was really great and gave a fantastic performance. I hope that *Deathbed* is successful so that there are sequels and maybe Dukey can be the next Freddy Krueger.

Fangoria: When is *Deathbed* going to hit?

Gordon: It's funny, because I just read in *Fangoria* that it'll be available in August.

Fangoria: How do you feel about not being involved in *Beyond Re-Animator*? At AFM [American Film Market], they had the new poster and all that, but then Jeffrey Combs also claimed he hasn't signed anything quite yet.

Fangoria: Yeah. When Brian made *Bride of Re-Animator*, I stayed out of it and I'm doing the same on this one. But I'm always there. As a friend of Brian's, if he has an idea he wants to run past me or show me a script and ask for suggestions, I'm always happy to help.

Fangoria: Do you want to stick with horror? After hearing what *King of the Ants* is about, that kind of answers that question.

Gordon: Yeah. It's not necessarily horror, but it is horrifying. There are some really *horrifying* sequences in that movie. Nobody uses a gun in that film. It's almost like on the Neanderthal level—there's a lot of bludgeoning. As a matter of fact, one person gets killed by having a refrigerator dropped on him. So, there's definitely some horrifying moments in it. I would call it horror, but not in your conventional, supernatural sort of way. I like to do other things as well. I think if you do the same things over and over again, you start getting into a rut and it's always good artistically to vary it as much as you can. I love horror, and I'm certainly going to be doing a lot of it, and coming back to it again and again.

Fangoria: What excites you these days? What are you looking for? I thought *Dagon* was an exciting movie.

Gordon: To me, I think the most important thing is a good story; something that really grabs you and has twists and turns that you don't see coming. So many of the movies that you see nowadays, you know everything that's going to happen within about five minutes. Those I get kind of tired of. What I like about projects like *Dagon* is that it is very different. It doesn't go where you think it's going to go. The ending is completely unexpected. *King of the Ants* is the same way. It doesn't play by the rules. That I always find interesting.

Fangoria: So much of your earlier movies have been at the forefront of miniature effects, yet in *Dagon* there's a lot more done with computers. Are you embracing that kind of technology or does it go from project to project?

Gordon: I think of it [this way]: they're all tools. The stuff you can do with computers is great, and I thought I'd hate to rely entirely on computers. What I tried to do with *Dagon* was do as much of it physically as I possibly could, to have it really right there, to have the actors to relate to. But when we couldn't, it became a digital effect. Originally, the whole sequence in the beginning of the film, where they discover the pit at the bottom of the ocean, I'd assumed it would be a miniature that we were going to have to use for that. But then the computer guys said, "We can do all this stuff. You don't have to build this." So, that was an eye-opener.

Fangoria: When do you think *King of the Ants* will hit?

Gordon: *King of the Ants* starts shooting in July, so it will probably be out next year.

Fangoria: Are you thinking of something beyond *Ants*? Something you might have in development?

Gordon: Oh, sure. We're always developing lots of things. We've got another Lovecraft script that Dennis Paoli wrote that I'd love to do. It's called *Envy*, and it's based on the Lovecraft short story "The Thing on the Doorstep" [written in August 1933, first published in January 1937]. It's a great project. We're working on a couple of other Lovecraft stories as well. I've got a Japanese project that I've been wanting to make for a long time called *Bug Lady*. So, there's still a file cabinet full of scripts that are next for me.

King of the Ants: It's No Picnic

Mark Wheaton / 2003

From *Fangoria*, no. 225 (August 2003), pp. 30–34. This is the first time the interview has been published in its unexpurgated form. Reprinted by permission.

"In *King of the Ants*, we've got everything from a golf club to a refrigerator," says director Stuart Gordon about the various weapons used to beat the hell out of people in his new gore-soaked film project. "We have sledge hammers, axes, gasoline—they pour gasoline on a guy and throw matches at him. The T-Rex tooth was a last-minute improvisation. In the book, the guy is hit with weights from a scale in the kitchen, but what we had come up with didn't really work for that. In the house we were shooting in, the guy collected Inca and Aztec pottery, things like that, and I thought, 'Wouldn't it be interesting if he got hit with that?' So, I asked them to find some stuff and one of the things they brought in was a T-Rex tooth from the museum. I thought it was really great because she hangs onto it and it looks like a hammer. I would say that tooth is about nine or ten inches long. The base is fossilized also as part of the jaw, so it's like a hammer. That was the change that we made."

Yes, Gordon is back with a new bloody-as-hell movie that, despite its buggy title, is *not* about giant ants eating their way through a small community. Instead, *King of the Ants* is a vicious, no-holds-barred thriller about a down-on-his-luck housepainter named Sean Crawley, who gets drawn into a world of crime when he's drunkenly offered $13,000 to kill a man. He does the job, and then finds out that not only will the guys who ordered the hit not pay him, they want to spend a week bashing his head in to make him a vegetable. Not unexpectedly, this doesn't sit well with Crawley, and this "ordinary housepainter" comes back to make everyone pay. The film stars George Wendt, Daniel Baldwin, Kari Wuhrer, Vernon Wells, Ron Livingston, and newcomer Chris L. McKenna as Crawley, the "King of the Ants."

"The title comes from the fact that at one time, when they're trying to scare Crawley, they show him an ant colony and they say, 'That's what you are—you're an ant and if we wanted to, we could just crush you,'" explains Gordon, talking to *Fango* on a park bench just off Sunset Boulevard near an editing studio where he's putting the finishing touches on the movie. "While they're beating the shit out of him, he's thinking, 'Well, he said I was an ant—an ant is tough, an ant has a skeleton on the outside, an ant is *strong*, and this ant is going to come back and get you guys for this! I'm King of the Ants!'"

Gordon, coming off one of the best horror films of last year—*Dagon*—has been developing *King of the Ants* for many years, since actor Wendt brought him the book on the set of *Space Truckers*. Written by British comedian Charles Higson, a veteran actor/writer on *The Fast Show*, *Randall and Hopkirk (Deceased)*, and other such programs, the hard-edged novel really appealed to Gordon, and even though it strictly isn't horror, he knew he wanted to turn it into a film.

"It was an incredible read—one of those books you just can't put down," says Gordon. "I talked to Charlie about adapting and Americanizing it, because the book is set in London. We worked with him for a year on the script, going through various drafts, making changes and tightening things up. He was great about it because—being involved in writing TV shows—he knows that you can't preserve everything from the novel. I was amazed at how brave the adaptation is, because he completely dumped entire sections of [his book]. Most novelists are married to everything they've written, and he was the opposite. He was really good about re-thinking it all in cinema terms. I think, in a lot of ways, we ended up strengthening the story with some of the changes that we made. I showed it to Dennis Hopper when we were working on *Space Truckers* and he said it was the best script he'd ever read. I asked him if he'd be in it and he said, 'No, man, I want to *direct* it!' The material is very compelling, strong stuff. You never know what's going to happen next."

King of the Ants might not have been a bestseller, but it did launch Higson's career as a novelist and led to the publication of three more of his hardboiled crime thrillers. All of them involve dirty deeds taking place in low-class situations but, interestingly enough, virtually no one ever gets shot. "People are murdered [in the books] with all kinds of blunt instruments, and *King of the Ants* is no exception," Gordon says. "I think there's one gun in the whole movie, and it fires two shots that don't hit anybody.

"The thing about a gun is that it can be really impersonal," he continues. "You pull the trigger and suddenly the person is dead. The way it's shown in movies, there's not even any blood. When you kill someone with a blunt instrument, it's personal, it's immediate, and you're face to face with that person when you do it—and, oftentimes, it doesn't work right away. You have to keep doing it and if there's a head injury, there's tons of blood. It's very caveman-like violence—disturbing violence."

Though he's the dispenser of mayhem for much of the movie, Crawley receives the most savage beating in the picture which takes place over the course of a week, when the bad guys—torturing him for killing a man they claim they didn't really want dead—decide to render him literally senseless rather than simply execute him. They take him out to the desert, wrap his head in foam to "avoid leaving too many marks" and proceed to lay into him with a golf club, day in, day out. When they're done, Crawley has been beaten virtually unrecognizable, into something out of a horror film . . . or, well, a Stuart Gordon movie.

"It really does change the way you perceive yourself, and the way you feel after looking at yourself in the mirror, at just how crappy you look," admits actor McKenna, who suffered through two-hour long daily stints in the makeup chair for a week to perfect his new post-golf-club smackdown visage. "It's amazing how easy it is to pretend you're all beaten up. I was really impressed by the prosthetics and the whole effects department on this film. They did an incredible job."

As Gordon was looking for that right "combination of innocence and toughness" in an actor to play Crawley, McKenna—who has been acting since age seven—put himself through a different kind of regimen to prepare for the role, which was awarded to him only twenty-two hours before the start of shooting, following a lengthy, six-month audition process. "I became pretty obsessed with it," says McKenna, who for part of the shoot was made to run bloody and battered through the desert in his underwear for hours on end. "I stopped working out, stopped dieting, and started letting myself go the best I could, which is not par for the course.

"Sean Crawley is a bit of a twisted person," McKenna continues. "He's bored, he's compulsive, but if you get to know him, he's not a bad guy at all—he simply doesn't have anything else going in his life, and when this opportunity comes along, he grabs it not knowing why. The character goes through such a transition in the movie. He's asked to kill somebody, but when he goes to do it, it just reads so real and it's painfully true, the way a person would react to killing a stranger."

With such a difficult role, even Gordon admits that it was a hard character to wrap his head around, particularly when it came to placing the audience on the side of a man who offs person after person. "I couldn't understand for years why it was that he's doing all these terrible things, but you still like him and care about him and are on his side," the director says. "But it's because it's about a guy finding himself. There's ultimately something positive about it.

"We had some big name actors who wanted to play the lead because it's a great role," continues Gordon. "Then they'd talk to their agents and their agents would talk them out of it. This happened at least a half a dozen times. I'd have meetings with these people and they'd be so excited about it and couldn't wait to start. They knew that there was no money because we were doing it at such a low budget, but then all of a sudden they'd talk to their agent and I'd never hear from them again. I think it was because of the violence. They were worried about the image of their clients and so forth. It takes some really brave actors to do it—people who are willing to take chances and risks."

The job of turning McKenna into the battered Crawley as well as creating the other numerous gore and, yes, creature effects on the movie went to Optic Nerve Studios, run by John Vulich, a longtime Gordon collaborator who first worked with the director when he was John Carl Buechler's assistant on 1987's *Dolls*. His other makeup effects credits for Gordon include *Castle Freak* and, in a lucky coincidence, some of the stuff on *Space Truckers*.

"[Vulich] did the square pigs and the robot woman whose head folds back, so he did a lot of great stuff," says Gordon. "One of the other things he did for *Space Truckers* was a dummy of George Wendt that was used when a window gets blown out by a gunshot and his whole body gets sucked through the hole. So, he had built George Wendt already. We knew in *King of the Ants* that we had to behead him, so it was like, 'Do you think we can use that George Wendt again?'"

Body prosthetics weren't all that Vulich was called on to build. As Crawley falls deeper and deeper into dementia brought on by the severe noggin-beating, he begins fantasizing about the wife of the man he first killed, Eric Gatley (Livingston). Coinciding with his newfound identity as the "King of the Ants," Crawley begins to imagine Gatley's wife, Susan (Wuhrer), in the guise of a giant maggot-monster, which was one of the more elaborate effects created by Vulich and his team. However, as Gordon jokes, some of the artist's recent jobs didn't exactly mesh with how far the director wanted to push the envelope on *Ants*.

"There was one gag where a guy takes a big chomp out of another guy's neck," he laughs. "I wanted to have blood showering out of him, which is probably what would happen. The guy came on set and the blood squirted out, but it wasn't what I wanted. I wanted it to be a real explosion of blood. I was kidding John, because his company had been working on *Buffy the Vampire Slayer* and *The X-Files*, and I said, 'You've been doing TV too long, man! I'm going to tell George Romero on you!'

"John built the maggot-monster, but I don't want to give too much of it away because it's really bizarre. The monster is tame compared to the other stuff they did. All of the gore in this movie is considerable and the great thing about Optic Nerve is that their stuff is very anatomically accurate. They get into all of the details and every time I go over there, Vulich is showing me some forensic text book that I can only look at a couple of pages of before I get sick. He uses all this stuff and it's very realistic."

With a film as extreme as *King of the Ants*, Gordon found it a hard row to hoe when looking for financing, which eventually came together through the indie house The Asylum. Financers simply couldn't accept a movie as graphically violent as *King of the Ants*, particularly where the lead character is committing the brutal acts. Some potential money people went so far as to suggest that the lead character's "brother had been murdered" at some point to "justify" Crawley's killing spree, but Gordon held true to his vision and made the movie he wanted to make.

"When I tell people about this, I say, 'Look at *The Godfather* [1972],'" he explains. "*The Godfather* is about a guy becoming the head of the Mafia. He's a murderer and you like him and want him to succeed—but the killings in that movie are very disturbing. I believe there's a similarity. The movie I kept coming back to on this one was *Psycho*. It's the most disturbing movie ever made. It was so disturbing that Hitchcock couldn't get the studio to produce it. They couldn't come up with the money. They thought it was too weird, too far gone, so Hitchcock ended up using his own money to produce *Psycho* at Universal, which is why it's in black and white, and there are no big stars in it like Jimmy Stewart or Cary Grant. He used his own money, he used his TV crew, and they shot the movie in twenty-two or twenty-four days, something like that. They shot on a very tight schedule and shot very fast. It's one of his greatest movies because he breaks so many rules."

Like Hitchcock, Gordon had around twenty-two days for his own shoot when *King of the Ants* went into production during late summer 2002. Gordon and Wendt both originally wanted to film the movie in their hometown of Chicago, where gangsterism and construction companies go hand in hand. However, after checking out some of the new local incentives around Los Angeles, the script was rewritten for Southern California.

"We started shooting on August 10 and had a four-week shoot," Gordon recalls. "We filmed all over the place because there's this new thing called California First where you're able to use things owned by the state, so we shot downtown at City Hall, on skid row, at a real homeless shelter, a dog pound, a zoo. The last night, we shot on a subway—they gave us our own train, which was fantastic! We are one of the first to take advantage of it. It's great. You're able to use all of these wonderful locations for free."

Though the creatures in *King of the Ants* are imaginary, Gordon still believes that the film's savage violence places it squarely in the fright genre. "When you've got so much mayhem in it, it's a horror movie," Gordon says. "The violence is really down and dirty. There's as much blood and guts in it as in any *Friday the 13th* film. It has all these hallucinations and monsters and, really, what is a horror film? It's something that's horrifying and this book, this script, and this movie are all horrifying."

Of course, those are hardly the ratings board's favorite words. "My biggest fear with this movie is the MPAA," he admits. "[*Ants*] is really disturbing, and we're pushing things pretty far. But the interesting thing is that with *Dagon*, they didn't ask for a single cut. I think if they like the movie, they're more open to letting it stand as it is. But all of the murder sequences in *King of the Ants* are really horrific—every single one of them—beginning with the murder of the accountant where Crawley starts with blunt instruments that don't seem to be working, and finally finishes by pushing the refrigerator over on top of him, crushing him. When we shot that, everybody in the room couldn't believe how horrific it was to see that happening."

As has been mentioned before, Gordon is a busy, busy man. He's currently set to produce Dave (*The Dead Hate the Living!*) Parker's film adaptation of Chas. Balun's novel *Director's Cut*, but is also trying to work up a new H. P. Lovecraft adaptation with his frequent collaborator, screenwriter Dennis Paoli, called *Envy*, based on the story "The Thing on the Doorstep." On top of that, as was recently announced at *Fango*'s Burbank Weekend of Horrors convention, Gordon hopes to bring the controversial David Mamet play *Edmond* to the screen with actor Lionel Mark Smith, who has acted in a number of Mamet-directed movies and plays Carl in *King of the Ants*.

"I've been trying to get this thing going involving a line of my own movies where I would produce them all, but I would direct every third one or so and get my friends involved in directing some of the other ones—people who have a lot of ability," Gordon says. "They'd be small movies, but they would not pull punches."

As for what's next on his plate to direct, Gordon himself isn't quite sure which will go first. "I've got a couple of things that I'm working on, but you're never certain until you're doing them, which is how it usually works out. The thing that's kind of cool is that both *King of the Ants* and *Dagon* were scripts that I'd been trying to get made for a long time. It's hard for me to believe that they're actually done now."

Though Gordon is famous for not making follow-ups to his own films, don't rule out seeing another installment of *King of the Ants* sometime in the future. "I've been kidding Charlie now that he should write a sequel to *King of the Ants*," Gordon says. "He said he'd been thinking about it, so maybe there will be one."

Screamography: Stuart Gordon

Tony Timpone / 2006

From the series *Screamography*. Transcribed by the editor and reprinted by permission.

Stuart Gordon: You know, Billy Wilder had the best line of all . . . people would come up to him and say, "What's your favorite movie?" and he would say, "My next one."

Narrator: When your body of work is as eclectic as writer-director Stuart Gordon's, it's easy to see why he would be pretty psyched for what lies ahead, because you know it's going to be something unconventional. This is Stuart Gordon, in his words, told to *Fangoria*'s Tony Timpone. This is his *Screamography*.

Gordon: When I was growing up in Chicago, my parents would not allow me to see horror films. So, of course, I had to see as many of them as I possibly could. They were afraid that they would give me nightmares—and they were right, they *did*. I would have terrible nightmares. It's very embarrassing to say that the very first movie that scared me was called *Abbott and Costello Meet Dr. Jekyll and Mr. Hyde*. I had nightmares for about three years after I saw that movie.

Narrator: It's hard to believe this is the same man that went on to direct *Re-Animator*. Wanting to entertain people is something Gordon wanted to do from an early age. In high school, he got bit by the theater bug and met longtime writing partner Dennis Paoli.

Gordon: Dennis and I met each other in high school, and we went to Lane Technical High School in Chicago. We formed a comedy group that was called the Human Race, and this was when we were just sort of in our senior year in high school. We actually got paid to perform at clubs and stuff, and I think we ended up losing one of our jobs because Dennis got a little too drunk and like fell off the stage at one of the performances. But what we were doing was not really stand-up comedy; it was more kind of like skit comedy—very influenced by the Second City, which is also based in Chicago. So, I had the theater bug for a long time.

Narrator: Gordon's passion for performance art would stick with him through his time at the University of Wisconsin. Always a fan of pushing the envelope, one of his plays, a psychedelic retelling of *Peter Pan*, even got him arrested.

Gordon: We did this production back in 1968, and we were making a political statement, kind of equating *Peter Pan*—using *Peter Pan*—as a way to frame what was going on at the time. That was the year of the Democratic Convention in Chicago, where there was all of the police attacking the protestors who were protesting against the war in Vietnam. So, in our production, Peter Pan and the Lost Boys are all hippies and yippies, and Captain Hook was Mayor Daley, and the police were the pirates. We had one sequence in it where they are going to fly off to Neverland—and we didn't change any of James Barrie's language—they say, "Well, just think lovely thoughts and up you go." So, we had them say those lines as they were dropping acid. (Chuckles) And the sequence we sort of got into trouble for was the trip to Neverland, which was a psychedelic dance sequence with a lightshow projected on the naked bodies of seven women dancers, and because of the nudity, the police came in and arrested us all.

Narrator: But there was a brighter side: he met wife and favorite leading lady, Carolyn Purdy.

Gordon: She was one of the seven dancers in the production of *Peter Pan*, and so once you get arrested with someone, I think it's a bond that lasts forever. (Laughs)

Narrator: College and run-ins with the law behind him, Gordon went on to form his own theater company, the Organic.

Gordon: Yeah, I did the first professional production of David Mamet's work, *Sexual Perversity in Chicago*, and he was just a young playwright at the time, who—every week—would come in with a new script, and say, "Stuart, you've got to read this! It's going to win the Pulitzer Prize!" And I'd say, "Yeah, right, David, sure." (Chuckles) And about three years later he *did* win the Pulitzer Prize.

Tony Timpone: That was a pretty amazing collaboration and meeting . . .

Gordon: It was.

Timpone: . . . launching both of your careers pretty much.

Gordon: It was a pretty exciting time to be in Chicago, because at the same time that we were doing our theater—and in my theater company, I had Joe Mantegna and Dennis Franz and André De Shields, I mean incredible actors. John Heard was [also] in our theater company. And then the Steppenwolf Company was there as well, with [John] Malkovich and Gary Sinise and Joan Allen; and at the Second City were John Belushi and Bill Murray. I mean, everyone was all there at the same time. It was incredibly exciting, and David Mamet just starting out, and William H. Macy, and I could go on and on . . . William Peterson . . . just an extraordinary time.

Narrator: Spending well over a decade working in theater, Gordon found his way into filmmaking when he was reintroduced to the work of an author that had captivated him as a child: H. P. Lovecraft.

Gordon: I thought I had read most of Lovecraft, when I met this friend, we were talking about horror movies one day—this was when I was still doing theater—and I was saying, "It's too bad someone doesn't do a new *Frankenstein* movie. They are the ones doing all these vampire pictures." She said, "Well, have you ever read 'Herbert West—Re-Animator?'" I had never heard of the story, I had never even seen it, and I was curious. So, I started looking around for it and I couldn't find it anywhere. I finally went to the Chicago Public Library and it turned out they had a copy of it, but it was in their special collections. I had to fill out a little postcard, and they sent it back to me and invited me to the library to come and read it. I couldn't take it out of the library. When I got there, it was like that scene in *Citizen Kane*, they sort of walked me into this room and they brought out this book and put it in front of me. It was a pulp magazine from the period, from the [1920s], and it was literally crumbling as I was turning the pages. I asked the librarian, I said, "Could I just xerox this, because I'm afraid that it's going to be destroyed?" and she let me do that. You know, Lovecraft wrote it as a serial, six little installments, and reading it, I thought, "Wow, this would make a great movie." Although, actually, to be truthful, I thought it would make a great TV series! (Laughs)

Narrator: Gordon pitched his idea to PBS with whom he had developed a relationship through his theater work. They passed, but Gordon quickly found hope with producer Brian Yuzna. The challenge now? How could Stuart Gordon bring his ambitious vision of Lovecraft's story to life with a tight budget and an even tighter shooting schedule?

Gordon: We used just about every trick in the book to make that film. The thing that was really kind of amazing is that there were no exteriors in the entire movie. Everything was shot on location, but it was all indoors. We never had to go outside, so there were no permits that were required for anything. It was after the film was finished that I think Brian looked at the movie, and said, "I think we need a couple of establishing shots of these places, just to sort of get a sense that there actually is a world out there."

Narrator: And what better way to get your actors into the spirit of a movie about the undead than taking them to the morgue.

Gordon: One of the things I like to do—and I did this in theater all the time—is do as much research as possible, and to go to actual places whenever I could. I called them "field trips." So, for *Re-Animator*, what I did was take all of the actors to the LA County Morgue to meet the pathologists there and actually to look at the bodies, and to get a sense of what it actually is like to be around—working—with dead people all the time. That freaked out several of the crewmembers and cast members, but it was a really important thing, I think, because it gave the whole movie a reality. Everyone could really—after they had been there—it wasn't this fantastical story anymore. They had to approach it as if it were really happening to them and so seeing the reality was a great thing. It also, I think, helped—everyone always talks about the very black comedy in the movie and where that comes from to a large degree is the pathologists themselves. You know, because if you are working in a morgue, you better have a good sense of humor, and it's a pretty sick sense of humor that you develop when you're working *there*.

Narrator: Working at breakneck speed also had consequences Gordon didn't count on . . .

Gordon: I remember the last day of shooting. Brian said, "We cannot go an extra day." So, it was literally a twenty-four-hour shoot. We never stopped shooting, and we got to the end of it and had finished the scene and I left the soundstage. Luckily, my wife, Carolyn, was there, because when I was driving back—we were staying at a hotel—my eyes stopped working. (Chuckles) I was on the freeway and, all of a sudden, I couldn't see. I was *blind*! I'm like driving the car and I could not [see] and it was like . . . you know, you get to a point, there's a total overload and they just sort of stopped working. I was able to pull over, luckily, and she took over and got us back. But it was absolutely insane.

Narrator: But good things come to those who almost go blind due to stress. Gordon's film went on to win the Critics' Prize at the Cannes Film Festival—no easy feat for a first-time movie director.

Gordon: It absolutely amazed me that it won that prize—and, it's funny, I didn't realize what that prize was until about a year or two ago. Someone explained it to me, what it was, because I couldn't understand. How could it win a prize because it wasn't in competition? The movie was shown at the market at Cannes and how could it win a Critics' Prize? It turned out that what the Critics' Prize is, for any movie that is shown in Cannes, whether it's in competition or not, and so the critics felt that *Re-Animator* was the best movie of that year, in 1985, of all the films shown at Cannes, which is really quite an incredible award. I had assumed that the critics would hate the movie. Originally, the movie was supposed to have been produced with the Organic Theatre Company, and even the board of the Organic Theatre refused to have anything to do with it. They said, "We don't want our name on *this*." So, I ended up taking a leave of absence from the theater and coming to LA, and directing it here. So, I assumed—I was hoping—my only goal was for the fans to enjoy it, and I just wrote off the critics. I think that turned out to be a good thing, because once you stop being worried about that stuff, it just sort of frees you up in a way.

Narrator: After the critical success of *Re-Animator*, Gordon was hired by legendary horror producer Charles Band for a three-picture deal that involved relocating his family to Italy. One of those films, 1986's *From Beyond*, was another adaptation of a H. P. Lovecraft story. In keeping with Gordon's no-holds barred approach to violence and sexuality, it wasn't long before he ran afoul of the MPAA.

Gordon: I requested a meeting with the MPAA and went in and talked to this lady and she started scolding me. It was like getting called to the principal's office. She was going [Gordon wags his finger sternly], "What were you thinking when you did this movie? What did you *think* we would say?" (Chuckles) She was talking about this one sequence where Jeffrey Combs is sucking Carolyn Purdy-Gordon's eyeball out of [its] socket, and then sucking her brain through her skull, and she said, "And here you are, with this disgusting idea, and the camera doesn't just stay there! The camera is pushing in, and pushing in, and pushing in! What were you thinking?" You know, it was like, [Gordon speaks in a *pleading* voice] "*I'm sorry, I'm sorry! Just give me an R rating!*" (Laughs) So, they really did a hatchet job on that movie. I mean, we had to cut almost, I think, five minutes of material out of the film. Then, when people started doing these director's cuts, people would come to me and say, "Can you put back in those minutes that the MPAA made you cut out?" And I went looking for them and I couldn't find them.

Narrator: But, twenty years later, Gordon's original cut will finally get to see the light of day.

Gordon: MGM, who now has the movie, called me up and they said, "We've found this film can with some trims in it. Could you come down and take a look at them and tell us what these are?" And it was all of the stuff that the MPAA had cut out—all of that "pushing in and pushing in!" (Chuckles) Now, we are going to restore the film and, hopefully, we'll be bringing out the unrated *From Beyond*.

Narrator: One of Gordon's next projects would get him back on the good side of the MPAA, an opportunity to direct a family movie that he and longtime collaborator Brian Yuzna were developing for Disney: *Honey, I Shrunk the Kids*.

Gordon: Well, I think that to Brian and me, *Honey, I Shrunk the Kids* is a horror film. (Laughs) You know, we never said we left horror; *it's* a horror movie. It's about a mad scientist who has this experiment that goes completely wrong that ends up turning his children into tiny little things. So, we have giant insects running around, and giant ants and giant bees. I mean, is this much different than *Starship Troopers* [1997], really, or *King Kong* [2005]? Those were the images that were in our minds. These little kids going through the blades of grass was like the guys in *King Kong* on Skull Island and these gigantic prehistoric monsters were things like an ant, or an ant colony, or a beetle, or whatever; and the idea that if you did the movie in a different way, it could be a very terrifying film.

It was interesting, when I was working on it at Disney, they were very nervous about it, because at one point, at one of the creative meetings, I said, "If this really happened, these kids would probably be dead in about two hours. If they were left in that world, which is probably more dangerous than the Amazon Jungle, if you dropped three or four little kids off in the Amazon Jungle they'd be dead in probably an hour." So, the Disney brass then started going, "You are *not* going to kill these kids! We cannot let you kill the kids in this movie!" I said, "Well, no, I'm not going to kill the kids, but I want the audience to think that they could die. I think there should be this sense of danger in this movie; there should be this fear. That's where the tension comes from: that these kids are in danger."

Narrator: But there were bigger stresses in the land of Disney than worries over the fate of the film's young leads.

Gordon: What happened was they were so nervous about this—and, again, it sounds amazing now to think about this—but this was when Michael Eisner had just taken over Disney. This is when this happened. The background on it was that the previous regime had run the studio into the ground making these bad family films. And so Eisner and his guys said, "Family films are death. We do not want to make any family films. We are not making *any* family films." They were even considering changing the name of the studio from Disney to Touchstone.

Timpone: Wow!

Gordon: And they decided they weren't going to make any animated cartoons either. I mean, it's amazing to believe. People don't believe this, but it's really true. It was Roy Disney who finally insisted that they continue to make the cartoons, and they said, "Alright, if you want to do it, then *you* do it." That's sort of what they said. So, he took on the animation division and when we pitched them this idea, they were so nervous about making a family movie. As a matter of fact, the weekend that *Honey, I Shrunk the Kids* opened, Jeffrey Katzenberg was interviewed in the *New York Times*, and he said, "*Honey, I Shrunk the Kids* is not a family film." (Chuckles) He was trying to sort of equate it with like *E.T.* [1982] or something, which *is* a family film, by the way. He said, "We're appealing to the child in the adults," it was some nonsense like that, but he was saying, "It is not a family film. No, no, no!" So, I was going up against this all the time with these guys, and it got to the point where the stress levels just got really out of control. I had a meeting with one of the executives once, and I got a nosebleed in the middle of the meeting. But it wasn't just a nosebleed that trickled down your face—the blood went *shooting* out of my nose onto his desk! (Laughs) He like *jumped* back! I mean, it was like something out of *The Exorcist* [1973]. I went home and told my wife what had happened, and she said, "You better see a doctor. That doesn't sound good." You know, she's Nurse Purdy. So, the doctor took my blood pressure and he said, "Holy smokes! You gotta take a break. You're not going . . ." It was one of those things where this was a big opportunity for me, and I didn't want to let go of it. But it was one of those things where, finally, I called my agent and I said, "What should I do? If I drop out of this movie, will I ever work again?" And he said, "Well, I don't know if you will, but I do know that dead directors do not work at all." (Laughs) So, that was what happened.

Timpone: Was that the hardest day of your professional life, when you had to make that decision—giving up this amazing opportunity [to do] this big-budget movie for Disney?

Gordon: It was really big. I think back now, and it's funny, *Honey, I Shrunk the Kids* was on like last week, and I was sitting there watching it. I hadn't seen it in a long time and it was bringing back all of these memories. The thing that was interesting was that they ended up using . . . I mean, I had storyboarded the whole movie, they had built all the sets, I had hired all of the people, the DP, everybody was like *there*, and I had to drop out about two weeks before it was supposed to start shooting. So, the movie, essentially—I mean, they made some changes—but I would say that 90 percent of it was exactly as I had laid it out. I keep thinking if I had made that movie, how would it have changed my life? I would have been making big studio pictures rather than making smaller films. But things happen for a reason. That's kind of the way I ended up at least justifying it to myself, and I'm not unhappy with the direction that I've gone. It could have been that if I had made that movie, the movies I would have ended up making wouldn't have been as fun or as interesting as the ones I have.

Narrator: And fun and interesting movies are what Stuart Gordon continued to write and direct, ranging from a remake of Edgar Allan Poe's "The Pit and the Pendulum" to 1996's camp horror favorite *The Dentist*, starring Corbin Bernsen. In 2005, Gordon reunited with some old friends from his theater days in Chicago to direct a movie whose horror stems not from the world of undead zombies or science fiction fantasy, but a harsh dose of reality: David Mamet's *Edmond*.

Gordon: *Edmond*, again, was one of those un-makeable projects. It was one of those scripts that had been around for fifteen years—longer actually, twenty years—that nobody wanted to do, because it really pushes all kinds of buttons. The thing that I think really freaks people out the most about it is that the main character is a racist, and so there are these like diatribes in it that are just absolutely horrific in that regard. It's, again, one of those stories that just goes places that you're not expecting. I don't want to give too much away about it, because the ending is very shocking and surprising. So, nobody wanted to do it, and the way that that movie ended up getting financed was by having a dozen—literally, a dozen—tiny companies band together to finance it. It's so funny, when a movie is shown and the companies are listed, it gets a laugh there are so many of them. But the thing about it is that David Mamet wrote the screenplay, it is one of the . . .

I think I'll say it's my favorite Mamet piece. His writing is brilliant, and the actors all responded to it. As much as the financiers were terrified of it, the actors embraced it and so we ended up with this incredible cast: William H. Macy playing Edmond; Julia Stiles, playing the girl that he murders; Mena Suvari; Joe Mantegna; Denise Richards. I mean, it's an incredible cast. We shot the whole thing in sixteen days. It was shot actually in less time than when we shot *Re-Animator*, because we had so little money. But everybody worked so hard. We actually rehearsed for a month before we started shooting and the performances are incredible. The thing that was such fun about it was just being on the set watching Macy work and everyone working with him. Everybody was at the top of their games. People always come up to me, and they say, "Was this more difficult than doing a horror film?" I say, "No, it was so much easier." There are no prosthetics really to speak of—I mean, there are some but not much. I said, "All I had to do was point the camera in their direction and that was about it," and it's really true. We showed it at the Venice Film Festival, it had its premiere there, and the audience just absolutely flipped. We had a fifteen-minute standing ovation at that first screening. The next day, I was being interviewed by all of these journalists there and they were saying things like, "This is the best horror film you've ever done." (Laughs) So, it's like—not that I'm trying to get away from doing horror films—but I think in a sense... there was one guy who even started comparing *Edmond* to H. P. Lovecraft, which was interesting, and the points that he was making about it were pretty true. I mean, there was a lot of similarity to some of the Lovecraft stories with *Edmond*, but it's about a guy who kind of... you know, there is that famous line of Lovecraft's where he says, "Man lives on an island of ignorance surrounded by forces that are beyond his control," and that kind of describes *Edmond* as well.

Narrator: And when Gordon got the chance to join the ranks of John Carpenter and Tobe Hooper to direct an episode of Showtime's critically acclaimed *Masters of Horror* series, it was back to H. P. Lovecraft, adapting his short story, "The Dreams in the Witch-House." The result was probably the series' most controversial and terrifying episode.

Gordon: It was a very ambitious script. I mean, my script had all kinds of stuff in it, and I broke the two basic rules of filmmaking, which is, they say, "Never work with babies or animals," and I worked with both of them in this. So, it made it really tricky, but I had a really good crew, and it was really well-organized. I was able to sort of—what I did was I split it off into a second unit and, in a sense, ended up with twenty days [instead of ten], because I had the two units working simultaneously.

Timpone: I thought that was one of the scariest hours on TV I had ever seen.
Gordon: Oh, thank you.

Timpone: And I think it's one the scariest things you've ever done. Was that one of your goals when you set out? You know, "Most of the other horror on TV just pussyfoots around, let's make something that *really* shocks people," including the death of a baby in the film.

Gordon: I know, I know. My wife threatened to divorce me. It's true.

Timpone: Some of the crew didn't even want to shoot that scene. Can you talk a little bit about that?

Gordon: No, it's true. The crew was really getting freaked out by it because we had these real—you know, you use twins when you are shooting with a baby—but it was like the idea that the baby was going to be . . . I mean, in the story, the baby is going to be sacrificed. This witch is forcing our hero to literally slice this baby open, and that was really freaking everyone out. But the thing about the series is, I think it is really a groundbreaking series. I think it's a historic thing. I don't think that there has ever been a series on television that has gone as far as this series has, and they've given us so much freedom. No one ever told me I could not do *this*. You know, they were worried about whether things would run over budget or schedule, but no one ever tried to censor the ideas of that story. And, of course, when you are working with all these great guys—John Carpenter and Tobe Hooper and Dario Argento—you feel like you are in this great club but, also, all of us kind of want to outdo each other, you know? Everyone wants to be able to do the scariest episode of *Masters of Horror*. So, in a way, it really set up a great dynamic.

Narrator: Stuart Gordon has given us three decades of movies that have taken the horror genre and turned it on its head, infusing humor, fantasy, and real-life drama to give each and every movie his own personal stamp. So, what could possibly be left to conquer for a man who has accomplished so much?

Gordon: You know, I'm almost sixty years-old now, and you realize that what it all comes down to is time. How much time is left, really? And how many movies are left to make? You don't want to waste your time doing stuff that's not important or that you don't care about. So, my only hope I guess would be that the next few movies—because I don't think that there are going to be too many more—are going to be my best. You know, Billy Wilder had the best line of all, which is sort of along those lines: people would come up to him and say, "What's your favorite movie?" and he would say, "My next one." (Laughs)

[As the end credits roll, Gordon shares one final anecdote with Timpone.]

Gordon: When I was shooting the first movie I did there [in Italy, which] was *Dolls*, and we were doing a scene and all of a sudden there's some guy hammering, a carpenter is hammering, you know, pounding nails while we were trying to shoot the scene. Finally, I yelled, "Cut," and went over to this guy and I said, "Excuse me, but we're shooting *sound*." And he says, "Senor Fellini always lets me work." I said, "Well, I'm not Fellini." And he said, "That's for sure!" (Laughs)

Inside Stuart Gordon's Urban Gothic: An Interview on *Edmond*

Matthew Sorrento / 2006

From *Film Threat.com*, August 29, 2006. Reprinted by permission.

While renowned for their zany treatments of horror, the films of Stuart Gordon succeed with the help of strong character portrayal. In an early scene in *Re-Animator*, which secured the director's place as a cult icon, gore flies when a cadaver is revived, and the mad creator Herbert West (Jeffrey Combs) cackles at an innocent's expense. But Dan Cain's (Bruce Abbott) shock at the sight realizes tension and elevates this scene from a splatter set piece. The menacing West turns into an immediate threat, and Gordon uses all the scene's players to make the threat real. In the hands of this Reagan-era Dr. Frankenstein, Gordon's corpses were no longer safely at rest.

Re-Animator's narrative continues to make nifty use of character, as two authority figures—Dr. Hill (David Gale, the infamous beheaded head) and Dean Halsey (Robert Sampson)—take on ironic characteristics of their previous selves. While dreaming of lechery when alive, Dr. Hill fulfills his perversion for the dean's daughter (Barbara Crampton) when he becomes undead. The articulate Dean Halsey transforms into a zombie who disrobes his own daughter before finally coming to understand that he is participating in her rape. When West finally takes some moral responsibility for what he has created, he completes the foundation that makes this horror comedy into a masterpiece worthy of repeat viewing.

Gordon drew similar credibility to the players in his lesser-seen follow up, *From Beyond*. The gruesome design of a hidden dimension—unlocked by the stimulation of the pineal gland—leaves quite a taste after viewing, but the characters' reactions to suspenseful situations make the film into a well-tuned gorefest. Gordon's 1995 video release of the Lovecraft-inspired *Castle Freak* used the characters' fear and desire to transcend the project's apparent lack of resources.

Aside from brief turns in different genres—stop-motion animation in *Robot Jox*, dystopia in *Fortress*, and magical realism in the Ray Bradbury-scripted *The Wonderful Ice Cream Suit*—Gordon has continued his affair with Lovecraftian horror that began with *Re-Animator*. He even chose to adapt the famed horror writer for "Dreams in the Witch-House," his first entry in the Showtime series *Masters of Horror*. But Gordon's recent feature-length project, *Edmond*, has allowed him to turn away from fantasy. His choice seems fitting, since he previously experimented with realistic horror in his 2003 feature, *King of the Ants*, a bizarre tale that transforms a contract killer into a torture victim. In *Edmond*, based upon the play by David Mamet, Gordon has created his strongest character yet, a man whose search for meaning turns violent.

"I've been getting into the banality of evil," Gordon said, in a manner both genial and contemplative, during a recent phone interview, "when terrible things are done by people who are more worried about their daily business." Indeed, Edmond Burke begins his story in banality, when he chooses to end his marriage and depart into the New York night. He wants honesty, but looks for it among sex workers trained in getting the better of their clients.

Edmond's anger at these failed attempts for sex, along with his other violent street encounters, brings out an especially disturbing "banal evil." And the director knew right away who should play the part. "I could hear [William H.] Macy doing all the lines as I read them," Gordon said. "I couldn't imagine anyone else doing them. It was the shortest conversation I've ever had with him when I asked him about doing it. He said, 'I've been waiting all my life to play this part.'"

Macy's knack for rage and vulnerability made him a clear choice to humanize this character. A Mamet veteran, Macy noted to Gordon that the role was the toughest of his career. And that's a lot coming from the man who realized Jerry Lundegaard in the Coen Brothers' *Fargo* [1996]. "He's the Fred Astaire of actors," Gordon said. "He makes it all look so easy."

But the project wasn't always so. Gordon had discussed the film with Mamet for twelve years before it came to fruition. When Gordon, who directed the original stage production of Mamet's *Sexual Perversity in Chicago* in 1974, first saw *Edmond*'s premiere stage run in Chicago, he never forgot it. "It's one of those things that burns itself in your mind."

Though interest among screen talent was strong when things finally came together, the script "scared the hell out of every studio in town," Gordon said. He notes that shooting was the easiest part of the project—quite an ironic description for a Mamet adaptation. But getting to the production was the most difficult. "When we started shooting, I don't think we had all of the money at that point. It was possible after the first couple of days of shooting that the whole thing could go down the tubes." Such a situation resulted, in part, from numerous investors backing the film, which left the producers' credit list nearly as long as the cast.

While the management had quite a job on its hands, Gordon attests that the shooting hardly suffered for it. "It's nice to know you have a great script, and that's how I felt about David's—what a gift it was." Though Mamet's impressive output makes him seem intimidating, he adapted to necessity. "His contract stated that we could not change one word without his okay," Gordon said. "I understood that, because we had meetings with studios who said that if we could make the prisoner [played by Bokeem Woodbine] who confronts Edmond near the end white, then they would be more interested in doing the movie. I told them, 'I don't think you're getting this.' David wanted to make sure that his script wouldn't get softened, or censored. But when I showed him the first cut, he gave me a script with all these lines cut from it. Some of them I agreed with, but some I didn't want to lose. He was much more open to [revising the script] after the movie had been shot."

It helped that Gordon had a history with the Pulitzer Prize-winning playwright, as a director of his works but also as his story collaborator. "*Sexual Perversity* was actually two [Mamet] plays that we put together," Gordon recalls. "The original *Perversity* was a series of unrelated blackout sketches—a scene between a couple of waitresses, then a couple of cops, with different people that had no real connection to each other. He had written another play called *Danny Shapiro and his Search for the Mystery Princess*, about this guy and girl having a relationship. I suggested we put the two together, and give the guy and girl [from *Danny Shapiro*] a friend, who could give them all this bad advice."

Mamet's approach during rehearsals also contradicts what legend would have you believe. "Mamet told the actors, 'Look, these are just words—you can do whatever you want with them,'" Gordon recalls from rehearsal for the original *Sexual Perversity* production. "The same goes for directors with Mamet. We rehearsed [*Edmond*] for a month, and I told the actors, 'Don't be so careful.' Everybody breathed a sigh of relief."

Gordon's advice calmed quite a range of performers. He immediately filled roles with old collaborators, including Joe Mantegna (a performer from Gordon's Organic Theatre in Chicago and a Mamet veteran), Jeffrey Combs, Debi Mazar, and George Wendt. However, there were still many more folks for Edmond to encounter on his journey, roles that presented a variety of risks. Gordon found himself relying on intuition, especially when casting the pivotal role of Woodbine's prisoner: "After you see so many people, then the one guy comes in and all of a sudden, it's like you're hearing [the part read] for the first time."

Having to fill a cast of professional girls for Edmond to encounter, Gordon found himself conflicted over his options. Mena Suvari, who appeared in the scene in *American Beauty* [1999] that tributes *Re-Animator*'s famous "head giving head" scene, approached him for a role. "It was exciting, because I really like her work a lot. But at first I thought, my God, she's too beautiful to be a whore. But then I got into an idea with all these gorgeous women, Bai Ling and Denise Richards—they are all unattainable. The more beautiful they are, the more tension there is. [Edmond] wants them so badly, but he can't have any of them. It's not realistic, but it works for the story."

Gordon credits Macy for fostering chemistry among the cast. "[He] created an atmosphere on the set that was so relaxed," Gordon said. "People were having fun being there with him. . . . He puts people at ease, that's one of the great things about him." And his example was just as inspirational. "Many times when we discussed the character, the actors asked, 'Is Edmond crazy? Angry? What is going on here?' But he was creating a character that you could really care about. In a way, I think [Edmond] wants what everybody wants. He wants honesty; he wants people to be straight with him, to cut the bullshit out of his life."

What he wants, however, is far from what he gets. Through Edmond, Mamet created an exhaustingly tragic figure. "He's sort of like [the playwright's] Hamlet—the biggest role he has ever written for an actor," Gordon noted. "Before this, [Mamet] did *American Buffalo*," in which Macy originated a role in the American premiere, "which all takes place in a pawn shop. He usually did work about a mentor and a kid, a student, and *Edmond* sort of broke him out of that. This whole thing about it being an odyssey, and following this guy on a journey—it's completely different than [what] he's done before. He's never done anything like that ever since, even."

Gordon found Mamet's adaptation of his episodic play especially cinematic, even though it was one of the first screenplays he ever wrote. "He put in a lot of stuff about camera directions, which is something directors hate to see in a script. Then I realized that he was describing how to cut from scene to scene. It was very dreamlike. For example, there's an early scene when he's looking at the tarot cards, and then he looks back down and there's a dinner plate. And suddenly he's at home at his dining room table. With that, I started really getting a sense of what [Mamet] was after. It opened things up, and I started to do even more of it than was indicated in the script."

The playwright also became quite a practical resource for Gordon. "It said in the script that Edmond punches a guy with a knife. I said [to Mamet], 'How do you punch someone with a knife?' Well, David Mamet collects knives—he's an expert," which is quite interesting for a playwright who named his essay on drama "Three Uses of the Knife." Gordon then found a knife with steel knuckles built in its handle, which Mamet identified as a "trench knife" from World War I, and agreed it was perfect. When Edmond purchases this curio from a pawnshop, the knife takes on a presence of its own, and promises unique mayhem.

Gordon captures this mayhem in a macabre fashion. When the knife is used to kill, he was none too restrained when he inserted a blood-drowning throat *gurgling* to death, voiced over a now-murderous Edmond. This moment pushes the film deep into the surreal, in which an everyman has trapped himself.

The director's treatment of *Edmond* has laid a path toward his next project. *Stuck* will feature a woman who, after hitting a man with her car, brings him back to her garage to die. Not only is it based on a true story, but the real-life woman was a caregiver at a senior citizen home. "When I was reading about it, I thought to myself, 'What would make someone like her do a thing like this?'" Gordon said. And soon he found himself musing on the depths of evil that can rise from the everyday. This two-character drama—a more restrained retelling of Stephen King's *Misery* [1990]—will allow the director to experiment in a new gothic mode and return to a contained, dramatic situation, natural for an experienced stage director.

While the restored cut of *From Beyond* is due out soon on DVD, Gordon will return to Showtime's *Masters of Horror* series for their second season when he begins filming Poe's "The Black Cat" this fall. This one-hour film, which is the director's follow-up to his "Dreams in the Witch-House" for the series, will insert Poe himself into his trademark story. And, quite fittingly, Jeffrey Combs will play Poe.

Indeed, Mr. Combs will be quite useful to the director in the future. Also on the horizon is *House of Re-Animator*, the fourth film in the series and the first sequel which Gordon will direct. While Combs returns as Herbert West, there will be promising newcomers to the series. William H. Macy will play the commander-in-chief, Gordon said, and he hopes his old friend George Wendt will sign on to ham it up as Dick Cheney. Gordon also wants Barbara Crampton to play the first lady to complete the *Re-Animator* reunion. He expressed interest in how re-animation could work as a metaphor for the current administration.

"What's amazing is that *they* are going over-the-top. And the reality is so insane that you have to go far to top it."

And, as Gordon noted, you can never go too over-the-top with *Re-Animator*.

Stuart Gordon

Paul Kane / 2007

Published in a slightly different form in *Voices in the Dark: Interviews with Horror Writers, Directors and Actors* (McFarland and Co., 2011), pp. 133–43. Reprinted by permission.

Paul Kane: Was William Castle quite a big influence on you?

Stuart Gordon: He was. His movies were always an event; he was an incredible showman. I remember one of his movies, I was waiting in line to get in, and you'd see people being carried out on stretchers and put into ambulances. He had another movie where he was advertising it as better than 3D—the monsters really come off the screen *into* the theater. That was *House on Haunted Hill* [1959], and he had a thing where at a certain moment in the movie this plastic skeleton came out of a box next to the screen on a wire over the audience, and everybody started booing and throwing their popcorn boxes at it.

PK: Have you ever thought about doing things like that with your films?

SG: You know, when we first screened *Re-Animator*, we did the old routine with the stretchers and the ambulances at a screening in San Francisco.

PK: What made you decide to set up the Organic Theatre Company?

SG: I had started a theater company when I was at college called Screw Theatre, and when I got out of school I realized I really loved theater and wanted to continue with that. So, Carolyn and I began the Organic Theatre Company in Chicago.

PK: Was any of it influenced by Grand Guignol Theater?

SG: Very much so—we always did a lot of blood effects on stage. We once did a pirate play where we hung one of the actors upside down, slit his throat, and put a bucket underneath him. We were expecting the police for the next ten minutes.

PK: Why weren't the Organic Theatre people behind you when you wanted to make an adaptation of [Lovecraft's] work?

SG: It's funny, but by the time we got to that point, Organic had really grown; it had become an institution. The yearly budget was over $1 million, and we had all these members of the community on our board. When I told them that I wanted to do a horror movie, they were saying, "No, no! We don't want the Organic Theatre name on a horror movie. We want to do an art film." By that point I'd met Brian Yuzna, and he had brought the financing and we were all ready to go. So, I took a leave of absence from the theater and directed the movie.

PK: *Re-Animator* started out as a series for TV, didn't it?

SG: That was our thought, because it was written as a serial. Lovecraft wrote it in six installments. It seemed like maybe it could be a miniseries or something. We took the first installment of the story and adapted it into a thirty-minute teleplay, but no one wanted to make it. Looking back on it, we must have been insane to think anyone would. Then we thought maybe it should be an hour long, so we took the second story and combined it, but we couldn't sell that either. Then, at that point, I was introduced to Brian Yuzna, who said, "This should be a feature." And I said, "Okay, I'll add the third story." He said, "No, no, no—add the fourth story in." So, we threw them all in.

PK: How did you first come across Yuzna?

SG: I met him through a friend, a guy named Bob Greenberg, and when I think back about this, it's kind of an incredible thing because Bob had been hired to direct another film, and that project had got derailed somehow. So, they were looking for something else to do, and Bob knew about the *Re-Animator* project so he suggested to Brian that we get together. I sent him the script we'd been developing and Bob was gracious enough to step aside and let me direct. I think back to that and ask, "Would I have been willing to do something like that, if I'd had my first chance to direct a picture? Give it up and let someone else direct?" It was very unselfish of Bob.

PK: When you first met Jeffrey Combs, what did you make of him?

SG: Jeffrey showed up for an audition for *Re-Animator*—that was the first time I saw him. He was sort of like a kindred spirit, as soon as I got to know him I realized he was exactly like the kind of people I'd been working with in the theater. Jeffrey's background is in theater as well. He has that sort of "go for broke, I'll try anything once" kind of attitude, which is what I really thrive on.

PK: Was he well versed in Lovecraft as well?

SG: I don't think he knew Lovecraft, actually. It was funny, Jeffrey was not really into horror films and was kind of disgusted by the amount of blood we were using during filming. There's a scene in the movie where a bone saw cuts through the zombie ["Melvin the Re-Animated," played by Peter Kent] and Herbert's in blood up to his elbow, and he *shakes* it off in disgust. That was genuine; that was the way Jeffrey felt about it all.

PK: You used the space very much like a theater set.

SG: There were people who said we were making movies for years, except we weren't on film; we were doing them on stage—live. So, what I discovered with movies was that in some ways it was actually easier than doing theater because we only did our plays in a round, a three-quarter round, and the audience could see three sides of the action, so it's much more difficult to hide the tricks. But with the movie camera you only have one audience member—and we were using techniques very similar to the ones we used on the stage.

PK: Were you aware that the "head giving head" scene would be as infamous as it turned out to be?

SG: (Laughs) We knew *that* was the scene that was going to make or break the movie. It's funny, because the very first piece of artwork that was ever done for *Re-Animator* was of that scene. That was the artwork Brian used to raise financing. It was done by a wonderful artist named William Stout.

PK: What did Barbara Crampton think about the idea at the time?

SG: She was very game. One of the things that a lot of people don't know is that, originally, I had cast a different actress to play that part. About two weeks before we were due to start shooting, this actress got cold feet. She said, "I've talked to my mother and I don't think it's a good idea for me to do this." So, we recast it and that's when I met Barbara. She just completely made that part her own, and she was just a great actress. We ended up making several more movies together.

PK: How did the three-picture deal with Empire come about?

SG: It was really based on the success of *Re-Animator*. After I directed *Re-Animator*, I went back to the theater, to Chicago. It was several months later that I got a call saying Empire Pictures was giving Brian and me a three-picture deal. They wanted us to come to Los Angeles and get started. It was at that point I actually left the [Organic] Theatre for good. The catch with the three-picture deal was that we had to make the pictures in Italy. I'd moved my family to LA and then a couple of months later told them, "We've got to move to Rome," which wasn't a bad thing. I mean, I loved going there. But while I was in Rome working on the first film, *Dolls*, there was an article in *Newsweek* in which Charlie Band, the head of Empire Pictures, was interviewed, and he was talking about *Re-Animator* and how worldwide it had made over $30 million. I had a two points profits or something, and I remember after I read it, I said, "Alright, drinks are on me! I'm a millionaire now!" (Laughs)

PK: In *From Beyond*, you explored the notion that there are creatures that exist around us all the time, we just can't see them. Do you ever think this might be true?

SG: Well, it really *is* true. Those creatures are called germs and viruses. They're living creatures that are invisible to us. I think sometimes that was where Lovecraft was coming from, he was kind of a hypochondriac and there was this fear of invisible things that could kill you.

PK: Is it true that you're very squeamish when it comes to blood and gore in real life?

SG: Yeah, it is. My wife started laughing at me, as there was this time one day when our dog stepped on a piece of glass and was tracking blood around the kitchen, and I passed out. As long as I know it's fake, I'm okay, but when it's real I've got a problem with that.

PK: Your wife, Carolyn, was cast in [*Dolls*]. How did she take to being killed off?

SG: Well, I try to murder her as often as I possibly can. (Laughs) At first she was a little disturbed by it. Then she finally got around to thinking, "As long as you only do it in movies, it's okay." A few years later, I did a movie and she was in it, and I *didn't* kill her, and she was very upset about that. She said, "Don't you love me anymore?" (Laughs)

PK: In your adaptation of "The Pit and the Pendulum," you explore Poe's fiction. In what ways does this differ from Lovecraft's fiction for you?

SG: Most of Poe's stories are set in the here and now. Lovecraft's work involved the idea of other dimensions, alien life-forms, and so forth. Most of Poe's stuff had to do with real people and real times. He also explores the senses; it's about characters that often have very acute senses. It means that little things can become very disturbing. Lovecraft was hugely influenced by Poe. If Poe had not existed, there would be no Lovecraft either.

PK: How did you get on with Lance Henriksen?

SG: Fine. He's an amazing actor, and also a method actor. He did a lot of research about Torquemada and discovered that he was ascetic, that he only drank water and only ate bread, and walked barefoot all the time. So, Lance did the same thing. Here he is in Italy, we're shooting this movie in a country that has some of the greatest food in the world, and Lance is not having any of it, not even the wine—until Oliver Reed showed up! (Laughs) The two of them ended up having a drinking contest. It was hilarious. Oliver drank Lance under the table. It was an amazing thing to see.

PK: What was Reed like as a person?

SG: He was wonderful, too. I mean, he was completely insane. He showed up on the weekend at this castle where we were shooting and the first thing that he did was say, "Bring out every bottle of wine you've got in the castle and put it on the table," this huge banquet table. Then he proceeded to drink himself around the table. I was thinking, "Oh, my God! What's going to happen when we get to Monday and we need to shoot the scene?" It was a nonstop binge and it went on all weekend. And when Monday morning rolled around, I went to the set and there was Oliver Reed. He was already in costume, all ready to go. He was completely sober, knew all of his lines perfectly. It was completely incredible. His attitude was: "The weekend is my time and I can do what I want, but Monday I'm ready to work." A phenomenal guy. We had great conversations. One of the things I learned about him was that he had never appeared on stage. He started in movies at a very early age; it was actually a horror film that got him going, *The Curse of the Werewolf* [1961], the Hammer film. But, no, he'd never appeared on stage. I remember sitting around the fire with him and he was reciting Byron. It was just the most beautiful thing I'd ever heard.

PK: *Castle Freak* brought Jeffrey Combs and Barbara Crampton back into the fold. What was it like working with them again?

SG: Oh, it was really great. They're both great actors. That was a movie that came together very quickly. Charlie Band financed it himself without a script. I was sitting in his office and there was a poster and it said *Castle Freak*, with a picture of a guy who looked like Quasimodo whipping some naked woman who's chained to the wall. So, I asked, "What's that movie about?" And he said, "Well, there's a castle and there's a freak." (Laughs) "Listen, you can do whatever you want with it, as long as there are those two elements in it." I had that conversation with him, I think it was in March, and we were shooting the movie in June. So, it was very, very fast. Dennis Paoli and I wrote the script very quickly—I think it's the only time I've ever shot the very first draft of a script, because it was that good.

PK: You adapted another Lovecraft story for *Masters of Horror*, "Dreams in the Witch-House." Why have you called this one of your favorite stories?

SG: It was also one of the very first Lovecraft stories I ever read; in fact, I think it might actually have been the very first one. That one really stayed with me, the idea of a witch coming through the wall of your room, grabbing you, pulling you out of your bed, and taking you off to do terrible things. It's a terrifying idea.

PK: For season two of *Masters of Horror* you explored the world of Poe again. How did you approach this new twist on "The Black Cat"?

SG: My daughter, Suzanne, is a teacher of high school English and she teaches Poe. Every year she has someone come in around Halloween to talk about Poe. So, last year I came in and I read them "The Black Cat" and scared the shit out of those kids! That story is just terrifying. It struck me afterwards that it would make a great episode of *Masters of Horror*. The other thing was that Jeffrey Combs and I had been talking about the idea of him playing Poe. It occurred to me that you could do that story and make Poe the protagonist. So, all of that just came together and Dennis Paoli and I wrote the script again. It came together very quickly.

PK: Can you tell us anything about *House of Re-Animator*?

SG: Again, this is one of these projects that we've been talking about for a while, but finding the money to make it has been difficult. The house in the title is the White House. And even though we have William H. Macy lined up to play the president, people are afraid, I think, to make that film. The story begins with the vice president dropping dead of a heart attack and, since he's running the country, they don't know what to do. Then the CIA suggests that they might be able to use this Herbert West fellow. So, that's kind of the premise.

PK: How did Macy become involved in the project?

SG: I worked on *Edmond* with Bill and we were having a great time. So, he said, "You know, I would love to do a horror movie." At that time, I was working on the treatment for *House of Re-Animator* and I showed it to him, and he loved it. So, he signed on.

PK: Is he a big *Re-Animator* fan?

SG: Yes. He got a chance to work with Jeffrey Combs in *Edmond* and they really liked each other, too.

PK: Is it going to pick up from the previous *Re-Animators*?

SG: In a way, it will. The idea is that West and Cain are estranged, but they're forced to work together to re-animate the vice president. I'm scripting it again with Dennis Paoli, who I did the first one with.

PK: Can you give us any more details about the story?

SG: I don't want to give too much away, but I've been talking to George Wendt about playing the vice president and Barbara Crampton about playing the first lady. I think that could be pretty great.

PK: So, will she be re-animated as well?

SG: It's kind of a chain reaction that gets set off. When people get re-animated, they never come back quite the same. There's also the thing in the *Re-Animator* movies that their libidos are completely unleashed; that they have no control over their sex drives.

PK: Will it be even wilder than the previous *Re-Animators*?

SG: I think it's going to pretty wild, it really will. I think that will be the fun part of it.

PK: How does Jeffrey feel about coming back?

SG: He's excited. And Bruce Abbott is coming back as well.

PK: Have you been in talks with all of them about it?

SG: Yeah, and they really like the idea. I will give you a scoop, actually, which is that in the story Dan Cain has a young son. I'm trying to convince Brian Yuzna that if there's another *Re-Animator* it should be called *Son of Re-Animator*. That would be after *House of Re-Animator*. If we're going to follow the Universal thing [from the 1930s and '40s], we have to then do *Ghost of Re-Animator*.

PK: That's right, and *Abbott and Costello meet Re-Animator*. (Laughs) How does it feel to be thinking about working on a new *Re-Animator*?

SG: For me, it's kind of like coming home. There's that part of it. It's such a wonderful feeling of being able to work with the same group of guys. One of the things I realized was that *Re-Animator* was one of those rare instances where everybody was on the same wavelength, which is probably the reason why it was as successful as it was. So, to be able to come back and join forces with those same folks again is something I'm really looking forward to.

PK: What have you made of the other *Re-Animator* films that followed yours?

SG: I thought they had their moments. There were things about them that I liked. I liked the re-animated penis and the rat [in *Beyond Re-Animator*, 2003]. (Laughs) There was some good work in those. My only quibble was that they kept referring to him as "Dr. West" and I can't imagine how he could have ever graduated.

PK: What can you tell us about *Stuck*?

SG: It stars Stephen Rea and Mena Suvari. It's based on a true story about a woman who hits a homeless man, and he goes through her windshield. She panics, and instead of taking him to the emergency room, she puts him in her garage—and the guy's still alive! She keeps him captive, kinda hoping he's going to die.

Stuart Gordon, *Stuck*

Nick Dawson / 2008

From *Filmmaker* magazine, May 30, 2008. Reprinted by permission.

Since the very beginning of his career, Stuart Gordon has set out to shock and disrupt. Gordon, a native of Chicago, began his assault on the public after developing a love of drama at the University of Wisconsin. He subsequently started the Screw Theatre—which made national news in 1968 when they performed a nude, psychedelic version of *Peter Pan*—and went on in 1970 to found the Organic Theatre Company in Chicago, where he was artistic director for fifteen years. Over that period, Gordon worked with Roald Dahl, Kurt Vonnegut, and Ray Bradbury, championed the work of the then-unknown David Mamet, and had Joe Mantegna and Dennis Franz as ensemble members.

In 1985, he left Organic to direct *Re-Animator*, based on an H. P. Lovecraft horror story, which won the Critics' Prize at Cannes and gained instant cult status. Gordon has since adapted three more Lovecraft works for the big screen, as well as works by Edgar Allan Poe ("The Pit and the Pendulum") and Ray Bradbury ("The Wonderful Ice Cream Suit"). In addition to horror and gothic, Gordon directed the futuristic prison drama *Fortress* and the campy *Space Truckers*, and wrote *Honey, I Shrunk the Kids* with his friend and fellow horror specialist Brian Yuzna. Recently, Gordon's work has shifted from the fantastical to the horrors of real life with the gritty thriller *King of the Ants* (2003), David Mamet's psychological drama *Edmond* (2005), and now his latest movie.

Stuck is based on the shocking true story of a care assistant from a senior citizen's home who, while drunk and on Ecstasy, hit a homeless man with her car, breaking his legs—and leaving him lodged firmly in her windshield. Rather than calling the police, she returned home, left her car in the garage, and regularly visited the injured man to check on his waning condition. In Gordon's film, the names of principal characters—played by Mena Suvari and Stephen Rea—have been changed, but much of what is presented here is true to the real-life events. Gordon and screenwriter John Strysik try to imagine the otherwise kind-hearted

Brandi's (Suvari) motives for not helping Tom (Rea), the man she hit. However, this is no dry psychological examination—Gordon takes every opportunity to play up the surreal and ridiculous elements of the story as well as, inevitably, the gory and unsavory parts. *Stuck* is a mixture of smart and silly, philosophical and flippant, as Gordon delivers an entertaining tale of the real-life macabre, and also a little food for thought for those who are looking for it.

Filmmaker spoke to Gordon about the true story behind the film, keeping Stephen Rea in a car windshield for most of the shoot, and making movies without film.

Filmmaker: *Stuck* is based on a true story. When did you first read about it and what was your initial reaction?

Stuart Gordon: When I read about it, it was in the newspapers for weeks, it was a huge story. The actual event took place in 2001, but I think the trial took place about two or three years later, so it was during the trial that most of the copy appeared about it. It was one of those jaw-dropping stories: here's a woman who's a caregiver in a senior citizen's home who hits a guy with her car and puts him in her garage, and keeps going in to see how he's doing, and talking to him and apologizing to him. This seemed like a fairly normal woman, so I kept wondering what would make her behave this way. That was really the question that we tried to answer with the movie.

Filmmaker: How quickly did you realize this was a story you wanted to tell?

Gordon: I was talking to John Strysik, who's a writer, and we were talking about ideas and I said, "What about doing a movie about this story?" He initially said, "Well, there's not a lot there, really. Is there enough for a feature?" I said, "Sure, I think there could be. Just let it play out—it's horrifying." So, we started working on it together.

Filmmaker: How did you get the rights to the story?

Gordon: Anything that's in the newspapers is public domain, so we just based it on what we were reading. We didn't talk to anyone, we didn't interview anybody; we saw some things that were on the television at the time on Court TV, but that was pretty much it. And then we started letting our imaginations run with it.

Filmmaker: With a story like this, were you concerned with the exact details of the case or did you worry that knowing what actually happened would inhibit your creativity?

Gordon: Actually, John visited Fort Worth and he saw the house and the garage where it happened, and he went to the highway and found the spot where she had hit the guy. Unlike our movie, it's out in the middle of nowhere, it's a highway. It was really kinda weird—what was this guy doing out there? We tried to get as much information as we could, and then some of it we ended up using and some of it we ended up changing. There were certain assumptions that we made that may or may not have been true. The whole idea in the movie of her being up for a promotion was something that we invented, but it was one of those things where the idea that she had something to gain by covering this up seemed important.

Filmmaker: How much did you manage to find out about Gregory Biggs, the real-life guy who was hit?

Gordon: We did find out that he had a son, and that kind of worked its way into the story. It was interesting, because the movie was just shown at the AFI Festival and, although I was not there, John Strysik and Stephen Rea were and this guy came up to Stephen Rea and introduced himself, and it was Gregory Biggs's son. Stephen's feeling was that this was a guy who was looking for his father and that he felt that by seeing the film he would maybe learn more about him. He got the feeling that Biggs's son did not know his father that well.

Filmmaker: Presumably you don't know how Chante Mallard, the woman who hit Biggs, feels about the film.

Gordon: Mallard's in jail serving a fifty-year term. I don't know whether she knows about the film, but I do know that there was a lot of press about it in Dallas-Fort Worth. I was contacted by someone from the radio station who had covered the trial and had heard about the movie after we had shown it in Toronto. She said, "You know, this woman is not a monster." I said, "Well, I don't think we portrayed her as a monster in the film."

Filmmaker: I think the idea that she is up for a promotion is somewhat forgiving towards her as it at least partly explains her actions, though in no way excuses them.

Gordon: The thing that we got into was that it was really about fear, this fear of ruining your life. Also, if people are in traffic accidents, it's never their fault. It's one of those things that you're schooled in, to never admit that you're to blame, so I think that's part of it too. I think that in our society now, people will just not admit to any mistakes, starting all the way at the top. There's a line in the movie where they say, "Look who's in the White House. Look, you can get away with anything now!" It's true, we've got this completely amoral president who sets the tone for everybody else. In talking about fear in our daily life, this is a guy who has done nothing but try to fan the flames of fear, to get us more afraid—afraid of terrorists, afraid of immigrants, afraid of gays, afraid of anybody. He's trying to keep everybody scared and under his thumb.

Filmmaker: When I was watching *Stuck*, I was aware of how unappealing the role of Tom must have been to actors because of its physical challenges. Did you have trouble finding someone willing to be stuck in a windshield for the majority of the movie?

Gordon: We didn't really approach that many people because we were lucky that we got Stephen Rea, who was at the top of the list, really. He's an actor whose work I've been admiring forever. There's just something about him and his face that just seems perfect for this. He's got this hangdog quality, and he's so sympathetic and you really care about him. Everything he does, he gets you to kind of become him, in a way, and for this movie that's what we wanted. He read the script and immediately signed on—we didn't have to convince him or talk him into anything. He was really taken with the script, and he said, "I realize I'm putting myself up for a world of pain here just to do this." There were times when he was regretting it, bitching about it, because every day was, like, two hours of makeup and then into the windshield for the rest of the day.

Filmmaker: Presumably the physical restrictions of the role had a psychological impact on him. Did you see the effect of that over the course of the shoot?

Gordon: I really did. As a matter of fact, we shot things in sequence and the day that his character pulls himself out of the hood of the car, I've never seen a happier man in my life. (Laughs) It was like, "Thank God, I'm out of that windshield!" He was in that windshield for three weeks.

Filmmaker: How firmly embedded did he have to be to appear genuinely stuck?

Gordon: Oh, he was really stuck. He couldn't move his arm, because it was wedged in there, it was that tight. And his head was hanging lower than the rest of his body and the blood would rush to his head. He would have to have something for him to lean on while we were setting up the shot. It was very uncomfortable. I would say to him, "Can you do one more take?" and he would say, "Ohhhhhh . . . oh, okay." He knew that we needed it, but he also got to the point where he said, "Don't put me in that windshield until everything is ready to go. I don't want to be in that windshield and have you fiddling with lights."

Filmmaker: The film is a strange companion piece to *Misery*. Was that in the forefront of your mind from early on?

Gordon: It was. When we were talking about doing it, I was saying, "Well, it would sort of be like *Misery*." It was one of those touchstones, and I know that Mena watched *Misery* several times before we started shooting.

Filmmaker: I think what makes this more interesting than *Misery* is that Mena Suvari, unlike Kathy Bates, is actually for the most part an extremely likable character on screen.

Gordon: I think that was one of the great things about Mena's performance; that she did not choose to make her crazy. This is a normal person, this is something that can happen to anybody, really. She makes a bad decision and then has to follow through.

Filmmaker: I may be reading too much into this, but I detected a possible nod to *Crash* [2004] when Suvari's character has sex with her boyfriend just after hitting Tom.

Gordon: This was actually true; this really did happen. Chante Mallard put Biggs in her garage and then immediately went in and had sex with her boyfriend. That really took place, and that's where we got this idea. I think that what was going on there—and we tried to get into it a little bit—was that this was a way for her to escape from what she's just done. It's like, "I'm gonna get drunk, I'm gonna get stoned, I'm gonna fuck my brains out, and I'm gonna pretend that this didn't happen."

Filmmaker: Looking at the arc of your career, there seems to have been a recent shift towards the grotesquerie of real life as opposed to horror grounded in science fiction or fantasy. Is there a reason for that?

Gordon: I don't know, except that as you get older you start realizing that real life is scarier than anything you can dream up, that the things that people actually do to each other are far more bizarre and horrifying than anything that Lovecraft could dream of. I have a friend who used to say that it's the little things that upset you the most. Godzilla destroying Tokyo is not a scary thing because it's so huge that we can't even imagine it, but a person cutting their finger with a razor is really upsetting because we've all done that.

Filmmaker: Looking at your bio, I was trying to find the common thread between your theater work in the seventies and eighties and the film work you've done subsequently. I suppose the crude conclusion that I came to is that in all of this you've given yourself the role of troublemaker or rabble rouser.

Gordon: That's accurate, I'd say. I like shocking people, I like waking them up, making them see things in a new way and pay attention. I think that's always a good thing. We spend so much of our life walking around in a daze. One of the things I liked about *Edmond* was that Mamet talks about that: he says, "How much of your life are you truly alive? Five minutes out of the year when you're in difficulties, or a traffic accident." That line, in a way, connects *Edmond* and this movie.

Filmmaker: When you were working in the theater, was it your ambition to move into film?

Gordon: It's funny, when I was a teenager I made little movies with my friends and when I went to university I wanted to take a film course, but it was full so I took an acting course instead. That acting course showed me the potential of theater, and I got *completely* into theater. But a lot of the plays that I did were sort of like movies on stage. I mean, we put on plays that had naval battles on stage, we did a police thing where we had gunfights on stage, a science fiction trilogy before *Star Wars* that went into other dimensions. I think, in a way, I was making movies without any film and so now to be able to make real movies is great. Although I still think theater is harder.

Filmmaker: What was the first film you ever saw?

Gordon: It was *The Greatest Show on Earth* [1952, directed by] Cecil B. DeMille, about the circus. I think I was about three years old. As a result, I wanted to be a clown. A lot of people say that I've succeeded. (Laughs) That movie made a big impression on me, the wonder of it all. It was a big movie.

Filmmaker: When was the last time you wished you had a different job?

Gordon: I think of a job as being something where you're being paid to do something you don't want to do, and the last "job" I had was when I was in college. I was working as a credit manager for Hertz Rent-a-Truck, and I had to call people up who hadn't paid their bills. That was one of those jobs where you wished you weren't doing it. I've been lucky since then never to have to work again.

Object in Mirror May Be Closer Than It Appears: Stuart Gordon Talks About Horror, the Absurd, and *Stuck*

Matthew Sorrento / 2008

From *Bright Lights Film Journal*, July 31, 2008. Reprinted by permission.

It isn't easy being the father of *Re-Animator*. This 1985 horror-comedy—Stuart Gordon's film debut after a career of directing for the stage—became an immediate cult favorite, and a giant that would loom over the rest of his career.

For his Chicago theater company, Gordon directed experimental plays and a nontraditional take on *Peter Pan* that got him jailed for obscenity. He had minimal experience in horror, though he'd soon bank on the market's box-office reliability to break into filmmaking. By the time he tracked down a withered copy of H. P. Lovecraft's "Herbert West—Re-Animator" in an archival collection, he knew he would revise a classic archetype, the Frankenstein/mad doctor tale, for his debut. But he wouldn't find his primary inspiration until he embarked on hands-on research. While observing decaying bodies at morgues, Gordon and his filmmakers encountered morticians whose wit was as dark as their profession. Hence, Gordon found what would make *Re-Animator* into a mix of screams and laughter.

Gordon's following projects often realized the wit lurking alongside his gruesome set pieces. Yet none of his films lit the sparks of his first, which showed a sensibility like James Whale's in maximizing the comic potential of its horrific subject matter. Gordon returned to Lovecraft throughout his career, including for his first project post-*Re-Animator*—1986's *From Beyond*, an enjoyably bizarre entry that grows routine halfway through. His producer, Brian Yuzna, directed the *Re-Animator* sequels in 1990 and 2003 that recycled the original film's style to lesser effect. Since 2001, Gordon spoke of returning to the series with *House of Re-Animator*, which would feature a president re-animated by Dr. West as a tribute to our current brain-dead head of state. But with financing trouble and Dubya soon to depart from office, the film was abandoned.

By the time *House* was announced, Gordon showed up with another film that sported a new gothic taste. *Edmond* (2005) was adapted from a stage play by David Mamet, whose *Sexual Perversity in Chicago* was directed by Gordon in its premiere stage production. Mamet's *Edmond* features a title character whose moral demise brings him into an urban landscape as nightmarish as it is realistic. Gordon cast William H. Macy as the title character who embarks on an episodic one-night journey through bars, brothels, and to a waitress's home, in which Edmond's swelling amorality results in murder. His final—and permanent—stop is a prison cell in which he finds blissful contentment in powerlessness.

With *Edmond*, Gordon realized a particular horror from crumbling humanity. It took him twenty years, but he had found a new style.

In his follow-up, *Stuck* (2007), Gordon grabs a story from the headlines to fashion another gothic tale stemming from the mundane, one showcasing an absurdist dilemma that offers a fresh take on the genre. The news story concerned the ultimate hit-and-run: after crashing into a pedestrian with her car at night, a woman raced home with the man still impaled in her windshield. "It was one of those stories that if it were made up, nobody would believe it," Gordon said during a recent phone interview, his attraction to this curious event evident in his voice. "It was a big story, and I was reading about it every day. Eventually, I started talking about the articles with my friend, John Strysik, and the story started turning into a movie."

The story as Gordon conceived it posed obvious challenges, since much of the action would take place in a home garage in which an injured man struggles, inch by inch, to free himself. But the director saw the project as a welcome challenge. "I've always been a big fan of Hitchcock's *Lifeboat* [a 1944 film which takes place completely on the eponymous location], and how it fully explores one location," says Gordon. "You always hear that rule of thumb—you have to open [a film] up with new locations. But [*Stuck*] is really about the people involved, and the tension rising from the two who are trapped."

One of the "trapped" is the victim, the recently laid off and homeless Tom, played with conviction by Stephen Rea. Yet Gordon sees the young woman, Brandi, played with wide-eyed panic by Mena Suvari, as another victim in this story. "She has this dead-end job," says the director, "and then a promotion gets dangled in front of her, and she has a future all of a sudden. And she won't let that be taken away from her."

As inexplicable as her actions may be, she also comes off as willfully irresponsible, stressing about the problem of having a dying man on her hands without a bit of compassion. Even one of Gordon's casting directors thought the character was despicable. "You could say the same thing about Lady Macbeth," says Gordon. Suvari's character in *Stuck* "is a great role, and she really appreciated it.

Mena and I are alike in that we both like dark subjects. I learned that we are kindred spirits when we worked on *Edmond*. She really liked the fact that this character [in *Stuck*] was so shocking. This is what drew her to the project." In *Edmond*, Suvari's innocent demeanor added depth to her disturbing portrayal of a prostitute, and Gordon knew she could bring the unsympathetic character in *Stuck* to life. "Mena actually contacted me [about being in the film]. She had received the script and then came to me and said, 'I definitely want to do this.' I knew how great she was [from doing *Edmond*], so I knew she would make the character real."

Gordon may have been destined to work with her, since she appeared in a scene in the 1999 Oscar-winner *American Beauty* that pays homage to *Re-Animator*, something of a film geek's treat. "That lovemaking scene [in *American Beauty*] is shot exactly like the ["head giving head"] scene in *Re-Animator*. Jeffrey Combs pointed out to me that they matched shot for shot. [Kevin Spacey's] head was in the bottom corner of the screen moving up her body." And the allusion is no mistake, since in another part of the film, Spacey's character refers to that "movie with the body walking around holding its own head. And then the head went down on that babe."

"It would have been easy to make Mena's character into a monster," Gordon says. "But that's not what we wanted, and [Suvari] didn't take that route. [Brandi] is just an ordinary girl who gets herself into a bad situation and makes some really bad decisions."

While Suvari acts an outrageous role with conviction, Gordon made another find by casting Stephen Rea as Tom, her antagonist in agony. *Stuck* begins with his firing and eviction, and Rea helps create a bleak tone of bureaucratic oppression. The actor's downbeat walk among the streets that results in his character's wounding accident-cum-kidnapping is a haunting one.

"[Rea] has such a hangdog face," Gordon says. "He could show that life has kicked his character around. I knew from his other performances that he could engage an audience this way. I've been a huge fan for years, and the idea of working with him was a dream.

"When we sent him the script, he got it right away. It turned out that both he and John Strysik are huge fans of Samuel Beckett. John started seeing Beckett elements in the script as we worked on it, like futile dilemmas about people who are buried in the sand. The absurd nature of the script appealed to Stephen." (Fittingly enough, Rea is now on stage in New York playing a Beckettian character for writer/director Sam Shepard in *Kicking a Dead Horse*.)

For much of the film, Rea's injured character struggles to dislodge himself from a broken windshield. "[Strysik and I] wondered if Tom should get weaker, since he's losing blood. But we knew that his survival instincts were kicking in," says Gordon.

Rea's character writhes in pain in scenes with surprising momentum for such limiting content. In these moments, Gordon couldn't resist incorporating some humorously gruesome bits akin to those in his gory shockers. At a point when Rea's character gains footing to pull himself from the shards of the windshield, he pushes them in deeper, in Sisyphean agony. Hence, viewers wince at his every movement in what becomes a uniquely tense, tongue-in-cheek moment. "Coming from a theater background," says Gordon, Rea "knew that this would be a real physical performance, and a test of his strength, really." While filming, the actor told Gordon that "Tom definitely wouldn't be out on the streets after all this—he'll somehow pull his life together."

Tom's ordeal recalls another bizarre and often gruesome tale. "*Misery* was a reference point for us," says Gordon. "[Suvari] actually watched the movie version a couple of times before we started shooting. The main difference, though, is that *Misery* has a psycho woman, and [Suvari] knew that she was playing just a normal woman in a bad situation.

"I think we've all done things like [what Brandi does]," says Gordon, without a drop of irony in his voice. "Nothing as bad as this, of course. These two people are stuck in life, beyond him being stuck literally in the windshield. They both get stronger. The film turns into a battle of survival for two desperate people—to the death, in a way."

Things No One Likes to Talk About: An Interview with Stuart Gordon

James Morgart and Robert Cashill / 2009

From *Cineaste* XXXV, no. 1. This is the first time the interview has been published in its unexpurgated form. Reprinted by permission.

Director-writer-producer Stuart Gordon burst onto the horror scene with 1985's *Re-Animator*, an adaptation of an H. P. Lovecraft short story, one of the great mad scientist films, and a refreshing change of pace after the decade's run of slasher movies. Spiced with quirky humor, kinky sex, and showers of body parts, *Re-Animator* found a fan in Pauline Kael, who rhapsodized about the film in the *New Yorker*. Gordon applied the same mixture to a second Lovecraft adaptation, *From Beyond* (1986). Witty and sophisticated without shortchanging on gore or lasciviousness, the two movies inaugurated a career in fantastic cinema that has encompassed a fractured fairy tale (1987's *Dolls*), a science fiction adventure about giant robots (1990's *Robot Jox*, made for a fraction-of-a-fraction of the budget of the *Transformers* movies), and Edgar Allan Poe adaptations (including 1991's *The Pit and the Pendulum*).

When Showtime rounded up filmmakers for its *Masters of Horror* series, it was only natural that it called on Gordon, who contributed a Lovecraft story for its first season ("Dreams in the Witch-House," 2005), a Poe for its second ("The Black Cat," 2007), and a third for *Fear Itself*, the series' continuation on NBC (2008's "Eater"). By then, Gordon's films had added politics to their witches' brew of ingredients. Co-written by noted science fiction author Joe Haldeman (*The Forever War*), *Robot Jox* takes place in a future where war is outlawed, and the two super nations that make up the world duke it out for resources with robots that fight gladiator style. In the US of 1993's *Fortress*, a one-child-per-family limit is strictly enforced; a couple that has broken the rule by conceiving a second after their first has died is imprisoned in a futuristic complex laden with nasty mind control and torture devices, including the dreaded "Intestinators."

2007's *Stuck*, a torn-from-the-headlines shocker, is based on a notorious 2001 crime. A hit-and-run incident leaves Tom (Stephen Rea), a homeless man, trapped in the windshield of a car driven by Brandi (Mena Suvari), a retirement-home worker. Brandi promises help once she parks the car in her garage, then reconsiders, triggering a cat-and-mouse game between the protagonists. Gordon also directed the 2005 film version of one of David Mamet's bleakest and most horrific plays, 1982's *Edmond*. Protagonist William H. Macy walks out on his comfortable life and into an ugly urban underbelly rife with racist taunts, casual brutality, and murder.

Gordon and Mamet came up together in the Chicago theater scene. While a student at the University of Wisconsin, Gordon was one of the 10,000 who participated in the protests against the 1968 Democratic National Convention in the city. He shaped the experience into a controversial student production of *Peter Pan*. The play's content was largely unchanged, but Pan and the Lost Boys were recast as hippies, Wendy and her brothers as straitlaced suburban kids, and Captain Hook and his band of pirates as, of course, Mayor Richard J. Daley and the Chicago police. Tinker Bell's fairy dust became LSD. But what really created controversy was the trip to Never Neverland in which a psychedelic light show was projected on the bodies of seven naked dancers.

Though a hit, *Peter Pan* caused Gordon and his wife (Carolyn Purdy-Gordon, one of the nude dancers, and a frequent co-star in his films) to be arrested for obscenity. . . . (Gordon plans to turn this story into a film, *'68*). All charges were withdrawn, and Gordon and Purdy-Gordon moved to Chicago in 1970, where they formed the groundbreaking Organic Theatre Company. The Organic made a name for itself with adaptations of *Animal Farm* and *The Adventures of Huckleberry Finn*, and original productions like the three-part sci-fi epic *Warp!*, *Bleacher Bums*, *E/R*, and the world premiere of Mamet's *Sexual Perversity in Chicago*. The company launched the careers of actors such as Joe Mantegna, Dennis Franz, Meshach Taylor, and John Cameron Mitchell.

Though his career has had brushes with Disney (notably the story for the 1989 hit *Honey, I Shrunk the Kids* and the 1998 Ray Bradbury adaptation *The Wonderful Ice Cream Suit*), Gordon maintains his independence. He was interviewed for *Cineaste* by aspiring filmmaker, James Morgart.
—Robert Cashill

James Morgart: I've heard that, while a student at the University of Wisconsin, you formed Screw Theatre and performed a *Peter Pan* production that gained recognition and landed you in jail. I was wondering if you could elaborate on that a little bit?

Stuart Gordon: Yes. It was 1968, the same year as the Democratic convention in Chicago where the riots broke out and the police beat up and tear-gassed the protesters outside the convention. My wife, Carolyn, and I were in the middle of that, and we got tear-gassed and arrested. So, following the incident, I decided that maybe *Peter Pan* could be used as an analogy for what was happening and we didn't change any of the dialogue from the original play. But we made Peter Pan and the Lost Boys these drug-experimenting hippies. Wendy and her brothers were these straight suburban kids. Captain Hook was Mayor Daly of Chicago, and the pirates were the police. In the original, when the kids fly off to Neverland, they get fairy dust sprinkled on them to make them fly, but for our production we had them drop acid. To portray this, we had a psychedelic light show, dancing bodies, and seven naked women.

JM: Wow, so was it the drugs or the nudity that landed you in jail?

SG: Well, it seemed the authorities were unhappy with the whole thing—the idea of sort of tampering with a beloved child's play. And, actually, the university backed our production, but I found out recently that following the play, they placed in their bylaws that there could be no nudity in any student production. It ended up as a felony offense for obscenity, so my wife, who was one of the nude women on stage, and I were arrested. Our attorney found out that the guy who brought charges against us was a convicted child molester. At that point, they withdrew their charges.

JM: Go figure.

SG: Yeah, it's funny because I've been writing a script about the whole thing called '68 and we're talking to the university about shooting it in Madison.

JM: That would be great, and the whole twist of the guy being a child molester is ironic.

SG: Yeah, that was great. Well, in order to arrest someone for obscenity, you have to have someone from the community saying that what you're doing is obscene. It can't just be the district attorney bringing charges without that. Yet they couldn't find anyone to come forward to complain even though there were literally thousands of people who had seen the play.

JM: So, from there you moved to the Organic Theatre Company in Chicago.

SG: Yeah, I started the Organic Theatre Company in Madison, actually. We still got harassed by the police for the content of some of our productions and we were threatened with being shut down. So, we decided to leave the university and take our company down to Chicago where we spent the next fifteen years.

JM: I was reading about some of your early productions, how they often had either a Marxist or Feminist slant, particularly *Bloody Bess* . . .

SG: Yes, that's true. *Bloody Bess*, in particular, was about the revenge of a woman on a man who raped her and murdered her father.

JM: Are those themes or ideas that you were consciously pursuing?

SG: Well, you have to remember that during these times, feminism was really kind of like a new thing. So, it was something that was in the air, and when you're doing theater, you're going to bring in what's happening around you.

JM: Is that something you feel is typical of the theater? That is, you're likely to overtly explore social forces and social values?

SG: Yeah. I mean, I think all art is political and your craft is going to naturally explore and react to society.

JM: According to the Organic Theatre Company's website, you ended up leaving in the eighties. I was curious as to how the founder of a theater company could effectively be pushed out of his own creation.

SG: Well, it was kind of what, I think, is typical with the arts scene. The theater was started by myself and a handful of interns, so it was kind of an artists' controlled co-op. But it came to a certain point where if we wanted a bigger performing stage, we needed fundraising, so we needed to put a board together. Once that happened, suddenly the board had the power and the artists did not. It got to the point where it really became frustrating towards the end, and so it was at that time that I did *Re-Animator*. Originally, I wanted to use the actors from the company for the film, but the board did not like the idea of me doing a horror film. They said I should be doing an art film, and they said they did not want the Organic Theatre Company's name on a horror film.

JM: Really? Because the website suggests that the initial cause of the rift was that they wanted more productions like *E/R*.

SG: Well, *E/R* was a huge hit and brought in a lot of money for the theater, so the board wanted every show to be that successful. I mean, I had been doing theater for fifteen years and that was the most successful production we ever had. So, I thought it was an unrealistic goal. When you're pursuing art, you can't expect every project to be "perfect" or commercially successful.

JM: How do you think your approach to storytelling changed once you moved from theater to film?

SG: I don't think it's changed that much, actually. One of the things we always tried to do in theater was to involve the audience directly. For example, in one production we did, we got the audience to get on stage with us. It was a show titled *Doctor Rat* and based off the William Kotzwinkle novel about animal experimentation. We had the audience in cages, which was our point: it was about a revolution within the laboratory. It climaxed with the lab doors being opened and the audience being released. You can't really do that with a film, but I try to get the audience involved in other ways. Any audience really wants to be engaged and really wants to get involved with the story being told. So, I try to do things in film that are going to require them to be carried into the work with their imaginations.

JM: When it comes to horror films, what do you think makes a Stuart Gordon film different from other films within the genre?

SG: Well, stories I'm drawn to are ones that are surprising and that take you to places you're not expecting. Most of the films in horror are rather formulaic in that you know what's going to happen, whereas with my work, I like to go places that are unexpected.

JM: That's interesting, because your films generally avoid the "slasher" genre of horror. That is, not only does it avoid the formulaic killer with a butcher knife, but also there's never that "final girl" whom Carol Clover talks about in her book *Men, Women, and Chainsaws* [Princeton University Press, 1992]. In fact, your portrayal of women comes across as very different from other horror films. Starting with your first film, *Re-Animator*, what was your vision for the main female character, Megan Halsey?

SG: Well, the character wasn't in the original story. When you're making a movie—especially when you're adapting Lovecraft because Lovecraft very seldom had female characters—you're not really sure of what you're doing. What I mean is that sometimes you do things sort of subconsciously. For example, I was being interviewed after *Re-Animator* came out, and he pointed out that there are basically three main types of monsters: a vampire, a werewolf, and a Frankenstein Monster. And he related all three to sex. The vampire story is about having sex with a stranger. The werewolf story is about having an inner sexual beast taking over. And the Frankenstein Monster story, he said, is about masturbation. So, immediately, I was like, "Whoa, whoa, wait a minute here . . ." So, there's always different ways in which people can interpret how a character functions in a given work. But I think with Megan, that sort of masturbation reading is fairly accurate though, in that she is a character who I intended to have a sort of pent-up sexual aggression surrounded by these three male figures.

JM: She also becomes a sort of object of protection in the film, whether it be her boyfriend or father . . .

SG: Yeah, that's quite true.

JM: Were you consciously seeking to show her as trapped in a patriarchal world?

SG: Actually, no, I never really looked at it in those terms. I saw her as a representation of the traditional role in society. You know, there's that scene towards the end where she is able to reach her re-animated father, and I think the message there is simply that love is stronger than death. That inside that re-animated brain of her father is the remembrance of her as his daughter and that need to protect her kicks in at that moment of realization.

JM: When it comes to nudity in *Re-Animator*, as in your other films, you handle it very differently than most other horror films in that it seems to be an almost equal-opportunity nudity film by having both men and women appear naked throughout. In fact, the first nude body shown is an obese corpse in an emergency room. What was your approach to using nudity in the film?

SG: I think we were trying to reflect reality. One of the things we did when we first began work on the film was to go down to the morgue. And what we found was that in reality there were dead naked bodies lying around, so we wanted to be sure to portray that. And, of course, where the majority of the nudity takes place is in the morgue, when the bodies are re-animated, so it only made sense that they would be naked.

JM: One of the only other female roles in the film is played by your wife. Her lines in the film consist of telling Dan Cain to stop attempting CPR on dead bodies on two separate occasions. Was there a purpose to having a woman in this role?

SG: No, not really. Again, I think that the scene is meant to be a reflection of reality. When we did *E/R*, we had a friend of mine who is an emergency room doctor give us technical advice on how emergency rooms actually operate. So, when it came to an emergency room scene in *Re-Animator*, we wanted to portray that realistically, and there are times when a doctor has done everything they can do to revive a body, but they can't. And so, for that scene, we wanted to show Dan's desire to not let these patients die. What was interesting was that while we were talking to various doctors before making the film, we found out that this idea we were exploring of re-animating bodies was something they were very much interested in doing and that there were people out there doing research seeking to re-animate dead bodies.

JM: So, the infamous scene with Megan tied to the table and Dr. Hill's head about to rape her . . .

SG: Ah, yes.

JM: Was there a social or political intent behind it?

SG: There was. We knew when we were making the movie at the time that scene would be a big deal. It had occurred to me while watching horror films before we shot the movie that there would always be that scene where the monster would drag the woman off with him and then the camera would cut, and you're left there wondering, "Well, what's he going to do with her?" So, our entire intention was that we would actually show what the monster would be doing in that scene that the audience is never shown. One of the things that we had added to the film was that these re-animated people would have their libidos fully unleashed, and that's part of the "problem," that they're not being held back by social constructs and values.

JM: Of *Re-Animator*, Pauline Kael wrote, "This horror film about a medical student with a fluorescent greenish-yellow serum that restores the dead to hideous, unpredictable activity is close to being a silly ghoulie classic—the bloodier it gets, the funnier it is. It's like pop Buñuel; the jokes hit you in a subterranean comic zone that the surrealists' pranks sometimes reached, but without the surrealists' self-consciousness (and art-consciousness) . . . Barbara Crampton is the dean's creamy-pink daughter (who's at her loveliest when she's being defiled)." What was your reaction to this review, which, along with other rave reviews, put the film on the map?

SG: I was amazed, because I made a film that I thought the critics would hate. In a way, the fact that I took that approach is one of the reasons why I think it worked out as well as it did. I wasn't worrying about the critics and I really didn't expect the critical success, because what I had set out to do was: first, to make a film that I wanted to make; and, second, to make a film that I thought the fans wanted to see. I think it was Roger Ebert who discovered the movie at Cannes, and his review wound up creating buzz for the film that resulted in other critics reviewing the film. I was pleasantly surprised at the responses that the film was getting. I have always been an avid reader of Pauline Kael, so when I read that she liked the movie I just loved what she had to say, especially about Barbara Crampton's character.

JM: In *From Beyond*, there's considerably less gore and considerably less nudity, and yet there are similar themes about control and sexuality. Was this a conscious exploration?

SG: I think to some degree, we certainly were. Though I think a lot of that is born out of adapting Lovecraft since I view his stories as already having control and sexuality embedded within the work.

JM: Though the character of Dr. Katherine McMichaels in *From Beyond* is played by the same actress, Barbara Crampton, who played Megan Halsey in *Re-Animator*, the characters are vastly different. Halsey is a traditional sort of straight-laced suburban middle-America young woman while Dr. McMichaels reflects more of that empowered go-getter values of say a J. C. Wiatt in *Baby Boom* [1987], or even elements of a Gordon Gekko from *Wall Street* [1987]. Was there a social critique being made with this portrayal?

SG: Well, again, she is another character we had to create since the Lovecraft original didn't have her in it. When we were working on it, I viewed her as sort of the female version of a Herbert West in that she has a similar drive to succeed the way Herbert does. One of her motivating factors is her father, which differentiates her from Herbert, but aside from that I definitely see similarities between them in terms of the greed and desire that drives them.

JM: In *Dolls*, Judy is left to carve out her own way of living due to the neglect of her father and her stepmother as they view her largely in economic terms. Did you intend the film to be more of a "good versus evil" [narrative] or as a work offering a critique on greed, as those who die in the story are largely obsessed with money?

SG: Honestly, my intention when it came to *Dolls* was this idea of maintaining the child within you; that getting wrapped up in the adult world will eventually wear you down and kill you, whereas those who survive in the movie are those who are still a child at heart.

JM: Do you find that, when it comes to horror, the fans tend to drive the industry more than other genres?

SG: The fans are definitely the most loyal of any genre. The horror fans are just incredible. The thing I keep discovering is that, first of all, they read everything. They're incredibly well read, so I've had great discussions with them on Poe or Lovecraft. And, secondly, they don't necessarily like everything. They're extremely discriminating. I think that when it comes to horror fans, they really do try to see and know everything within the genre.

JM: It seems that almost all of your films deal with ambition, power, and greed, from *Honey, I Shrunk the Kids*, where ambition both literally and metaphorically shrinks a scientist's children, to *Re-Animator*, where it leads to horrific scientific advances. Are these statements about ambition's negative effects intentional?

SG: I think these films are about dreams, and how incredible dreams can be. And the horror about dreams is that you have to be careful, because sometimes they can wind up becoming nightmares. Basically, at their root, they follow that old adage: "You've got to be careful what you wish for."

JM: What do you think of the phrase "torture porn"?

SG: I hate it. First of all, there's the phrase "porn" being thrown in there, and there's always been that stigma of horror being likened to porn. Secondly, torture is something that's existed in drama since the very beginning. Shakespeare uses it effectively in *King Lear*. Honestly, I think whoever uses this phrase just doesn't like horror very much.

JM: Given their explicit violence, could films like *The Pit and the Pendulum* and *Dagon* be considered "torture porn" though they're derived from classical sources?

SG: There's torture in them, but I think horror reflects society. The fact that for decades we've had horror films that have torture in them reflects the fact that for years we've had a government that endorses torture. Most recently, torture has been on the front page of the newspapers almost every day, and you've got people like Dick Cheney defending torture as something that's necessary for our national security. So, of course, you're going to see it reflected in art.

JM: The films mentioned in reference to torture porn are films like *Saw* [2004] or *Hostel* [2005], which came out just after details about Abu Ghraib were starting to surface in the press. Does the backlash against a film like *Hostel*, where humans are commodities, or its director, Eli Roth, come from torture just being too stark of a reality for some people to face?

SG: The thing about horror is that it deals with issues that we don't really want to talk about—starting with the most basic idea, which is death. All horror films deal with death, which is a topic that most people don't usually discuss. To have the ability to discuss or explore things that society wants to avoid is what makes the horror industry a very great and powerful thing.

JM: Do you find the trend toward remaking horror films of the seventies and eighties derivative or inspired in its own way?

SG: I think it's pointless. I don't like these movies at all. I think when the movie was made, the filmmaker had something to say. When a studio goes out and hires some music video director to remake a film, it's largely a commercial enterprise.

JM: If you or someone else were planning to rework your older films, what might you do differently?

SG: What I'd do differently is that I wouldn't rework any of my older films. And I'm not that big into sequels. I think that once you've done something, you should go on to something else. Unless, after the first film, you feel that there's still more to say about the subject, which sometimes can happen. I was planning to make *House of Re-Animator*, but we missed our chance for the film to be relevant as it was to be centered on the Bush administration. So, in a way, I'm kind of delighted that I don't have to make it.

JM: How has the marketplace changed for your films?

SG: I'm just lucky that people keep watching them. So, at the end of the day, it's really a matter of whether or not you're proud of your work and the projects you've put forth.

JM: What does it mean to be considered a "Master of Horror"?

SG: Well, you know, that term started out as a bit of a joke. It came from a documentary being made that was called *Masters of Horror* and they were interviewing all of us for it. It was Mick Garris who realized that none of us were getting to meet one another, as we were being interviewed separately, and invited us all to dinner together. So, that label, "Masters of Horror," was basically born out of that first dinner. Here we were, sitting at this big table at a restaurant, and at a table near us they brought a cake for someone celebrating their birthday. Guillermo del Toro got all of us to stand up and sing "Happy Birthday." And it ended with him saying, "The Masters of Horror wish you a happy birthday." It was really fantastic. Then we started meeting every couple of months, and eventually Mick got the idea to do the series so we could all work together.

JM: *Edmond* was an unusual choice to bring to the screen. How did you and David Mamet collaborate on the adaptation?

SG: It was something we had been talking about for years. In fact, I think he had written the screenplay shortly after he had written the play back in the eighties. When it came to actually make the movie, we worked closely with one another, but the film actually wound up staying fairly close to the original, as it was quite brilliant.

JM: What about the play attracted you?

SG: Again, I think it's tackling something that people really don't want to talk about. The topic being, of course, racism, which is always a difficult one to broach. And the film addresses the idea that everyone is racist, which is something that people don't want to admit, but it's true. It's just a part of the human condition. All you have to do is get into a bad traffic situation and you'll find yourself saying things that you never would've expected could come out of your mouth.

JM: *Edmond* and *Stuck* show horror erupting in everyday surroundings. Is there such a thing as "normal life"? Are we all fated to become monsters?

SG: I don't think there's such a thing as normal. (Laughs) I think that's something that everyone likes to be. I think everyone has monsters within them and are, in one way or another, trying to contain them. And a lot of my movies are about monsters, but they're not about fighting monsters, they're about being one.

JM: What drew you to the fact-based story of *Stuck*?

SG: It was about an ordinary person, this caregiver of senior citizens, who becomes a monster. How did that happen? After reading about it in the newspaper, I just couldn't stop thinking about it. I'm influenced by both film and theater, but what I try to be most influenced by is real life. I really think that it's an artist's job to take life and put it into an artistic framework.

JM: Why did you alter the race of the main character, Brandi?

SG: My intention was to make it unclear what the race of the main character was. In fact, the character was named after someone I knew who was a light-skinned Black girl with green eyes. And so, with her character, there is that element of, "Is she a Black girl or is she a white girl who is maybe a Black wannabe?"

JM: *Edmond* and *Stuck* present a harsh portrait of race. Does the election of President Obama inspire hope or deepen the fissures?

SG: I think it's a great thing, an amazing thing. In fact, I think it's the only good thing that came out of the Bush administration. Because it never would've happened if things hadn't gotten as fucked up as they did. But I don't think his election is going to stop racism. People will always have that irrational fear and that's not going to go away.

JM: Those fears are surfacing now.

SG: I grew up in Chicago and, while I was there, Martin Luther King Jr. decided to march in the streets, and Mayor Daley said, "Well, this is Chicago, there isn't any racism here." King's response was, "Then there shouldn't be a problem, should there?" But, of course, there wound up being a huge problem as the protesters had stones and bricks and objects hurled at them by my neighbors as they marched. People who didn't think there was racism in their city found out that, when confronted with the issue, there was a ton of racism within the city. I think it's better to get it out there and to discuss it, [rather] than to keep it bottled up and behind closed doors.

JM: I've seen photos of you online out at the picket lines during the Writers Guild of America strike. Do you consider yourself an activist?

SG: Absolutely. I think I did a lot more back then than I do now. The writers' strike was the first time I was out on the picket lines in years and years. But I do consider myself an activist.

JM: How does your background in theater and politics of the sixties inform your work?

SG: I think the sixties were a time of us realizing for the first time that all art is political. We had a lot of turmoil going on around us and we were constantly reacting to that in our work. It's just something that's been part of my art ever since. That is, anything I'm going to do is going to be political in one way or another.

JM: On the drawing board is '68.

SG: I'm hoping to get that made, but it might be a bit of a challenge as it's the first time I'll be making a love story. My wife and I are part of the story, so it'll involve how we met and fell in love. But it'll also involve our being tear-gassed at the convention and our arrest following the adaptation of the *Peter Pan* play.

JM: So, it'll extend the politics of your work?

SG: Absolutely. It'll be focused on the politics of the sixties, as I really don't think there's ever been a great film about the sixties that's been able to capture the turmoil and turbulence of the time.

JM: Edmond says, "Behind every fear is a wish." Do you agree?

SG: I think your fears change throughout your life, but I think that you always wish the best for the people you love. So, there's always that fear that something bad will happen to them. There's this whole subgenre of horror films emerging right now about children who are killing their parents, and I think that's one of the new fears, that we're becoming afraid of our own children. I don't know why that is. Maybe it's a Boomer thing; that my generation is now getting old and should just get out of the way of the younger generations. Maybe it's technology that's become a dividing line between us and our own children. "Oh, Dad is too dumb to figure out email!"

Mortal Wisdom: Stuart Gordon

Danny Draven / 2009

From *The Filmmaker's Book of the Dead: A Mortal's Guide to Making Horror Movies* (Routledge, 2015), pp. 175–81. Reprinted by permission.

Danny Draven: How did your background in the theater help you as a director?

Stuart Gordon: I had a lot of experience in theater working with actors, writers, and playwrights. All of that was very useful to me. We did a lot of plays that were fantasy or horror based, and we did a lot of the effects live on stage. A lot of those effects were used in *Re-Animator*, which was my first film. I didn't know anything about filmmaking, not even the basic things like screen direction and crossing the line. On the set of *Re-Animator*, I was run over several times by the dolly because I didn't know where to stand.

Draven: Your film *Re-Animator* is a classic because of its combination of extreme gore, sexuality, and dark humor. The film masterfully balances gross-out horror and macabre humor. Why is laughter an important element in horror films?

Gordon: It's great to have those moments when you can break the tension with a laugh and then crank the suspense again. . . . The humor comes out of the characters; it's not winking at the audience. You have to be careful not to mix comedy with horror or they will cancel each other out. I think you have to take the movie seriously. Your audience wants you to do that. If they sense that the director thinks the whole movie is silly, or that he thinks he is slumming by doing a horror movie, they will have nothing to do with it. They want to know the people who made the movie are fans of the genre and take it seriously.

Draven: How important is sexuality in horror films?

Gordon: I've always felt that sex and horror go hand in hand. They are basically two sides of the same coin. You can go back to some of the old drawings in the Middle Ages and they have something called "Death and the Maiden." They would use the character "Death" as a picture of a skeleton caressing a beautiful naked woman. I think what it is, is life and death. Sex symbolizes life and procreating. Horror movies are really about death, and it's the conflict between the two. Even in the older horror movies there are scenes of the monster picking up the woman and carrying her off. They never used to show you what happened when they carried her off, but now we do. I am sensing a backlash recently. Kids are getting more puritanical. In one of my movies I was looking at some of the comments about it on IMDb, and one of them wrote, "How bad is the nudity?" It was somebody who wanted to watch it with his girlfriend, but was afraid if it was too sexually explicit she might think he was a pervert or something. It was just really weird. I think now there is sort of an anti-sex feeling in horror movies as well. I think things are changing. I feel if there is a reason for the nudity in terms of the story, fine; then do it. If the audience feels that you are doing it just to add T & A to your movie, they tend to turn off to that.

Draven: What are the mechanics of a successful scare?

Gordon: It depends on what you are calling a scare. Stephen King once said, "The strongest emotion one can create is horror, a sense of dread." The sense that something awful is going to happen is *true* horror. The next level, he said, was "shock," when something jumps out at you and goes, "*Boo!*" The lowest level is the "gross-out," something that is just plain disgusting. Those are the ways he broke it down. I think, for me, in regards to scaring an audience, it is creating characters and a story you care about. Once your audience is involved, you can put your characters in dangerous situations and they will get scared for them.

Draven: What is the best way for a new director to communicate with an actor on set?

Gordon: I think it's helpful if the director knows what goes into acting. I always advise new directors to do some acting or theater classes. If you take an acting class, you will know how to speak the language of the actor. It's important for the actor to know that the director understands what they are going through. The thing I have learned over the years is to ask questions of the actors and let them solve the problems, so it's coming from them. You ask questions like, "What would you do if *this* were to happen?" The actor has to believe that this is all really happening to him and put himself in that situation. Giving an actor a direction by saying, "Be more scared," isn't helpful, because you are just asking him for the results of what you are looking for, as opposed to asking, "What is it about the situation that would scare *you?*" Something you can also do is the "what if?" situation. "What if you are being followed by somebody? Suppose you heard the person breathing, not knowing if it was human or animal?" By this, you're putting their imaginations to work, putting them in that situation.

Good directors don't say a lot to the actors, but they say just enough and encourage them. The director is kind of a surrogate audience for the actor. So, it's encouraging to say, "Wow, you did great!" to the actor to put them at ease. It's important for them to be relaxed, to create a comfortable environment on the set, even though you are under a lot of pressure to work quickly. You should never rush the actor. You try to make them feel like they have all the time in the world to do what they have to do. I think in moviemaking, the actors are the most important part of the process. It's all about the acting for me. The technical part is important, but movies are all about the actors; that's what makes them so powerful. Actors become like family to the audiences, and we care about them.

Draven: When directing horror films, what criteria do you use when determining where to put the camera?

Gordon: The best answer I've heard came from Steven Spielberg, who said that he likes to put the camera where he sits to watch the rehearsals. I think that's a very practical way to look at it. I also recommend rehearsing with your actors before production to work out all the character motivation and other details. For *Re-Animator*, I was influenced by Roman Polanski's work. He shoots his movies by making his audiences feel they are a character in the film. One of my favorite shots is the over-the-shoulder shot. It gives the audience a real sense of being in the movie instead of watching it from a distance. Alfred Hitchcock had a great line, too. He said, "I want to be on the train; I don't want to be a cow in the pasture watching the train go by." What I like in movies is when you forget you are watching a movie. You're engaged, and you're *in* it. As an audience, you want to forget that these are actors and there is a script. When you start to say to yourself, "Wow, what a great shot!" you're out of the movie. The positioning of the camera can really have an effect on how the audience takes in the scene. One of the other things I've learned is that horror is slow. Horror is about anticipation. The longer it takes someone to walk up the stairs the better, because you know something is at the top waiting for them. You need to slow it down. I read somewhere that when David Cronenberg makes movies, his scripts are very short because he knows he will play things as slowly as he possibly can.

Draven: Do you storyboard?

Gordon: Yes, I do storyboard, but not everything. I storyboard effects sequences and stunt scenes. I think it's important to show departments what you have in mind and how you are planning on shooting it. When dealing with special effects or mechanical prosthetics, they will know where the camera is going to be. This way they can hide the machinery or see how they can accomplish the shot. In one of my earlier movies, [*From Beyond*], we had an effect where we had a thing coming out of this guy's forehead. Sometimes we used a dummy and sometimes we used the actor, puppeteering from the side of his face the camera couldn't see. So, we had to have a drawing on how we planned on shooting it. It's a good idea to sit down with the effects guy before you storyboard, so you know what the effects are and how they are planning to accomplish them. I usually don't storyboard everything because I like to see what the actors are going to be doing. They may not want to come through the window and would prefer a door. Well, then your storyboard ends up in the trash can. That's why I think rehearsals are important. I don't even do my shot list until after I rehearse with the actors.

Draven: In today's digital revolution, there are more horror films than ever being made. What do you think are the biggest mistakes new filmmakers commit when making their first horror film?

Gordon: I see more movies concerned with the gore effects than the actors or the story. The most important thing—and this is true about all movies, not just horror movies—is the script. You really have to get your script right and create a story that is really captivating, and where every scene flows into the next one. I've seen a lot of movies where the script is just nonexistent, but you can tell that they spent a lot of time focusing on the makeup effects. This is not only true with little films, but big Hollywood blockbusters. No matter how wonderful your actors and effects are, if the script is bad, you're doomed.

Draven: In your experience, what do you think are the most vital elements a horror film must have to be successful with an audience?

Gordon: A story with characters that you care about, I think, is one of the most important. One of the things I see a lot are people that make movies about other movies. They borrow scenes from other films. You think you are seeing retreads from other movies and scenes you've seen a million times. What's important is to come up with something fresh and new. I also think you need to go beyond what has been done before in the past. I think good horror movies are transgressive and do things that are taboo. There are so many horror movies out there. You have to do something that separates your film from the rest of the pack, something that has people talking about how they can't believe what they just saw.

It's interesting how time has a way of dulling everything down. Amazingly, about thirty or forty years ago, *Night of the Living Dead* was being shown at midnight screenings, with scenes of zombies eating flesh and intestines. No one had ever seen this before, and it was very disturbing. Audience members vomited and fainted. Now, that movie is shown uncut on television at 3 p.m. in the afternoon. In *Psycho*, Hitchcock sets up the whole story with Janet Leigh stealing money from her company and being on the run. This whole storyline builds up to her getting stabbed to death in the shower. The stabbing in the shower was a famous scene, but the scene would not be as powerful as it was had he not done all the setup for it, getting us involved with the character's predicament. This makes the audience feel as if they are getting stabbed in the shower. That's why it's so shocking.

The greatest tool that a filmmaker has is the audience's imagination. If he can manipulate, tease, and engage them, he will get their imaginations spinning.

With a great filmmaker, you feel you are in the hands of a guy who is not going to stop. He is going to go way beyond anything you have ever seen before. You get this weird feeling where you are excited and also terrified, wondering if you can handle this. I think that is the goal of the filmmaker. When you realize that the filmmaker is smart and talented, and that you are under his spell, it's a great feeling. In *Alien*, you don't see the whole monster until one of the last shots in the movie. You see little pieces of it, a little mouth or pieces of a hand. You're not even sure what you are looking at half the time. It makes it mysterious. The idea is that once you show the monster, the movie is over. It's the fear of the unknown that is the strongest fear. Once the unknown becomes known, then you can handle it.

Draven: In 2002, I produced and directed a film with you for Full Moon Pictures called *Stuart Gordon Presents Deathbed* for a budget of only $35,000 that was shot in eight days in Los Angeles. As someone who regularly works on larger projects, this was somewhat of a different world you entered into, working under these constraints. What kinds of things did you learn from working at this ultra-low budget level with fast-paced schedules?

Gordon: I learned a tremendous amount. That was a really good experience for me. I felt like I was seeing the future of filmmaking. Seeing how you produced and directed *Deathbed* was a revelation to me. It made me realize that the whole world that I had known was about to change in a big way. I remember you guys were making movies out of an apartment complex, which seemed to be a mini production studio. We did Foley and ADR in the bathroom, sound design in another apartment, and our commentary in your living room. What I feel that will never change is the importance of story, strong performances, and imagination. That is what you need no matter what the format is. It all comes down to the script, actors, and the director being able to tell that story.

I always tell my students that the problems are always the same no matter what the size of your budget. You never have enough time or enough movie. When James Cameron did *Titanic* (1997), he wanted to build the whole Titanic full-size and couldn't do it. He had to build half of it. There was a scene where he had to show the other side, and he ended up just flipping the negative. He had all the signage written in mirror image because he knew he was going to flip it. The whole scene where the passengers were boarding the ship was all shot with a negative flipped because the ship was facing the wrong way. Amazing! My mother used to always say, "There are two ways to solve a problem: one is to throw money at it; the other way is to be clever."

Stuart Gordon Talks *Nevermore: An Evening with Edgar Allan Poe*

Robert V. Galluzzo / 2009

From *ShockTillYouDrop.com*, September 28, 2009. Reprinted by permission.

In July of 2009, Stuart Gordon teamed up with his *Re-Animator* co-writer Dennis Paoli and star Jeffrey Combs to put on a one-man play titled *Nevermore: An Evening with Edgar Allan Poe*, a fitting tribute to the famous horror fiction author and poet who, in October, will celebrate his 200th year. What started out as a simple four-week run has been expanded three times now and is going on into its fourth month. Having seen the show numerous times, *Shock Till You Drop* sat down to chat with Stuart Gordon about the surprise success of his stellar play.

Robert V. Galluzzo: What were the origins for the *Nevermore* play? I imagine this stemmed from working with Jeffrey and Dennis on the *Masters of Horror* episode, "The Black Cat"?

Stuart Gordon: Yeah, you're absolutely right. We had such fun working on that that we thought we should do something more with Jeffrey Combs as Edgar Allan Poe. This year, being Poe's bicentennial, it struck us that a one-man show would really be the thing to do. And, ideally, we'd like to take it on tour around the country to celebrate Poe's 200th birthday.

RVG: Are you guys really taking this show on tour officially?

SG: Well, that's our plan. We don't have any definite plans to do so yet, because this show has just really taken off here in LA. What started as a four-week run is now going into its fourth month!

RVG: That's funny, because I literally just moved into town the first week it started playing and I've already seen it twice, and plan to catch it again this weekend. It's been a great show. And the neat thing is every single time I've gone to see it, there's always recognizable faces in the audience. The first time I saw Joe

Dante sitting a few seats over. Another time, I sat behind Angus Scrimm. That's part of the fun of seeing the show here in LA.

SG: I know. It's an amazing audience. Besides having celebrities showing up, we have a very mixed group—everybody from very young kids to oldsters. With Poe, everyone loves him. And his work is for everyone, really.

RVG: The thing I find interesting is that this is based upon the type of show that Poe had done on stage in the last year of his life, correct?

SG: That's right. Yeah, he did recitals, often in very large auditoriums with 2000 seats and so forth. He'd become famous as the author of "The Raven" [1845], so he was really taking advantage of it. It was like a rock star going around doing his greatest hits. (Laughs)

RVG: Were any of Poe's last shows documented? What kind of research did you do?

SG: Well, there were reviews of some of them and, it's funny, because the reviews were varied. Some reviews said that he was absolutely magnetic and he was like an actor, but others said he was very quiet, reserved. He also did things in smaller venues where he'd perform with the light of a single candle for effect and we used that in our show as well.

RVG: Let's talk about Jeffrey Combs for a minute. Obviously, I'm a big fan of his work on the screen, but this play is a true testament to what an incredible actor he is.

SG: Absolutely. People forget how great he is, and I think part of it is because he's so versatile that oftentimes you do not even realize it is Jeffrey Combs.

RVG: By the time he gets to the midway point of "The Raven," I'm blown away by the fact that an actor can not only memorize that poem, but perform that entire show for an hour and a half by themselves.

SG: I know!

RVG: It makes me realize how hard acting really is.

SG: Well, Jeffrey says that it's like climbing a mountain every night. It really is a marathon for him. He's exhausted by the time it's done, but he really does give it his all.

RVG: Both of you guys have worked on stage and on screen. Any thoughts on stage work versus the screen work?

SG: Well, the thing that's fun about theater is that it really involves the audience directly, unlike a movie which is shadows on a wall. In a live performance, you can interact with an audience, which we do in the play. I remember one night there was someone sneezing, and Jeffrey would say, "Do you need help, dear sir?" and things like that. It was great acting because, from then on, every sneeze started getting laughs. But I think that's what the charge is. You feel as if you're in the same room as Edgar Allan Poe.

RVG: Within the first ten to fifteen minutes, I completely forget it was Jeffrey and I felt like I was sitting there watching Poe.

SG: I know. It really is incredible, because it doesn't look like Jeffrey; it doesn't sound like Jeffrey. It's Poe that's up there.

RVG: The show initially was only set for four weeks, but I believe it's been extended three times now.

SG: It has, yeah. It's now running up until Halloween. And it's possible it may even go beyond that.

RVG: Were you surprised by the overwhelming response to the show? When did you know that you guys had something special with this play?

SG: Well, we knew it, I think, from the first few performances, because my fear was that we would end up with an audience of four or five people. Coming and listening to someone recite poetry is kind of a hard sell. But Jeffrey just is so incredible and I think he does channel Poe. Once the word got out about what we were doing, suddenly there were crowds there every night and we were turning people away.

RVG: You mentioned earlier that you're hoping to tour this show. I believe there's a celebration for Poe's 200th birthday taking place in Baltimore in October where they plan to throw him a proper funeral. Were you invited to do the play there for that event?

SG: Yeah. We'd been talking with the organizers in Baltimore, but, unfortunately, we opened the show in July and they already had a lot of their plans in place. It didn't seem like it'd work for us to join them there, although we have discussed it with them.

RVG: Obviously, there's no photography or videotaping allowed during the actual show. Hopefully you guys will get to take it on the road. But, for those of us who can't come out to see it, have you ever given consideration to taping it for perhaps a DVD release?

SG: We are talking about that, and I think it's very possible that that could happen.

RVG: You're there every night for the play. Does it ever get old for you? (Laughs) Or are you taken aback by Jeffrey's performance every night?

SG: No, because Jeffrey is constantly growing and trying new things, and every night is a little different. And, I say again, that's one of the great things about live theater, that the audience is always different. So, he changes the show each night and makes little adjustments, and adds things, and gets inspiration, and so forth. That's the great thing about Jeffrey Combs as an actor. You never get tired of watching him.

An Interview with Stuart Gordon

Christopher O'Neill / 2010

From *10k Bullets.com*, April 16, 2010. Reprinted by permission.

With his cinematic debut *Re-Animator* in 1985, Stuart Gordon instantly proved himself to be a filmmaker with a unique style and vision. Now a quarter of a century old, the picture still shocks with its graphic violence and splatter effects, which are infused with a jet-black sense of humor that simultaneously enhances the sense of brutality yet makes it too absurd to be truly offensive. This disarming mixture, along with a strong control of working within limited budgets and a deft handling of actors, puts Gordon head and shoulders above many other directors working within the horror genre.

Having forged a filmography that includes such off-kilter classics as *From Beyond*, *Dolls*, *Castle Freak*, and *Dagon*, Gordon has recently changed tack and gone from such fantasy-based pictures to a series of films characterized by what he calls "the banality of evil." *King of the Ants* (adapted from a novel by the British writer Charles Higson) and *Edmond* (based on the controversial stage play by David Mamet) are dark, shocking, and thought-provoking pictures that put ordinary people into extreme situations where they respond in the most horrific yet plausible ways.

His last feature film, *Stuck*, follows the same pattern and is all the more disturbing because it was inspired by a true story which took place in 2001 in Fort Worth, Texas: an intoxicated young woman was involved in a car accident where the victim went through the windshield and the driver continued home, parked her car in the garage, and left the man, still stuck through the windshield, to die. Gordon has taken this event and created a film that may be his masterpiece. In *Stuck*, Mena Suvari portrays the driver while Stephen Rea is the accident victim, and they both deliver magnificent, multilayered performances that must rate as among their best work on celluloid. With solid support from Russell Hornsby, Rukiya Bernard, and a wickedly funny appearance by Carolyn Purdy-Gordon, plus a solid screenplay by John Strysik, *Stuck* cannot be praised enough and deserved wider distribution than the token mini-theatrical releases that it received in America and Britain.

For the third MOTELX Film Festival in Lisbon, Stuart Gordon was honored with a retrospective of his work and the director was in attendance to introduce his movies. It was here that I met Gordon, a charming, intelligent, and humorous gentleman who, for the benefit of my Dictaphone, introduced himself by saying, "My name is Steven Spielberg."

Christopher O'Neill: With your most recent feature films, you have veered away from the fantastical and into a reality-grounded kind of horror. What brought about this change?

Stuart Gordon: It was quite gradual. It started with *King of the Ants*, which is a book my friend George Wendt brought to me, and said, "If you like this, I'll option it." I read it and I was completely blown away, because it was about an ordinary guy who is hired to kill someone, and I kept thinking at some point he was going to change his mind. But he actually does the murder, yet somehow you end up still caring about this guy. I said, "George, we've got to make this movie." So, we got the writer Charlie Higson to adapt the book into a screenplay and took it to every studio in town. But they all said, "This is totally amoral! I don't think we can do this movie." I started realizing things that happen in real life are far more disturbing than the things that people dream up for horror stories.

O'Neill: Beyond the horrific elements with these films you are also able to explore issues such as race, gender, class, and sexuality. Is this something that appeals to you?

Gordon: Yes, it does. All these things are interconnected, that's the thing you realize about life. You know, someone may say, "You are making political movies now," but I never thought of these films as being political. But because they are about society, they are. All three movies are about ordinary people who end up doing terrible things and these things happen. You read about them every day in the newspaper.

O'Neill: What is most impressive about *Stuck* is that it expands on a true story both to further explore the moral issues at hand and to invest in characterization.

Gordon: We did several drafts where we did follow the story closer to what actually happened, but what we realized was we wanted this character to become *active*. The question we started asking ourselves was did the guy realize what was happening to him, and did he try to escape and to get out of this situation? Suddenly, this made the story open up into a whole new dimension that was exciting to us, so we went in that direction. I think it was Joshua Logan, a stage and film director, who said in his autobiography that the protagonist always has to change, that the events that happen in the course of the story have to change this person's life in a major way. With the character that Mena Suvari plays that was the case, and by opening up the idea of the Stephen Rea character becoming active, then it came through for him too. What we ended up with, I think, is interesting since we now have a story with two protagonists. It becomes this life and death struggle between the two of them, and they are both sympathetic in their own ways.

O'Neill: *King of the Ants*, *Edmond*, and *Stuck* are tautly paced and tightly scripted, recalling the film noir of the 1940s and '50s. Do such pictures influence you?

Gordon: Well, I love those movies. With *King of the Ants*, I was aware that it was sort of a "noir" story, but while I was making the other films I never quite thought of them that way. But it's true, they do follow that pattern. One thing that I learned, even before I made them, is that movies should be very compact and economical, and shouldn't have any waste. Part of this is because when you're working on a low budget, you don't want to shoot anything that you don't have to. So, you keep honing that script down to what exactly is essential to make this movie work.

O'Neill: By doing so you learn more about the characters by having them respond to situations rather than through dialogue.

Gordon: Yes, you discover who they are by their actions. My writing partner, Dennis Paoli, always likes to tell me about how when he's on an airplane he watches the movies without buying the headphones—since you should be able to follow the story completely without any dialogue—and I think that's really important. That's one of the things about movies that I like; it's really about action.

O'Neill: Stephen Rea has a physically demanding role in *Stuck*. Throughout the film, I kept being reminded of the fly-in-the-spider-web scene from the 1958 version of *The Fly*.

Gordon: Well, Stephen was always joking, "I know my lines for today: 'Help me! Help me!'" He is incredible. And I have to say it was a dream come true to work with him, because he's been one of my favorite actors for so long and he really responded to the material. One of the things that was interesting is that it turned out that both he and the writer John Strysik are huge Samuel Beckett fans—and Stephen had actually worked with Beckett. There was something about this story that he could relate to it in Beckett terms, with characters buried up to their necks in sand and so forth, and this is kind of like that. Stephen also knew that it was going to be a very uncomfortable role to play. I mean, he was literally in that windshield day after day after day when we were shooting, and I think he really appreciated the spareness of it all.

O'Neill: Your films are rich with moments of black humor. What are your thoughts on this?

Gordon: My films always end up being funny and I often describe them as comedies. I think *King of the Ants* is funny, and *Edmond* is funny. I would have meetings with studio executives, and they would go, "What is funny about *this*?" and I'd give them a couple of examples. A friend of mine once said, "Life is too important to take seriously."

O'Neill: It is twenty-five years since you made your first feature, *Re-Animator*. How do you think the film holds up today?

Gordon: I look at it and I'm pretty proud of the way the film came out. One of the things I didn't realize at the time when I made it, was it was one of those rare situations where everybody was making the same movie and everybody was really giving it their all. Brian Yuzna, the producer, says it was "beginner's luck," because it was our first film and I thought all movies were going to be like that. But we soon found out how incredibly lucky we were.

O'Neill: Is it true that you are involved in a fourth *Re-Animator* film?

Gordon: I was, but, unfortunately, that's not going to happen. It was called *House of Re-Animator*, and it took place in the White House. The plot involved re-animating Dick Cheney's corpse, which was the basic idea. Bruce Abbott was going to come back, we had William H. Macy lined up to play George Bush, we were even talking about Barbara Crampton doing Laura Bush, which would have been interesting, and George Wendt to be Cheney. We had an amazing cast, but we couldn't get the financing for it. I think people were afraid of offending the Bush administration. Now, thank God, those days are over, but the idea of doing another *Re-Animator* movie was appealing.

O'Neill: What ultimately makes the *Re-Animator* films so successful is Jeffrey Combs. He is such a versatile actor who can adapt to and play any role.

Gordon: He's a total chameleon. We were doing *Masters of Horror* ("The Black Cat," in which he played Edgar Allan Poe), and, when he was in his Poe makeup, he didn't look like Jeffery, he didn't sound like Jeffrey. He *was* Poe. There was one day when we were staying in the same hotel and he got into the elevator with me and he looked like this sort of redneck character. After a few minutes, I realized, "It's *Jeffrey Combs!*" He's amazing in his ability to become all these people. I'm working with him now, doing a live evening with Edgar Allan Poe, and it's just astonishing what he does. What a fantastic actor he is. One of the things I learned doing theater is when you find someone whose work is great, and you're on the same wavelength, that you should hang onto that person and not let go.

O'Neill: What is the concept behind the Edgar Allan Poe play, *Nevermore*?

Gordon: It's set in 1848, the year before Poe died, and during that time he was doing recitals in big auditoriums and reading his poetry. So, it's based on one of those evenings with Poe dealing with what he would have called "The Imp of the Perverse." There was always something in him that had to destroy whatever it was that he was doing, so he starts drinking heavily during the course of this recital and all hell breaks loose. Jeffrey is just astonishing. It's a one-man show, and although there are other characters involved in the story, the only one that we see is Poe.

O'Neill: Finally, you are here in Lisbon for a retrospective of your work at the MOTELX Film Festival. How do you feel about being at this festival?

Gordon: Well, it's funny, because when they do retrospectives it usually means that you're dead. So, I keep pinching myself!

DG Interviews Stuart *"Re-Animator"* Gordon

Joe Bannerman / 2011

From *DailyGrindhouse.com*, September 7, 2011. Reprinted by permission.

One of my most surreal film experiences was watching *Re-Animator* with my grandmother. I was just a stupid kid, but, whenever I visited, she'd let me rent any damn thing I wanted. Grandma wasn't crazy about horror movies—or "Spooky-Doos," as she called them—but she'd nonetheless sit on the couch with me, chain-smoking like Denis Leary, and watch whatever crap I happened to pick up at the nearest Mom 'n' Pop Shop. I will never forget the moment David Gale was holding his own decapitated head between Barbara Crampton's exposed thighs. Grandma, never missing a beat, took a long drag off her Winston Light and exclaimed in her thick Southern drawl, "I never did like these here Spooky-Doos!" Thanks, Stuart Gordon!

Daily Grindhouse: Last week we spoke with Diane O'Bannon, wife of the legendary screenwriter Dan O'Bannon, and she told us you're working on a script written by her late husband. I was wondering if you could talk a little about Dan O'Bannon, his work, and what established him as one of the best screenwriters of our time?

Stuart Gordon: Well, Dan O'Bannon was a genius. I got to meet him back in the eighties, and he was quite a character. The first time I met him, a friend of mine brought me to his apartment. We knocked on the door, and it took a long time for anyone to answer. Finally, there was this voice on the other end going, "Who is it?" We told him who we were, and then heard about twelve locks being unlocked. And then the door opened and he was just standing there, wearing a bathrobe—this was around three in the afternoon—and he's holding a Taser in his hand, which was the first time I had ever seen one of those. I didn't know what it was. I thought it was a ray gun or something. He explained what it was, exactly what it could do, and that all he had to do was shoot an intruder and then plug it in. He could have the guy on the floor convulsing while he called the cops. He was a strange fellow. He kept his apartment super air-conditioned, so it was *freezing* in there. We had a wonderful talk, and got to be friends. When he married Diane, and had Adam, they came over to our house several times for barbeques and things. He was just a terrific guy. The most incredible imagination of anyone I've ever met.

DG: What do you think it is about his work that makes it so timeless [and produces] such great movies?

SG: Well, he really understands what scares people. He always used to say that he would start with himself and whatever were the things that would scare him. He would always take a fresh take on everything. I remember him talking about *Alien* and, in most movies, the monster wants to eat you, but he came up with the idea that the monster wants to reproduce with you. Actually, it doesn't even want to reproduce with you really; it just wants to use you as a host for laying its eggs, essentially. He was basing that on nature. He said that the things that you find in real life are much more disturbing than anything that you could dream up. That idea, I thought, really was unique: the idea that they were just using the humans as hosts for their reproductive function.

DG: Right, that sounds fascinating. Now, from what I understand, the project is called *The Men*. Were you surprised when Mrs. O'Bannon brought it to you, and what is your take on the project? Can you take us a little bit into that?

SG: Brian Yuzna and I were hanging out with Dan one day, and he just started talking about this idea. He hadn't even written it yet. It just knocked us out; we thought it was just such a funny idea. We worked with him on it for a while—for like a year, I think—while he was developing outlines, and did a draft or two. Then, for some reason, he decided this might be a project he wanted to direct himself, and so he kind of withdrew it from us. I guess he was unable to get it set up at a studio, unfortunately. When he passed away, I was at his memorial service and I was talking to Diane about that script, and she said, "You want to take a shot at it? Get it made?" And I jumped at the chance.

DG: Is this a sure deal? Is this something that's going to happen?

SG: We're pursuing it. We're talking to producers. It's looking like it may happen [and will] be shot in Europe. That's one of the things that is shaping up right now. We don't have a start date yet, so it's still not 100 percent.

DG: Okay. Are you still working on a film entitled *The Thing on the Doorstep*?

SG: On and off. That's a project I've been trying to get made for a long time. It looked like we were getting close there a couple of years ago, but, unfortunately, things kind of fell apart. So, we're starting over again. It's a great script, written by Dennis Paoli, who wrote all of the Lovecraft movies that I did. He's my writing partner. We go way back—all the way to high school together. Gosh, we've been trying to get it made for almost twenty years now.

DG: Wow, that's amazing. That's some diligence on your part, sir.

SG: Well, *Dagon* took fifteen years to get made. The thing about Lovecraft is that his ideas are so bizarre that it's not your typical vampire movie, or something that studios would understand. They're much more posh and unique. These days, studios are very afraid of anything that's new. It seems like all they want to do is remake things or do sequels.

DG: Your fascination with Lovecraft goes without saying, and a lot of his themes provide a strong undercurrent to your work: insanity, an impending sense of doom, trying to comprehend the incomprehensible. Is that a challenge as a filmmaker—conveying somewhat abstract ideas visually?

SG: I think, in some of Lovecraft's stories, he gets very specific about things, and then there are some where he's very abstract or vague. I think it's about choosing the right story. There are some of his stories that are very clear, very action-packed, and those are the ones that I gravitate towards.

DG: Now, if we can step back a little bit, can you tell us a bit about the first film that changed your life, and made you say, "Wow, *this* is why I want to get into movies"?

SG: I think the first film I ever saw was called *The Greatest Show on Earth*, which was a circus movie. I must have been about four years old when I saw it. My response to it was it made me want to become a clown. But the movie that really changed my life was Stanley Kubrick's *2001*. I got very excited about that film and the idea of making movies—you know, realizing that you could get across some really complex ideas in film. That movie changed my life.

DG: When people like me are bothering you, what movie do they bring up the most? I think I know the answer, but thought I would hear it from you . . .

SG: (Laughs) *Re-Animator* has become my middle name. I'm cool with that. I think if it weren't for *Re-Animator*, I wouldn't be making movies. I'm always happy to talk about that film, but I like it when I get questions about some of the other movies that I've done as well.

DG: That's kind of a follow-up for me. Is there a film that you dig, or think may have fallen undeservedly under the radar?

SG: The one film that I really wish had gotten a better release was a movie called *The Wonderful Ice Cream Suit*, which is so different from the other movies I've done. It's not a horror film at all. It's a comedy, and it was written by Ray Bradbury. I had a chance to work with Ray on the film. He wrote the screenplay. We produced it for Disney studios, but it never really got a good DVD release, unfortunately.

DG: I did read up a little about that film, but I must have missed—I don't know how—that you collaborated with Ray Bradbury. What was it like working with him?

SG: He was fantastic. He had written the script, and it was beautiful. It was like poetry. As a matter of fact, he wrote it not in the typical format of a screenplay at all. There were no breaks for scenes. It was like he was describing the finished film. I told him, "Ray, in order to budget this and schedule it, we're going to have to break it into scenes." He said, "Oh, sure. Of course, go ahead." I did, and showed it to him. He said, "What did you do to my script?!"

DG: I would be terrified if I brought something to Ray Bradbury and he said, "What did you do to this?"

SG: He was very funny. Sometimes I would suggest ideas, changes and things, and he would say, "Stuart, I'm the tailor that made this suit; I know where all the buttons are supposed to go," which I realized was the nicest way that anyone had ever told me to go fuck myself.

DG: (Laughs) I'm assuming you didn't argue very much with him, right?

SG: No, we're still great friends. As a matter of fact, I just saw him a couple of days ago and wished him a happy ninety-first birthday. Ray told me he feels that *The Wonderful Ice Cream Suit* is the best film that's ever been done of his work.

DG: Well, now I'm going to have to go watch *The Wonderful Ice Cream Suit*. That's on my to-do list. Now, looking at your writing resume, we have *Re-Animator* in 1985, *From Beyond* in 1986, and then *Honey, I Shrunk the Kids* in 1989. I wanted to know if you caught anyone off guard with such an abrupt transition.

SG: Well, you know, I always say I don't think it's that abrupt of a transition because I think *Honey, I Shrunk the Kids* is a horror movie. I really do. It's about a mad scientist, and his experiment goes terribly wrong. The kids are being attacked by giant insects. It has all of the earmarks of a horror film. It's just that the tone of it is more family-friendly. We wanted that movie to be scary. We wanted the audience to be worried about those kids. I think that's the reason it was successful; there's a lot of tension in that movie.

DG: You know, I never thought of it that way. But, now that you mention it, if you can actually take Rick Moranis out and put in Jeffrey Combs, suddenly it's a horror movie.

SG: Absolutely. I mean, Rick Moranis is great, and I like the comedy that's in the film, but we really wanted the sense of danger. There are moments in there where you think they're not going to make it.

DG: Speaking of Mr. Combs, you once said that the whole process of making a movie really hinges on having a great cast. Of course, I think Jeffrey Combs is an extraordinary actor, but you guys work with each other *a lot*. Does he have incriminating photos of you, or is he simply the De Niro to your Scorsese?

SG: (Laughs) Every director has his favorite actor. Jeffrey's one of mine. We are on the same wavelength about so many things that we can almost read each other's minds now. So, it makes working together very easy and fun. He can do anything, he can be anybody. He's a chameleon really, so he's always surprising me. I'm always amazed at the stuff he comes up with.

DG: It has always perplexed me as to why he never got that much mainstream success. I know he was in *House on Haunted Hill* [1999], but mostly his work is a little left of mainstream. You think that's just a choice of his, or ... ?

SG: Jeffrey has really become today's version of Vincent Price. He's a genre actor. There's a certain group of people—Boris Karloff, Bela Lugosi, Lon Chaney—these are people who are giants of the world of horror, and I think Jeffrey is one of those people now. I think he would've liked it if he could get into some big studio pictures from time to time, but he's constantly working. He's constantly doing really interesting stuff. I think he's pretty pleased with his career.

DG: I do love his work. I know he starred in another Lovecraft adaptation that you were once attached to, called *The Lurking Fear* in 1994. Stuart Gordon, Jeffrey Combs, Lovecraft—it sounds like a sure thing and, suddenly, you see C. Courtney Joyner take the helm. Could you tell me maybe what happened?

SG: I think it was a project that originally we were talking about doing for Empire Pictures, which was Charlie Band's company before Full Moon. I think when Empire went down, that project kind of ended for us. But Charlie had always wanted to do an adaptation of "The Lurking Fear," and I think that's what he finally did, getting Courtney to direct it in '94. Courtney went in a very, very different direction than we were planning to go. We were thinking of actually making it a period piece, and having Lovecraft as the main character in it—the main character is a writer of horror stories. It's almost like Lovecraft describing himself.

DG: Jeffrey Combs has already proven himself being able to play Edgar Allan Poe, so I'm assuming he could probably do justice to Lovecraft as well.

SG: He actually did play Lovecraft in a movie called *Necronomicon* [1993]. It was sort of a wrap-around story. The movie was directed by Brian Yuzna and several other directors. Brian directed the framing story, which was about Lovecraft going to the library and reading the *Necronomicon*.

DG: Keeping in line with collaborations, I'm a huge fan of your work, obviously, and also of David Mamet's, but your respective filmographies are, in my opinion, pretty different. How did you end up collaborating with him on *Edmond*?

SG: David Mamet and I go way back. As a matter of fact, I produced and directed the first professional production of his work on stage, which was *Sexual Perversity in Chicago* back in 1974. So, we met each other when Mamet was just beginning as a playwright, and we stayed friends throughout the years. I had seen *Edmond* when it was first done on stage and thought that it would make a great movie. I've been pestering David ever since, and we finally got it to happen a few years ago.

DG: Making sure you have a wonderful cast definitely starts with getting somebody of the caliber of William H. Macy. I really love his work.

SG: He's just amazing. It was a part he'd always wanted to play, too, and had never actually done it on stage, which was very interesting to me. William Macy also is a very old friend, back from our days of doing theater in Chicago.

DG: Speaking of writers, is it frustrating to see your words interpreted by others? In that vein, is it frustrating when you're actually directing the film, because I'm assuming there are some logistical issues that play a hand in what transpires between the page and the screen?

SG: Usually, when I'm directing, I'm able to keep things pretty close to what I had in mind. When you write something and you end up not directing it, sometimes things go in directions that you never expected, which sometimes can be good and sometimes not so good.

DG: I've read that you were given carte blanche to do what you wished when making *Masters of Horror*. How does contributing to an anthology like that compare to the restrictions of feature filmmaking?

SG: Well, actually, it was very much like making a feature film. When I do a feature film, I've got the final cut. So, I'm able to do what I want to do.

DG: You don't get a lot of studio interference, or anything of that nature?

SG: No, not lately. Not in the last fifteen years, really. I'm pretty much able to do what I want to do. That was what made that series so wonderful. In television, it's usually the opposite. In television, the director is really just a hired gun, and it's really the producers that control television—producers who are usually the writers of the shows themselves. What made *Masters of Horror* different was that they let the directors have the power, and that really was spectacular. It was great to work on that series and to hang out with some of the directors who I idolized. It was great to be able to meet them and to get to know them as friends.

DG: You mentioned television, and I was going to ask if the transition was tough when you did "Eater" for *Fear Itself*—which I loved, by the way. I loved the claustrophobic police precinct, the *feel* to it. Working at NBC, though, I know you can't really go back to a lot of your standard tools.

SG: No, and that was really kind of rough, because NBC was very worried and very scared and nervous about the idea of doing horror on network television. I had to fight for every drop of blood that appeared in the final cut of the film.

DG: When Stuart Gordon goes to the movies, is there a director—or anyone currently working in mainstream cinema, I guess you'd say—who excites you? Or did you see anything good at the theater lately?

SG: There are several directors whose work I really like. David Fincher is one. I think he does fascinating work and I loved *The Social Network* [2010]. I thought that was a great film. It should have won Best Picture, I believe. I like P. T.

Anderson a lot. I wish he did more movies. I love the work of Àlex de la Iglesia, the Spanish director. I saw his most recent film [*The Last Circus*, 2010], which was hilarious and very twisted. And I love Gaspar Noé. I just saw *Enter the Void* [2009], which I thought was an absolutely mindboggling movie.

DG: His movies intimidate me. I'm almost afraid to go see them. They seem to push the boundaries of film itself.

SG: He does great work, and I love *Irreversible* [2002]. I think that's his best film to date, actually.

DG: Is there an anecdote, or a fact, that never gets touched on during these types of interviews, something you'd like to pass along—maybe a *Daily Grindhouse* exclusive?

SG: Well, we were kind of talking about movies that kind of blow our minds. The one that blew my mind last year was *A Serbian Film* [2010]. I don't know if you've seen that movie yet, but it really goes beyond anything you've ever seen before. I met the writer and director at a festival last year. They told me that my films inspired them to make that movie. I couldn't have imagined what they meant until I saw it.

DG: That's another one I just read about. I don't know if I have the constitution to put up with it.

SG: It's really, really powerful. It's extremely well-made, and it's about something—it really is about Serbia. It's about the atrocities that the Serbs did during the Bosnian war. It's really making a very strong political statement.

DG: Do you see yourself collaborating with [Srdjan Spasojevic] the gentleman who made *A Serbian Film* at some point?

SG: Well, that would be cool. I'm looking forward to see what he does next. He's a very, very interesting filmmaker, I think.

DG: That movie, along with films like *The Human Centipede* [2009], kind of take me back to the glory days of VHS—the Video Nasties, the "we dare you to watch" kind of movies. It seems like we're kinda going back to that era.

SG: Isn't that what horror is supposed to do?

DG: Exactly, especially considering mainstream fare like *Twilight* [2008]. I'm not going to get on a rant about that, but it just seems like movies aren't dangerous anymore. You have nothing to fear when you sit down in the auditorium and the lights darken.

SG: It's always been those little movies—that were done independently and for no money—that are the ones that blow you away. Movies like *The Texas Chain Saw Massacre* or *Evil Dead* [1982]—those are the kinds of films that come out of nowhere, and the filmmakers are ready to do things that you've never seen before. That's what I like about people who are still making those kinds of movies.

DG: The fringe films—the dangerous films—I think that's what the horror genre is all about. I think you're absolutely correct, sir. Finally, I was going to ask if you have any projects you want to plug or anything you want to let our readers know about before I let you go.

SG: I've just finished working on *Re-Animator: The Musical* here in Los Angeles. We're hoping to take that on the road soon. Maybe that'll be coming to a theater near you sometime soon.

DG: I live in Nashville, and something cool like that very rarely comes by. So, if you could pencil that in, I would be forever in your debt.

SG: Also, I should mention that we're talking to the public library in Nashville about bringing our show *Nevermore*, which stars Jeffrey Combs as Edgar Allan Poe, sometime next year. We *will* be bringing something to a theater near you.

DG: And we will plug away on the site. Anything we can do to help. That'd be great. It sounds awesome.

SG: Yeah, it is. He's amazing as Poe. He played Poe in the *Masters of Horror* episode "The Black Cat." He looked so extraordinary that I really felt like I was hanging out with Poe. He came up with this idea of doing a one-man show, live on stage. We've been doing that for the last couple of years. We did it in honor of Poe's bicentennial in 2009, and it's still running.

DG: Do you have any thoughts about the upcoming film with John Cusack as Poe? I believe it's called *The Raven* [2012].

SG: John Cusack's a friend of mine, and I'm curious to see what he's going to do with Poe. It doesn't seem like they're really sticking to the facts about Poe's life. It's kind of a fantasy inspired by Poe's work. But, sure, I'm curious about it. I look forward to seeing it.

DG: I love [Cusack's] work as well. He really made *1408* [2007]. That was kind of a one-man show, and he pulled it off with flying colors.

SG: That's a great movie.

DG: I appreciate you taking the time to talk to us today, sir.

SG: It's a pleasure.

DG: Thank you, Mr. Gordon.

Stuart Gordon: H. P. Lovecraft, Ray Bradbury and the Museum of Jurassic Technology

Jeremy Rosenberg / 2012

From *KCET.org*, posted as a segment of their "Arrival Stories" series, on May 31, 2012. Reprinted by permission.

"What's your or your family's Los Angeles arrival story?" This week we hear from movie and theater director and writer, Stuart Gordon:
"I came to Los Angeles to direct a movie, *Re-Animator*.

"Both of my parents were born in Chicago and so was I. I did theater in Chicago for many years. I was the artistic director of a theater company called the Organic Theatre when I took a six-month leave of absence to test the Los Angeles waters. I've been here now for twenty-seven years.

"*Re-Animator* was a project I originally thought I was going to do in my hometown, but as things turned out, it was shot in Hollywood at a little studio called S&A that had been in existence since the days of Charlie Chaplin and Mary Pickford.

"As a result of the success of the film, I ended up being offered a three-picture deal. I moved my family here. This was in 1985. We left on a Friday the 13th.

"We packed everything up into our Toyota Corolla. I drove cross-country and went across Oklahoma and Texas. I think the most sort of dramatic part was when we went through Death Valley at noon—which was probably the worst thing I ever did!

"My wife and I had two small children with us. My youngest daughter—who was three at the time—was lying in the back seat and my wife looked at her and thought that she had passed out from the heat. My wife threw a cup of water on her and she immediately woke up and started crying, 'Mom, why did you do that?' So, that was our trip here—our journey.

"One of the first things I remember when we got to town was we were having a bite to eat—I think it was on Ventura Boulevard—and we saw a guy dressed as Jesus carrying a cross. He was dragging it along past the window of the coffee shop. That's when we knew we were in LA.

"Over the years, I've shot about a third of the movies here. The other ones I've done all over the world. As a matter of fact, it turned out that the three-picture deal that I was first offered involved shooting pictures in Rome.

"So, we had just moved the family here and then suddenly we're heading off on an airplane to Rome. So, yeah, I've shot movies all over—in Spain, Hungary, Australia. Make a movie and see the world!

"Los Angeles is a place that can take some getting used to, because it is very different from any other place. It's one of those cities which the longer you're here, the more you appreciate it.

"It was funny, when I first moved here it always seemed like it was summertime, so my sense of time got kind of messed up. I would say, 'Well, it must have happened last summer,' and it would turn out it was in February or something.

"But the longer you're here the more aware you become of the changes of the seasons. It's much more subtle, but there are those changes. My wife is always kidding me because I'm very much into the idea of *this* is in season, *this* is tomato season; *this* is corn season.

"The other thing about LA is that there's never a dull moment. There's always some sort of crazy thing going on. I often think of LA as being like a big circus, that there always are some things that you just cannot believe are happening, taking place here.

"I also love the history here. You go on a movie lot, or to Musso & Frank, and realize that all of these great people hung out at that bar, like Orson Welles and Raymond Chandler. The deal to make *Frankenstein* [1931] was supposedly made in Musso & Frank with James Whale.

"I've really started to fall in love with Downtown LA and the fact that you're right next to Chinatown, and you're right next to Boyle Heights, and you're right next to Little Tokyo—it's kind of like being on the yellow brick road, it's wonderful.

"You asked me to name a few places in LA that I think have a Lovecraftian feel. Well, I just was at one of them for the first time a couple of weeks ago. It's the Museum of Jurassic Technology, which I think is very Lovecraftian.

"You kind of feel like you've gone back into one of his stories with these kind of crackpot scientists coming up with all these weird ideas, and there's a mood that kind of settles over you when you're there that is very much like being in one of Lovecraft's stories. It's kind of this creepy, very sort of serene kind of feeling. It's weird and otherworldly.

"The other place that I think is very Lovecraftian is the La Brea Tar Pits. You know, they have been there for literally millions of years and you just get this sense of—you see all these weird bones and these animals, and statues of giant sloths and things that have been found there. It's like going into another dimension.

"One time I was there and I was thinking, 'How could these animals be so stupid as to *walk* into a tar pit?' And, as I was walking across the grass, my foot got stuck in some tar. Okay, that's how it happened!

"You also asked about another writer, Ray Bradbury. Well, Ray is a good friend of mine, and I'm very proud to know him. I met him thirty years ago when we did theater back in Chicago. We did one of his plays called *The Wonderful Ice Cream Suit*, and we brought it on tour to Los Angeles and did it at UCLA, and he came to see it. The story involves five Mexican-Americans who all share a white suit and when they wear the suit it makes their dreams come true.

"At the end of the play, the audience started yelling, 'Author,' because they knew Ray was in the house. He got up on stage and said, 'I want to put on the suit,' and he literally stripped down to his boxer shorts right in front of the whole audience. When you see somebody in their skivvies, you're friends for life.

"Ray is amazing. I think of him as a holy man, because when I go to see him I'm always inspired and see things in a new way. One time he told me his two rules of life, which I thought were great. He said: 'Rule number one is get your work done and rule number two is to hell with it!'"

[Editor's note: Ray Bradbury died on June 5, 2012, at the age of ninety-one, just five days after this article was uploaded.]

Stuart Gordon: Gentleman of Splatter

Barbara Crampton / 2012

From *Fangoria*, no. 317 (October 2012), pp. 36–42. Reprinted by permission.

When *Fangoria* first approached me about doing a journalistic turn, focusing on my frequent director Stuart Gordon, I asked him how he felt about the cover photo involved. "They want me to be holding your bloody severed head," I said. "Is that okay with you?" There was a momentary pause. "Will you be holding it between your legs?" he beamed.

Much has been written about this master of blood-spattered terror. Best known for his seminal 1985 movie *Re-Animator*, in which I appear (and which made its Blu-ray debut this month from Image Entertainment), Gordon is often credited with converting many horror fans to the wonders of H. P. Lovecraft. Grounding the atmospheric author's strong tales of fear and desire in multidimensional characters, his films *Re-Animator*, *From Beyond*, and *Dagon* have become modern classics. He has occasionally veered into science fiction with *Fortress* and *Robot Jox*, comedy with *Honey, I Shrunk the Kids* (he was the writer and originally intended director), and thrillers such as *Stuck* and the David Mamet-penned *Edmond*—and with all of these pictures, he displays a knack for exposing the dark, the sinister, the cruel, the human, and the absurd.

Rightly inducted into the Masters of Horror by the innovative Mick Garris, Stuart enjoyed first camaraderie and then monthly dinners with other notable directors such as Tobe Hooper, Joe Dante, John Landis, Wes Craven, Guillermo del Toro, Dario Argento, Rob Zombie, Eli Roth, and others. Subsequently, many from this group took part in a highly successful anthology series for Showtime, produced by Garris; Stuart's contributions were the Poe-riffing "The Black Cat" (with Jeffrey Combs) and the Lovecraft revisit "Dreams in the Witch-House."

"Stuart really is one of a kind," Garris says. "He has managed to continue to bend the rules and move in new directions, or even make things new again in directions he's already trod. He's an incredibly sweet and affectionate friend, and a really proud family man, gentle and funny, yet he loves being able to outrage you with his art, to really make you feel something, and give you an experience that you'll remember. He's a true artist, without the so-called 'artist's disposition.' He's a guy I really like and admire a lot."

Who's to argue with *that*?

In the last few years, Stuart went back to his roots on the stage (he was the founder of Chicago's Organic Theatre), first with the one-man Combs/Poe show *Nevermore*, then by redirecting *Re-Animator* into a raucous, bloody, award-winning sing-a-long musical that won an LA Drama Critics Circle Award, six *LA Weekly* Theater Awards, and an Ovation Award.

I visited with him recently, reminiscing about our work together and talking about his new projects. I asked him questions about certain genre collaborations, and they in turn shared their insights about him with me. Some call him a visionary—sentimental, intoxicatingly courageous, ensemble-minded, the Buddha of the horror world. Others confide that he is stubborn, rebellious, a dictator (sort of), and sick, as he murders his wife (actress Carolyn Purdy-Gordon) in every movie!

But at the end of the day, Stuart is simply my friend, warm, and engaging. I know him to be an insistent storyteller with a keen sense of character and motivation. Whether his tales are of a vicious killer, a magical toymaker, or a far-gone madman, his stories are consistently rich, uncompromising, smart, and always amusing.

Here, then, for your reading pleasure, is Stuart Gordon, the man behind the lens . . .

Barbara Crampton: You have a wide body of work dealing with both real and imagined horrors. Why do you think *Re-Animator* is the movie you're most identified with?

Stuart Gordon: *Re-Animator* deals with conquering death. We all face it, and horror movies are always about that. This movie is about a guy who has a dream to cheat death. I think that resonates with a lot of people.

Crampton: In working with you as a director, I've found you to be incredibly prepared in terms of your vision, down to the minute details of a character's backstory. How rewarding or frustrating is that when working with an actor if they disagree with your vision of a role as a whole or in a certain scene?

Gordon: Francis Coppola once said that the actor is the expert on the character, so he or she is going to know far more about the role than the director does. I'll have ideas of what the backstory may be, but if the actor has ideas of their own, oftentimes they're better than the ones I thought of. I feel it's important to let the actor lead the way.

Crampton: We both adore Jeffrey Combs. You've worked with him on how many projects?

Gordon: Gosh . . . I wanna say eight or nine.

Crampton: How would you describe your relationship with him?

Gordon: It's sort of similar to the relationship you and I have, which is that we know and trust one another, can almost read each other's minds. We think in similar ways. Both you and Jeff are fearless, and that's fantastic.

> "Not only is he my key director, he's also my good friend. But that doesn't mean we can't disagree. We respect and listen to one another. I have gratitude for all the work he's given me. And he's an actor's director. He loves our process. He is gleeful around us. Some directors can be technical and wary of these creatures who get in the way of getting the project done. He embraces us. During the filming of *Re-Animator*, Bruce Abbott and I made a decision that this movie was so gory and graphic, the only way we could get through it was to find the humor whenever possible. Stuart kept telling us throughout to play it straight, not for laughs. So, between us, the balance was achieved."
> —Jeffrey Combs

Crampton: The tone of *Re-Animator* is just right—you really found the balance of humor and horror.

Gordon: We didn't play it as though it was obviously funny, and I believe that's what made it funny. Mel Brooks has this line about the difference between comedy and tragedy: he says, "Tragedy is when I cut myself shaving; comedy is when you fall into a sewer and die!"

> "A lot of our humor is in the outrageous; not just crossing over, but *way over* the line, and that comes from Stuart's courage. If a joke or a scene tells some truth, it's in, and you'll have to fight him to get it out."
> —Dennis Paoli, Gordon's frequent writing partner

Crampton: Were you surprised that I would commit so wholeheartedly to that "special" scene in *Re-Animator*?

Gordon: (Laughs) I was actually very surprised and happy that you did, because we knew in advance that it would be the most provocative moment in the movie.

Crampton: I thought it was a funny scene on paper, and also very much in keeping with how much creepier Dr. Hill had become after being re-animated. I was definitely nervous to do it, but it's the scene that everyone remembers, so now I have a sort of perverse fondness for it!

"Stuart clams he would never ask an actor to do anything he himself would be unwilling to do. So he says ... I've never put him to the test, but I've been tempted. [He also] does not believe in censorship. This has led to some contentious dustups in our house ..."
—Carolyn Purdy-Gordon

Crampton: You've given me some great roles to play: a mature victim in *Re-Animator*, a tormented, grieving mother in *Castle Freak*, and my favorite: Katherine in *From Beyond*. That movie was a luxury. We had money, time, and location. What was shooting that like for you?

Gordon: Part of the adventure was that we were in Italy ...

Crampton: We also had a great special effects team.

Gordon: Yes. Far more elaborate than *Re-Animator*. Also, our production designer, Giovanni Natalucci, was able to make it seem as if it were taking place in New England. Mac Ahlberg, our DP, did a stunning job. I saw it projected last time with you, I believe. It's ...

Crampton: ... beautiful. Did you cast Ken Foree as Bubba because of what he'd done in *Dawn of the Dead*?

Gordon: I was aware that he'd been in the film, but he was really just the best guy for the part.

Crampton: He came in and auditioned?

Gordon: Yeah, and he really nailed it. He has a good-natured quality. I've never seen him in a bad mood. You can believe he used to be a pro football player. He was the character.

Crampton: You took me shopping for my leather outfit. How many did I try on?

Gordon: About two or three hundred or so. (Laughs) I think we realized none of them fit you perfectly, so we ended up going to someone who made it for your body, and it was perfect.

Crampton: I gave it away.

Gordon: You did?

Crampton: There were so many things I should have saved from certain productions. After we did *Re-Animator*, Bruce gave me his scrubs and his jean jacket. I later sold them at a yard sale ... along with the leather. Damn!

Gordon: Wow!

Crampton: I hope someone's enjoying it. Were you disappointed that Brian Yuzna took over the reins on *Bride of Re-Animator*?

Gordon: No. All the sequels had to be R-rated, and I knew that would make it impossible to top the original. Dennis and I had a very different idea for *Bride*, focusing on Dan living with his re-animated wife: you!

Crampton: Oh, darn! That would have been fun.

"I'll always think of Stuart when I hear Dr. Hill's line in *Re-Animator* regarding the afterlife: 'Maybe it takes desire, an obsessive desire . . .' That's because when it comes to making movies, Stuart has that obsessive desire. He can be incredibly focused on getting a scene done just the way he wants it. A great example of this was on the very last day of shooting *Dolls*. The Italian line producer was becoming increasingly frustrated with his determination to get every last shot he possibly could, in spite of the schedule having come to an end. In an attempt to assert his authority, the line producer called on the rental company to collect the set dressing. But Stuart evidently didn't feel he was done with that set, and refused to stop shooting.

"Then the line producer did something I had never seen before, nor have I ever seen it since: he ordered the workers to take away the furniture while the shooting continued. Of course, he had no idea just how determined Stuart could be, even in the face of this adversity. Stuart ignored the interlopers and just kept setting up shots. At one point, as he was lining up an angle of a doll on an overstuffed chair, the workers walked right in, picked up the chair and took it away! But Stuart didn't miss a beat. He quickly moved the doll onto the bed, positioned it carefully, called for the lights—and very calmly, in his best Italian, said, 'Accione!'"
—Brian Yuzna

Crampton: You and Dennis Paoli have an amazing ability to channel Lovecraft. *Dagon* is my favorite movie of yours that I haven't been in—the mood, the atmosphere.

Gordon: Thanks. That was written as a follow-up to *Re-Animator*. We brought it to Charlie Band and he said, "No, this is too goofy."

Crampton: You had a hard time raising funds for it because the financiers didn't think something from the sea could be scary. But I love the fish people. They are far more freaky to me than any zombie!

Gordon: It was frustrating. We even had one studio tell us that if they turned into werewolves, they would finance it. They laughed at us.

Crampton: Why do you constantly gravitate toward Lovecraft?

Gordon: Brian Yuzna and I both loved Roger Corman's Poe films. When I see those movies, it makes me want to read Poe. We had a plan in mind: if *Re-Animator* was successful, we would do a whole series of Lovecraft adaptations. We felt he was a neglected writer.

Crampton: I think you've popularized Lovecraft more than any other filmmaker.

Gordon: That makes me really happy.

Crampton: I had never heard of Lovecraft before I made *Re-Animator* with you.

Gordon: Neither had Jeff. He always said he thought I was talking about a boat!

Crampton: (Laughs) You once said your films are about dreams, how incredible they can be and how you have to be careful because they can turn into nightmares. Are the monsters of the mind more horrible to you than real monsters?

Gordon: Real life is much more disturbing than dreams. You read about things in the newspaper that are far beyond anything you could dream up.

Crampton: That brings me to [the fact-based] *Stuck*. That movie is dark, profiling the worst of someone's character. Mena Suvari totally gave herself over to feeling she was justified in victimizing Stephen Rea's character.

Gordon: Yeah. *She* was feeling like the victim.

Crampton: Her line to him is, "Why are you doing this to *me*?"

"Not only is Stuart a man of great talent, he is a sweetheart to his core. He is an interesting mix of wild imagination for the dark, twisted, and sinister, and a kind of father figure at the same time. I have always been a fan of horror movies, and upon working with him, I came to realize he directed a film called *Dolls* that literally terrified me as a child! That was one of the first horror movies I had seen, and it ruined my relationships with dolls from that point on!"
—Mena Suvari

Crampton: What was it like working with Lance Henriksen on *The Pit and the Pendulum*?

Gordon: He was in character all the time. He was Torquemada the Inquisitor, so people were terrified of him. I remember at one point, the focus puller blew one of the shots, and he fell to his knees and begged forgiveness from Lance.

Crampton: Did he forgive him?

Gordon: Well, we did another take. But he was a scary guy. We were constantly arguing about every little thing.

Crampton: That's painful. Maybe he was doing it on purpose?

Gordon: We got to the very end of the shoot, and I was exhausted. Finally, he was arguing about something and I said, "Alright, do whatever you want, I don't care."

Crampton: You had to have been at the breaking point.

Gordon: Yeah. But then Lance said, "Don't give up on me, man!" which was kind of wonderful, because what it said to me was: "This is my process. This is how I work, and if you're gonna work with me, don't give up. We need to keep fighting!" I ran into him at a convention recently, and he gave me his book [*Not Bad for a Human*, 2011]. He talks about how he had a nervous breakdown after he did *The Pit and the Pendulum*. It took him months to release himself from Torquemada.

> "Stuart and I were so deep into the story that we were at each other's souls. Living in a drafty Italian castle, Stuart confessed to me that I almost gave him a heart attack. I was living the character day and night: a cloistered monk. I loved him for never giving up. We moved through the Inquisition together.
>
> "Recently, I saw his direction of the Poe play with Jeff Combs. I was blown away by his skill and respect for what is important about telling a story. Jeffrey was brilliant. The form Stuart contained was like light shining through a glass of sherry. I respect Stuart immensely, although he murders his wife in every movie he makes. In ours, he choked her to death."
> —Lance Henriksen

Crampton: You directed David Mamet's screenplay for *Edmond*, and also his play *Sexual Perversity in Chicago* at the Organic Theatre. How difficult was it bringing that kind of dialogue to the screen?

Gordon: When we were doing *Sexual Perversity*, Carolyn was playing the lead and she said to David, "I don't get this speech, help!" He said to her, "Oh, those are just the words; you can *do* whatever you want." I loved that. What a freeing thing to say to an actor.

Crampton: The *Edmond* performance was a tour de force for William H. Macy. It was perfection.

Gordon: I always call him the Fred Astaire of actors, because he makes it look so easy. He set the tone for everyone. He's one of the sweetest, nicest people. The other thing that was great was his approach. He embraced the character and didn't treat him as some sort of monster. That's the point of the Mamet script: we are all like this, we all have racist tendencies. He was just letting it all out.

> "Stuart is a jolly fellow with a wicked sense of humor. He is not one to lose it. It's hard to throw him. He always has a smile on his face. He makes an actor feel comfortable because he is so prepared. He is bold and imaginative, but also decisive. He listens to all ideas, and says, 'Okay, now this is what we are going to do!' Filmmaking isn't a democracy, it's a dictatorship! It should be."
> —William H. Macy

Crampton: For me, prison movies are always about the relationships between the guys stuck there. You had a great ensemble in *Fortress*: Kurtwood Smith, Tom Towles, Vernon Wells, Jeff Combs . . . Do you have a favorite story from that movie?

Gordon: Village Roadshow produced it. They had just bought this studio in Australia from Dino De Laurentiis; they were turning it into a theme park and wanted a movie shooting there for the opening. They had these trams like the ones at Universal. So, one day at lunch, Vernon and Jeff climbed onto the tram in their prison uniforms and hijacked it with their fake guns. The park people said, "The tourists loved it! Can you do it every day?" (Laughs)

Crampton: Did you?

Gordon: No.

Crampton: You were kinda busy! *The Wonderful Ice Cream Suit*, written by your friend Ray Bradbury, was such a sweet movie and a departure from horror. Do your fans know about this movie, or does it fall into a whole different category for you, along with your screenplay for *Honey, I Shrunk the Kids*?

Gordon: This movie was buried by Disney. I don't know what happened. I think it got caught in the war. Roy Disney was the producer, and he and I worked on it. Michael Eisner and Roy got into a big fight. It ended up with Eisner throwing Roy off the board, and then Roy coming at Eisner with the stockholders and getting Eisner tossed out of the studio.

Crampton: Too bad. It's adorable. More people should see it.

Gordon: I agree.

Crampton: You're in development on a project with one of my favorite people, A. J. Bowen; he and I are in *You're Next* [2011], which is coming out from Lionsgate soon.

Gordon: That's a film called *Purgatory*. I'm hoping we'll be able to get the financing. A. J.'s a great actor. I keep thinking he's the next Jack Nicholson.

> "Stuart is different from a lot of his contemporaries; he keeps getting better at storytelling. He keeps learning, honing his craft. He does this with a lot of love in his heart, which translates directly to the screen. I'd probably work for him for scale!"
> —A. J. Bowen

Crampton: You watched *A Horrible Way to Die* [2010] at Fantastic Fest, and Simon Barrett, who wrote both that movie and *You're Next*, was in the audience during a showing of *Re-Animator*. I believe I popped into his head to play the mother in *You're Next* because you were there. So, really, I got that part because you reminded him of me. You were instrumental in my comeback to the horror genre!

Gordon: I think you were responsible for your comeback to horror, absolutely.

Crampton: Which leads me to my next question: what other projects are you developing, and is there anything for me?

Gordon: We're not done! I have several projects I'm working on. I don't want to say too much about them, because I don't want to jinx them. But we're definitely going to be working together again.

Crampton: That's good news. Back to your current big baby, *Re-Animator: The Musical*. You began your career in theater, and *Re-Animator* is arguably your most popular movie. How satisfying is it to combine the two in a production that is so critically acclaimed?

Gordon: It's just great fun. I love theater. I've always managed to keep my hand in it. It all came full circle. We had extensions and sold out houses in LA, and by the time you read this, we will have played at the New York Musical Theatre Festival and Scotland's Edinburgh Fringe Festival.

Crampton: You've said you're not a fan of remakes; you call *Re-Animator: The Musical* a "revisit." Has the story changed or been altered a bit, aside from the singing and dancing?

Gordon: I think it's pretty true to the movie. We took the actual dialogue and set it to music. The thing about musicals is that people can sing about what they're feeling. You really can't have characters describe their feelings too much in films. You have to show things.

> "Stuart gave me the outline, which was basically each scene from the film with his suggestions of lines from the script that could possibly be songs. I was nervous, because I knew how much the fans love that film and I didn't want to disappoint. So, we hammered away at it for almost three years! I'd grab inspiration from whatever source seemed appropriate: Bernard Herrmann, Sondheim, Gilbert and Sullivan. Eventually, we ended up with a script that's about 90 percent music. It's more like an operetta, but most people don't seem to mind."
> —Mark Nutter, composer, *Re-Animator: The Musical*

Crampton: *The Musical* is fantastic; fast, fun, and campy. But I must admit that the first time seeing it was very strange. The dialogue is pretty intact, and this isn't *Romeo and Juliet*—something done by others *ad infinitum*—so it was strange to hear another person speak *my* lines!

> "Stuart is surprisingly calm, and dresses like an Ivy League English professor. I have never heard him raise his voice, and he talks about violent, uncomfortable details as though he's giving directions to the 405."
> —Rachel Avery, Meg Halsey in *Re-Animator: The Musical*

> "Stuart is a lot of fun, and a real bulldog. He won't give up until he gets it! I remember we were doing *King of the Ants*; it was hot, I was getting sunburned. I left the set to get some sunscreen. He was yelling, 'Where's George?' When I came back, he said, 'I had no idea you were such a pussy!'"
> —George Wendt, Dean Halsey in *Re-Animator: The Musical*

"He's very ensemble-minded, and starts each rehearsal with a theater game. I haven't done that since college! He's not only a master of horror, but also trying to make people feel something on a visceral, primal level. What better way to shake someone out of their complacency than to spray them with blood or send a re-animated zombie into the audience?"
—Jesse Merlin, Dr. Hill in *Re-Animator: The Musical*

"He's the Buddha of horror. But underneath is this sick imagination that perfectly understands how a scare should be played or when more blood is needed—which is always."
—Graham Skipper, Herbert West in *Re-Animator: The Musical*

Crampton: Where would you like to see *The Musical* ultimately mounted?
Gordon: If we can get some backers, off-Broadway would be great.
Crampton: You really have a special relationship with your wife, Carolyn. Has your forty-three-year love affair kept you sane in this crazy world of horror filmmaking?
Gordon: I feel like I'm lucky where it counts. The thing about Carolyn is that she's still constantly surprising me. We've been together all these years and I'm still discovering new things.

"Stuart is unabashedly sentimental. I receive flowers every year on each of our daughters' birthdays, just to thank me for giving him such lovely children. I get beautiful and sometimes hilarious poems and love letters . . . still. He surreptitiously weeps during sad movies he's seen many times over. *Cinema Paradiso* [1988] is one that never fails to tug at his heartstrings. You get the picture?"
—Carolyn Purdy-Gordon

Yes, Carolyn . . . I think we do.

What Lies Beneath, What Dwells Beyond: The Pleasures and Perils of Adapting Lovecraft

Michael Doyle / 2012

Sections of the following interview, conducted on October 4, 2012, were published in *Rue Morgue's 200 Alternative Horror Films You Need to See* (2012). Reprinted by permission.

Michael Doyle: What is the most pertinent challenge in adapting the works of H. P. Lovecraft?

Stuart Gordon: Well, the problem with making any film based on Lovecraft's work is, when you read his stories, so much is left to the reader's imagination. His work is very internal and it can be hard to read, because his characters are always dealing with things that are too horrible to describe. Lovecraft's stories are all about what lies beneath, what dwells in the beyond, and how Man is fortunate that he "lives on an island of ignorance" surrounded by forces he cannot hope to control. Lovecraft felt the most powerful fear was fear of the unknown. That's great for the reader, but cinema is primarily a visual medium. So, in film, you must show the audience something. But with Lovecraft how much is *too* much?

MD: You are Lovecraft's greatest cinematic champion, having brought no less than five of his works to the screen over the years, beginning with *Re-Animator*. Back in 1985, no filmmakers were actively tapping these properties.

SG: That's true. There have been movies that have acquired some of Lovecraft's themes and ideas, or have been greatly influenced by him, but, yeah, nobody was really digging into that treasure trove of stories. I think that's changed over the years. More people are reading Lovecraft now and more filmmakers are adapting his stories for film, but back when we did *Re-Animator*, they really weren't. I think you can trace the current popularity of Lovecraft's work to the growing sense many of us have in the world that we are surrounded by forces we cannot control, and that's a scary idea.

MD: I'm aware that you had a long-term plan from the beginning of your filmmaking career to direct a series of Lovecraft movies in the tradition of

Roger Corman's Poe movies for AIP. But did you always have a clearly defined, premeditated approach to tackling a Lovecraft movie, or was it something that evolved or was adjusted for every individual project?

SG: It depends on the story, and what we had to do to make it work as a movie. I've taken ideas from different Lovecraft stories and incorporated them or used them as a launching point. Like on *From Beyond*, the original story was only seven pages, so that became our prologue and we went from there. In an early draft of the script, the creature that eats Dr. Pretorius at the beginning was a Shoggoth, but you never saw it. The Shoggoth is described in *At the Mountains of Madness* [1931] as a protoplasmic sphere about fifteen feet in diameter that can turn itself into anything it needs to be. So, it's an extremely utilitarian monster in that if it needs a mouth to devour someone, it develops a mouth; if it needs arms or legs, it develops arms and legs, that kind of thing. Lovecraft has this idea that the Shoggoth were bred to be mindless slaves by the Old Ones, the beings that once populated the world, as a labor force used to build their cities and so forth. But the Shoggoth mutated over millions of years, accidentally developing intelligence, and became these independent creatures that rebelled against their masters. When we were writing *From Beyond*, we seized on the idea that the Shoggoth got intelligent when it ate someone, acquiring the knowledge or brainpower of its victims, and that was how it evolved. We reasoned that it must have eaten one of the Old Ones and absorbed their intelligence. So, when the Shoggoth ate Pretorius it kind of became Pretorius; it took his physical shape, spoke with his voice, everything. But the Lovecraft purists have enjoyed admonishing me over the years for the way I've kind of taken what I wanted. They feel these films should be period films, but I believe you have to find a way to make these films work. Again, you also have to deal with the problem of what you show.

MD: You tend to show an awful lot though, don't you?

SG: I do. (Chuckles) But you don't want to cheat the audience, you know?

MD: Does the will or influence of the Lovecraft purists ever touch you?

SG: No, you can't think like that when you're making a movie. You have to make the movie that *you* want to make.

MD: And, of course, Lovecraft's stories haven't gone anywhere.

SG: Right. People can read them anytime they want. What I like to do is take the words on the page and try to create my own vision of the story, but you can't please everybody. I remember, many years ago, I was working on an adaptation of *The Sirens of Titan*, the Kurt Vonnegut book. Vonnegut actually came to see it when the play was in previews, and he said something to me that I've never forgotten. In fact, it pretty much sums everything up. Vonnegut said, "You know, you really have to pretend that I've been dead for ten years!" (Chuckles) When I heard that I thought, "Yeah, that's exactly what you have to do." What he was saying was we were being too slavish to his book, too devoted to it, and we had to make some changes. We had to take some chances and some liberties, and instead capture the *essence* of the material. That's how you should approach Lovecraft, too, in my opinion: capture the essence of his stories but in your own way. With *Re-Animator*, because it was the first movie, I did not want to cheat the audience. So, we just kind of threw everything in there and really went for it.

MD: "Herbert West—Re-Animator" is not representative of Lovecraft's work though, is it?

SG: No, and Lovecraft had no particular regard for it. Reading the six installments, you could see how they could easily be adapted in comparison with some of Lovecraft's other stories. So, it was a case of compression; sort of telescoping the events of the stories and modernizing them. The other thing about Lovecraft is he wasn't a writer who explored relationships much or was preoccupied with character development. That meant we had to build up the part of West's accomplice in our script, make him seem more real, somebody that you cared about. Dan Cain then became our protagonist, as his character is really the audience.

MD: I've spoken to several of your contemporaries—John Carpenter, Larry Cohen, Joe Dante—about the manner in which critics devalued several horror movies of the 1980s. Works such as *The Howling*, *The Thing*, *Videodrome* [1983], and *From Beyond* were criticized for supposedly allowing the special makeup effects to dictate the content and even the narrative of certain films. How do you respond to that charge?

SG: Well, I think a lot of effects can unbalance and overwhelm a movie, but each of those films you mentioned has a good story, good performances, good direction, *and* good special effects. So, the effects are just one aspect of the movie. What I find interesting is nobody really cares about having a lot of special effects in movies anymore—certainly not in big Hollywood movies. It's just accepted and expected now.

MD: David Cronenberg was once castigated in a review that cited the scene in *Videodrome* where metal tendrils erupt from a handgun, piercing the flesh of a character's hand and transforming it into a literal *hand*-gun. The critic felt the film came to a grinding halt in that moment just to concentrate on the juicy details of the effect.

SG: I know the scene you're talking about. I never feel that way when I see *Videodrome*; I think the effects work beautifully within the context of Cronenberg's themes and ideas—and that's how effects should work. They should always have a reason for being.

MD: Is that how you utilized the makeup effects in your early films?

SG: Yes, absolutely. You mentioned *The Thing*: back when I was preparing *From Beyond*, I know that was definitely in my thoughts. The effects in that movie are pretty mind-blowing in their inventiveness and outrageousness. Talk about pushing things far out, John Carpenter really did that in *The Thing*. I wanted to take that same approach on *From Beyond*, but make it a very thoughtful approach. I wanted the monster to be something different every time it appeared, always evolving and changing its form, like the Shoggoth.

MD: Mark Shostrom, who created the fabulous Pretorius Monster, told me it was sometimes difficult to coordinate between the various makeup effects crews on *From Beyond*, and a concerted effort had to be made to ensure a modicum of creative continuity and cohesion was maintained in the work. Is that how you remember it?

SG: Well, we had four effects teams doing the monsters for *From Beyond*, and I think a lack of communication was inevitable. There was definitely a competitive feeling between the different effects people as they were trying to outdo each other. That was a good thing for the movie because it raised the level of everybody's game. You know, effects people are like magicians in that they keep a lot of their creative secrets to themselves, which is not always helpful. But I think Mark would agree that everybody came together as one at a certain point and made it all work. I mean, the Pretorius Monster was just terrific. Mark and his crew did a great job on it, and Ted Sorel really played the hell out of that character.

MD: In the 2006 director's cut of *From Beyond* you restored some of the graphic content excised from the original theatrical release. How did that opportunity arise?

SG: It came about from Monsters HD, which was a twenty-four-hour horror channel in the States [that went] out of business [in 2009]; they were the ones who paid for the restoration of *From Beyond*. MGM saw the workprint and immediately became concerned about the cost of restoring the movie for a DVD release. Initially, they wanted to include the lost footage as extras [on the disc]—they didn't want it incorporated back into the film. To me, they were throwing away a wonderful opportunity to do something special. I argued that even if the footage was of a noticeably poorer quality than the release print at least it was *there*, you know? I felt it was important to reinstate this stuff as it brought the film closer to my original vision for *From Beyond* before the MPAA started going at it. It was at this point that Monsters HD contacted me as they had recently made a deal to show the film and somehow they'd heard about the new material we'd unearthed. They asked me what it would take to create a director's cut and I explained the situation to them, and they decided they wanted to contribute financially to restoring the movie. I don't think it would have happened without their involvement. The costs were just too prohibitive for MGM to absorb alone.

MD: How complete is this version of *From Beyond* in your estimation?

SG: It's very close to being complete. There was something I cut back in '86 that occurred during the opening of the film: Crawford Tillinghast gets the Resonator working and knocks on Pretorius's bedroom door to tell him about it. That's still in the movie. What isn't in the movie is what comes after: Crawford goes inside and sees a naked young woman who has obviously been involved in a violent S&M tryst with Pretorius—she is trussed up and a large nail has been pounded through her tongue. Crawford frees her; she throws on a robe and runs out of the house. That all happened at the beginning. I now wish I had kept that moment. I cut it because I thought it was a little too much. Nowadays, tongue-piercing is everywhere, and it doesn't seem so strong or weird anymore. There are lots of girls who have pierced tongues. Unfortunately, that footage is still lost or I would have included it in the restored cut of *From Beyond*. Nobody could find that particular piece of film, although we looked for it.

MD: In an interview you did back in 1986 with John Gallagher, you talked about literally "fighting over frames" with the MPAA during deliberations on the film.

SG: It's true. Yeah, that's what it came down to. We were looking to get an R rating on *From Beyond* as *Re-Animator* going out unrated the year before had held the film back from becoming even more successful than it was. Part of our plan was—unlike our approach on *Re-Animator*—to hold back on seeing gallons of blood. Our solution on *From Beyond* was to go with slime instead of blood, as we felt that was a little more inoffensive. But slime proved to be even more of a problem for the MPAA. They were like, "No, this is *worse*! Slime is even more disgusting than blood!" So, that became a problem. The first time we submitted the film to the MPAA, they said we had no chance of getting an R rating. This is the point when you enter into discussions about the "cumulative effect" of a film, which is a term I kept hearing again and again. I asked what had troubled them in *From Beyond*, and they said, "*Everything*!" That wasn't helpful. I then said, "Yeah, but what things specifically?" "It's the whole movie—it's all just too weird and disturbing." We ended up submitting the film to the MPAA at least half a dozen times and then they started to get specific regarding certain scenes, certain shots, certain *frames*, they wanted removed. It was just depressing.

MD: Exactly what were the things they objected to?

SG: There were several things—and not all of it was the horror and violence, it was the sexual aspects of the movie. There was a sequence where Dr. Pretorius is fondling Barbara Crampton's breasts and his hand, which has these elongated penis-like fingers, drops below the frame-line towards her vagina. They certainly objected to that and some of the other sexual things. We also had a scene where Dr. Bloch, who is played by my wife, is examining Crawford's pineal gland, which is moving around like a worm. She tries to grab it with her forceps and its sort of eluding her grasp. In the release version, that is a very brief moment, but we found some extra material that we put in which extended it. That scene is now a little more unnerving, I think, which is good.

MD: By virtue of their prudery, was it difficult reasoning with the MPAA?

SG: Yeah, it was a very puritanical attitude they had. I remember requesting a meeting with them; I wanted a dialogue about what we could do to avoid an X rating. There was no NC-17 rating back then—that came later [in 1990]—so *From Beyond* was going out with an X. So, I went in there and was confronted by a woman who I believe was a retired librarian. Right off the bat it became confrontational. Basically, for the first hour or so of our meeting, she berated me for even making the movie. She highlighted several shots I'd done, and said, "Look at what you did here, this is wrong: you should be panning *away* in this shot, but instead you're always pushing *in!*" (Laughs) The scenes that suffered most during this process were things like Dr. Bloch having her eyeball sucked out of her skull by Crawford. He then spits it out of his mouth and the eyeball looks up at the camera from the floor. We didn't see much of that until the director's cut came out and it was finally restored. Another scene that was tampered with is the one where Crawford repeatedly smashes the woman [paramedic's] head against the ground during his escape from the hospital. The MPAA felt it was too excessive: "One blow is enough! Why does he have to hit her head one-two-*three* times?" So, we had to keep chopping out stuff until they were satisfied.

MD: Do you feel you were an intended target of the MPAA?

SG: Definitely! Yeah, they really had it in for me. I've always had this feeling that they were punishing me for *Re-Animator*. With that film going out unrated, we had sort of bypassed the MPAA and they never forgot that. I think they were pissed at us for getting away with so much on *Re-Animator* and so they pounced when *From Beyond* came around. I was informed by somebody at the MPAA that if *Friday the 13th* and *The Thing* had been made just a few years later, they would never have gotten away with the stuff that they did. I simply tried the best I could to preserve the intentions and integrity of *From Beyond*, but it took twenty years for audiences to see all that I wanted them to see.

MD: Two primary concerns for censors have always been sex and violence, two consistent elements of your cinema. Would you concede there is a sickening perversity about some of the villains in your films, a sexual perversity in the cases of Dr. Hill and Dr. Pretorius?

SG: Definitely. Both of those characters do take an obscene delight in their perversity. They really love doing these terrible things! (Laughs)

MD: For those characters, particularly *Re-Animator*'s Dr. Hill, death appears to free them entirely from any residual sense of propriety or obligation.

SG: It does. You know, horror stories can be about shaking off the ropes that tie us down to conventionality. Horror often has an anarchistic quality that questions traditional systems of authority and morality. There are horror films that warn against that kind of behavior, and the characters that transgress are punished: so, if you don't follow the rules of society and the status quo, you basically *die*. What's interesting about Hill and Pretorius is that once certain things happen to them—death and a kind of rebirth—their ids go completely nuts. I think we tend to equate intellectuality with a reluctance to enjoy the carnal aspects of life. One assumes that great thinkers have no interest in affairs of a physical or sexual nature, as they are perceived to be a distraction, a detriment to the mind. I don't believe that is the case at all. Just because you are a scientist or an intellectual, it doesn't mean you aren't governed by the same needs and desires as everybody else. It's like you have the same kinds of thoughts floating around inside your head as the next person.

MD: Pretorius is defined as a sexual sadist in *From Beyond*, though, isn't he? He is forced, or perhaps submits, his flesh to a remarkable process of physical transformation in this unholy union he shares with the forces from beyond, and fully indulges himself.

SG: Well, the whole idea with Pretorius was to take an extremely intelligent human being—a genius—and have him undergo this incredible transformation. Only he is a sadistic man who sees his metamorphosis into a monster as a wonderful opportunity. He understands the range of possibilities it gives him to explore all the dark and sordid impulses he has, because the five senses just aren't enough for him anymore. He can now, as a Shoggoth, literally transform himself into whatever he wants just by thinking and imagining it. We based Pretorius on the Marquis de Sade, thinking, what if all this happened to a human being who was totally immersed in depravity? What would he do? What would he choose to be? Of course, he really would be kind of debauched. (Chuckles) Dr. Hill does the same thing in *Re-Animator*: he still has this craving for fame and immortality, but more than anything he wants to have his wicked way with the dean's daughter. He no longer has any control over himself. His libido is unleashed and he's going to do what he wants to do.

MD: You originally wanted to make *Dagon* in 1986, shortly after completing *Re-Animator*. What were the circumstances that prevented that earlier incarnation of the film from happening?

SG: The company that was originally going to produce the film did not like the story. They thought it was ridiculous and, as a matter of fact, that was the problem we had for fifteen years. People would start laughing when they heard the idea of a movie where people started turning into fish. That's why it took so long to get *Dagon* made. Nobody really appreciated or understood the concept. They just thought it was absurd and not a particularly scary notion for a horror film.

MD: How did the project eventually get reactivated?

SG: It was really because Brian Yuzna started the Fantastic Factory for Filmax and was able to pick and choose the projects he wanted to do. He called me up, and said, "I think we can finally get this movie made."

MD: Were any significant changes made to the screenplay in the time between the first version of the picture sinking and the eventual shooting of *Dagon* in late 2000?

SG: For the most part, the script stayed the same, but as we got closer to shooting we did make some changes. It's really based on two Lovecraft stories; one is "Dagon" and the other is "The Shadow Over Innsmouth," and we really brought it a little closer to the latter. "Innsmouth" is one of Lovecraft's most action-packed stories in that it involves a guy who comes to a fishing town and all the weird, shambling locals that inhabit that place come after him. So, it's essentially a tense and paranoid chase story in that it's really *moving*. That quality lent itself to a more cinematic story.

MD: It's interesting to think what *Dagon* would have been had you made it back in the 1980s.

SG: Well, for one thing, it would have starred Jeffrey Combs and Barbara Crampton! We even named the heroine Barbara in honor of Barbara Crampton. By the time we were ready to make *Dagon*, both of them were a little too old to play Paul and Barbara, but those were the two people I initially had in mind for it. But if we had made *Dagon* back in the 1980s, I don't think it would have been all that different.

MD: I presume, then, that you always had a strong sense of what the visual style of *Dagon* should be?

SG: I did, yeah. When we were originally going to do the movie I had been thinking that the creatures should look exactly as Lovecraft had described them—half-human, half-frog-like beings—but whenever we did concept drawings they always looked like the Creature from the Black Lagoon. When I was in Galicia, Spain, where we shot *Dagon*, I discovered a dish called Pulpo Gallego, which is octopus. I suddenly thought, "Wouldn't it be interesting if these creatures were octopus-like and had no skeletons?" That idea changed our whole direction, where we went with the fish-people.

MD: Why is the film shot almost entirely with a handheld camera?

SG: I felt that it should have a documentary-like feeling, and I was very interested in Lars von Trier's "Dogme 95" concept. I thought it would be cool to use that approach and make *Dagon* look like a Dogme movie, but have it be about something that was completely unnatural and preposterous. There is no dialogue for large stretches of the film, and I think we took our lead from Lovecraft on that. I mean, *Dagon* starts with a couple and then we get rid of Barbara pretty early on, so Paul is alone and there is nobody for him to talk to. You may also notice there are no subtitles in the movie, which gave it an alienating, mysterious quality.

I wanted the audience to feel what Paul was feeling—that he didn't understand what people were saying. The film really has the quality of a nightmare in that regard, in that it feels like nobody can help or understand you, and you're simply wandering from one unnerving situation to another with no place to go. That's very scary, I think, but it all began with the idea of presenting something totally unreal within a realistic form.

MD: One aspect that achieves that feeling is the distinctly queasy, roaming quality of the camera.

SG: Yeah, the camera is pretty much always on the move. Again, that was an effort to capture the confusion that Paul feels as he drifts through the town. Of course, when you move the camera a lot, and do 360-degree takes and everything, it causes a lot of lighting problems for the cameraman, but I think the effects you create are very unsettling. I was fortunate to have a good DP [in Carlos Suárez].... You really get that queasy feeling on the boat scenes, too. We were on a sailboat for a lot of the time in that movie. When we were doing the handheld stuff on the boat, the camera operator was a woman, and I believe the camera actually weighed more than she did. There were a couple of real-life scary moments when she almost went overboard and into the ocean.

MD: Speaking of the character's inability to be understood, did you have the same problem when working with the Spanish actors and technicians?

SG: The truth is me, Brian, and Ezra [Godden] were the only English-speakers on the set. Everybody else, the entire crew, was Spanish. I've shot films in various countries—Italy, Hungary, Australia, Ireland—and you do encounter certain linguistic and cultural differences when you're working on location. But you can learn a lot of interesting things when you're shooting in a different country. I don't speak Spanish fluently, but enough of the actors I cast in the film spoke English—pretty good English—so I could make myself perfectly understood to them. My DP spoke very little English, but we worked well together. You know, there are five different languages spoken in Spain and each of them possess their own sort of unique structures and meanings. I was out in Barcelona and they speak Catalan there; they don't speak Spanish. So, a little like Paul's situation in the movie, I never really knew what people were saying. In the region where we shot *Dagon*, they didn't speak Spanish there either; they spoke Gallego.

MD: There's an authenticity about the location you used for the town of Imboca, the fishing village where Paul and Barbara seek refuge after their boat is scuttled on rocks.

SG: That town was a really atmospheric, foggy place. There was something about it that seemed very Lovecraftian. It's actually called Combarro and we ended up using that name for the character in the film. It means "marshland," and in the original story the character's name is Paul Marsh, so it seemed like

Combarro would be the Galician equivalent. Interestingly, in Spanish, Imboca means "in the mouth," which was a joke on "Innsmouth"—Lovecraft's name for the town. Lovecraft's story is set in New England, and rather than trying to recreate Massachusetts, we decided on Galicia. On a sunny day, Combarro was charming, but when it was overcast it took on this sinister, creepy feeling. Naturally, we had our art department come in and make it a little scarier, just to push that feeling of dread. We boarded up some of the windows to make it look even more threatening than it normally would under different conditions.

MD: How did the locals feel about a film company washing up on their shores?

SG: We had the cooperation of the town. They were very friendly. They actually appear in some scenes. In the flashback sequence, where you learn what happened in Imboca many years earlier, and you see the villagers pulling in the nets, those are the real inhabitants of the town. You know, that place was an ancient fishing village that goes back to medieval times, and is literally built on rock and granite. So, it's a place where certain things and feelings have long remained the same in some ways. What's funny is, when I was working on the film and we were looking to secure the financing to shoot from the Arts Council of Galicia, we had to submit the script to them for their approval in order to get it. I was nervous about this, thinking they were going to flip out when they read all the twisted stuff that was supposed to happen in *Dagon*. I didn't know whether or not they thought the project might potentially destroy all the tourism in the area. So, we sent them the script and were waiting nervously for their response. I later received a message saying they had some notes, so I was expecting the worst. It turned out that we got only one comment back from them, which was an instance where we had referred to Gallego as a dialect. They corrected me: "No, it's not a dialect; it's an actual language." That was *it*.

MD: I'd like to talk about some of the cast, beginning with Macarena Gomez, who plays Uxía. What was she like to work with?

SG: Great. Macarena looked like a young Barbara Steele—she had that same unearthly beauty that Steele had. Macarena was perfect for the role as she had that combination of evil and innocence that was so necessary. Uxía had to be seductive and terrifying at the same time, which is not an easy combination for an actress to make, but Macarena managed it. Her background is in dance, she was originally a ballerina, and she was able to incorporate some of her dance skills into the performance. At the end, where she is doing all the graceful underwater stuff with Ezra, Macarena had to act while she was swimming and convey certain emotions. That's where her ability as a dancer was really useful.

MD: Another fascinating bit of casting in the film is Francisco Rabál, who plays the elderly Ezequiel, the last human inhabitant of Imboca. Were you a fan of his work?

SG: Oh, yeah. He was a terrific actor, one of the greatest stars of Spain. He'd worked several times with Luis Buñuel, so it was an honor to work with him. People kept asking me, "How did you get Paco Rabál for this film?" What's interesting is he campaigned for the role. When I first met Paco, I discovered he was a huge Lovecraft fan and we ended up talking about it for three hours. Paco loved the script and kept saying, "I *have* to do this movie!" He was a real trouper, too. I mean, *Dagon* was a hard shoot, one of the most physically demanding movies I've ever made, as we were extremely cold and wet the whole time we shot it. We decided early on that it should be raining all the time in the film. I wanted it to be oppressively wet, almost like this unending downpour would drain the audience on some level. Looking at the film now, you really do get the sense that you want to find some place warm and dry. But there were times when I was pissed off with myself for having made that decision, as we shot *Dagon* in November and December, and we'd be constantly dumping water on everybody. We were all freezing our asses off, just trying to get through it. Of course, Paco was not a young man at the time, but he never complained. He and Ezra set the tone for the whole production. If Paco wasn't complaining how could anyone else? I tried to protect him as much as I could, tried to make some things go easier for him, but he had to be in the rain for some scenes. He was so passionate about the project. Paco even wrote a poem about being in *Dagon*, which we included in the press kit. Unfortunately, he died a few months after we finished shooting. My big regret is that Paco never got to see the finished film, but we did dedicate it to him.

MD: Presumably, the rest of the cast weren't as familiar with Lovecraft as Rabál. How did you communicate to them the distinctly intangible qualities of his work?

SG: I encouraged them to read Lovecraft, and most of the actors did read the stories the film is based on. Although, I'll say it again, I think it was shooting in Galicia that helped them to understand the weirdness of the story. It was such an interesting place to be, and the unique atmosphere it generated helped the actors get into that world. I mean, for one thing, there is a rich mythological tradition there, tales of sea monsters and witches, and there have been all these shipwrecks off the coast. As a matter of fact, when you land at the airport, there are all these toy witches they are selling as souvenirs. So, you didn't have to do much to get into that Lovecraftian feeling. It really was like stepping into another world.

MD: It's my understanding that Dagon is a real deity.

SG: That's correct, yeah. A lot of Lovecraft's gods were created by him—Cthulhu, for example—but Dagon is an actual sea god: half-human and half-fish. One of the Ten Commandments is "Thou shalt have no other gods before me," which is interesting when you think about it, because it acknowledges that there were other gods kind of floating around. Dagon was one of those other gods. He is the god of the Philistines, and his followers were into committing human sacrifice. Dagon is mentioned several times in the Bible—it was the Temple of Dagon that Samson brought down as the followers were preparing a human sacrifice inside. One of the things the Dagon worshippers would do is murder their first born son and bury him under the doorway of the house in order to bring good luck.

MD: How lovely...

SG: Yeah! (Laughs) Of course, that practice hasn't continued, but it's amazing how certain things have survived and even made their way into the rituals and vestments of Roman Catholicism. Researching Dagon, I found out the priests would wear these fish-heads that looked like the mitre that the pope and bishops wear. I discovered that the papal mitre originated from the Dagon worshippers, looking as it does like a big fish-head with the mouth open and the fish-skin flowing down their backs like a cape. I thought it would be interesting if we turned that around and made the inhabitants of Imboca wear garments of human skin as they gradually transformed into fish. Doing the research, I learned that Christianity is very inclusive, everyone is welcome, and the Dagon worshippers were welcomed in, too. Even the symbol of the fish that was used in early Christianity comes from Dagon, and this was a way of us saying, "We have all these things that you are used to, traditions that are observed, and here's where some of them came from." Even the whole thing about Christians only eating fish on a Friday comes from Dagon as well.

MD: Do the transforming townsfolk wear human skins in an effort to consciously preserve some remnant of their vanished humanity?

SG: I think it can be understood that way, as some echo of their lost humanity. The skins idea is not in Lovecraft's stories, but maybe one of the things the film touches on is the power of religion to transform people into something else entirely. That transformation can be positive and it can be destructive. I mean, people do terrible things in the name of religion. We see it happening in the world now with extremists and terrorists.

MD: Do you believe in God?

SG: I do, and another interesting thing about the film is it's like a war between the gods. During the skinning scene, Paco and Ezra recite the Twenty-third Psalm, and so each god is being pitted against the other. But, in Lovecraft's world, our God is powerless against the older gods. Ezequiel is being killed in such a horrific way—having his flesh torn off—in those moments he and Paul are sort of clinging to the hope of some kind of salvation. But it's like one thing's evil is another thing's good. I thought that was such a disturbing idea, that one is truly alone in a sense, and the only thing that is real in that moment is the pain and death being inflicted on this old man. So, our God is simply not present; He can't intervene and save them. They just have to face it on their own. You know, to me, that feels pretty real as the apparent absence of God is something that has troubled humanity for a long time.

MD: The evisceration of Ezequiel is a deeply shocking and unpleasant scene, perhaps the most shocking and unpleasant in your entire filmography.

SG: Yeah. Well, Ezequiel is a character the audience has hopefully come to like and to see him experience such a terrible and protracted death is kind of tough for them. Actually, that scene was the only time Paco ever complained, and I don't blame him. He was a frail seventy-five-year-old man and was having some pulmonary problems. As I said, he died only a few months later. I do recall that he didn't like the prosthetics he had to wear, and, of course, we had to have them. So, it was an intense scene to shoot for those reasons. I can recall thinking to myself when I was doing it, "Okay, *this* would be the point where I'd leave the theater!" (Laughs) I walk out of a lot of movies. I'm a total coward.

MD: The violence in *Dagon* is more intense than in your early films and played with less humor. It marks a shift in your work towards a more disconcerting realism in your portrayal of brutality, a trend that would continue with your next three movies: *King of the Ants*, *Edmond*, and *Stuck*.

SG: Well, the violence in those movies is intense, but it's not violence for the sake of violence. Each of those movies has a point to make, so the violence had to be more real. In *Dagon*, even though it is fantasy, what's amazing is I wasn't asked to make a single cut in the entire film. After all the problems I'd had with the MPAA, they left it alone. I thought they'd have big problems with the skinning scene. Clearly, they weren't paying attention.

MD: One subtle moment in the film is the hotel clerk turning around to get Paul the keys, revealing that the wrinkles in his neck are actually—

SG: [Interrupting] Fish-gills! (Laughs) Yeah, the actor who plays the clerk [José Lifante] is wonderful. You'll notice that the fish-people don't blink in the movie, an idea taken directly from Lovecraft's story. It was difficult for the actors not to blink—especially in the constant rain—but it adds to the weird air that surrounds them. Something is clearly very wrong about them, and the fact they don't blink does register with a lot of viewers.

MD: It's been a decade since *Dagon* was released, and I'm curious about your feelings towards it. After struggling for so long to get the film made, were you satisfied with the results?

SG: Yeah, and I was actually grateful that we hadn't made *Dagon* earlier, because the original idea was to show a lot more of the creatures. I think it was better not to because with Lovecraft the more you leave things to your imagination, the better it works. It took about a year to make the film, edit it, score it, put it all together, and it was like coming to the end of a long journey.

MD: At present, your last Lovecraft adaptation is "Dreams in the Witch-House," which you made for the first season of *Masters of Horror* in 2005.

SG: Yeah, and that story has always been one of my favorites. It was the first Lovecraft story I read and has always stayed with me. What I find fascinating about "Dreams in the Witch-House" is its firm basis in physics—the pentagram used in witchcraft, which has been around for thousands of years, is pure geometry. What Lovecraft suggests is that if you have the right series of angles you can travel inter-dimensionally and visit other realms and realities. That's a brilliant concept—one that resides more on the side of science fiction than it does horror—but it's still very scary. Lovecraft was always looking for ways in his stories to combine science with magic, logic with the occult, and nobody does it better than him. I think "Dreams in the Witch-House" is really one of the best illustrations of that.

MD: Was "Dreams" always going to be the first film you were making for the series?

SG: Yes. When Mick Garris first put *Masters of Horror* together with Showtime, and got all these great horror directors like John Carpenter and Dario Argento involved, I was encouraged to do a Lovecraft story. There was definitely a desire expressed for each of us to make something that was kind of in keeping with our own individual style and trademarks. I think nearly all of us had a pet project that we wanted to do. Since I'd always loved "Dreams in the Witch-House"—as a matter of fact, after Charlie Band rejected *Dagon* in '85, it was one of two choices for my next film along with "From Beyond"—it was perfect for me. The story has the quality of a child's nightmare: there's a witch that comes creeping into your room in the dead of night and takes you off to these distant places to do terrible things. It's just terrific. Each director had ten days in which to shoot their films and, as long as we stayed within our budgets [of $1.2 million], we could do whatever we liked. It was pretty exciting having that high level of freedom.

MD: Did you lose anything from Lovecraft's story due to budgetary concerns?

SG: Yeah, but it was negligible. The film is pretty faithful to Lovecraft's story, one exception being the sequence where the Witch takes the student that is renting the attic room in Arkham to another planet. We couldn't afford to do that, so we lost it, but I don't think that loss hurts the film at all. I'm real happy with how it turned out.

MD: How do you feel about other directors tackling Lovecraft adaptations, and those films that retain a Lovecraftian flavor, like John Carpenter's *In the Mouth of Madness*?

SG: Fine. *In the Mouth of Madness* is probably the best Lovecraft movie ever made that isn't actually based on one of Lovecraft's stories. I think it's underrated. John did a really good job on it. I also consider *The Blair Witch Project* [1999] to be kind of a Lovecraft movie, too.

MD: Of course, we still wait, more in hope than expectation, for Guillermo del Toro to make his adaptation of *At the Mountains of Madness*.

SG: Yeah, that would be great. We all want to see that movie become a reality.

MD: Apparently, if it ever happens, it will be the world's first $150 million R-rated horror movie. A truly extraordinary prospect.

SG: And there's the rub, because the studios don't want to risk that kind of money on a big-budget Lovecraft picture. Having had my own problems in trying to get various Lovecraft projects off the ground, I feel for Guillermo. People just don't understand [Lovecraft's] work; they don't think it has any mass commercial appeal. I don't agree with that, actually. I think *At the Mountains of Madness* has the potential to be a huge movie, one that could change the way Lovecraft is viewed for a long time. So, it's a real heartbreaker for Guillermo. I've talked to him a little about that project and it sounds fascinating.

MD: Tom Cruise was announced as starring in del Toro's film, which one assumes would have assisted the commercial potential of the project considerably.

SG: Yeah. It's funny, I believe at one point Guillermo was considering Jeffrey Combs for a role in it—not the Tom Cruise role, some other role. You know, that idea makes sense to me. I mean, Jeffrey is now so closely associated with Lovecraft after *Re-Animator* and *From Beyond*, and he has also played Lovecraft in the wrap-around story of *Necronomicon*. I consider it a compliment to the work that Jeffrey and I have done, that Guillermo was considering him. It sort of acknowledges us.

MD: Are there any future Lovecraft movies you have cooking in the pot?

SG: I always have projects I want to do. I'm afraid sometimes that if I talk about these things too much, they'll be cursed by a witch and thrown into the black abysm from which there is no return! (Chuckles) So, let's save all that for another conversation.

Stuart Gordon on Polanski and Kubrick

Michael Doyle / 2014

Portions of this interview, conducted on January 16, 2014, were published in *Rue Morgue's Horror Movie Heroes* (2014). Reprinted by permission.

Michael Doyle: When did you first become acquainted with the cinema of Roman Polanski?
Stuart Gordon: It was when I was in college and I first saw *Knife in the Water* [1962]. I was hugely impressed with the skill and maturity he displayed with what was his debut film. I subsequently followed Polanski's career very closely and became a big fan of his work.
MD: In your mind, what are the strongest characteristics of his movies?
SG: I don't think anyone is better at making a subjective film in which you directly perceive things from the point of view of the main character. When you watch Polanski's movies, you feel like you are the main protagonist and I think that is his greatest strength as a filmmaker. In fact, when I made *Re-Animator*, I used *Rosemary's Baby* as sort of my model. I had never made a film before, and I was very taken with the way Polanski shot that movie. You almost never see a close-up of Mia Farrow and are always looking over her shoulder. So, when people are talking to Rosemary, they are almost talking to the camera and that's a technique I've used in a lot of my films. I often say that *Rosemary's Baby* was my film school, because I ended up adopting several of Polanski's methods in my filmmaking.
MD: That approach is very effective in unsettling the viewer.
SG: Yeah, and I think another good example of that subjective approach is in *The Pianist* [2002] where the character played by Adrien Brody, who is a Polish Jew, is hiding in an apartment from the Nazis. There are all these battles going on outside, tanks and guns and soldiers coming down the street. A lot of directors would want to go down into the street and cover the action, but Polanski never does. He keeps the camera in the apartment, and the audience is watching these events through a window just as Brody's character is. That approach really

succeeds in building the growing sense of tension and apprehension that we are also hiding from the Nazis. Because Polanski is such an inventive filmmaker, he doesn't go for the obvious approaches that other directors do. There are some things that Polanski does even in his darkest films that I think are very funny. He has a real black comedic streak, which is something I often strive for in my own work.

MD: There is a concentration on paranoia and claustrophobia in *Repulsion* [1965] and *The Tenant* [1976] in the way both those films chart the bleak descent of an isolated individual into madness and violence.

SG: Yes, and, again, Polanski really puts the audience in the mind of Catherine Deneuve in *Repulsion*. You are seeing things the way she sees them, as opposed to a movie like *Psycho* where Hitchcock keeps you at somewhat of a distance. We don't ever get into the mind of Norman Bates in *Psycho*, but in *Repulsion* and *The Tenant*, Polanski really leads us into that dark and lonely place—inside the mind of an insane person who is hallucinating and so forth. It's incredibly disturbing.

MD: A lot of critics have difficulty separating the depictions of violence in Polanski's work from the tragedies of his personal life. Would you agree?

SG: Well, I certainly think that Polanski has experienced the real thing. Unlike most of us directors, the stuff that he's gone through personally has been hellish—starting with his traumatic childhood during World War II, and moving on to the Manson murders where his wife and child were brutally murdered. Polanski has really known violence and death firsthand, and maybe that's another reason why his films contain such remarkable power.

MD: It's difficult to watch the disturbing slaughter of Macduff's family in *Macbeth* [1971]—which is perhaps Polanski's most violent film—without immediately thinking of the Manson murders that occurred just two years prior.

SG: Yeah, absolutely. Polanski's *Macbeth* might be the best *Macbeth* I've ever seen, actually, but yeah, it's hard not to recall the murders when you view that particular sequence. What strikes me most about Polanski's work is that he doesn't ever flinch. He just plunges right into the heart of darkness. When I make my own films, I always do the same. I mean, you have to decide what you want to do as a director, what the audience should be seeing and feeling, and you shouldn't hold back. Polanski is the master at confronting audiences with the horror, but doing it in sort of an intimate way, a way that really gets under your skin. You look at it, and say, "Gosh, how did he do *that*?" Another interesting thing is that I read his autobiography where he talks about studying the way human beings actually see things. It's a book about vision and how the eye works and so forth. Polanski incorporates certain details into his films which give them an extra sense of reality, and this knowledge is probably why they feel so ruthlessly subjective. He also likes to really play with the audience.

MD: Can you give me an example of his playfulness?

SG: There's a famous story about when he was making *Rosemary's Baby*: Polanski was shooting a scene where [Ruth Gordon] is on the telephone in the bedroom and Mia Farrow is in the foreground. Polanski kept telling the cameraman [William A. Fraker] to move the camera to the right, but the cameraman replied, "If I do that we are not going to see [Ruth] very well." Polanski insisted that he do it and I think in the finished film all you can see in the shot is [portions of her head and body]. When *Rosemary's Baby* eventually played in the theater and that scene arrived, the whole audience were leaning and straining to look around the corner and see [Gordon]. (Laughs) That clearly demonstrates how Polanski can not only capture reality as we experience it, but playfully manipulate the audience on a psychological level.

MD: I've always admired Polanski's grasp of the small sensory and auditory details present in his filmmaking.

SG: Yeah, he's the best at that. Polanski is not only conscious of how we see, but how we hear, how we feel, how we dream—the use of silence in the dream sequence in *Rosemary's Baby* was so groundbreaking. Nowadays, there are movies which are just wall-to-wall music, the music never ever stops, but Polanski uses silence extremely well in his films. I don't think there are many filmmakers that can compete with his understanding of those things. So, it's not just the way we see, but the way we experience reality. One of the most famous stories I've discovered involves the scene in *Chinatown* [1974] where Jack Nicholson is looking at a man who is standing on a dam at a great distance. The man is suddenly shot, and Nicholson is watching this execution through a pair of binoculars. We see the man fall and then we hear the gunshot ringing out. When the studio heads saw that scene, they said, "Shouldn't we hear the gunshot *before* the man falls?" Polanski said, "No, Nicholson is so far away from this incident, and light travels faster than sound. So, from his relative position, you're going to see the gunshot [hit the victim] before you hear it." Like you said, it's those small details, that understanding of the way things actually are, that gives his films such a devastating sense of reality.

MD: I'm intrigued by the way Polanski effortlessly moves from experimental personal projects to more commercial films. For example, *Repulsion* was followed by the avant-garde *Cul-de-sac* [1966]; *Rosemary's Baby* was followed by the intensely violent Shakespearean adaptation, *Macbeth*; and *Chinatown* was followed by the blackly comic *The Tenant*. Is that difficult for a director to do, to balance those types of varying projects?

SG: I don't imagine it was for him, because he's made so many great movies across so many different genres. For me, in my own work, all my films are personal films. I think as a director you have to be personally involved with a film in order to make a really good film. You have to have this burning desire—you know, like this is the movie I *must* make. Without that desire, it's hard to make a movie—and making a movie is hard enough. I've always felt that way about my movies, and no doubt Polanski does, too. Even the films that people may think are my more commercial or impersonal films, things like *Robot Jox* or *The Wonderful Ice Cream Suit*, or whatever, are mine. They are deeply personal films, because I don't even think in terms of commerciality really, not in the sense that, "Okay, this is just a job." Neither was I trying to change my image; I just think in terms of the movies I'd really love to see. I never make any other kind of distinction.

MD: What do you make of Polanski's later films?

SG: I wasn't crazy about *Carnage* [2011]. That one was based on a play [*God of Carnage*] and felt a little too constricted and contained as a movie. The interplay between the four main actors was excellent, but its theatrical origins were very evident to me, so it just felt like a play. I don't think Polanski had a chance to really do his thing with that material and open it up. But I really liked *The Ghost Writer* [2010], his political thriller with Ewan McGregor and Pierce Brosnan. I thought that was great, very tense and stylish.

MD: You must have watched *The Ninth Gate* [1999] with a great deal of interest.

SG: I did, yeah. I guess *The Ninth Gate* was sold as Polanski's big return to horror after many years away from the genre, but I thought that movie was just okay. Aside from one or two creepy moments, and a nice performance from Johnny Depp, I didn't think it was great—nowhere near the quality and effectiveness of *Rosemary's Baby* and *Repulsion*. But, you know, Polanski is still very much around. You often hear that a director's powers kind of disappear or dwindle with age, but he is still just knocking 'em right out of the park. Of course, he won an Academy Award for *The Pianist*, so he remains an important filmmaker.

MD: As a director whose later works are routinely compared to your earlier efforts, do you have some sympathy for Polanski?

SG: Absolutely. I get it sometimes with *Re-Animator*. People will say, "I liked *Edmond*" or "I liked *Stuck*, but it's no *Re-Animator*." I think Polanski's early horror films—*Repulsion*, *Rosemary's Baby*, *The Tenant*, even *The Fearless Vampire Killers* [1967]—are so great, he is almost competing with himself, with his own reputation, like many directors are. *The Tenant* is spectacular, and what a *weird* movie that is! Again, that film makes it feel like the horrors are all happening to you. I just didn't think *The Ninth Gate* had the same kind of power as his early stuff, but I'd love him to make another horror film. I think a lesser Polanski horror film is still superior to 90 percent of the horror movies that are out there.

MD: Have you ever met Polanski?

SG: No, never. I'd love to meet him at some point. Of course, he's not allowed to come to America after his problems with the law, and I don't know how I could ever meet him in Paris where he lives. I've never run into him at a film festival in Europe or anything, but I wish I could.

MD: It's well documented that the reason Polanski cannot enter the US is because of his fleeing the country after the rape allegations made against him in 1977. Do you have trouble reconciling his alleged crimes with the work or can you separate the two?

SG: I separate the two, because I don't know Polanski the man, I only know his work. It's sort of the same situation with my love of Lovecraft: it's now been confirmed that Lovecraft was a racist and anti-Semite who had some very distasteful views on other races. I find those views horrifying and sickening, but I love Lovecraft's writings. So, I tend to separate the artist from the art, although I do understand why some people have difficulty doing that.

MD: Do Polanski's films still inspire and unsettle you?

SG: Yes, and I continue to watch and rewatch them. It's funny, but every time I see *Rosemary's Baby* on television, I simply cannot turn it off. No matter how many times I've seen that movie, it's so compelling I just have to sit there and deal with it all over again. Every aspect of *Rosemary's Baby*—from the casting and performances to the direction and score—is amazing and an endless source of inspiration to me.

MD: Would you say that Polanski is your primary influence as a filmmaker?

SG: Yeah, Polanski and Hitchcock. As a matter of fact, just before I made *Re-Animator*, I also reread Francois Truffaut's book [*Hitchcock/Truffaut*, 1966] just to gather as much information and inspiration as I could. That's a really great book. It gives you so many invaluable insights into Hitchcock's whole approach.

MD: I understand that another of your cinematic heroes is Stanley Kubrick.

SG: I adore Kubrick! Yeah, I just find him and his movies fascinating.

MD: Kubrick worked under some fairly unique conditions—the enviable amounts of control he enjoyed over his works, the considerable budgets and casts he worked with, and the sheer diversity of the films he made across a number of genres.

SG: Yeah, it was a pretty amazing career he had. I love reading books and articles and opinions on Kubrick. I try to devour as much of that stuff as I can. You know, Larry Cohen once told a great story about Kubrick at one of these "Masters of Horror" dinners we have over here. Has Larry ever mentioned it to you?

MD: No.

SG: You should ask Larry about it the next time you talk. It would make a terrific addition to your book [*Larry Cohen: The Stuff of Gods and Monsters*, 2015]. I'm sure he can tell this story better than I can, but, basically, back in the early sixties, Larry was walking through Times Square when he saw a rather disheveled-looking guy—one he might have even mistaken for a homeless person—digging through the contents of a trashcan. As Larry got closer, he recognized this person to be none other than Stanley Kubrick—I believe Larry had once visited the set of *Spartacus* [1960], so he knew what Kubrick looked like. Larry asked him what he was doing and, without even looking up to see who it was addressing him, Kubrick replied, "I'm looking for my reviews." (Laughs) I believe *Lolita* [1962] had only just opened that same weekend, and Kubrick was desperately trying to get hold of each and every review so he could see what the reactions to the picture had been. Larry said that Kubrick was very calm, even nonchalant, when he suddenly came upon him like that, like it wasn't a big deal that this great director should be caught burrowing through a trashcan on Times Square. Anyway, he and Larry talked for a little while and then Kubrick, satisfied that he had found what he was looking for, straightened up, said his goodbyes, and then just walked away. I don't think Larry ever laid eyes on him again.

MD: (Laughs) That *is* a wonderful story. I'll have to ask Larry to relay it to me.

SG: I actually collect Kubrick stories. I never met him, but I've met a lot of people who have worked with Kubrick. They all have fascinating stories to tell. One of the best ones I ever got was from Zalman King, the director of *Wild Orchid* [1990] and the erotic TV series *Red Shoe Diaries* [1992–97]. When Kubrick was doing *Eyes Wide Shut* [1999] over in England, Zalman got this phone call at two in the morning from a guy claiming to be Stanley Kubrick. Zalman thought it was some ridiculous joke and was about to hang up, when the guy succeeded in convincing him that he really was Kubrick. It turned out that Kubrick was calling Zalman to ask him about how best to shoot sex scenes. Zalman told me that he and Kubrick had stayed up all night discussing this, and then afterwards Zalman woke up his wife and told her what had happened. She couldn't believe it, but then, the next night at two in the morning, the phone starts ringing. Zalman picks it up and it's Kubrick again, who proceeds to continue the conversation exactly where they had left it the previous night. This situation went on and on, for like weeks, with Kubrick always calling at precisely two in the morning. At first Zalman was flattered, but then, after a while, it started to be a real pain in the ass as he couldn't get any sleep. Eventually, he just blew up and told Kubrick: "Look, just make the damn movie! Leave me alone!" (Laughs)

MD: There was an excellent documentary made by Jon Ronson called *Stanley Kubrick's Boxes* [2008], where they went through an extensive archive of scripts, photographs, correspondence, and other documents. Have you seen it?

SG: Yeah, I've seen it. That's a great documentary. My wife is always kidding me about it because there was this thing in it about a note [Kubrick once wrote] that says, "We must have three melons in the house at all times." I said to her, "Well, right there is the reason why I'm not a great director. I don't have enough melons in the house." (Laughs) So, whenever we go to the grocery store, I say, "Okay, now we've got to get *three* melons!"

MD: Kubrick is a filmmaker from which many enduring myths and legends have arisen over the years. No doubt some stories are true and others are not, but most generally agree about his fastidious and meticulous approach to filmmaking—including the multiple takes he does.

SG: There was a great quote by Kubrick about chess that possibly explains his doing multiple takes. I think I've got it here somewhere. Let me just find that quote and I'll read it to you. [Gordon searches intently for something] Ah, here it is! Now, Kubrick was a chess player, and at one time in his life he used to make his living hustling chess in Central Park. One of the things people who worked with him would say is Kubrick would never give them a reason for why he was doing another take; he would never tell them to do something different. He would just say, "Let's do it again." I think the following quote explains why he always did so many takes. Kubrick said: "You sit at the board and suddenly your heart leaps. Your hand trembles to pick up the piece and move it. But what chess teaches you is that you must sit there calmly, and think about whether it's really a good idea and whether there are other, better ideas." Now, that quote says a lot about what was going on in Kubrick's head, why he did all those takes: he kept waiting for something better to happen. It was as if he was waiting for some sort of inspiration to arrive. Basically, he was asking himself, "Is this really the *best* move? Is this the *best* shot I can get? Is this the *best* way to do this?"

MD: What did you make of Kubrick's final film, *Eyes Wide Shut*?

SG: I liked it, but I don't think he ever quite finished *Eyes Wide Shut*. Kubrick would fiddle with his movies—even after they were released sometimes. He once cut around fifteen minutes from *2001* after that picture had been released for a week. There was also a sizable portion of *The Shining* cut from some release prints, including a different ending that he lost. I just have this feeling that Kubrick would have returned to *Eyes Wide Shut* and refined it slightly in the time between his death in early 1999 and the release of the film later that same year. I also have this theory that his death was brought about by the reaction of the guys at Warner Bros. when they saw it. This thought is based purely on nothing; it's just a feeling I have about what went down. I think the studio was appalled that some of the sex in the film was so explicit they wouldn't be able to secure an R rating for it. I believe that when they told Kubrick that, the stress of it might have been a contributing factor to pushing him towards his demise. I think he died four days after screening the movie for the studio, something like that. When they released *Eyes Wide Shut* in the States, Warner Bros. put these figures in to block the action so you couldn't see all the sex that was going on during the orgy scenes. Literally, the studio digitally created figures that were placed on screen to be standing in the way. This was done because Kubrick had had it written in his contract that they couldn't edit or cut out his stuff, but the executives at Warner Bros. felt this was something they could get away with. So, I've never actually seen the version of *Eyes Wide Shut* that was shown in the UK and some other countries with all the sex completely visible.

MD: I remember that in the months prior to the release of *Eyes Wide Shut* there were all sorts of wild rumors about what was to feature in the film. For instance, I read somewhere that Tom Cruise was to appear in drag and participate in orgies with dubious-looking extras.

SG: Yeah, and there were also these stories about how Kubrick had hired somebody to teach Tom Cruise how to have sex with the girl in it. I believe Cruise then successfully sued the British tabloid that printed that story, or some other allegation which painted him in an unflattering light. But there have always been a lot of crazy stories associated with Kubrick and the making of his films. I don't know whether you've read it or not, but there's a book called *Blue Movie* [1970] by Terry Southern, who also wrote the screenplay for *Dr. Strangelove* [1964] among other things. Have you read *Blue Movie*?

MD: No.

SG: It's a work of fiction, but it's really about Kubrick—a Stanley Kubrick-like director [named King B]—who is making a mega-budget hardcore porno movie using big Hollywood stars. This film can only be shown in one theater on Earth, which is located somewhere like Luxemburg—no, Liechtenstein! *Blue Movie* is a vicious satire of Hollywood and the monster egos some people have in the industry. The thing about *Eyes Wide Shut* is I think Kubrick was into the idea that Tom Cruise and Nicole Kidman would really be having sex on camera. I believe it was one of the things he talked about with certain people, and was the reason he cast a married couple to play the leads. Kubrick felt they could actually be fucking for *real*. There was this feeling that Kubrick had felt he'd been hoodwinked, that Cruise and Kidman would not literally be doing it—the implication being they weren't having sex. The story goes that Kubrick then called up R. Lee Ermey, who'd played the drill sergeant in *Full Metal Jacket* [1987], and was bitching about this to him. So, there were a lot of crazy rumors flying around. I think the tabloid had implied that Cruise wasn't interested in having sex with a woman, and that he was gay. Cruise won that case in court, won damages and an apology. But I do think Kubrick was trying to get the reality of the relationship between Cruise and Kidman within the film, perhaps forgetting they were just actors. I read a fascinating book called *Eyes Wide Open* by [Frederic Raphael] the screenwriter of *Eyes Wide Shut*, who also gets into the idea that Kubrick wanted them to have real sex on camera.

MD: Last year, I read an article online in which David Cronenberg said that he considered *The Shining* "not to be a great film" and also felt that Kubrick had no understanding of horror. I presume you don't share Cronenberg's view?

SG: No, I don't. I know Stephen King doesn't like Kubrick's film either as it deviates from his novel, but I consider *The Shining* to be a brilliant film. In fact, with that movie, I think Kubrick proved he had a grasp on what is truly scary: madness, isolation, despair, and so forth, horror that is rooted in the family. When you think about it, what's scarier than having a member of your own family, somebody you love, going insane and trying to kill you? Here's Daddy coming through the door—grinning horribly—with an axe in his hands. It's terrifying! So, yeah, I think Kubrick had a complete understanding of horror, and you can see it in some of his other films, too, that are not horror films: for instance, the breakdown of HAL 9000 in *2001* is terrifying.

MD: Did you ever see the documentary *Making The Shining* [1980] shot by Kubrick's daughter, Vivian, for the BBC?

SG: Yeah, that was really something. It was fascinating watching Kubrick at work, sort of jousting with Shelley Duvall and everything. I actually spoke to Vivian Kubrick once. She was also a composer and had written the haunting score for *Full Metal Jacket* under the pseudonym Abigail Mead. I had really liked that score and wanted her to compose the music for my movie *Fortress* back in 1992. So, I contacted Vivian and she asked me to send her a copy of the film, which I did. I had this feeling that she was watching it with her dad, you know? Then, later, she turned *Fortress* down, and I was like, "Oh, well, okay." I mean, you never know how these things are going to turn out. I was reading about her just recently, actually, about the whole thing with her becoming a Scientologist and breaking off from the family. Apparently, some say that estrangement may have been what killed Kubrick and not Warner Bros.' response to *Eyes Wide Shut*. It just broke his heart. He wrote Vivian a long letter, pleading with her to come back to England from the States before he died. I believe Kubrick had also wanted her to score *Eyes Wide Shut* before she left and there was some acrimony about that, because she didn't end up doing it for some reason.

MD: Do you find it somewhat ironic that Kubrick, a man who exerted such rigorous control over his work and working environment, could seemingly not do the same in his private life?

SG: Well, you can't control everything, you know? Life and relationships have a way of just happening and, oftentimes, you have to roll with it. It's funny, I was talking recently with somebody about the human element of filmmaking; when you work with all these different people they end up contributing to your vision and changing it in some way. I like that about making movies, the feeling we're all in this big pot of unpredictability together, and you have different personalities and situations you must deal with on a daily basis. But I imagine that was sort of problematic for Kubrick. I'm sure he wanted to control *everything*, no matter what. I think he got closer than most of us directors to achieving that goal, but real life is very different to movies. The human element of life is that people are free to be dicks! (Laughs) They can be impulsive, stupid, cruel, and we all have to accept that at some point, whoever we are and whatever we do. It's like we all have to be free to make our own mistakes.

The Grimmest of the Grim: Stuart Gordon on *Taste*

Michael Doyle / 2014

This interview was conducted on August 22, 2014. Printed by permission.

Michael Doyle: What can you tell me about your most recent play *Taste*?

Stuart Gordon: *Taste* is a two-man play we did at the Sacred Fools Theatre in Hollywood about a guy who puts an ad on the internet for someone he can kill, cook, and eat. It's about the meeting of these two men in what turns out to be their first and their last encounter. The play takes place in real time, so it's the course of this rather bizarre and extraordinary relationship playing right in its entirety before the audience's eyes.

MD: Who are essaying the two leads?

SG: Chris McKenna, who I worked with on *King of the Ants* and *Re-Animator: The Musical*, plays Vic, the guy who has consented to being eaten, and Donal Thoms-Cappello plays Terry, the guy he has met online. I needed two talented actors to make this story work, and that's what I got. I enjoyed working with both actors. They each had terrific ideas and were very committed. Chris and Donal were open to all the different ways of playing it.

MD: How did the project first come to you?

SG: It was sent to me by Adam Goldworm, who was a producer on *Masters of Horror*. Adam is the manager of Benjamin Brand, the author of *Taste*, so that's how I came to receive the material. Adam thought *Taste* would be something that would appeal to my sensibilities, so he sent it along to me. I'm very happy that he did. When I read it, I thought, "Wow, this is interesting."

MD: What was it about the script that captured you?

SG: The strength of the writing. Ben is a writer who I think is going to have an amazing career. I had to put his script down a few times, actually, as it had so many moments in it that made me feel uncomfortable and woozy. I realized that if it affected me that way, it must be something good. The two characters really leapt off the page and the interaction between them felt totally authentic. You see their relationship develop and change over the course of an hour and a half, and you get a tremendous sense of who these men are. They meet as perfect strangers and depart just about as close as two people in this world can possibly be.

MD: Did *Taste* exist first as a screenplay?

SG: Yes, Ben originally wrote it as a movie. At some point, somebody read the script and convinced him that it would probably work better—and be more impactful—if it were done as a play rather than as a film. And I agreed with that, that it would be perfectly suited to the theater.

MD: What elements made it more fitting for that medium in your view?

SG: Well, for one thing, *Taste* takes place in a working kitchen, so it's sort of a cooking show. I thought if we did that in reality, the aromas would reach the audience and enrich the experience for them. The idea was people would smell it and have a strong reaction, and that's pretty much what happened. There is a real directness about theater that, in some ways, film cannot match. I mean, in film, you can cheat the audience by using different cuts and angles. The fact that you are seeing it happening *live* in front of you, and there is not so much distance between [the event] and the viewer, makes *Taste* a more powerful experience for the audience than if it had been a movie. We actually had people pass out during the show! I enjoy saying that theater separates the men from the boys, but there's a lot of truth in that. You have to be a little tougher and more resilient to sit through something like that.

MD: So, you went the way [Hans] Laube and [Michael] Todd [Jr.] did with "Smell-o-vision"—which John Waters later exhumed with his "Odorama" process, the scratch 'n' sniff cards audiences were handed [when they saw *Polyester*, 1981].

SG: Not quite! (Laughs) What we did was not so much a gimmick. It's funny, I was reading about how our senses work in relation to food, because so much of food is about sight, about our visual perception. How we see, touch and taste is fascinating, but, oddly enough, smell is something that also comes from the mouth. This [article] suggested that if you hold your nose while eating something it affects your taste, and so a lot of different things are going on in terms of our senses. But if you combine the sight of something with the smell of something, it can have even more potency.

MD: For you, is theater more satisfying than film when it's done right and what you have worked towards as a director has come off?

SG: Well, theater is harder, but the great thing about it is the immediacy of it, how it generates a unique kind of energy and excitement. Because theater is a living thing, and the audiences are different with each performance, every night is different. That makes it special. You can make adjustments as you go along with a play, because living things grow and change, but you can't do that with movies. You have just the one chance to get it right.

MD: It's my understanding that *Taste* is based on the real-life 2001 case of "the Rotenburg Cannibal," Armin Meiwes.

SG: That's correct, yeah. It's an amazing story. Armin Meiwes was a German guy who was looking for a willing volunteer to be murdered and eaten by him—and somebody [named Bernd Jürgen Armando Brandes] just stepped right up. He really wanted this terrible thing to happen to him; he wanted to die and for his flesh to be consumed.

MD: Are you aware there is a compelling documentary about the case that was screened on Channel 4 in the UK [in 2004], which chronicled in detail the encounter these men had?

SG: What was that show called?

MD: "The Man Who Ate His Lover."

SG: I heard about that. I might have seen it.

MD: One of the things that struck me was the claim that, at first, the victim requested that Meiwes literally *bite* off his penis.

SG: Apparently, that's true, and then they decided to use a knife to get the job done. The victim then tried to eat some of his own penis, but the taste and texture wasn't to his liking. Some effort was made to cook the penis to make it more palatable, I guess, but then it was chopped into smaller pieces and fed to Meiwes's dog. You know, what happened that day just went so far beyond the scope of what most people can imagine...

MD: One disturbing detail I recall—I can't forget it, actually—is that after the emasculation occurred the victim trotted off upstairs minus his member, climbed into a hot bath that Meiwes had run for him, and simply waited to bleed to death.

SG: Yeah, and, meanwhile, Meiwes was downstairs quietly reading a [*Star Trek*] book. I guess, finally, he just killed the guy because he was probably taking too long to die or something. He wanted him out of the way. Meiwes then spent the following months—or however long it was—going back and eating various parts of the victim's body. I think he ate quite a bit of it. You really can't make this stuff up. Real life is so much stranger than fiction.

MD: Whatever way you examine or approach this story, the removal of a man's penis followed by the shared eating of it before death makes for grim entertainment.

SG: I know. It's kind of the grimmest of the grim. I think that's why I like *Taste* so much! (Laughs) You know, it's interesting, I have a weak stomach, but I'm attracted to stories like this. They speak to me because they're about people, about human desire and behavior, and there's something quite funny and moving about the play. But it is a disturbing story and disturbing things do happen. We had Tony Doublin and Gabe Bartalos—I first worked with Tony way back on *Re-Animator*—doing our special effects, and they did a terrific job.

MD: In the past, you've spoken of striving for authenticity in terms of detailing the realities of death, and how that was a reaction to the manner in which corpses were portrayed in cinema. Is that attention to detail more difficult to sustain in theater than in film? Is it even needed?

SG: I definitely think it's needed. I'd say it depends on what you're doing.

MD: How *bad* you want it to look *good*?

SG: Exactly. Like, before I made *Re-Animator*, for example, I talked to a lot of morgue attendants and pathologists and learned all about the individuality of death. The pathologists gave me slides of actual corpses, which I then passed on to our makeup effects people as reference, so we could get as close to reality as possible. The thing I noticed was how unique we are in death. Depending on how a person died, the body will react differently. Corpses are never just one color—white, like we saw in most movies—they're all sorts of colors. As a matter of fact, we used to call the zombies in *Re-Animator* our "rainbow corpses" because they were like an explosion of colors. The only reason we got that attention to detail was because I asked pathologists different questions about the physical and chemical changes a body undergoes after death. I discovered that a person would turn bright red if they died of a heart condition and yellow if they died of a liver condition, and there were also shades of blue, black, green, and purple. Knowing we achieved a degree of realism in the effects always pleases me, but I make no distinction if it's a movie or a play. *Taste* was a little different, though—there were no close-ups [as in film]—but I always want to know that we got everything anatomically correct. It had to be right, because people get so many things wrong.

MD: The theme of cannibalism has been explored in countless paintings, books, and films. Why do you think there is an enduring fascination with this act?

SG: It's really the last great taboo. If you look back throughout history, and not just the history of the arts, there have been many, many acts of cannibalism recorded: the Aztecs performed ritual sacrifice and cannibalism as a matter of course; there was the Donner Party, who were a bunch of pioneers who got snowbound in the mountains in the 1840s and were reduced to eating each other; there have been serial killers like Jeffrey Dahmer who consumed their victims. I think [the Meiwes] case is just one of the more modern cases we know of, but, yeah, cannibalism has been with us since the dawn of Man.

MD: *Taste* is further evidence I see of a trend in your work where you are depicting more decidedly human monsters.

SG: Well, a human being is just about the worst monster there is.

MD: I agree. How does the play address the notion of human evil?

SG: Something I try to convey to actors is the idea that monsters don't consider themselves to be monsters. They just don't think that way. Monsters don't get out of bed in the morning and say, "I'm a really *evil* person!" I'm sure Hitler and Stalin never once did that. I tell actors all the time: "Don't think the character you're playing is evil. No matter what, don't think what you're doing is a bad thing." An actor has to find the humanity in a character, even if everybody else sees them as a monster. [They have to] walk in their shoes, look through their eyes, because the actor begins from the inside—with themselves—and then goes from there. So, they have to believe the character is doing a bad thing for a good reason—maybe not even on that level of understanding. I mean, [what happens in] *Taste* is entirely consensual. There are no monsters in it, really.

MD: Does the play make some attempt at explaining why this extraordinary thing may have occurred?

SG: I'm sure there are reasons why it happened and you glimpse clues through the characters as the play progresses. These are two lonely people and they find each other for only a short time, but one of the things that fascinates me about Vic and Terry is they are really kind of stuck in an early phase of their development. Again, the story is an exploration of who they are, and they are like babies in a way. Babies are fixated with their mouths; it's their primary sensory organ. They are always putting things in their mouths as a way of exploring and understanding the world around them. Babies put objects in their mouths to see what something feels and tastes like. These guys have never really left that phase. It's all about the mouth for them. They are still very oral.

MD: I once queried you about the fact your movies often show audiences the unspeakable horrors in fetid detail. How did you reconcile that impulse in *Taste* with the need to avoid what could possibly be construed as an exploitative misstep or contentious stereotype?

SG: Really, you just have to trust your instincts, and those of the people you are collaborating with, that this is the way we should go. But I don't ever like taking a backward step. I just love going *way* out there! (Laughs)

MD: Did the actors always respond to that inclination you have to agitate?

SG: Yeah, they were great. We rehearsed for six weeks, which is a quite a long rehearsal period, and they both brought their best games. I think, together, we achieved a real balance in *Taste* between sort of provoking the audience and taking them on this emotional journey. You know, all theater aspires to create a world, and this particular world is Terry's apartment, his kitchen, and that's where these men fulfill this incredible arrangement. What the story builds towards is totally incomprehensible to most of us, but for these two men it's a very real and desirable thing.

MD: It seems obvious to say, but I think all committed lovers tend to create their own little worlds where many things seem to make perfect sense to them.

SG: Right, and if you exist outside of that world you might begin to kind of question it. There's a tendency in society to look from afar at certain relationships and say, "What is *this*? What are they doing here?" We just can't understand it. As perverse as this play might seem, we know it's based on something that actually happened. I think that's one of the things that makes *Taste* so powerful; it's truth.

Stuart Gordon Discusses *Re-Animator: The Musical*

Tyler Doupé / 2014

From *Wicked Horror.com*, October 3, 2014. Reprinted by permission.

Stuart Gordon has been involved with some of the most iconic horror films of the past thirty years, and he continues to find new ways to innovate and delight fans of genre film. So, we naturally jumped at the opportunity to speak with him about the upcoming revival of *Re-Animator: The Musical*. In this exclusive interview, we discuss fan reaction to the *Re-Animator* stage play and delivering practical effects before a live audience; then we take a moment to reminisce on *Fear Itself*.

Wicked Horror: Your background is in theater. Was that a driving factor in your decision to adapt *Re-Animator* for the stage?

Stuart Gordon: Yeah. I've always loved theater. That's how I began my career; I was artistic director for the Organic Theatre Company in Chicago. I worked in theater for fifteen years before moving to California to do movies, and I have continued doing plays ever since. Someone suggested the idea of *Re-Animator* as a musical, and I thought the idea was silly at first. But the more I thought about it, the more I realized that the movie is very contained. There are only a few characters. The effects we used in the movie were all practical and could be done live on stage. I realized that it was actually a great idea and I started working with Mark Nutter, the composer.

WH: Did the success of stage productions like *Evil Dead: The Musical* have any influence on your decision to bring *Re-Animator* to the stage?

SG: I have come to realize that there is a whole subgenre of musicals based on horror movies. There's *Little Shop of Horrors*, *The Phantom of the Opera*, *The Evil Dead*, and even *The Silence of the Lambs* has been adapted for the stage. I think horror kind of lends itself to musicals because it's very emotional which is common to most musicals.

WH: What made you want to put together a revival of *Re-Animator: The Musical*?

SG: We actually hadn't really retired it. The last time we produced it we took it to the Musical Theater Festival and then to the Edinburgh Festival in 2012. After that, I sat down with the composer because we wanted to do some more work on it. We've actually added some new songs. It's a different production now than when we did it two years ago and we wanted to try it out.

WH: In adding the new songs, did you remove any from the previous version?

SG: We took out a couple of songs, but nothing major. I think that the replacements are far better than what was there before. We also took some of the other songs and expanded them, so they are better than ever now. I'm really looking forward to getting it in front of an audience and trying out the new stuff.

WH: How did the tone from the film translate to the stage? It seems like the darkly comedic overtones from the picture would be perfect for a stage adaptation in the sense that the cast is singing about re-animated corpses. There's a bit of humor inherent to that.

SG: It does lend itself really well to the stage. The movie was funny and I think the play is even funnier. Mark Nutter, the composer, has incorporated a lot of that into the music. I think that only about ten minutes of the play's dialogue is actually spoken word.

WH: It must be very lively to have so much of the production done in song. That's bound to be good for audience engagement.

SG: It is! We've had people come to see the show so many times that they even sing along on some of the songs. There's a [Miskatonic] University fight song that people will sing along to and they even bring pompoms to wave during the show. There's a lot of blood flying around as well. We call the first three rows the "splash zone." We've actually had audience members show up wearing all white. One time, a couple sitting in the very first row arrived wearing a tuxedo and a wedding dress. They were covered in blood by the end of the show. There's a lot of audience involvement with the play.

WH: Speaking of the splatter zone, how have the practical effects from the film translated to the stage production? Has it been difficult not being able to use cutaways and not having the benefit of multiple takes?

SG: We've had a couple of misfires. But for the most part—I would say 99 percent of the time—it's been on target. We've been lucky to have had the same guys who did the effects for the movie doing the effects for the play.

WH: Is the process of rigging special effects for a play significantly different than how you would do them in a film?

SG: Most of it is pretty similar. There were a couple of things we had to figure out for the play. But we've used a lot of devices similar to what was used in the movie. Back in the day when we made the film, there was no CG. So, everything was done practically, and, when you're live on stage, it's a similar situation.

WH: Is there any chance that you will take the show on the road?

SG: Actually, we may at some point. That's one of the things we were talking about. We would like to start a touring production of the show.

WH: I know that this might be a sticky wicket because of the difference in pay for a stage actor versus a screen actor, but I am curious if you have considered bringing back any of the original cast members?

SG: I did talk to Jeffrey Combs and Bruce Abbott about joining the production at one point. But they are both busy and it didn't work out. They've both come and seen it though, which has been really fun. They said that watching it really brought them back.

WH: I noticed that Chiller TV is gearing up to re-broadcast *Fear Itself*. I've always kind of wondered why that show didn't seem to resonate with mainstream audiences. I really enjoyed it, but it only lasted for one season. As someone involved with the series, what do you think went wrong?

SG: It actually did pretty well. It was a fairly highly rated show. What actually killed it was the [Beijing] Olympics. The network took the show off the air when the Olympics came on and they never ended up bringing it back. Out of the twelve episodes that were done, I think they only aired six or seven of them.

WH: I had assumed it must have been a ratings issue because, typically, a highly rated show doesn't go off the air for no reason. That's interesting.

SG: Yeah, I know. It was frustrating. I think my episode was the highest rated of those that aired, and it was one of the last ones that they showed. So, it seems that the audience was building. I still don't quite understand why they didn't bring it back.

Talkhouse Film Contributors Remember Stuart Gordon

Nick Dawson / 2020

From *Talkhouse.com*, March 25, 2020. Reprinted by permission.

In the following post, *Talkhouse Film* contributors and other filmmakers share their tributes to Stuart Gordon, the great genre filmmaker behind such films as *Re-Animator*, *From Beyond*, *Dagon*, and *Dolls*, who passed away yesterday, aged just seventy-two. He was a contributor to *Talkhouse Film* from its inception, and was both a brilliant writer and a warm, lovely human being. He will be deeply missed.

Richard Stanley [director of *Hardware* (1990), *Dust Devil* (1994), and *Color Out of Space* (2020)]: We are deeply saddened here at Shadow Theatre HQ by the news of Stuart Gordon's passing. Stu was the founder of Chicago's Screw Theatre who staged a notorious 1968 antiwar adaptation of *Peter Pan* (inspired by the Democratic National Convention riots of that year) that got him and his then-girlfriend (and later wife), Carolyn Purdy, arrested on obscenity charges. The case received national attention before the charges were finally quashed. Stu capitalized on the publicity generated by this case to launch the Organic Theatre Company, described as "take-off-your-clothes, scream-and-bleed theater," whose legendary excesses included the premiere production of David Mamet's *Sexual Perversity in Chicago* (1974). He is perhaps best remembered by contemporary audiences as the director of *Re-Animator* (1985), a darkly comedic reimagining of H. P. Lovecraft's classic story cycle that served to unleash a further slew of hugely popular adaptations on the world, including *From Beyond* (1986), *Dagon* (2001), and "Dreams in the Witch-House" (2005) for the *Masters of Horror* anthology series.

His work played a pivotal role in widening the reach of Lovecraft's mythos and cementing its place in popular culture. I had the good fortune of meeting Stu in the early twenty-first century when I appeared as an uncredited extra in *Dagon*, playing one of the inhuman denizens of the cursed village of Imboca, indeed the only one to be seen wearing a hat. We took meals together many times during the course of the troubled production as I suspect Stu needed a sympathetic listening ear, being somewhat adrift in Galicia at the time and relatively unfamiliar with the Spanish language. I will always cherish the memory of those conversations. Now Lovecraft's Old Ones have recalled their tireless publicist and cinematic spokesperson to the great beyond. Iä! Iä! Cthulhu fhtagn! In pace requiescat, maestro. This world will never be the same without you.

Rodney Ascher [director of *Room 237* (2012) and *The Nightmare* (2015)]: There's a quote from Flaubert I've always found inspirational (one I've misattributed for years to J. G. Ballard): "Be regular and orderly in your life, so that you may be violent and original in your work." Although I can't claim to have known Stuart Gordon closely, my brief meeting with him at the 2015 Stanley Film Festival (where he was generous enough to speak well of my film *The Nightmare*, and more importantly, to talk at length with my five-year-old son about *Honey, I Shrunk the Kids*) left me with the impression that the quote was written specifically for him. *Re-Animator* is a film I've watched and rewatched countless times (and even showed clips from when I was teaching at a film school), but the trio of neo-noirs he directed in the 2000s (*King of the Ants*, *Edmond*—or as I like to call it "David Mamet's *Eyes Wide Shut*"—and *Stuck*) riveted and shocked me in ways that are increasingly rare. All four of those films did things I assumed couldn't be done, broke rules that I assumed were carved in stone, and delighted me as they did it. My brief in-the-flesh encounter with him suggested that these uncompromising works of transgressive art (that were also often very funny) were all the work of a kind and generous man and I've been heartened to see it confirmed in the countless testimonials to him exploding online this morning.

Jim Hemphill [director of *Bad Reputation* (2005) and *The Trouble with the Truth* (2011)]: Stuart Gordon was a god to me for almost thirty years before I ever met him. Like many of his fans, I first discovered his talent via his debut feature *Re-Animator*, a movie I still consider to be one of the ten greatest horror films of all time. When it was released in 1985, I was a rabid thirteen-year-old movie nut who pored over Roger Ebert's and Pauline Kael's reviews like a rabbi studying the Talmud. They were sacred texts, and I vividly remember both Ebert and Kael championing *Re-Animator* in reviews that made me salivate for the film. (The fact that it had been released unrated because no cuts imaginable could make it palatable to the MPAA made it even more appealing.) When I finally saw it after what seemed like an eternity of waiting (it was probably about two weeks), the most shocking thing about *Re-Animator* wasn't its explicit violence or sex, but the fact that it exceeded my stratospherically high expectations; it was smart, hilarious, scary, and as philosophical as it was visceral—the work of a true visionary.

I don't have the space here to go through my ongoing relationship with Stuart's films, but I'll just say that after *Re-Animator* I looked forward to every new Stuart Gordon release with the same breathless anticipation that I met each movie by Scorsese, Eastwood, Bigelow, Demme, and the other masters in my personal pantheon. In 2015, I finally had the opportunity to interview Stuart for *Paste Magazine*, and the experience proved that whoever said you should never meet your heroes was an idiot. Stuart was every bit as intelligent and funny as one of his films, but with a soft side that might surprise some. (It didn't really surprise me, since in my experience meeting filmmakers like Wes Craven and Sam Raimi, I've often found that directors who make the most savage movies can be the nicest, most well-adjusted human beings on the planet.)

We struck up a friendship via email and then in person, and I found out what a special man Stuart was. He seemed genuinely interested in me and my work, taking the time to watch my movie *The Trouble with the Truth* and giving me advice about where to go next. Making films is such a brutal and difficult business that many people who do it are too busy treading water in their own careers to help others, but Stuart always had time for me and my questions, no matter how dumb or frivolous. When you finished a conversation with Stuart, you always felt better about yourself and the world than when the conversation began; he was a man of faith and empathy, and I think that's the key to the greatness of his films—they were dark movies by a pure soul, giving them a complexity and resonance that makes them endlessly rewarding on repeat viewings. I felt honored and flattered by Stuart's mentorship and generosity, and in the hours since he passed away I've discovered that he had a similar relationship with dozens of other filmmakers. I thought I was special, but it turns out Stuart was the one who was special.

Darren Lynn Bousman [director of *Saw II* (2005), *Saw III* (2006), and *St. Agatha* (2018)]: A few years back, I was invited into the inner horror circle by way of an exclusive event known as the "Masters of Horror" dinner. This was something put together by our maestro, Mick Garris. This event was held a couple of times a year at various restaurants around Los Angeles. In short, it was an excuse for a bunch of horror lovers to get together and geek out about all things macabre. I remember at one of these events, I was sitting by myself at the bar. Truth be told, I didn't know many of these legends outside of their movies I idolized as a kid. In the beginning, I was scared to approach them, so the majority of that first event I sat by myself, trying to work up the courage to introduce myself and inject myself into their conversations.

So, cut to me sitting at the bar, sipping on a cheap beer, when over walks Stuart Gordon. Holy fuck, this dude is a legend. As I sat there, trying to figure out what to say to him, he turned to me. "Darren Bousman?" he says. "Yes!" He extends his hand, "Stuart Gordon, wanted to introduce myself to you." I flipped the fuck out. Stuart Gordon is introducing himself to *me*! We chatted, and he walked me over to the group and invited me into his conversations. Stuart was a fucking insanely talented artist. Most will fawn over his movies *Re-Animator*, *Castle Freak*, or my personal favorite, *Stuck*, but my favorite Gordon production hands down was his directing of *Taste*, the nasty and gut-wrenching play based on the true account of a man who put an ad online looking for someone he could kill, cook, and eat. Sitting in that theater, revolted at the content, I couldn't help but smile. Gordon was jumping and shifting narrative mediums and still finding a way to disgust and entertain me, decade after decade.

Brian Trenchard-Smith [director of *The Man from Hong Kong* (1975), *Turkey Shoot* (1982), and *Dead End Drive-in* (1986)]**:** I met Stuart Gordon when he came to Australia to make the Christopher Lambert sci-fi actioner *Fortress*. I had been a big fan since his gloriously Grand Guignol *Re-Animator*, one of several H. P. Lovecraft novellas he brought to the screen. He was kind and gracious to me personally. We would meet periodically at "Masters of Horror" dinners. He was a warm-hearted, energetic man, with a keen intellect and a love of actors born of many years working in theater. He loved movies and relished the challenge to make them bigger than their budgets. He knew how to build tension, then break it with a laugh. He enjoyed turning clichés on their heads, while chopping off a few heads along the way. But he also understood what would make family audiences laugh, as the co-creator of the *Honey, I Shrunk the Kids* franchise. There was, in fact, no genre he could not handle. It was a pity the studios did not recognize that. But he will always be remembered as an icon in the Horror Hall of Fame. *Vale*, Stuart, you will be missed.

Barbara Crampton: I met Stuart when the actress originally cast as Meg in *Re-Animator* dropped out, after her mother read the script. I guess the role was thought to be too racy and provocative. But that's what I loved about it, those boundary-breaking leanings and the humor, of course. The casting director, Anthony Barnao, called me in on the second go-round to read for Stuart with Jeffrey Combs and Bruce Abbott, who had already signed on for their respective roles. There were a few other young gals there too, but after a few hours, it was just us three actors. Stuart had us run through the scenes and offered a lot of directives for us to try. I remember him calling out specific prompts to me personally: "You love him more than anything in the world," meaning Dan. "You don't trust this guy, he's hiding something," meaning Herbert West. I felt like I was rehearsing a play. We went on like this for a long afternoon.

The next day, I received the happy news that I'd been picked for the role. I was ecstatic. This was the biggest part I'd been asked to play up until this point. We continued to rehearse for the three weeks leading up to filming. We didn't get paid for that time, but I didn't care. It was about the work, and I was so happy to be in the company of a real director and talented actors, honing the words and the play of each scene. We were so prepared going into production for our twenty-two-day shoot that it felt like we actually had more time than that. Yet, surprisingly, we also went into overtime almost every day. Stuart never wanted to stop filming, or for that day to end. Wrapping shortly before the Christmas holiday, many days we went fourteen or even sixteen hours. I made more money in overtime on *Re-Animator* than my original salary.

The film was a hit and called "pop Buñuel" by Pauline Kael. Janet Maslin said it had "grisly vitality." Roger Ebert walked out of the theater saying he was "surprised and reinvigorated." Most agreed it was daring, exciting and original. The success of the film spawned a working relationship with Stuart Gordon and a deep friendship which lasted more than thirty years. He pushed me into uncomfortable and vulnerable places as Meg, he encouraged me to celebrate my bravery and heroism in *From Beyond*, and to search for my deep love as a mother while simultaneously examining the horror of an unforgiving marital relationship in *Castle Freak*. He, along with his longtime writing partner Dennis Paoli, wrote thought-provoking and long-lasting stories of men and women thinking and acting on impulses others dare not utter. He was the bravest and kindest creator; gentle, funny, and illuminating of our darkest fears and greatest hopes.

Joe Dante [director of *The Howling* (1981), *Gremlins* (1984), and *The 'Burbs* (1989)]: Stuart was a longtime attendee at the "Masters of Horror" dinners in Hollywood, a gathering of (usually out-of-work) genre filmmakers, which allowed me to recruit him as a valued *Trailers from Hell* Grindhouse Guru. His taste in commentaries was eclectic, running from the expected *Cannibal Holocaust* [1980] to the unexpected *Calamity Jane* [1953]! Which serves to highlight a divide in his media profile—although beloved for his iconic and witty horror films like *Re-Animator*, he was just as dedicated to the theater, cofounding Chicago's Organic Theatre Company and defying the University of Wisconsin to stage a notorious nude version of *Peter Pan*. More recently, he'd been active in the LA theater scene with his staging of *Nevermore* with Jeffrey Combs as Edgar Allan Poe and, most riotously, *Re-Animator: The Musical*, during which the first several rows of audience were supplied with plastic sheeting to ward off the gouts of gore splattered from the stage. Despite a number of health issues in recent years, he never lost his sense of humor. He will be missed.

Larry Fessenden [director of *Wendigo* (2001), *The Last Winter* (2006), and *Depraved* (2019)]: I had known Stuart Gordon through his work since *Re-Animator* came out. I was always charmed by that film's wry sensibility and the theatrical panache with which he pulled off the special effects. It instantly felt like a new voice in horror had arrived. I remember sitting with my future wife watching *From Beyond* a few years later. In my memory, we were in some sleazy theater on Forty-second Street, but that's just the spell cast by the movie. And I remember watching *Stuck*, from 2007, and wishing he had gotten to work more. Years later, in 2010, I found myself corresponding with Stuart about collaborating on a movie together. My company, Glass Eye Pix, had specialized in producing low-budget horror, and Stuart felt maybe we could get a project off the ground. He had a sort of "Old Hollywood" workman's approach to the business which I found grounded and appealing. We went out with two different scripts that he liked, but never quite landed the big bucks. And indeed, I feel like Stuart's idea of low-budget was a bit elevated from the sort of fare I had been able to pull off with young first-time directors.

Then, almost in a conciliatory gesture, I invited him to direct a radio play ["The Hound"] for the series I had launched with Glenn McQuaid, *Tales from Beyond the Pale*. Stuart agreed, and we mounted a lovely production in which he brought on many old collaborators—writer, composer, and cast members, including the radiant Barbara Crampton—and with Glenn on board as sound designer, they created something quite wonderful. (I even got to be directed by Stuart in my role as the Demon Hound Itself!) Stuart was always very convivial and supportive, generous with a compliment but never pandering. He was an artist and workman who had his own struggles with the industry, despite his iconic contributions. (Recall that he also penned the story for *Honey, I Shrunk the Kids*.) Just last month, I was working with Ms. Crampton on a film and our thoughts turned to Stuart. Our reminiscences were warm, our admiration deep. He was a mentor and friend and fellow traveler, all at once. Godspeed, Stuart.

Charles Band [head of Empire Pictures and Full Moon Entertainment, and director of *Parasite* (1982) and *Trancers* (1985)]: Everyone in our Full Moon Features family is deeply saddened by the passing of Stuart Gordon. Our history with Stuart goes back over thirty-five years, when he and Brian Yuzna came into the Empire Entertainment office and found a home for *Re-Animator*. Films like *From Beyond*, *Dolls*, *Robot Jox*, *The Pit and the Pendulum*, and *Castle Freak* followed, and throughout all of them, Stuart and I remained good friends. He and my dad had an especially great relationship and hung out until my dad left us in 2002. Beyond his talent, Stuart was a super sweet man: if you had met him on the street you would never imagine that he was the creator of such compelling, yet depraved work. Lovers of our genre have lost a unique kindred spirit and we will miss him very much.

Jackson Stewart [director of *Beyond the Gates* (2016)]: I'm totally devastated from the news about my longtime friend and mentor Stuart Gordon passing away. The impact he had on the lives of friends, fans and, most importantly, his family, is impossible to measure. He was one of the smartest, funniest, most articulate and kind-hearted people I've ever had the pleasure of knowing. Those who knew him knew his health had been in the decline for a while, but also what an incredible amount of creativity was still bursting from him. Stuart had such a wonderful, unique point of view and an incredible filmography under his belt.

I remember talking to him the weekend that *Inception* and *Dinner for Schmucks* came out [in July 2010] and he told me, "One was excellent and the other was absolutely terrible." I asked, "Oh, so I'm guessing you liked *Inception*," and he said, "No—hated it. *Dinner for Schmucks* was terrific!" He never backed down from holding court with an unpopular opinion. He also had a whole slew of awesome movies he developed that unfortunately never got made with him at the helm—*House of Re-Animator*, *Iron Man*, *Kingdom Come*, and *American Psycho* amongst them. I loved the man like another father and I'm going to miss him forever. I thank God I got to chat with him a few weeks back and he sounded like his old, wonderful self.

He told me a bunch of great stories about Jack Kirby, Neal Adams, and Stan Lee, and still seemed totally full of life and happiness, which is how I want to remember him. His brilliant movies will live forever. My heart goes out to his wife, Carolyn, daughters Jillian, Suzanne, and Margaret; as well as his terrific grandchildren. I know he's landed safely wherever he's gone in this big universe of ours. Rest in peace, genius. I am so lucky I had the fortune of knowing you.

Axelle Carolyn [director of *Soulmate* (2013), *Tales of Halloween* (2015), and *The Haunting of Bly Manor* (2020)]**:** I met Stuart fifteen years ago, as a young film reporter aspiring to make movies of my own. When I nervously confessed the huge impact *Re-Animator* had had on me, he volunteered his time to discuss filmmaking, keeping in touch over the years, and advising me on occasion. He was attached to direct an early version of my first movie, *Soulmate*, and when I decided to make it myself, had nothing but encouragement. We met at festivals around the world, then, when I moved to LA, at dinner parties with our families and friends. He was generous with his knowledge, time, and praise; a true mentor, a true friend.

Graham Skipper: I, with no exaggeration, have Stuart to thank for my entire career. He took a chance on me when I was a complete nobody, and treated me like a total equal from day one. I spent four years on stage as the musical Herbert West in *Re-Animator: The Musical*, and was always in awe as he would direct with precision, but an eye for collaboration. He would listen to all the actors, but would never lose sight of his vision. He was always kind, never cruel; always supportive, gentle when he needed to be, and forceful when he needed to be. He was a total master of his craft. After the musical ended, he and I remained close friends and would have lunch often. I'll cherish those days and conversations the most. He was a brilliant man and a force of artistic genius, that deserves to be in the pantheon of the all-time directorial greats—not just cinematically, but for the stage as well. Don't forget the man was a theatrical pioneer in Chicago in the seventies as well! I'm so thankful—more than words could ever say—for my time with him. I send all my love to his family, and I hope that people are able to rediscover not only his well-known work, but some of his lesser-known masterpieces, and allow his work to inspire now more than ever.

Ernest Dickerson [cinematographer of *Do the Right Thing* (1989) and director of *Tales from the Crypt: Demon Knight* (1994), *Bones* (2001), and *Masters of Horror: The V Word* (2006)]**:** I became a big fan of Stuart Gordon's films after first seeing *Re-Animator* then *From Beyond*. I became an even bigger fan of Stuart, the man, after meeting and spending time with him at the Masters of Horror dinners, and bumping into him and Carolyn at the Encino Farmer's Market. Such a brilliant, funny, warm, and generous human being. I always got a big kick knowing this teddy bear of a man gave us some of the most adventurous, genre-bending and -stretching films and theater of the last thirty-five years. His stage production of *Re-Animator* was so abso-fucking-lutely amazing! That "splash zone" was 100 percent Stuart Gordon. So sad that there won't be any more Stuart Gordon movies. I guess we'll have to console ourselves with the fact that we were lucky to have him while we did. I never got the chance to know him better, but I miss him already.

Dennis Paoli: I have collaborated with Stuart Gordon since 1963, when we had a satire group called—wait for it—the Human Race that played the coffeehouse circuit in Chicago. I was his college roommate when he wrote and directed his first play, *The Game Show*, in which the audience was locked in the theater, surveyed by helmeted and truncheon-carrying ushers, and abused by a demented TV host who taunted and tortured contestants until the audience revolted and rushed the stage. Back in Chicago, he founded the Organic Theatre, which established a brand another collaborator-turned-critic-now-crime-novelist Lenny Kleinfeld christened "take-off-your-clothes, scream-and-bleed theater." No one took their clothes off or bled in *Bleacher Bums*, a play about screaming Chicago Cubs fans built from improvs—based on an idea by Joe Mantegna—that I got to collaborate on with the company of the Organic that included Joe, Dennis Franz, Keith Szarabajka, and Stuart's wife, Carolyn Purdy-Gordon. (Ask me how they met, sometime.)

It illustrates two characteristics of Stuart's theatrical genius: his strong narrative sense, and his ability to bring together a group of actors who were not only talented and very smart but brave and lots of fun. It was true of his crews and collaborators, too. We all became friends, friends to this day. This sad day.

It's true of his film work, too. The writer is the first person off a film project and I've never been on a set, but I'm friends with Jeffrey Combs and Barbara Crampton and Brian Yuzna, the *Re-Animator* gang. And with Mark Nutter, who composed the score for the highly unlikely and hugely entertaining *Re-Animator: The Musical*, the large cast of which meets up regularly. Stuart's work was always about community, what creates it and what imperils it, and how the hard work of making one, and saving one, is worth it. His audiences, his fans, his friends miss him, but he's left us a great gift: each other.

Additional Resources

Magazines, Newspapers, and Websites

Alexander, Chris. "*Stuck* Up and Run Down." *Fangoria*, no. 274 (June 2008).
Associated Press. "Authorities Split on Nude Co-eds." *Waukesha Daily Freeman*, October 1, 1968.
Associated Press. "Official Opinions of *Peter Pan* Show Featuring Nudes Unclear." *Sheboygan Press*, October, 1, 1968.
Balun, Chas. "*The Pit and the Pendulum*." *Fangoria*, no. 84 (July 1989).
Balun, Chas. "The Unmaking of *The Shadow Over Innsmouth*." *Fangoria*, no. 91 (April 1990).
Blake. "*Stuck*: Interview with Stuart Gordon, Mena Suvari and John Strysik." *Screen Anarchy*, January 6, 2008.
Carnell, Thom. "Stuart Gordon." *Carpe Noctem* III, no. 3 (1997).
Colander, Pat. "An Update on Things Organic." *Chicago Tribune*, July 9, 1976.
Collis, Clark. "Director Stuart Gordon Talks *Re-Animator: The Musical*." *Entertainment Weekly*, May 3, 2012.
Cozzalio, Dennis. "Throwing Punches: *Re-Animator* Director Stuart Gordon Talks About His Upcoming Film Series at the New Beverly Cinema." *Sergio Leone and the Infield Fly Rule*, January 11, 2010.
Curci, Loris. "The *Castle Freak*." *Fangoria*, no. 148 (November 1995).
Despatis, Pierre-Alexandre. "Interview: Stuart Gordon." Ioncinema.com, August 2, 2006.
Dollar, Steve. "Talking *Stuck* with Stuart Gordon." *New York Sun*, May 30, 2008.
Doughton, K. J. "*King of the Ants*." *MovieMaker Magazine*, February 3, 2007.
Eisenthal, Bram. "Not Horror, But Harrowing." *The Gazette*, July 15, 2006.
Ensley, Mike. "King of Horror." *Pensacola News Journal*, March 16, 2004.
Faraci, Devin. "Exclusive Interview: Stuart Gordon." *CHUD.com*, September 14, 2006.
Feinblatt, Scott. "*From Beyond* . . . And Back Again!" *Screem*, no. 26 (April 2013).
Ferrante, Anthony C. "Storming the *Fortress*." *Fangoria*, no. 124 (July 1993).
Fiorentino, Francesca. "Stuart Gordon: Memoirs of an Eternal Peter Pan." *MoviePlayer*, June 6, 2011.
Fischer, Dennis. "A Moist Zombie Movie." *Fangoria*, no. 46 (August 1985).
Fischer, Dennis. "*RoboJox*." *Cinefantastique* 19, no. 2 (January 1989).
Fischer, Dennis. "Stuart Gordon's *Castle Freak*." *Cinefantastique* 26, no. 4 (June 1995).
Forbis, Will. "An Interview with Stuart Gordon." *Acid Logic*, August 1, 2002.
Garris, Mick. "Stuart Gordon." *Post Mortem with Mick Garris*, June 7, 2017.
Gilpin, Kris. "Sound of Thunder, Scream of Metal." *Starlog*, no. 145 (August 1989).

Gire, Dan. "*Re-Animator.*" *Cinefantastique* 15, no. 4 (October 1985).

Gire, Dan. "Stuart Gordon on *From Beyond.*" *Cinefantastique* 17, no. 2 (March 1987).

Gordon, Stuart. "Bret & Me, Or How I Didn't End Up Directing *American Psycho.*" *Talkhouse*, June 10, 2016.

Gordon, Stuart. "Things I've Learned as a Movie Maker." *MovieMaker Magazine*, February 3, 2007.

Gudino, Rod. "A Weird Tale." *Rue Morgue*, no. 28 (July–August 2002).

Hemphill, Jim. "Horror Master Stuart Gordon Talks *Re-Animator*, Lovecraft and MPAA Ratings." *Paste*, July 21, 2015.

Herman, Jan. "The Indie Jones." *Los Angeles Times*, March 27, 1998.

Hodges, Mike. "Fear Today, *Dagon* Tomorrow." *Fangoria*, no. 213 (June 2002).

Howard, Ben, and Dan Auty. "Stuart Gordon: Laughter is the Antidote to Fear." *MovieScope* 2, no. 6 (March 2009).

Howe, Michele. "Horrors, It's Halloween." *Daily Record*, October 30, 1986.

Hughes, Mike. "Spotlight Shines on the Sultans of Scary." *Sacramento Bee*, October 26, 2005.

Humphrey, Alex. "*Re-Animator the Musical*: An Interview with Stuart Gordon." *Love Horror*, July 10, 2012.

Jankiewicz, Pat. "Baby Boomer." *Starlog*, no. 181 (August 1992).

Jones, Alan. "H. P. Lovecraft's *Dagon.*" *Shivers*, no. 94 (January 2002).

Jones, Alan. "Reservoir Hogs." *Starburst* 19, no. 4 (December 1996).

Kane, Joe. "Stuart Gordon Goes for the Gut." *New York Daily News*, November 5, 1986.

Kogan, Rick. "The Selling of a Thriller of a Film." *Chicago Tribune*, November 16, 1986.

Koyama, Christine. "Organic's Gordon Keeps Head High as Others Fall in *Re-Animator* Debut." *Chicago Tribune*, October 13, 1985.

Lambie, Ryan. "Stuart Gordon Interview: *Re-Animator*, *Pacific Rim*, *Fortress.*" *Den of Geek*, May 30, 2014.

Lovece, Frank. "Tamer *Re-Animator* Available on Video." *Marysville Journal-Tribune*, January 12, 1987.

Marcinko, Bill Dale. "Close Up: Stuart Gordon." *American Film* XII, no. 5 (March 1987).

Martino, Sam. "*Peter Pan* Leaves Never-Never Land to Face Obscenity Charge." *Star Tribune*, October 6, 1968.

Matthews, Kevin. "An Interview with Stuart Gordon." *Flickfeast*, August 18, 2012.

McDonagh, Maitland. "Interview with Stuart Gordon." *Mad Movies*, no. 39 (October 1985).

McDonagh, Maitland. "Interview with Stuart Gordon." *Mad Movies*, no. 45 (January 1987).

Mesling, Pete, "Q&A with Stuart Gordon." *Film Fodder*, 2003.

Mólgaard, Kristian. "Re-Animating the Horror." *Trauma: Splatter Movie Magazine*, no. 1 (1993).

Nobile, Phil, Jr. "The Badass Interview: Stuart Gordon." *Birth. Movies. Death.*, November 14, 2014.

Northmore, Henry. "Interview: Stuart Gordon, Director of *Re-Animator*, *From Beyond* and *Castle Freak.*" *The List*, May 20, 2014.

Nutman, Philip. "The Man Who Collected Lovecraft." *Fangoria*, no. 59 (December 1986)

Nuwer, Hank. "Two Gentlemen of Chicago: David Mamet and Stuart Gordon." *South Carolina Review* 17, no. 2 (Spring 1985).

O'Brien, Joseph. "Back . . . *From Beyond*!" *Rue Morgue*, no. 56 (May 2006).

O'Brien, Joseph. "Filming the Unfilmable." *Rue Morgue*, no. 50 (October 2005).

Phipps, Keith. "Stuart Gordon." *The Onion*, October 10, 2002.

Pouncey, Edwin. "*Re-Animator*: Labor of Lovecraft." *Sounds*, December 21/28, 1985.
Preston, Marilynn. "The Organic Theatre Survives the Worst, Shoots for the Best." *Chicago Tribune*, January 16, 1976.
Price, Michael H. "*Dolls* Maker Heads for Broader Audience." *Fort Worth Star-Telegram*, April 28, 1987.
Rebello, Stephen. "Stuart Gordon: The Genre's Re-Animator." *Cinefantastique* 17, no. 1 (January 1987).
Rochon, Debbie, and Peter Schmideg. "Keeper of the Castle." *Samhain*, no. 58 (September–October 1996).
Rollans, Scott. "So Much to *Fear Itself*." *Fangoria*, no. 274 (June 2008).
Rosell, Rich. "Stuart Gordon: The Re-Animator Speaks!" *DigitallyObsessed.com*, 2002.
Salza, Giuseppe. "*From Beyond*: Special Make-up Effects." *Cinefantastique* 17, no. 2 (March 1987).
Salza, Giuseppe, and Dennis Fischer. "*RoboJox*." *Cinefantastique* 18, no. 4 (May 1988).
Scapperotti, Dan. "*Dagon*." *Cinefantastique* 34, no. 6 (October 2002).
Scapperotti, Dan. "*Fortress*." *Cinefantastique* 24, no. 2 (August 1993).
Schultz, Ian. "Interview with Stuart Gordon." *Psychotronic Cinema*, May 13, 2016.
Schweiger, Daniel. "*The Pit and the Pendulum* Swings Again." *Fangoria*, no. 101 (April 1991).
Terry, Clifford. "RoboPlot." *Chicago Tribune*, November 23, 1990.
Thomas, Rob. "Film Director Returns to Old Haunts." *Capital Times*, April 23, 1999.
Thomas, Rob. "Film, Stage Director Leads Dream Course." *Capital Times*, March 15, 2000.
Thomas, Rob. "Swimming with the (Mutant) Fishes." *Capital Times*, July 24, 2002.
Waddell, Calum. "Master of Horror: Stuart Gordon." *Videoscope*, no. 64 (Fall 2007).
Waddell, Calum. "Re-Ant-Imator." *The Dark Side*, no. 108 (April 2004).
Worland, Gayle. "No Guts, No Glory." *Wisconsin State Journal*, March 30, 2008.

Books

Draven, Danny. *Talk You to Death: Filmmaking Advice from the Mavericks of the Horror Genre*. Lukan Books, 2017.
Gordon, Stuart. *Naked Theater and Uncensored Horror*. FAB Press, 2022.
Gregorits, Gene. *Midnight Mavericks: Reports from the Underground*. FAB Press, 2007.
Jay, Dave, Torsten Dewi, and Nathan Shumate. *Empire of the B's: The Mad Movie World of Charles Band*. Hemlock Books, 2014.
Larson, Mark. *Ensemble: An Oral History of Chicago Theater*. Agate Midway, 2019.

Audio Commentaries

Dagon (Lionsgate Home Video, 2003); two commentaries: the first with screenwriter Dennis Paoli, the second with actor Ezra Godden.
Dolls (MGM, 2005) with screenwriter Ed Naha.
Edmond (First Independent, 2006) with writer David Mamet.
From Beyond (MGM, 2006) with actors Jeffrey Combs and Barbara Crampton, and producer Brian Yuzna.
King of the Ants (Mosaic Entertainment, 2004) with actor Chris L. McKenna.

Masters of Horror: "The Black Cat" (Anchor Bay, 2007) with actor Jeffrey Combs.

Masters of Horror: "Dreams in the Witch-House" (Anchor Bay, 2006) with actor Ezra Godden and DVD producer Perry Martin.

Re-Animator (Elite Laserdisc, 1995); a second audio commentary (minus Gordon) features actors Jeffrey Combs, Bruce Abbott, Barbara Crampton, and Robert Sampson, and producer Brian Yuzna.

Robot Jox (Scream Factory, 2015) with DVD producer Michael Felger.

Space Truckers (Sterling Home Entertainment, 1999).

Stuck (High Fliers, 2009) with writer John Strysik and actress Mena Suvari.

Index

Abbott, Bruce, xxv, 27, 137, 147, 181, 196, 197, 237, 241
Abbott and Costello Meet Dr. Jekyll and Mr. Hyde (1953), 61, 128
About Last Night (1986), 14, 37
Accident on Hill Road (2009), xix
Adams, Neal, 35, 244
Addams Family, The (1991), 106
Ahlberg, Mac, 12, 16, 18, 41, 107, 108, 197
AIP (American International Pictures), 57, 204–5
Alien (1979), 12, 15, 91, 100, 174, 184
Alien Nation (TV series), 92
Aliens (1986), xxiv, 15
Aliens: Ride at the Speed of Fright (1995), xxiv, 106
Allen, David, 20, 21, 42, 47, 53, 54, 56–57, 106
Allen, Joan, 129
All the Right Moves (1983), 54
Altiere, Kevin, 55
Amazing Colossal Man, The (1957), 82
American Beauty (1999), 140, 157
American Buffalo (play), 140
American Psycho (novel), xxiii, 244
American Werewolf in London, An (1981), 76
Anderson, Paul Thomas, 188–89
Animal Farm (play), 35, 160
Ardmore Studios, xxiv, 105–6, 108
Argento, Dario, 136, 194, 217
Ascher, Rodney, 239

Assembly Line (unproduced film), xxii
Astaire, Fred, 138, 200
Asylum (unproduced TV series), xxiii, 57
At the Mountains of Madness (novella), 205, 218
At the Mountains of Madness (unproduced film), 218
Avery, Rachel, 202

Baby Boom (1987), 165
Bad Taste (1988), 85
Bailey, Bunty, 12
Bakker, James, 72
Baldwin, Daniel, 122
Balsam, Martin, 64
Balun, Chas, 127
Band, Albert, 28, 243
Band, Charles, xi, xvii, xxiii, xxiv, 9, 19–20, 28–29, 32, 41, 53, 54, 57, 69, 71, 73, 74, 77, 79, 83, 95, 96, 98, 99, 118, 119, 132, 144, 146, 187, 198, 217, 243
Band, Richard, xxvii, 7, 41
Band of Brothers (2001), 116
Barbarella (1968), 19
Barker, Clive, 59
Barnao, Anthony, 241
Barrett, Simon, 201
Barrie, J. M., xxi, 3, 26, 34, 129
Bartalos, Gabe, 231
Bates, Kathy, 152
BBC, 227

Beckett, Samuel, 157, 180
Beckoning Fair One, The (play), 38–39, 61
Belle de Jour (1967), 78
Belushi, Jim, xxii, 27, 37
Belushi, John, 12, 129
Bernard, Rukiya, 178
Bernsen, Corbin, 134
Berserker (unproduced film), xxii, 23, 29, 42
Bettelheim, Bruno, xii, 20, 42
Beyond Re-Animator, xxv, 120, 148
Bible, The (1966), 19
Bigelow, Kathryn, 240
Biggs, Gregory, 151, 153
"Black Cat, The" (2007), xv, xxv, xxvi, 141, 146, 159, 175, 181, 190, 194
Blair Witch Project, The (1999), 218
Bleacher Bums, xxi, xxiv–xxv, 14, 27, 32–33, 38, 160, 245
Bloody Bess (play and unproduced film) xxi, xxii, 22, 25, 27, 36, 42, 51, 161
Bloomfield, John, 101–2
Blue Movie (novel), 226
Body Politic, The, 33, 35
Body Snatchers (1993), xxiii, 91, 94–95
Borrower, The (1991), 85
Bousman, Darren Lynn, 240–41
Bowen, A. J., 201
Bradbury, Ray, xiii, xxiv, 36, 109–10, 111, 138, 149, 160, 185–86, 191, 193, 201
Braindead (1992), 84, 85, 89
Brand, Benjamin, xvi, xxvii, 229–30
Brandes, Bernd Jürgen Armando, 231
Bride of Frankenstein, The (1935), 15, 18
Bride of Re-Animator (1989), xxiii, 5, 13, 15, 20, 41, 42, 79, 98–99, 120, 197–98
Briggs, Joe Bob, 63
Brody, Adrien, 219
Brooks, Mel, 196
Brosnan, Pierce, 222
Buechler, John Carl, 12, 16, 41, 125

Buffy the Vampire Slayer (TV series), 125
Bug Lady (unproduced film), 121
Buñuel, Luis, xi, 165, 214, 242
Burg, Steve, 55–56
Burgess, Anthony, 26
Burns, Bob, xxv
Bush, George H. W., xii–xiii, 48, 50, 92
Bush, George W., xxv, 167, 168, 181
Bush, Laura, xxv, 141, 147, 181

Calamity Jane (1953), 242
Cameron, James, xxiv, 174
Cannes Film Festival, xi, xxii, xxiii, 7, 9, 14, 87, 110, 131, 149, 165
Cannibal Holocaust (1980), 242
Cannom, Greg, 71
Carnage (2011), 222
Carolyn, Axelle, xxvii, 244
Carpenter, John, xiv, xvii, xxv, 13, 48, 135, 136, 206, 207, 217–18
Cartland, Barbara, 63
"Cask of Amontillado, The," 70
Castle, William, 61, 75, 90, 142
Castle Freak (1994), x, xiii, xxiv, 95, 96–99, 110, 119, 125, 137, 146, 178, 197, 241, 242, 243
Castle Freak (2020 remake), xxvii
Chandler, Raymond, 29, 192
Chaney, Lon, 97, 187
Chaplin, Charlie, 191
Cheney, Dick, xxv, 141, 146, 147, 166, 181
Chiller TV (network), 237
Chinatown (1974), 221
Chinese Ghost Story, A (1987), 106
Citizen Kane (1941), xvii, 63, 130
Civil Wars (TV series), 100, 103
Clarke, Arthur C., 17
Cleopatra (1963), 19
Clover, Carol, 163
Cobb, Ron, 42, 55, 91, 101
Cohen, Larry, x, xiii–xiv, xxv, 206, 223–24

INDEX   253

Combs, Jeffrey, xv, xxiv, xxv, xxvi, 22–23, 24, 28, 31, 45–46, 69, 87, 89, 97, 120, 132, 137, 139, 141, 143, 146, 147, 157, 175–77, 181, 182, 186–87, 190, 194, 196, 199, 200, 201, 211, 218, 237, 241, 242, 246
Conan the Barbarian (1982), 42, 91
Coppola, Francis Ford, 195
Cops (play), xxii, 27, 37, 42
Corman, Roger, 7, 11, 23, 29, 32, 46, 51, 57, 60, 69, 70, 71, 74, 89, 198, 205
Coscarelli, Don, xxv
Crampton, Barbara, xii, xxv, xxvii, 20, 22–23, 27–28, 30, 46, 78, 85, 97, 104, 137, 141, 144, 146, 147, 165, 181, 183, 194–203, 208, 211, 241–42, 243, 246
Crash (2004), xv, 153
Craven, Wes, x, xiv, 84, 90, 194, 240
Cronenberg, David, xiv, 49, 66, 76, 172, 206, 227
Crowley, Aleister, 52
Cruise, Tom, 54, 218, 226
Cul-De-Sac (1966), 221
Curse of the Werewolf, The (1961), 146
Cusack, John, 190

"Dagon" (short story), xiv, 30, 112–13, 210, 211, 214
Dagon (2001), x, xiv, xv, xxiv, xxv, 112–21, 123, 127, 166, 178, 185, 194, 198, 210–17, 238, 239
Dagon and Other Macabre Tales (book), 9, 11
Dahl, Roald, 38, 149
Dahmer, Jeffrey, 232
Daley, Richard, xxvi, 26, 34, 129, 160–61, 168–69
Dance, Charles, 101, 104
Danny Shapiro and His Search for the Mystery Princess (play), 37, 139
Dante, Joe, xxv, 76, 89, 175–76, 194, 206, 242
Daughter of Darkness (1990), xii, xxiii, 63–64

Davis, John, 92
Dawn of the Dead (1979), xiii, 197
Dead Alive. See *Braindead*
Dead Hate the Living!, The (2000), 127
Dead Ringers (1988), 49
Deathbed (2002), xxv, 118–20, 174
de la Iglesia, Àlex, 189
De Laurentiis, Dino, 19, 29, 201
del Toro, Guillermo, xxv, 167, 194, 218
DeMille, Cecil B., 154
Demme, Jonathan, 240
Deneuve, Catherine, 220
De Niro, Robert, 186
Dentist, The (1996), xxiv, 98, 116, 134
Depp, Johnny, xxiii, 222
De Shields, Andre, 27, 129
Devil Doll, The (1936), 11–12
Dickerson, Ernest, 245
Dinner for Schmucks (2010), 244
Director's Cut (novel), 127
Dirty Harry (1971), 37
Disney, Roy E., 110, 133, 201
Disney, Walt, 48, 82, 83–84, 85
Disney Studio, xii, xiii, xxii, xxiii, xxiv, 25, 42, 47–48, 57, 73–74, 80, 81, 82, 83–84, 85, 109, 110, 132–34, 160, 185, 201
Doctor Rat (play), 39, 162
Dolls (1987), xii, xxii, 11–12, 14, 19, 20, 21, 25, 32, 35, 41, 42, 46, 53, 59, 66–67, 69, 73, 77, 80, 81, 106, 112, 125, 136, 144, 145, 159, 165–66, 178, 198, 199, 238, 243
Don't Look Now (1973), 12
Dorff, Stephen, 100, 103
Doublin, Anthony, 16, 231
Dracula (1979), 40
Dracula (novel), 61, 75
"Dreams in the Witch-House" (2005), xv, xxv, 135–36, 138, 141, 146, 159, 194, 217, 238
Dr. Strangelove (1964), 226
Duvall, Shelley, 227

Eastwood, Clint, 240
"Eater." See *Fear Itself*
Ebert, Roger, xi, 165, 239, 242
Edinburgh Festival, xxvi, 202, 236
Edmond (2005), ix, xiv–xv, xxv, 127, 134–35, 137–41, 147, 149, 153, 156, 157, 160, 167–68, 169, 178, 180, 181, 187–88, 194, 200, 216, 222, 239
Eggby, David, 94
Eisner, Michael, 81, 133, 201
Empire Pictures, xi, xii, 7, 9, 10, 16, 19–20, 21, 22, 23, 24, 25, 28–29, 31, 32, 41–42, 47, 53, 54, 56–57, 69, 73, 74, 77–79, 98, 144, 187, 243
Empire Strikes Back, The (1980), 21
Enter the Void (2009), 189
Envy. See *Thing on the Doorstep, The* (unproduced film)
E/R (play and TV series), xxi–xxii, 14, 27, 33, 39, 73, 160, 162, 164
Ermey, R. Lee, 226
E.T. the Extra Terrestrial (1982), 133
Evil Dead, The (1982), 189, 235
Evil Dead II (1987), 68
Exorcist, The (1973), 133
Exorcist III, The (1990), 71
Eyes Wide Open (book), 226
Eyes Wide Shut (1999), 224, 225–26, 227, 239

Face of Fire (1959), 20
Fantastic Factory/Filmax, 112, 113, 211
Farrow, Mia, 219, 221
Fast Show, The (TV series), 123
Faust: Love of the Damned (unproduced film), xxiii, xxiv, 88
Fear Itself, "Eater" (2008), xv–xvi, xxvi, 159, 188, 235, 237
Fearless Vampire Killers, The (1967), 222
Fellini, Federico, 18, 64, 136
Fenn, Sherilyn, 99

Fernández, Julio, 113
Ferrara, Abel, xxiii, 94
Fessenden, Larry, 242–43
Fincher, David, 188
Fly, The (1986), 49, 50, 66
Fly, The (1958), 180
Flyswatter, Dukey (Michael David Sonye), 119–20
Foree, Ken, 197
Forever War, The, 39–40, 54, 91, 159
Fornicopia (play), 39
Fortress (1992), ix, xiii, xxiii, 74, 79–80, 86–88, 91, 92–95, 106, 110, 138, 149, 159, 194, 200–201, 227, 241
1408 (2007), 190
Fox, Terry Curtis, xxii, 26, 27, 37
Fraker, William A., 221
Frankenstein (1931), 5, 30, 97, 130, 192
Frankenstein (novel), xii, 11, 40, 155
Franz, Dennis, 27, 110, 129, 149, 160, 245
French Connection, The (1971), 37
Friday the 13th (1980), 12, 62, 126, 209
From Beyond (1986), ix–x, xi–xii, xxii, 11, 12, 14, 16, 17–20, 22, 24–25, 28, 29–31, 32, 35, 41–42, 48, 50, 52, 54, 59, 69, 71, 74, 77–78, 85, 86, 96, 97, 112, 116, 132, 137, 141, 144, 155, 159, 165, 172–73, 178, 186, 194, 197, 205, 206–10, 217, 218, 238, 242, 243, 245
Fuller, Jonathan, xiii, 69, 97
Full Metal Jacket (1987), 226, 227
Full Moon Entertainment, xii, xxiv, 53, 69, 79, 83, 95, 97, 98, 99, 118, 174, 187, 243

Gale, David, 27, 137, 183
Game Show, The (play), 33–34, 39, 245
Garres, Rafael, 114, 116
Garris, Mick, xviii, xxv, 167, 194–95, 217, 240
Gentry, Paul, 93, 106, 107
Ghostman, The, xxiii, 89
Ghost Writer, The (2010), 222

INDEX 255

Glass Eye Pix, 243
Godden, Ezra, xxvii, 115–16, 212, 213, 214, 215
Godfather, The (1972), 126
God of Carnage. See *Carnage*
Goldblum, Jeff, 49
Goldworm, Adam, 229
Gómez, Macarena, 116, 213
Gonzalez Gonzalez, Clifton, 109, 110
Goodman Theatre, xxii, 33, 37, 41
Gordon, Bert I., 85
Gordon, Jillian, 36, 39, 77, 144, 191, 244
Gordon, Margaret, 244
Gordon, Ruth, 221
Gordon, Stuart: actors and acting; 15, 33, 84, 103–4, 170, 171–72, 176, 203; censorship, xvi, xvii, 3, 10, 18–19, 23, 28, 62, 66, 72, 78, 95, 96, 136, 139, 197, 209; childhood, xxi, 25, 33, 60–61, 75–76, 100; comedy, xvii, 5, 15, 19, 65, 66, 71–72, 76, 84, 96, 111, 116, 131, 170, 186, 196; death and fear, 6, 8, 17, 23, 48, 50, 60, 61, 66, 77, 95, 130–31, 136, 144–45, 151, 153, 163–64, 167, 168–69, 170–71, 195, 209–10, 220, 232; directing, 14–15, 153–54, 170–73; influences, 15, 60–61, 64, 70, 72, 100, 128, 142, 172, 180, 205–6, 223, 235; nudity, sex, and violence, ix, x, xii, 3–4, 6, 8, 18, 25, 26, 29–30, 31, 34, 37, 39, 41–42, 49, 59, 62–63, 71, 74–75, 78, 85, 90, 93, 123–27, 129, 132, 138, 143, 147, 153, 161, 163–64, 165, 166–67, 170–71, 179, 208–10, 215–16, 220, 224, 225–26; politics and art, ix, x, 26, 30, 31, 39, 47, 48, 129, 153, 159, 162, 164, 169, 179, 189; religion, 21–22, 70, 72, 214–16; remakes, 15, 167, 185, 202; special makeup effects, 5–6, 34, 38–39, 46, 50–51, 61, 71, 84, 89, 97, 104, 114, 124–25, 172–73, 206–8, 236. See also MPAA (Motion Picture Association of America)
Gordon, Suzanne, 36, 40, 144, 146, 191, 244
Graham, Gary, 54, 92
Grant, Cary, 126
Greatest Show on Earth, The (1952), 154, 185
Great Switcheroo, The (play), 37–38
Greenberg, Bob, 41, 143
Gris-Gris (unproduced film), xxii, 21–22, 25, 42, 49, 95, 98

Haldeman, Joe, 39–40, 54, 55, 91, 92, 159
Hammond, Wendy, xxiii, 89
Haunted Palace, The (1965), 11
Heard, John, 27, 129
Heavenly Creatures (1994), 85
Hemphill, Jim, 239–40
Henriksen, Lance, 69, 71, 99, 145, 199–200
Henry: Portrait of a Serial Killer (1986), 85
"Herbert West—Re-Animator," xi, 7, 9, 10–11, 17, 27, 40, 85, 113, 155, 206
Higson, Charles, xiv, xxv, 118, 123, 178, 179
Hill Street Blues, 27, 37
Hitchcock, Alfred, xi, xvii, 9, 12, 49–50, 64, 65, 66, 76, 126, 156, 172, 173, 220, 223
Hitchcock/Truffaut (book), 223
Hoberman, David, 81
Home Brew (magazine), 7, 9, 113
Honey, I Blew Up the Kid (1992), xxiii, 82–83, 91, 94, 110
Honey, I Shrunk the Kids (1989), xii, xxii, 25, 42, 43, 47–48, 69, 74, 81–84, 92, 110, 132–34, 149, 160, 166, 186, 194, 201, 239, 241, 243
Honey, I Shrunk the Kids (TV series), xxiv
Hooper, Tobe, x, xiii, xxv, 135, 136, 194
Hopper, Dennis, xiii, 100, 102–3, 110, 123
Hornsby, Russell, 178
Horrible Way to Die, A (2010), 201
Hostel (2004), 166–67
House of Re-Animator (unproduced film), xxv, 141, 146–47, 155–56, 167, 181, 244

House on Haunted Hill (1959), 142
House on Haunted Hill (1999), 187
Houser, Ron, 103–4
Howling, The (1981), 76, 206, 242
Huckleberry Finn Part 1 (play), xxi, xxii, 26, 36, 41, 160
Human Centipede, The (2009), 189
Humanoids from the Deep (1980), 51
Human Race, The (satire group), 65, 128, 245

Inception (2010), 244
In the Heat of the Night (TV series), 55
In the Mouth of Madness (1994), 217–18
Into the West (1992), 73
Invasion of the Body Snatchers (1956), xxxiii, 94
Iron Man (unproduced film), xxiii, 244
Irreversible (2002), 189

Jackson, Peter, 84, 85, 89
Johnson, Anne-Marie, 55
Johnston, Joe, xxii, 57, 81
Journey of Natty Gann, The (1985), 80
Joyner, C. Courtney, 187

Kabbalah (play), xxiv
Kael, Pauline, 28, 32, 159, 164–65, 239, 242
Karloff, Boris, 97, 187
Katzenberg, Jeffrey, 81, 83, 133
Kent, Peter, 143
Ketchum, Jack, xxv
Kidman, Nicole, 226
Kid Safe: The Video (1988), xxii
King, Stephen, 61, 141, 171, 227
King, Zalman, 224
Kingdom Come (unproduced film), 244
King Kong (2005), 132
King Lear, 166
King Must Die, The (novel), 39

King of the Ants (2003), ix, x, xiv, xv, xxv, 117–18, 120, 121, 122–27, 138, 149, 178, 179, 180, 181, 202, 216, 229, 239
Kirby, Jack, 28, 244
Kleinfeld, Larry, xxi, 40, 245
Knife in the Water (1962), 219
Koslo, Paul, 55
Kotzwinkle, William, 39, 162
Kubrick, Stanley, 64, 65, 100, 185, 219, 223–28
Kubrick, Vivian, 227

Ladies Night (unproduced film), xxv
Ladyhawke (1985), 18, 42
Lambert, Christopher, 74, 86, 87, 88, 241
Landis, John, xxiv, xxv, 76, 194
Lane Technical High School, xxi, 33, 128
Lang, Fritz, 51
Last Action Hero (1993), 106
Last Circus, The (2010), 189
Laube, Hans, 230
Laveau, Marie, xxii, 21–22, 49
Lawrence of Arabia (1962), 79
Lear, Norman, xxi–xxii, 33, 39
Leary, Denis, 183
Lee, Stan, xxiii, 244
Lee, Stephen, 12
Lifeboat (1944), 156
Ling, Bai, 140
Little Shop of Horrors (musical), 235
Little Sister, The (play), 39
Livingston, Ron, 118, 122, 125
Locklin, Loryn, 86
Logan, Joshua, 179–80
Lolita (1962), 224
Lorraine, Carrie, 12
Love at First Bite (1979), 40
Lovecraft, H. P., ix, xi, xiii, xiv, xv, xxii, xxv, xxvii, 5, 7–8, 9, 10–11, 13, 14, 17, 18, 22–23, 27, 29, 30, 32, 40, 41, 42, 46, 50–51, 59–60, 61, 67, 69, 70, 74–75, 78, 85, 95, 98, 99,

110, 112–14, 116, 117, 118, 121, 127, 130, 132, 135, 137–38, 142–43, 144, 145, 146, 149, 153, 155, 159, 163, 165, 166, 184–85, 187, 191, 192, 194, 198–99, 204–6, 211, 212–13, 214, 215, 216–18, 223, 238, 239, 241
Lucky (unproduced film), 40
Lugosi, Bela, 187
Lurker in the Lobby, The (book), 118
Lurking Fear, The (unproduced film), xxii, 22, 30, 42, 50, 74, 187

Macbeth (1971), 220, 221
Macy, William H., xv, xxv, 129, 135, 138, 140, 141, 146–47, 156, 160, 181, 188, 200
Mad Max (1979), 21
Madsen, Michael, 85
Making The Shining (1980), 227
Malkovich, John, 33, 129
Mallard, Chante, xv, 151, 153
Malone, William, xxv
Mamet, David, xiv, xxi, xxv, 14, 27, 33, 37, 73, 127, 129, 134–35, 138–39, 140, 149, 153, 156, 160, 167–68, 178, 187, 194, 200, 238, 239
Man Bites Dog (1992), 89
Mann, Ted, xiii, 100–101, 103
Mantegna, Joe, xv, xxii, 27, 109, 110, 129, 135, 139, 149, 160, 245
"Man Who Ate His Lover, The" (documentary), 231
Marat/Sade, 33
Marquis de Sade, 52, 210
Martí, David, 114
Martindale, T. Chris, xxv
Marx Brothers, 64, 111
Maslin, Janet, 242
Mason, Hilary, 12, 46
Masters of Horror (dinners and TV series), xv, xxv, xxvi, 135–36, 138, 141, 146, 159, 167, 175, 181, 188, 190, 194, 217, 223, 229, 238, 240, 241, 242, 245

Matinee (1993), 89–90
Mazar, Debi, xv, 100, 103, 104, 139
McCall, Bruce, 91, 101
McGregor, Ewan, 222
McKenna, Chris L., xiv, xxvii, 122, 124–25, 229, 233
McNaughton, John, 85
McQuaid, Glenn, 243
Mead, Abigail. *See* Kubrick, Vivian
Meet the Feebles (1990), 85
Meiwes, Armin, xvi, xxvii, 231, 232
Men, The (unproduced film), xxvi, 183–84
Men, Women, and Chainsaws (book), 163
Merlin, Jesse, 203
Meroño, Raquel, 116
MGM, 132, 207
Mighty Morphin Power Rangers (TV series), 106
Miquel, Llorenç, 114
Misery (1990), 141, 152, 158
Mitchell, John Cameron, 160
Monsters HD, 207
Morales, Esai, 109, 110
Moranis, Rick, 186
Moroff, Mike, 109
MOTELX Film Festival, xxvi, 179, 182
MPAA (Motion Picture Association of America), xii–xiii, 10, 18–19, 24, 25, 28, 31, 42, 62–63, 77, 78, 82, 93, 126–27, 132, 207, 208–9, 216, 239
Mrs. Bixby and the Colonel's Coat (play), 38
Muppet Christmas Carol, The (1992), 106
Murray, Bill, 129
Murton, Simon, 101, 105, 107
Museum of Jurassic Technology, 191, 192
Musical Theater Festival, xxvi, 236

Naha, Ed, 11, 20, 41, 42, 81
Natalucci, Giovanni, 18, 42, 197
Naulin, John, 16

NBC, xv, 159, 188
Necronomicon (1993), 187, 218
Nevermore: An Evening with Edgar Allan Poe (play), xv, xxvi–xxvii, 175–77, 181–82, 190, 195, 200, 242
Newman, Peter, 95, 104–5
Nicholson, Jack, 201, 221
Nightmare, The (2015), 239
Night of the Living Dead (1968), xiii, 59, 68, 85, 173
Ninth Gate, The (1999), 222
Noé, Gaspar, 189
Norris, William J., 25, 27, 41, 75
Nutter, Mark, xxvi, 202, 235, 236, 246
NYPD Blue (TV series), 100, 110

O'Bannon, Dan, xxvi, 183–84
O'Bannon, Diane, 183, 184
Odyssey (play), 35
Old Dark House, The (1932), 20, 42
Old Yeller (1957), 82
Olmos, Edward James, 109, 111
Once Upon a Time in America (1984), 18, 42
Organic Theatre Company, The, x–xi, xvi, xxi–xxii, xxvii, 9, 14–15, 23, 24–25, 26–27, 28, 30, 32–33, 34–40, 41, 42, 59, 61, 73, 85, 110, 129, 131, 139, 142–43, 144, 149, 160, 161–62, 191, 195, 200, 235, 238, 242, 245
O'Toole, Peter, 69, 70, 79, 99

Paoli, Dennis, xv, xvii, xxiii, xxiv, xxv, xxvi, xxvii, 19, 21, 23, 27, 30, 36, 40, 41, 54, 57, 59, 65, 70, 75, 85, 95, 97–98, 112, 116, 121, 127, 128, 146, 147, 175, 180, 184, 196, 198, 242, 245–46
Parker, Dave, 127
PBS, xxi, 38, 130
Perfect Storm, The (2000), 115
Perkins, Anthony, xii, xxiii, 64
Peter Pan (play), x, xxi, 3–4, 26, 34, 73, 129, 149, 155, 160–61, 169, 238, 242

Peterson, William, 33, 129
Pet Sematary Two (1992), 88
Phantom of the Opera, The (musical), 235
Pianist, The (2002), 219–20
Pickford, Mary, 41, 191
Pirates (1986), 51
Pit and the Pendulum, The (1991), x, xii–xiii, xxiii, 44–47, 48, 49, 50, 51, 52, 57–58, 60, 69–72, 79–80, 88–89, 96, 97, 99, 134, 145–46, 149, 159, 166, 199–200, 243
Poe (play), xxi, 35
Poe, Edgar Allan, xii, xv, xxi, xxv, xxvi, 7, 23, 35, 44, 45, 46, 51, 57, 60, 61, 69, 70, 74, 79, 134, 141, 145, 146, 149, 159, 166, 175–77, 181–82, 187, 190, 194, 195, 198, 200, 205, 242
Polanski, Roman, xvii, 51, 64, 65, 172, 219–23
Polyester (1981), 230
Price, Vincent, 23, 46, 57, 60, 71, 187
Progeny (1999), xxiv, 116
Psycho (1960), xvi, xvii, 7, 8, 12, 15, 49–50, 64, 65, 66, 76, 126, 173, 220, 244
Purdy-Gordon, Carolyn, x, xviii, xxi, xxvi, 12, 24, 25, 26, 31, 34, 40, 69, 129, 131, 132, 133, 136, 142, 145, 160, 161, 164, 169, 178, 191–92, 195, 197, 200, 203, 208, 224–25, 238, 244, 245
Purgatory (unproduced film), 201

Rabal, Francisco, 213–14, 215–16
Raimi, Sam, 60, 68, 240
Randall and Hopkirk (Deceased) (TV series), 123
Raphael, Frederic, 226
"Raven, The" (poem), 176
Raven, The (2012), 190
Rea, Stephen, 148, 149–50, 151–52, 156, 157, 160, 178, 180, 199
Reagan, Ronald, xii, 92, 137
Re-Animator (1985), ix, x, xi, xii, xvi, xvii, xviii, xxii, xxiii, xxv, 5–6, 7–8, 9–11, 12, 13, 14, 15, 16–17, 18–19, 20, 22, 23, 24, 25,

27–28, 30, 32, 33, 37, 39, 40–41, 42, 48, 54, 59, 61, 62–63, 64, 66, 68, 69, 73–75, 77, 78, 80, 82, 84, 85, 89, 92, 96–97, 98, 106, 110, 112, 113, 117, 119, 128, 130–32, 135, 137, 138, 140, 141, 142, 143–44, 147, 149, 155, 157, 159, 162, 163–65, 166, 170, 172, 175, 178, 181, 183, 185, 186, 191, 194, 195, 196, 197, 198, 201, 202, 204, 206, 208, 209–10, 218, 219, 222, 223, 231, 232, 235, 238, 239–40, 241–42, 243, 244, 245, 246
Re-Animator: The Musical, xvi, xxvi, 190, 195, 202–3, 229, 235–37, 242, 244, 245, 246
Red Badge of Courage, The (1951), 20
Red Shoe Diaries (TV series), 224
Red Sonja (1985), 19
Reed, Oliver, 69, 145–46
Reich, Wilhelm, 51–52
Renault, Mary, 39
Repulsion (1965), 220, 221, 222
Reservoir Dogs (1992), 84, 90, 118
Return of the Jedi (1983), 15
Richards, Denise, 135, 140
Richard III (play), 34–35
Ridges, G. Michael, 28
Robot Jox (1989), ix, xii, xxii, xxiii, 14, 19, 20–21, 25, 42, 47–48, 53–57, 59–60, 65, 69, 78–79, 91–92, 106, 138, 159, 194, 222, 243
Rolfe, Guy, 12
Romeo and Juliet (1968), 19
Romeo and Juliet (play), 202
Romero, George A., x, xiii, 59, 65, 66, 68, 125
Ronson, Jon, 224
Rosemary's Baby (1968), xvii, 64, 219, 221, 222, 223
Roth, Eli, 167, 194
Roth, Tim, 90

Sacred Fools Theatre Company, The, xxvii, 229
Sagansky, Jeff, 37
Sampson, Robert, 137

Saw (2004), 166
Schwarzenegger, Arnold, xxii, 23, 42, 86, 92
Scorsese, Martin, 186, 240
Screw Theatre, x, xxi, 26, 142, 149, 160–61, 238
Scrimm, Angus, 176
Second City, The, 33, 128, 129
Serbian Film, A (2010), 189
Seven Deadly Sins of Horror, The (unproduced film), 98, 121
Sexual Perversity in Chicago (play), xxi, 14, 27, 37, 73, 129, 138, 156, 160, 187, 200, 238
"Shadow Over Innsmouth, The," xiv, 8, 50–51, 60, 74, 95, 98, 112–13, 211
Shakespeare, William, x, 26–27, 166, 221
Shepard, Sam, 157
Sherman, Tom, 55
Shining, The (1980), 64, 225, 227
Shostrom, Mark, xviii, 207
Sierra, Gregory, 109, 110
Silence of the Lambs, The (1991), xxiii, 235
Sills, Paul, 26, 33, 35
Sinise, Gary, 129
Sirens of Titan, The (book), xxvii, 37, 205–6
Sitges Film Festival, xxii, xxiii, xxiv, xxv, 9, 84, 108
'68 (unproduced film), xxvi, 160, 161, 169
Skipper, Graham, 203, 244–45
Smith, Dick, 50–51, 60
Smith, Kurtwood, 88, 200
Smith, Lionel Mark, 127
Snail Boy (2000), xxiv
Social Network, The (2010), 188
Sorayama, Hajime, 101
Sorel, Ted, 18, 30, 207
Soulmate (2013), 244
Southern, Terry, 226
Space Truckers (1996), ix, xiii, xxiv, 91, 92, 94, 95, 100–108, 110, 123, 125, 149
Spacey, Kevin, 157

Spanish Inquisition, The, xii, 44–45, 48, 50, 51, 57–58, 69, 70, 71, 72, 89, 200
Spartacus (1960), 224
Spasojevic, Srdjan, 189
Spielberg, Steven, 172, 179
Spolin, Viola, 35
Stanley, Richard, 238–39
Stanley Kubrick's Boxes (2008), 224
Starship Troopers (1997), 132
Star Trek (TV series), 91, 100, 231
Star Wars (1977), 15, 36, 39–40, 91, 153
Steele, Barbara, 213
Steppenwolf Theatre, 33, 129
Stewart, Jackson, 243–44
Stewart, James, 126
Stiles, Julia, 135
Stoker, Bram, 63
Stone, Oliver, 60, 61
Strysik, John, xxvi, 118, 119, 149–50, 151, 156, 157, 178, 180
Stuck (2007), ix, x, xiv, xv, xix, xxvi, 141, 148, 149–53, 155–58, 160, 168, 178, 179, 180, 194, 199, 216, 222, 239, 241, 243
Suárez, Carlos, 212
Susan's Plan (1998), xxiv
Suvari, Mena, 135, 139–40, 148, 149, 150, 152–53, 156–57, 158, 160, 178, 180, 199
Swaggart, Jimmy, 72
Sweetheart (unproduced film), 40
Switch Bitch (play), 38
Szarabajka, Keith, 245

Tales from Beyond the Pale ("The Hound"), xxvii, 243
Tales from the Darkside (TV series), 41
Tales of Halloween (2015), xxvii, 244
Taming of the Shrew, The (1967), 19
Tarantino, Quentin, 90
Taste (play), xvi, xxvii, 229–34, 241
Taylor, Meshach, 110, 160

Teenie Weenies. See *Honey, I Shrunk the Kids*
Tenant, The (1976), 220, 221, 222
Texas Chain Saw Massacre, The (1974), xiii, 85, 189
Thoms-Cappello, Donal, 229, 233
Titanic (1997), 174
Titus Andronicus (play), 34
They Live (1988), 48
Thing, The (1982), 13, 206–7, 209
Thing from Another World, The (1951), 23
Thing on the Doorstep, The (unproduced film), 121, 127, 184
Tingler, The (1959), 61, 75–76
Thriller (TV series), 60
Todd, Michael, Jr., 230
Tor (unproduced film), xxiii
Torch Song Trilogy (1988), 50
Torres, Liz, 109
torture porn, 166
Towles, Tom, 85, 87, 200
Trailers from Hell (website), 242
Trancers (1985), 20, 243
Trenchard-Smith, Brian, 241
Trouble with the Truth, The (2011), 239, 240
Truffaut, Francois, 223
Twilight (2008), 189
Twilight Zone, The (TV series), 12, 60
2001: A Space Odyssey (1968), 91, 100, 101, 185, 225, 227

Uncle Oswald (play), 38
University of Wisconsin, x, xxi, 3–4, 25–26, 33–34, 42, 73, 77, 129, 149, 160–61, 242
Urban Gothic (TV series), xxvi
Uses of Enchantment, The (book), 20, 42

Vidal, Lisa, 109
Videodrome (1983), 206
Video Nasties, 93, 189

Village Roadshow, 80, 86, 92, 201
Vis. See *Titus Andronicus*
Vonnegut, Kurt, xxvii, 37, 149, 205–6
von Trier, Lars, 211
Vulich, John, 125

Wall Street (1987), 165
Warp (play), xxi, 27, 35–36, 160
Waters, John, 230
Weird Tales (magazine), 9, 113
Welles, Orson, 63, 192
Wells, Vernon, 88, 101, 122, 200
Wendt, George, xv, xxv, 100, 101, 118, 122, 123, 125, 126, 139, 141, 147, 179, 181, 202
Whale, James, xii, 155, 192
Where the Chill Waits (unproduced film), xxv
White Zombie (1932), 22
Who's Afraid of Virginia Woolf? (play), 34
Wilder, Billy, 128, 136
Wild Orchid (1990), 224
Williams, Ian Patrick, xxiii, 12
"William Wilson" (short story), 51

Wizard of Oz, The (1939), 18
Wonderful Ice Cream Suit, The (film), ix, xiii, xxiv, 109–11, 138, 149, 160, 185–86, 201, 222
Wonderful Ice Cream Suit, The (play), 36, 110, 193
Woo, John, 90
Woodbine, Bokeem, 139
Wrightson, Bernie, 51, 60, 91, 101
WTTW, 38
Wuhrer, Kari, 122, 125

X-Files, The (TV series), 125

Young Sherlock Holmes (1985), 20, 42
You're Next (2011), 201
Yuzna, Brian, xxiii, xxiv, xxv, 7, 9, 10, 16, 41, 43, 59, 75, 76–77, 79, 80–81, 98–99, 112, 113, 116–17, 120, 130, 131, 132, 143, 144, 147, 149, 155, 181, 184, 187, 197–98, 211, 212, 243, 246

Zombie, Rob, 194

About the Editor

Credit: Siân Doyle

Michael Doyle lives in Wales and is the author of the books *Larry Cohen: The Stuff of Gods and Monsters*, *Hancock on Hancock*, and *Conversations with Carpenter*. His writing has appeared in such publications as *Fangoria* and *Rue Morgue*.

www.ingramcontent.com/pod-product-compliance
Lightning Source LLC
Chambersburg PA
CBHW021834220426
43663CB00005B/241